George Washington Versus
the Continental Army

George Washington Versus the Continental Army

Showdown at the New Windsor Cantonment, 1782–1783

MICHAEL S. MCGURTY

McFarland & Company, Inc., Publishers
Jefferson, North Carolina

Library of Congress Cataloguing-in-Publication Data

Names: McGurty, Michael S., 1964– author.
Title: George Washington versus the Continental Army : showdown at the New Windsor Cantonment, 1782-1783 / Michael S. McGurty.
Description: Jefferson, North Carolina : McFarland & Company, Inc., 2023. | Includes bibliographical references and index.
Identifiers: LCCN 2023039264 | ISBN 9781476692371 (paperback : acid free paper) ∞ ISBN 9781476650838 (ebook)
Subjects: LCSH: Washington, George 1732-1799—Military leadership. | United States. Continental Army—History. | United States—History—Revolution, 1775-1783—American forces. | New York (State)—History—Revolution, 1775-1783. | Hudson River Valley (N.Y. and N.J.)—History, Military. | New Windsor Cantonment Site (New Windsor, N.Y.)—History. | New Windsor (N.Y. : Town)—History, Military.
Classification: LCC E255 .M35 2023 | DDC 973.3/447—dc23/eng/20230905
LC record available at https://lccn.loc.gov/2023039264

British Library cataloguing data are available

ISBN (print) 978-1-4766-9237-1
ISBN (ebook) 978-1-4766-5083-8

© 2023 Michael S. McGurty. All rights reserved

No part of this book may be reproduced or transmitted in any form or by any means, electronic or mechanical, including photocopying or recording, or by any information storage and retrieval system, without permission in writing from the publisher.

Front cover image: "Washington and His Generals" drawn and engraved by A.H. Ritchie, 1870 (Library of Congress); *background* The Winter-Cantonment of the American Army and It's [sic] Vicinity for 1783 (map reproduction courtesy of the Norman B. Leventhal Map & Education Center at the Boston Public Library and New-York Historical Society Collection)

Printed in the United States of America

McFarland & Company, Inc., Publishers
Box 611, Jefferson, North Carolina 28640
www.mcfarlandpub.com

Table of Contents

Preface   1

Chapter 1. "The camp behind Snake Hill": Introduction   5

Chapter 2. "The Timber was heavy and the work very fatiguing": Constructing the Log City—Lieutenant Ebenezer Elmer, 2nd New Jersey Regiment   18

Chapter 3. "Our God and Soldier we like adore": The Diverse Residents of the Camp   33

Chapter 4. "The service is much impeded, desertion vastly encreased, and the disposition of the Troops extremely soured, by the frequent want of Provisions": The Failure of the Country to Provide for the Army and the Effect on Soldier Health   43

Chapter 5. "A tolerably decent appearance": Clothing, Gear, Flags, and Identity   57

Chapter 6. "So usefull a Scheme": The Temple of Virtue   77

Chapter 7. "Had this day been wanting, the world has never seen the last stage of perfection to which human nature is capable of attaining": The Newburgh Conspiracy   92

Chapter 8. "Awakening again the spirit of Emulation and love of Military Parade": Manning the Force and Training for Battle   118

Chapter 9. "No Military neglects or excesses shall go unpunished": A Decline in Discipline and Increased Challenges to Authority   126

Chapter 10. "Retiring from the field of Glory with Joy in their countenances, but poverty in their pockets": The Shameful Disbandment of the Continental Army   140

Chapter 11. Denouement: The Conclusion   147

Appendix 1. Organization of the Continental Army in New York and Northern New Jersey in 1782-83   165

Appendix 2. Paying the Continental Army   168

Appendix 3. Duty for the Lines   171

Appendix 4. Deaths at the New Windsor Cantonment	173
Appendix 5. The Two Anonymous Letters to the Officers of the Army and General Washington's Response	175
Appendix 6. The Mountainville Hut	180
Chapter Notes	183
Bibliography	213
Index	221

Preface

With the war nearing its end in early 1783, General George Washington, in his Hudson Highlands stronghold, had to keep a wary eye on not only the large British force in New York City, 60 miles to the south, but also his increasingly disgruntled soldiery chafing under martial authority and the country's broken financial promises. A nationalist faction in Congress seized upon this discontent to instigate the Newburgh Conspiracy, the attempt of Continental Army officers to menace civil officials who opposed the Impost of 1781, a 5 percent tax on imports. Through this collusion, the plotters sought to vest the central government with the authority to raise a revenue, the source of real power and the means to satisfy all the nation's creditors. "A dangerous instrument to play with," the army, by this point a long-dreaded professional force, was provoked into threatening the very liberties that the war was fought to defend. Standing between his men and the American people, the stalwart commander in chief extricated the republic from this last major crisis of the American Revolution.

The purpose of the present work is to address the limited historiography on the American military at the end of the Revolutionary War and challenge the notion that no perils remained after the purported war-ending victory at Yorktown, Virginia, in 1781. Two more contentious years followed, the major threat being internal. The lessons learned from the acrimonious civil-military relations during this time are as relevant today as they were in the 18th century.

Only one book has been written specifically about the New Windsor Cantonment. Janet Dempsey's *High Time for Peace*, published in 1987, is a solid description of the historical events at this location in the final year of the American Revolution, but by focusing on the nature of military society, I analyze what factors influenced the people living in this encampment. This area, covering two and a half square miles and comprising the second-largest city in New York in 1782–83, was more than soldier-built huts of wood and stone. The New Windsor Cantonment was a contrived community of people who would never have willingly associated with each other in any other context. In their shared suffering and quest for justice, however, they also shared a bond that transcended sectional differences and race. Although the pride of the nation, the Continental Army was a sword of Damocles hanging over the public's head. General Washington increasingly questioned whether he could maintain control of his troops and feared what they might do. He was incredulous when his officers exploited this anger and utilized it to intimidate the Continental Congress. A far more capable and lethal instrument than earlier in the war, this disconsolate legion was ripe for use by demagogues, demonstrating why there was a traditional fear of standing armies.

Examining the command structure, composition, equipment, training, and operation of the Continental Army in the Hudson Valley, I provide a context for the diverse camp population facing the grim visage of returning to civilian life impoverished and broken in body and spirit. Through the prism of their military service, the New Windsor Cantonment residents viewed the American people as unworthy benefactors of their suffering. Lashing out against this ingratitude, they too wanted to share in the prosperity that the realization of independence promised.

With the 250th anniversary of the American Revolution fast approaching, this book is a study of reckless ambition during a tumultuous time in our nation's founding.

If Historiographers should be hardy enough to fill the pages of History with the advantages that have been gained with unequal numbers (on the part of America) in the course of this contest, and attempt to relate the distressing circumstances under which they have been obtained, it is more than probable that Posterity will bestow on their labors the epithet and marks of fiction; for it will not be believed that such a force as Great Britain has employed for eight years In this Country could be baffled in their plan of Subjugating it by numbers infinitely less, composed of Men oftentimes half starved; always in Rags, without pay, and experiencing, at times, every species of distress which human nature is capable of undergoing.

—General George Washington, February 6, 1783.[1]

CHAPTER 1

"The camp behind Snake Hill"
Introduction

At the end of October 1782, over 7,000 soldiers marched into New Windsor, New York. Located along the Hudson River 10 miles north of West Point, this community hosted most of the northern Continental Army through the spring of 1783. Camping on the rolling hills west of town, troops from New York, New Jersey, New Hampshire, Maryland, and Massachusetts built around 600 log buildings, which with peace at hand became their last winter encampment. After New York City was captured in 1776, the natural defenses of the Hudson Highlands to the north and nearby northwestern mountains of New Jersey sheltered American forces for the remainder of the war except for three weeks in October 1777. From this mountain bastion, part of the Appalachian chain, they challenged British forces operating in southern New York and northern New Jersey and sent reinforcements to all points of the compass. The base of its main army and most important headquarters, no other position served Continental Army leaders' purposes so well. Situated within this American Gibraltar was West Point. Built on top of frowning rock cliffs, the fort, started in 1778, was actually a series of fortifications that guarded a huge chain stretched across the Hudson River to block enemy shipping. Dominating every approach, West Point was so strategically located that Washington referred to it as the "key which locks the communication between the Eastern and Southern states."[1] The mountains screened their movements, so the Americans could suddenly debouch out of the passes anywhere along this range. With Washington's numbers estimated more to indulge British ego, the dark peaks kept their secret well, because the enemy seldom ever knew exactly what was behind them. Large numbers of American soldiers defended and operated out of this region. The struggle to control the Hudson River was the longest campaign of the war. New York's lakes and rivers were fought over since man first set foot on the landscape. Created by glacial activity over a span of more than two million years, no other state had so many inland watercourses. The Mohawk, Susquehanna, and Delaware rivers gave ready passage into the western interior and the Great Lakes beyond. The Lake Champlain–Lake George–Hudson River corridor cut through the state like a dagger. For millennia, native war parties followed these ancient courses. France and Great Britain struggled for a century to control these historic invasion routes. Many forts were constructed along the lakes and rivers, but there were so many important locations that it was not possible to defend them all. Whoever controlled these strategic waterways held a decisive military advantage, but how could America defend them against the preeminent naval power on the globe? British control of New York would cut the United States nearly in half.

With the fall of New France at the end of the French and Indian War, Great Britain took possession of Canada. The objective of the first American offensive of the war, launched in 1775, was to drive the British out of the north. When that invasion failed, for the remainder of the war the United States had to commit a substantial force to defend upper and western New York. Though the British Army, royalists, and their native allies to the north and west posed a serious threat, the greatest danger to New York came from the sea. Having nearly as many ships as France and Spain combined, the two next most powerful national fleets, the Royal Navy figured prominently in Great Britain's military plans. British vessels could attack anywhere along the Atlantic seaboard and navigable inland waterways with virtual impunity. There was also no better means to move troops and supplies. Keeping large numbers of ships on station, however, depended on having bases. With one of the finest natural harbors in North America and extensive port facilities, New York City was the best anchorage in the rebellious colonies besides Narragansett Bay. Strategically, there was no better target. Simultaneous thrusts from Canada up Lake Champlain, across Lake George, and down the Hudson River and from the sea to seize the lower Hudson would subjugate New York in one stroke. Losing New York City in 1776, the Continental Army, with difficulty, defended the rest of the state the following year. Reestablishing its dominant central position with the construction of West Point, the army's Highland defenses were never again seriously threatened. In an increasingly desultory strategy, stalemate in the north made the British turn to the south. Their capture of Savannah, Georgia, at the end of 1778 and Charleston, South Carolina, in the spring of 1780 was hoped to bring out enough royalists, the British ministry's will-o'-the-wisp, to complete the subjugation. Costly defeats in the interior and one Pyrrhic victory, however, severely diminished the British Army's strength and dampened the enthusiasm of many potential supporters. Unable to continue, British general Charles Cornwallis eventually led his army to the Tidewater region of Virginia in the late spring of 1781. Reinforced, he was eventually ordered to fortify a port. Selecting Yorktown, where the York River empties into Chesapeake Bay, he was safe if the Royal Navy controlled the eastern seaboard, but the French fleet arrived first and blocked any rescue from the sea. From the Highlands, Washington led a portion of the Continental Army to Virginia and succeeded, with the cooperation of his French ally the Comte de Rochambeau, commander in chief of the French Expeditionary Force, to besiege and capture the British army at Yorktown.

West Point, 1783, by Pierre L'Enfant (Library of Congress Prints and Photographs Division).

The allied forces of France and the Continental Army's capture of the principal enemy southern army at Yorktown, Virginia, in the fall of 1781, broke Great Britain's resolve to wage an offensive war in the 13 colonies. This capitulation eventually brought down the Lord North government, and the new ministry that succeeded his administration in March 1782 conceded that it would recognize American independence. By the fall of that year with the peace negotiations still dragging on, British forces still clung to New York City, Maine, the western frontier posts, and Charleston, South Carolina. The question was whether the spring of 1783 would see an end to the war or continued fighting. This choice, however, was not that of Great Britain and the United States alone. The war had also drawn in France, Spain, and the Dutch Republic, which diverted a substantial portion of British military strength away from America's shores. In their quest to avenge their humiliating defeat in the French and Indian War, the Seven Years' War in Europe, France from the outset of the conflict sent over thinly veiled shipments of arms, gunpowder, and other war matériel that helped sustain the Continental cause. France entered a formal diplomatic and military alliance with the United States in 1778. Although the first efforts at cooperation were the defeats at Newport, Rhode Island, in 1778 and Savannah, Georgia, in 1779, the promise of this pact gave the Americans added hope, which helped them to persevere through the darkest times. This was not, however, an open-ended commitment. French king Louis XVI needed to conclude his obligations to the United States as quickly as possible. Beside fighting for the independence of America, France also had to protect an extended coastline and its colonial possessions as well as fulfill its promise to Spain.

In order to entice Spanish king Charles III to enter the war, France pledged to act in concert with his military to take Gibraltar, the southern tip of the Iberian Peninsula, which was captured by the British in 1704. That rocky promontory jutting out into the sea dominated the entrance to the Mediterranean. Spain became a French ally and an American cobelligerent in 1779 only after France agreed to keep fighting until Gibraltar was retaken. While the Continental Army camped at Verplanck's Point in September 1782, the Bourbon powers made one last desperate attempt to carry that fortress. Holding out for four years, it never fell. Only the announcement of the preliminary articles of peace in February 1783 lifted the blockade. Spain had to settle for retaining Minorca, the British Mediterranean base buttressing Gibraltar, which Spain and France seized in February 1782, and the return of East and West Florida. The cost of this conflict had a ruinous effect on the French treasury. Eventually, the massive war debt would bankrupt the kingdom and start the chain of events that led to the French Revolution. Only Great Britain possessed the financial resources to fight a war on such a scale, but even its economy was straining under the burden, so Great Britain declared war on the Dutch Republic at the end of 1780 to stop its trade with the Americans and France. Baltic naval stores, carried in United Provinces of the Netherlands shipping, enabled the French to maintain such a large fleet. With all these nations involved, fighting raged not only in America, Europe, and the Mediterranean but also in the Caribbean, where those imperial powers possessed islands, and on the high seas throughout the world. The last major battle of the war was fought in India between British and French forces. Memory of this period might have prompted Washington in his farewell address as president to warn future generations to "steer clear of permanent Alliances with any portion of the foreign world."[2]

Internal politics was unsettled as well. The Articles of Confederation, the proposed plan for administering the new nation, was not ratified until 1781, but this did little to bolster the effectiveness of the government. Though theoretically a national legislative body, Congress was powerless to act without sanction from the states. Tenaciously hanging on to their power of the purse as they had done in colonial days, the state assemblies were backward in voting funds to support the war. With the British ministry propagating its desire for peace in the aftermath of Yorktown, the states were not motivated to appropriate the money to pay for the recruiting incentives necessary to fill their Continental lines. The legislatures would not even approve the additional funds for Continental Army pay, which was normally months in arrears, let alone appropriate the money for additional forces. Washington warned the states in a circular letter in May 1782 that Great Britain's offer of the olive branch was "merely delusory" to temporarily quiet the opposition among their own people and to undermine the U.S. alliance with France. He closed with the sage rejoinder that "no Nation have ever yet suffered in Treaty, by preparing, even in the Moment of Negotiation, most vigorously for the field."[3] Many of the best and brightest had left Congress by this point because of the endless partisan bickering and the lack of authority to tax, the basis of real power.

The Continental Army moved north to New Windsor from Verplanck's Point, opposite Stony Point, on the east side of the Hudson River. With the British in the process of evacuating the remainder of their southern force, substantial portions of which were bound for New York City, Washington deployed the army that summer in the lower Hudson Valley. Vulnerable to attack from the reinforced enemy, Washington prevailed upon General Rochambeau to move north from his encampments in the vicinity of Williamsburg and Yorktown, Virginia, for a juncture with him along the Hudson. In the heady days following Yorktown, the Continental commander in chief held out hope that in the spring of 1782 the two armies would undertake the reduction of New York City. Since it was lost, its recapture shaped his strategy. Personally a humiliating defeat in which half of his army was nearly lost, Washington planned every year to attack New York City, only to be frustrated by circumstances beyond his control. He was disappointed once again as French naval superiority, so decisive at Yorktown, proved fleeting. Without the support of a substantial French fleet, the enterprise was not practical to undertake, as were the lesser objects of Charleston, South Carolina; Savannah, Georgia; and Penobscot, Maine. A coveted 14th addition to its national confederation and haven for royalists and native warriors serving alongside British forces, Canada was an option. Washington queried Rochambeau about the feasibility of giving it another try with the combined might of both of their armies. Needing permission from his government to undertake any new operations, the French commander could agree only to a union with the Americans. His men encamped at Crompound (Crompond), 10 miles east of Verplanck's Point, so as not to compete for the same forage and wood. Trying to impress the French officers, Washington staged an elaborate field exercise to show them the military preparedness of his command. Powerless to do more than politely decline Washington's requests for concerted action, Rochambeau at the end of October marched his soldiers to Boston, Massachusetts, for embarkation to the West Indies.

The Continental forces then headed north to establish their winter quarters, or cantonment. Serving as military cities, cantonments were temporary barracks fashioned out of standing timber. Soldiers in the northern part of the United States normally went into cantonment when cold weather brought an end to the campaign season. Besides being in a strategic and protected area, these campsites had to have enough trees to construct huts and provide firewood, had to have access to potable water, and had to be situated on a road network that facilitated the movement of supplies. The Connecticut Line and the artillery attached to the infantry at Verplanck's Point moved up to augment the Invalid Corps and the 2nd and 3rd Artillery Regiments at West Point. Major General Henry Knox commanded this fortress. The Massachusetts, New Jersey, and New York Lines and the Rhode Island Regiment marched north to the vicinity of New Windsor. Guarding prisoners of war near Lancaster, Pennsylvania, the Canadian Regiment was ordered to posts in southern New York and northern New Jersey after being relieved by recruits from the Pennsylvania Line. Captain Bartholomew von Heer's mounted provost, the Marechaussee Corps, was sent to Chester, New York. As part of its military police duties, the corps also sometimes provided the force whenever quartermasters had to impress supplies from local inhabitants. Fortunately, by this point in the war the army rarely had to resort to this most distasteful measure. The mounted troops of the 2nd Light Dragoons were posted in the vicinity of Danbury and Reading, Connecticut, while the two dismounted troops were posted "contiguous to the [Long Island] Sound."[4] The rest of the troops from Pennsylvania south to Georgia were with Major General Nathanael Greene, commander of the southern theater.

Before moving to its winter campground, the Continental Army maneuvered for the secretary of war, Major General Benjamin Lincoln, on October 24. Two days later the left wing, commanded by Major General William Heath, marched north in the rain. They encamped near the north redoubt, opposite West Point, and suffered in the damp woods because they had no tents. The following day, the troops crossed the Hudson River in boats to the fort. In the afternoon, they "ascended Butter Hill" and camped that night on the opposite side. Resuming their march, at 7:00 a.m. the following day, October 28, they headed north, turned west onto the current Forge Hill Road, and arrived at their hutting ground three hours later. Major General Arthur St. Clair's right wing, a day later, followed the route of the left wing, arriving at New Windsor on October 29. Along the way, the left wing relieved the 10th Massachusetts and the 2nd New York garrisoning West Point with all of their Connecticut troops.[5] Coming up from the south via Pompton, New Jersey, the 3rd Maryland Regiment was ordered to march to New Windsor. The regiment was to leave a detachment at the blockhouse in the Clove, beyond Suffern, if the men from Hazen's Regiment were not there yet. Arriving at the hutting ground about a week after the main body of troops, the Marylanders were attached to the New Jersey Brigade.[6] With the local population of approximately 1,300, the appearance of the Continental Army made New Windsor the second-largest city in New York.

Consolidated in 1781 with the 2nd Rhode Island into a single regiment, the 1st Rhode Island for a short period in 1778 aggressively recruited Black soldiers, both free and enslaved. Native Americans were also enlisted. However, the 1st Rhode Island was never exclusively African American. Washington in 1780 wanted those soldiers divided between the two regiments "to abolish the name and appearance of a Black Corps." The Rhode Islanders tarried at New Windsor for less than a week. After arriving on the ground west of town, they were ordered to encamp near the mouth of Murderer's (Moodna) Creek to await transportation to Albany. Stormy weather slowed the embarkation, but by November 4 the entire regiment had boarded boats and sailed north to relieve the New Hampshire Line that was watching the northern and western approaches to that city. In poor condition after their duty on the northern frontier, the New Hampshire troops arrived at New Windsor in mid–November.[7] The Rhode Islanders would have cause to regret their new posting. In January and February 1783, General Washington lent them to militia colonel Marinus Willett, formerly of the New York Line, for use in his expedition against the enemy fort at Oswego, in central New York. Thwarted in his plans to attack New York City, Washington proposed a surprise attack on this British frontier outpost, located where the Oswego River flows into Lake Ontario. Feeling practically alone in pressing for attacks despite British overtures to suspend hostilities, he wanted to dictate the course of affairs, not wait on events. Continued aggressiveness would not only deter the enemy from detaching some of its garrisons in this country to attack the French, Spanish, or Dutch, which if successful would strengthen the British position in the peace talks but would also provide a focus for an increasingly disgruntled American soldiery. Traveling through heavy snow, the expedition arrived within four miles of the fort, only to blunder into a swamp, as their Indian guide had become lost. With many of the men's feet frozen, the whole debilitated by the cold, and having been on the move for 36 straight hours, Willett called off the attack. During the expedition and the insufferable return forced march, one man froze to death, and many others had frostbite.[8]

Washington selected New Windsor because it was the choice of quartermaster general Colonel Timothy Pickering. Accompanied by two other colonels, Heman Swift and Henry Jackson, and Lieutenant Colonel David Cobb, the Salem, Massachusetts, native examined several other sites on both sides of the river before making his recommendation. First settled in the 17th century, the village was a thriving community of approximately 1,300 when the cantonment was established. This number included enslaved Africans and refugees from British-occupied areas. Located on the west side of the Hudson River just south of Newburgh, New Windsor was astride the trade routes heading into New England and those via the water to Albany and New York City. To the west of the village, there were farms, orchards, and woodlots. The terrain is dominated by Snake Hill, the granite eminence that rises more than 200 feet above the surrounding countryside. Several gristmills and at least one sawmill were located along the streams in the vicinity. Though the rocky terrain precluded fitting large numbers of soldiers in proximity, the preferred campgrounds were situated in the vicinity of the Albany Post Road on the eastern side of the Hudson River, south of Fishkill and opposite West Point. By 1782, however, that region did not have enough trees left to meet the needs of the army.

The reasons for choosing this site were based on several factors. Unlike other places where the number of trees were insufficient or too big or too small, the woods around New Windsor could provide the necessary timber for both hut construction and firewood. Moreover, the location was relatively secure, as West Point stood between New Windsor and British forces to the southward, and was large enough to accommodate most of the army in one place, making supply and discipline easier. From nearby Beaver Dam (Silver) Stream, there was a plentiful supply of water. There were also military supply activities already operating in the vicinity, and the area boasted a well-developed road system. Operating since 1781, the nearby army hospital utilized the remaining huts constructed by the Continental artillery during the previous winter. The major drawback to New Windsor was its location on the west side of the Hudson River. Except for the artillerymen, no large groups of soldiers encamped in this location for any length of time. Supplying a few hundred men was one thing, but the nearly 8,000 souls who arrived in the late fall of 1782 put a strain on available resources. By necessity, some of the provisions were gathered to the eastward and faced a perilous winter crossing of the ice-choked river. Pickering wrote to Washington's aide, Lieutenant Colonel David Cobb, in early October urging that the army go into winter quarters as soon as possible. Not only did the tents sustain more damage at that time of year than the entire season, but the soldiers could also do the work in their linen hunting shirts, thereby saving their uniform coats, and "would go thro' it with a degree of cheerfulness." Waiting until

Chapter 1. "The camp behind Snake Hill"

the weather turned worse for no apparent reason made the building of huts so much harder, and "both officer and soldiers... already [had] sufficient causes of discontent." Also, for Pickering, his agents, and contractors, it was far easier to sustain a stationary force. Though ever hopeful of last-minute opportunities to accomplish some military feat, Washington acceded to the quartermaster's reasoning. With the French gone, there was no justification for remaining any longer in the field.[9]

The map of the New Windsor Cantonment in the collection of the New-York Historical Society, *Winter-Cantonment of the American Army and it's* [sic] *Vicinity for 1783*, executed by Simeon De Witt, geographer of the United States, shows the prominent features familiar to all camp residents and visitors. Immediately after the war, De Witt was appointed surveyor general of the State of New York, a

Quartermaster General Colonel Timothy Pickering (1745–1829) by Charles Willson Peale, from life, 1792–1793 (INDE 14131) (courtesy Independence National Historical Park).

position he held until his death 50 years later. The villages of Newburgh and New Windsor were clustered along the Hudson River. Beaver Dam Stream, currently Silver Stream, located in the center of the map, flows south and merges with Murderer's Creek, currently Moodna Creek. Murderer's Creek then flows east into the Hudson at Plum Point, the first European settlement in the vicinity. The Clove Road coursed south, and the Goshen Road coursed southwest. By either route, the army could march to the strategic heights around Morristown, New Jersey, the site of a few previous Continental Army encampments. Some of the roads were built by the Continental Army to improve communication between the three main encampment sites. The new road that connected the adjutant general's quarters and Commissary William Bell's issuing location was "made practicable for Waggons, by removing the Stumps, loose stones and rubbish." It was later extended to the "interval between the first and third Massachusetts Brigade[s]." Once communications between the various encampments were opened, soldiers were "forbidden to cross or lay open the fencing of inclosed Meadows or field."[10]

General George Washington stayed at the home of the widow Tryntje Hasbrouck, south of Newburgh. This modest fieldstone house was used for 16 months, his longest occupation of any headquarters. Just north of the junction of the Beaver Dam Stream and Murderer's Creek is the John Ellison house. Constructed in 1754, the elegant English-Dutch–style house was military headquarters in the summer of 1779, for the then quartermaster, Major General Nathanael Greene, and artillery commander General Henry Knox. Knox returned that fall and stayed again from the end of 1780 to the following July. He last used the home from May to September 1782. General Horatio Gates, commander of the encampment at New Windsor, resided there from November

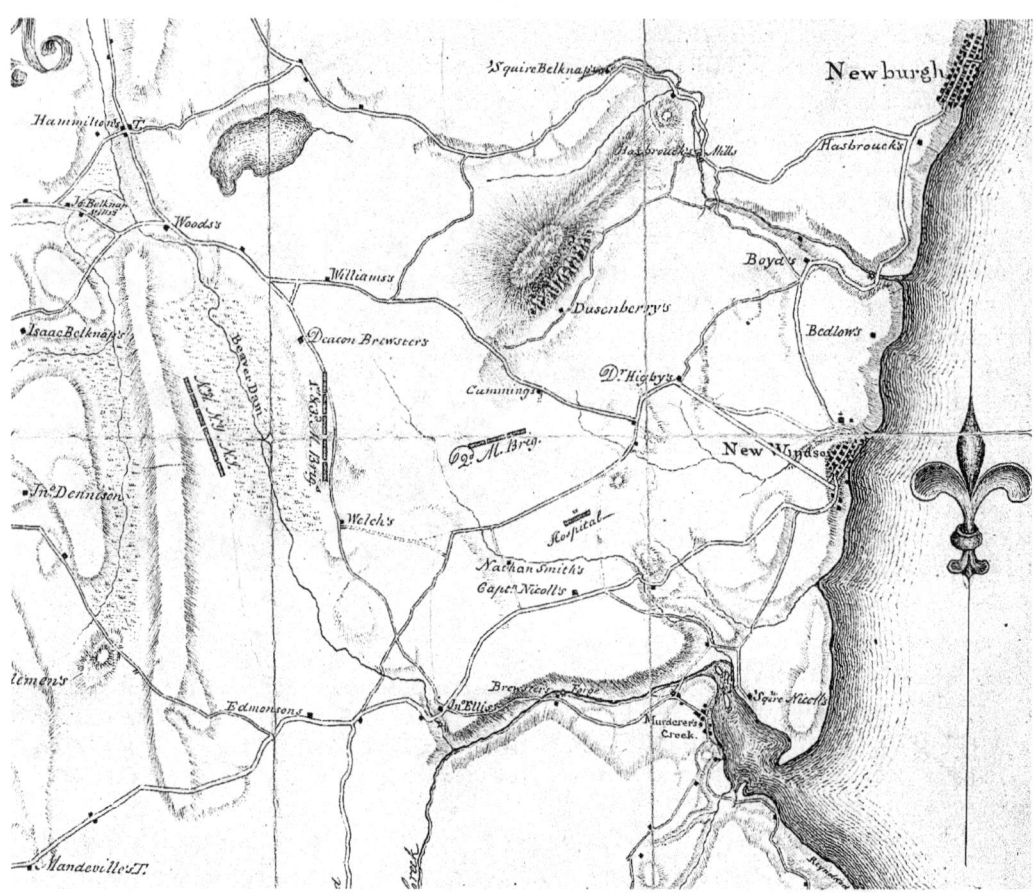

Detail from the *Winter-Cantonment of the American Army and It's* [sic] *Vicinity for 1783*, by Simeon De Witt (1756–1834). Pen and ink on laid paper, 28×38 cm, New-York Historical Society, maps M30.1.30, digital image 54675 (© New-York Historical Society).

1782 to the end of March 1783. First billeted at the James and William Edmonston house just west of the intersection of the Clove Road and the Goshen Road, Gates complained directly to Washington that "your Excellency's dog kennel at Mount Vernon, is as good a Quarter as that I am now in." If the Edmonston house was anywhere near as bad as Gates intimated, it was fortunate that the New Hampshire, New Jersey, New York, and Maryland division commander, General Arthur St. Clair, the next intended occupant, never took up residence. After escorting his troops to New Windsor, St. Clair left for Philadelphia and never returned. Though acknowledging that "the Discipline and Dress of the Army ... [was] indeed almost beyond belief" and that he commanded in his opinion "as fine a Body of Men as ... [he] ever beheld," the quality of his troops could not assuage his desire to avoid the drudgery of camp, so he made excuses to Washington why he could not come back.[11]

The Deacon Samuel Brewster house, in the center of the De Witt map, was headquarters for Major General Robert Howe, commander of the Massachusetts Line. Expected to go on leave immediately after the army arrived at the ground designated for their winter quarters, Pickering arranged no quarters for General Heath, which sparked a heated exchange. Amused by the spat, aide-de-camp Captain William North wasted little time in relaying the details to his commander, Friedrich von Steuben: "Heath spoke in a high tone. Pickering in a higher told him he might procure quarters for himself; if he could not do it within one mile, he might in four," which the indignant general did at the Squire Abel Belknap house west of Newburgh. Heath stayed there again when he replaced Gates as the commander of the New Windsor encampment in April 1783. Pickering was at the house formerly occupied by Captain Uriah Mitchell, deputy quartermaster, in Newburgh. Martha Washington and Katherine Hand, wife of the adjutant general Brigadier General Edward Hand, ate dinner with him there on January 18, 1783. Hand established himself and his wife and children at the Samuel Byard house in New Windsor, taking up residence shortly after Washington moved into the Hasbrouck house.[12] French engineer in the American service Colonel Jean

General George Washington (1732–1799) by James Peale, after Charles Willson Peale, c. 1787–1790 (INDE 14171) (courtesy Independence National Historical Park).

Widow Tryntje Hasbrouck house (General Washington's headquarters). The Jonathan Hasbrouck house, Washington's Headquarters State Historic Site, Newburgh, New York, c. 1906. Library of Congress Photographs and Prints Division.

Baptiste Gouvion stayed at Samuel Wood's tavern, just north of the encampment area, from January 22 to June 16, taking over "two Rooms and a Kitchen." His commander, Major General Louis le Bègue de Presle Duportail, stayed there previously for two months beginning in May 1781 and was expected, but he did not leave Philadelphia after both of them returned from France in December 1782. The John Denniston house, located on the hilltop in the center of the De Witt map, was occupied by Colonel Francis Barber, commander of the 2nd New Jersey Regiment. He was killed nearby on February 11, 1783, when he rode into the path of a tree felled by soldiers in the camp. Field Commissary of Military Stores Richard Frothingham and his assistants stayed at the widow Mandeville's on the Goshen Road, a little more than a mile west of the Edmonstons. Geographer of the United States Simeon De Witt was at the home of James Latta, and Deputy Paymaster Hezekiah Wetmore resided

Major General Horatio Gates (1728/29–1806) by Charles Willson Peale, from life, 1782 (INDE 14053) (courtesy Independence National Historical Park).

John Ellison house (Gates's headquarters). Knox's Headquarters State Historic Site, New Windsor, New York. The letters instigating the Newburgh Conspiracy were written in this house (author's collection).

at the Samuel Brewster, Jr., house by the forge along Murderer's (Moodna) Creek, just west of Gates's headquarters.[13] Major General von Steuben, the inspector general, was at the Samuel Verplanck house in Fishkill, directly opposite Newburgh on the eastern side of the Hudson.

The largest concentration of Continental soldiers was in the valley of the Beaver Dam Stream, in the center of the De Witt map. The Maryland, New Hampshire, New Jersey, and New York Lines built their huts west of the stream, facing to the east. The 1st Massachusetts Brigade, composed of the 1st, 4th, and 7th Regiments and the 3rd Massachusetts Brigade's 3rd and 6th Regiments, were encamped along the dirt road, east of Beaver Dam Stream. Before they were disbanded and dispersed among the rest of the Massachusetts Line to fill vacant positions, in accordance with the reforms that were to take effect by January 1, 1783, the 9th Regiment encamped between the 3rd and 6th Regiments. However, they were redistributed before construction of the huts began. The 1st Massachusetts Brigade camped in order facing west toward their parade from right to left: the 1st, 7th and 4th Regiments. As in the 3rd Brigade, the two senior regiments were arrayed on the flanks, with the junior one in the center. The 1st and 3rd Massachusetts Brigades' huts were along the dirt road, east of Beaver Dam Stream. Directly east on the opposite side of the hill, the 2nd Massachusetts Brigade faced south, with the senior 2nd Regiment on the right, the 5th Regiment on the left, and the junior 8th Regiment in the middle.

Major General Frederick William Augustus, Baron Von Steuben (1730-1794), by Charles Willson Peale, 1781-1782 (INDE 11876) (courtesy Independence National Historical Park).

During the New Windsor Cantonment, the artillery, the Connecticut Line, and the Invalid Corps were at West Point and its dependencies. Dependencies were smaller outposts that included the north and south redoubts on the eastern side of the Hudson River, opposite that fortress. The Invalid Corps was composed of soldiers who had been wounded or were in some other way incapacitated as to make them unfit for normal service. They were, however, capable of performing garrison duty, which made available more able-bodied soldiers for the field. Stationed south of West Point in posts that extended into New Jersey, Brevet Brigadier General Moses Hazen's Canadian Regiment interdicted suspicious persons and Americans attempting to sell goods to the British. Hazen's regiment relieved a detachment from the 3rd Maryland that then marched to New Windsor. Hazen's positions were at the blockhouse guarding the Dobbs Ferry Hudson River crossing and the one in the clove "a little beyond Sufferans."[14]

Beginning at the fort at Stony Point and crossing over the Hudson River and generally following the course of the Croton River, "the lines" were forward outposts manned by the Continental Army. They were there to "cover the Country from the incursions of the Enemy" and prevent "all manner of illicit intercourse and commerce between the Citizens of this State and the Enemy." Though directed to prevent livestock and other foodstuffs from passing into British-controlled territory, Ensign Ricker Sedam of the 1st New Jersey Regiment took it upon himself to not only seize but also sell a cow he thought was intended for the enemy. The court did not dispute his right to take the animal but pointed out that he should have had a magistrate condemn it prior to the sale. Realizing that his actions were the product of youthful zeal, the court thought that his conduct was excusable. Convinced that unless the states surrounding New York City made this illegal trade punishable by death, Washington believed that the entire American army could not enforce this prohibition. To exit or enter American lines, individuals had to receive written permission from a government official. Only Congress, the secretary at war, the supreme executive of the states, and General Washington could authorize the issue of a flag. This white cloth only showed the bearer's peaceful intention and desire to communicate. It was the authorizing document that accompanied the signal that determined whether individuals or correspondence could pass into or from American lines. By January 1783, enemy communications were only accepted at the New Bridge crossing of the Croton River. Except for those addressed to American government officials, all letters and dispatches coming from enemy lines had to be inspected at Continental Army headquarters. Captain Aaron Ogden, also from the 1st New Jersey, was involved in "a step of inadventure" when he entered New York City in March to assist Continental Congress emissary Lewis Morris with the delivery of dispatches announcing the general peace to British commander General Guy Carleton. Washington wanted an immediate investigation of the "unprecedented conduct he has adopted." When informed by Ogden of the aid he afforded Morris in entering British lines, the commander in chief desired that he should "entertain no further apprehension of his displeasure."[15]

When the camp at New Windsor was established, the light infantry was occupying these positions. Eventually they were relieved, and a new regiment from the cantonment, beginning with Colonel Matthias Ogden's 1st New Jersey, rotated through the duty every two weeks. A company was stationed at both Stony Point and Verplanck's Point, and the remaining seven companies, which included that regiment's light infantry, were posted along the Croton River. Ogden was allowed to extend his patrols east to Bedford or station a company at that place. Remembering the fate of 1st Rhode Island Regiment commander Colonel Christopher Greene and 30 of his men, killed in a royalist attack at the Pines Bridge crossing of the Croton in May 1781, Washington warned Ogden to "keep each Company as compact as may be, changing position very frequently, and taking every precaution to prevent the Enemy from making a stroke at any of your Detachments."[16]

Initially watercraft were used to transport soldiers to the lines, probably the flatboats secured in Murderer's Creek, in late October. The 1st New Jersey sailed in early December to relieve the light infantry. This mode of travel ended, however, with the buildup of ice in the river. The following month, Washington dismissed his own barge crew and sent them back to their regiments and told everyone else with boats to do the same.[17] When the Hudson River froze there were the ice boats fitted with runners or skis, operated by the quartermaster department, but the regiments walked the entire way to the advance posts beginning in mid–January 1783. Leaving on Thursdays until the end of March, the day was changed to Tuesday in April. Taking longer to reach the positions, the regiments were preceded by their quartermaster, who arranged lodging along their route of march as well as accommodations during their tour of duty. Empowered by the "Act of this State for Billeting Troops," they were assisted in identifying places by local civil authorities, who could force residents to house them. Making the quartermasters coordinate with local officials prior to the arrival of the soldiers was in response to the complaint of Pelatiah Haws, justice of the peace in Westchester County at Peekskill, who wrote to Washington that 19 soldiers showed up at his house and that before he went to bed the number had risen to 30.[18] Even when the Hudson was navigable again in the spring, the regiments continued to march to the lines.

By the end of March 1783, the commander of the lines assumed responsibility for the blockhouse at Dobbs Ferry, relieving the Canadian Regiment of that duty.[19] About a dozen miles north of Manhattan, the Dobbs Ferry crossing was too close to enemy lines for the Americans to make use of it for most of the war. Beginning at this location, beacons were positioned on prominent rises on both sides of the Hudson River heading north to provide early warning of armed enemy vessels. The Invalid Corps manned the stack of logs ready for firing above Fishkill Landing, now Beacon, New York, while a detail from West Point watched the signal station on Butter Hill, later Storm King Mountain. In mid–November 1782, Knox asked Washington whether to maintain these positions over the winter and reported that his artillerists were putting together some rockets to provide another mode of alarm. Expecting to meet with Governor Clinton in a few days to discuss the matter, the commander in chief told him to continue the beacons in the meantime.[20] With no further mention of the signal fire locations, they were probably abandoned. Anyway, ice would shortly prevent ships from sailing the river until the spring.

Chapter 2

"The Timber was heavy and the work very fatiguing"

Constructing the Log City—Lieutenant Ebenezer Elmer, 2nd New Jersey Regiment[1]

> We are busily employed completing our Town. It will I suppose contain of Honest men—Women—and Rogues and the progeny of both, ten thousand souls.[2]
>
> —Lieutenant Colonel Tench Tilghman to John Bingham, November 28, 1782

MILITARY DUTY WAS DESIGNED to increase soldiers' readiness for battle, protect their person, promote greater efficiency, and keep them busy. Some of the work parties, called fatigues, did activities whose only purpose was to employ the soldiers. When stationed at West Point, much of the garrison's time was spent mending and improving the fortifications. Compromised daily by the elements, forts were always in need of repair. Roads were built in the camp at New Windsor that were handy to have, but they probably would not have been constructed had there been more useful ways for the soldiers to spend their time. Discouraging enlistments and promoting desertion, life in the Continental Army was tedious and strictly regulated. Drummers played the various calls, which regulated the day. Reveille told soldiers to wake up, and tattoo told them to go to their tents and remain in them until the following morning. Just after reveille, troop was beat "for the purpose of calling the role and inspecting the men for duty." Prior to tattoo, the roll again was taken at the retreat call, and the soldiers were warned about their duties for the following day. In emergencies, "to arms" was the signal to quickly put on your accoutrements, grab your weapon, and assemble in your unit area for further instructions. "The general" was the call to take down the tents and prepare to move. At the assembly call the troops formed, and the march call sent the column in motion. A convention of attacking a fortified place, the parley call was a request to speak with the enemy. In the beginning of a siege, attackers usually tried to intimidate the defenders into surrendering without a fight during this conference. Defenders played the parley call when they could no longer mount an effective resistance. At the investment of Yorktown, a British drummer mounted the parapet and beat the parley call until the allied forces finally recognized his summons and stopped firing. There were calls for adjutants and noncommissioned officers to gather, to summon fatigue and wood-gathering parties, to announce church call, and to tell drummers to assemble. To prevent unnecessary alarm, musicians were to practice at a set time during the day.[3] There is no information regarding how proficient they were. Giving someone a fife or a drum no more made him a musician than did having a gun make one a soldier. Unskilled drummers and fifers caused confusion. Lieutenant John Hiwell, from the 3rd Continental Artillery, was the inspector and superintendent of music. In the spring of 1783 he held at least one session at his hut, where he inspected and then instructed the musicians, who were not on duty. Drum Major William Loudon, of the 1st New York, held daily practice sessions, weather permitting. Presumably, the rest of the regiments followed suit.[4] Acknowledging the desperate want of infantry, at the end of December 1781 Congress barred the enlistment of any more drummers and fifers. Men were performing the easy duty and getting the extra pay, while boys were thrown into the ranks. When additional musicians were required, they were to come from the infantry. Any subsequent infantry performing this duty would have the extra pay normally accorded to musicians set aside for the repair of the regiments' instruments or for replacements for those that were missing, because they were responsible for any loss or damages. They could also have their regular pay stopped to make good any deficiency. Most of the units, however, maintained nearly their full complement of music until the end of the war, facilitated by the disbandment and consolidation of the Connecticut and Massachusetts Lines at the end of 1782. Though the nation tried to provide a full complement of instruments, there were still so many musicians that there was a great shortfall of drums.[5] At least for the ones in possession of drums, they were issued protective cases.

The typical day at New Windsor started with reveille, beaten by the drummer. Reveille varied by season. In the winter months, the time was usually one hour later because of the cold and shorter hours of daylight. Since there was no standard time, the adjutant general was the official timekeeper. He set his watch off the clock at headquarters or the commander in chief's timepiece and synchronized the hour and minutes with other officers, especially the brigade majors.[6] The brigade majors, who oversaw the conduct of daily activities within their brigades, made sure fellow officers, especially the regimental adjutants, were operating on Continental Army standard time. Morning roll call was then taken to ensure that no soldier had left camp during the night. Enlisted men were forbidden to leave camp without a pass or unsupervised. Some of them left to take food from local farmers and then returned before reveille because it was a set time every day. Eventually, catch rolls were called at different times in the middle of the night to discourage marauding. Individuals not present at the calling of the rolls were punished upon their return. After the morning roll call, the soldiers started to prepare their food ration and clean their persons. Personal hygiene was limited to possibly just washing the face and hands. Shaving was done every few days because facial hair was not allowed. Some might brush their teeth, but that was about it. Eighteenth-century people in general did not wash themselves extensively in the wintertime for fear of getting sick. This was why impetigo, a bacteriological skin disease called "the itch," was common in the ranks. Following breakfast, the soldiers started to do their work. When the weather improved, there was military drill as well.

Besides work on the huts, the army performed many fatigues designed to improve the camp. Removing the obstructions in front of their hutting ground and clearing a roadway for the passage of the provision wagons was of primary importance, especially for the isolated encampment site on the western side of Beaver Dam Stream.[7] Every day there was one regiment on guard duty and another on fatigue. Other regiments or a portion thereof were sometimes detailed to perform specific tasks. In the construction of the Temple Building, the causeway, the firework stand, and the illumination frame, every brigade was assigned a portion of the work. Following the day's activities, the soldiers returned to their tents or huts and consumed the evening meal. With the beating of the drum at night called "tattoo," the soldiers retired for the evening. This routine continued every day. There were, however, some events that broke the monotony. On November 6, 1782, four soldiers from the 10th Massachusetts assisted engineer Major Etienne de Rochefontaine, a volunteer from the French service, in "surveying the environs of the Camp." The following day, 29 soldiers from the 1st New Jersey Regiment were led by a subaltern officer to William Ellison's wharf in New Windsor. There, they took charge of some of prisoners of war and escorted them to Philadelphia. A few days later, a trustworthy veteran soldier from each regiment was assigned to the adjutant general's office to carry orders to West Point and perform other duties. Generals Gates, Howe, Knox, Hand, and John Paterson met on December 19, 1782, at the Horton house, near where Murderer's Creek empties in the Hudson, to resolve the disputes stemming from the reorganization of the Connecticut Line.[8] At the end of November 1782, a dozen 10th Massachusetts soldiers, led by a sergeant, marched to Fishkill Landing, opposite Newburgh, to assist John Ruddock, deputy commissary of military stores, in transferring the supplies located there and at the Fishkill depot to West Point. Expected to be on this duty for several days, the detail was to carry enough provisions for that length of time.[9] They actually were there for only three days, because a fatigue from the 9th Massachusetts arrived to replace them. Colonel Benjamin Tupper then led the 10th Massachusetts south to Verplanck's Point. At this time, both the 9th and 10th Massachusetts Regiments were in the process of being disbanded, so the strength of each was considerably reduced. After setting up tents and affixing chimneys to them, the 10th Massachusetts, under the direction of Rochefontaine, started to repair the fortifications at Verplanck's Point, sometimes referred to as Fort Lafayette. Returning to New Windsor after completing the work, they left their tents behind to provide quarters for the companies that would occupy that post while serving on the lines. Appreciative of their effort, the commander in chief authorized the distribution of an additional liquor ration to these men.[10] In January, a small detail from the 4th Massachusetts Regiment was ordered to take charge of a number of naval prisoners at West Point and conduct them to Philadelphia.[11]

Modeled after European militaries, the Continental Army was a conventional force intended to engage the enemy in the linear tactics of the day. While capable of fighting small-unit actions, sometimes referred to as *petit guerre*, the Americans' goal was to decisively win battles and sieges and avoid serious defeats. In such a vast territory, however, tactical losses on individual battlefields did not often have large-scale or strategic implications, because the country lacked a location whose capture or destruction meant ultimate defeat. Napoleonic military theorist Carl von Clausewitz later referred to these crucial national places as centers of gravity. Every major city in the country was occupied by British forces at some point during the war and availed them little other than denying their use by the Americans and having the cities as bases of operations. Vital resources could also be centers of gravity. In trying to avert a war, British officials attempted confiscation of stockpiled colonial weapons and ammunition precipitated one instead. Challenging every enemy action to wear them down to show the futility of continuing the war was paramount. Victories were not essential to accomplish this goal, but maneuvering the armies so they could live to fight another day and resilience was. Mentoring his impetuous young protégé, the Marquis de Lafayette, who was anxious that the American army do something right away to reverse the deteriorating military situation following the disastrous fighting in South Carolina in 1780, Washington patiently explained to him that "to endeavour to recover our reputation, we should take care that we do not injure it more."[12]

General Washington was commander in chief of the entire Continental Army, but the coalition nature of the American union interfered with his ability to place the best officers in leadership positions or marshal the nation's resources, needlessly protracting the conflict. Washington commanded from the northern department, while General Greene led the forces in the south. For both armies, the core was composed of Continental regulars who could be augmented by organized state units of full-time soldiers, called levies, and the militia. Sometimes, individual replacements were taken from the militia to fill the depleted ranks of their state's Continental Line regiments. They were also called levies because they too were drawn out of the ranks of the militia. There were also entire units of them raised for a specific period by the individual states for service that was in their interest. Some state formations were so powerful that they could undertake singlehandedly offensive operations. George Rogers Clark's successful campaign, in 1778–79 that drove the British out of the Illinois Territory was organized and financed by Virginia because it claimed that region. Amassing the largest American naval flotilla of the war, containing its own navy and army and three Continental Navy vessels, Massachusetts tried to retake its territory in Maine from the British in 1779 but suffered a disastrous repulse. During the winter of 1782–83, New York employed two state regiments of levies to defend its settlements along its northern and western frontier. A number of these men took part in the abortive expedition against Fort Oswego in February 1783.

The militia performed military duty only when they were needed. After the crisis passed, these reserve forces returned to their civilian pursuits. Brought over with the first wave of settlement, the militia system would be the British undoing. Communities were expected to embody their men into units, instruct them in the soldierly arts, and enforce the requirement for individuals to provide themselves with a firearm and accoutrements. Initially intended as an economy measure, requiring little involvement from the mother country, this expedient created a large pool of rudimentarily trained manpower with the means to resist. Also, most of the officers cut their teeth in the militia. At numerous critical moments in the war, they proved decisive. One can, however, wax too much on their importance. Usually difficult to mobilize and indifferently trained and led, these temporary soldiers were too slender a reed upon which to anchor a line of battle, but in a supporting role or as a recruiting ground for the regular Continental forces they were invaluable. "Militia service … [was] preferred by the peasantry to the Continental, the pay being greater, the duty less, and the discipline more relaxed." Most states throughout the war had certain numbers of its full-time force or militia on extended service manning posts on the frontiers, guarding and transporting supplies, and augmenting the Continental Line during the campaign season. For the unemployed or underemployed, prolonged militia duty provided decent pay, especially when bonuses and bounty clothing were offered, without the long-term commitment and uncertainty of Continental Army service. Washington, however, feared trusting the survival of the country to the vagaries of the militia given "how precarious and uncertain the aid is." In many cases, the militia would not stay beyond their short-term of service no matter how dire the situation was. Washington wanted a dependable regular force so that the militia would not be called out "except on the most extraordinary occasions." Those citizens, who were drafted by their states, were thrown into a life in which they were not accustomed and inclined, while calculating individuals did several short enlistments to collect the substantial incentives offered at the beginning of each term of service. "The sums expended in bounties, waste of Arms, consumption of Military Stores, Provisions, Camp Utensils &ca; to say nothing of Cloathing which temporary Soldiers are always receiving, and always in want of, are too great for the resources of any Nation; and prove the fallacy and danger of temporary expedients."[13] Militiamen engaged in vital wartime employment were sometimes excused from service. Moreover, considering that most of them were farmers, the timing of the call-ups had to be ideally after spring planting and before harvest time. This severely limited the time that army commanders had to accomplish their missions. But other reasons for poor militia turnout was that it was difficult to invigorate them unless the danger was immediate and close at hand. Even then, if prospects were unfavorable, they would not mobilize, and if there was a nearby threat the states would not release them for service elsewhere. Moreover, too many false alarms and transitory enemy incursions were over before they could gather, which did not encourage alacrity.

The army at New Windsor was from the regular Continental Line, a few members of which were short-term soldiers levied from the militia. In the middle of December 1782, the levies, having completed their work, began to leave. That month 89 soldiers were discharged from the New York Line, compared to five others from the rest of the army encamped here.[14] All or nearly all of those discharged soldiers were levies. The main forces at New Windsor were from Massachusetts, Maryland, New Hampshire, New Jersey, and New York. In the beginning of the camp, the Rhode Island Regiment stayed for a few days at the mouth of nearby Murderer's Creek along the Hudson before going north to relieve the two New Hampshire regiments garrisoning the frontier north and west of Albany. A company from the New Jersey Line serving in Pennsylvania's Wyoming Valley was ordered to rejoin its line at New Windsor in February 1783. For the sake of discipline, Washington wanted this company withdrawn the previous fall, but Pennsylvania authorities were convinced that the Connecticut settlers would then seize the post and dominate the region. Both Connecticut and Pennsylvania vied with each other to lay claim to this rich land. Over the winter, commissioners tried to settle the dispute. Isolated and living off the country due to the failure of the ration contractor, Captain Abel Weyman, commander of that company of about 50, equally drawn from both the 1st and 2nd New Jersey Regiments, wrote to headquarters at the end of November requesting again the relief of his unit. Telling Weyman that a resolution was expected shortly, Washington did not believe that a garrison would then be necessary. If Congress was determined to still keep troops in the region, he would replace his unit with another company. In the interim Washington promised to try to fix the supply situation.[15] Though ownership of the Wyoming Valley was finally decided in favor of Pennsylvania, this conflict persisted for nearly two more decades.

The Massachusetts Line was one division of the Continental Army at New Windsor, and the New Hampshire, New Jersey, New York, and Maryland Lines were the other. Each division was composed of several brigades. The brigades were typically composed of two to three regiments. A regiment consisted of "one colonel, one lieutenant colonel, and one major, where full colonels continued: or one lieutenant colonel commandant and two majors, where the colonels are not continued: 9 captains, 22 subalterns,

1 surgeon, 1 surgeon's mate, 1 serjeant major, 1 quartermaster serjeant, 45 serjeants, 1 drum major, 1 fife major, 10 drums, 10 fifes, 612 rank and file." Each company had one captain and two subalterns, officers who were below the rank of captain. The four extra lieutenants, known as supernumeraries, were assigned the duties of paymaster, quartermaster, adjutant, and recruiter.[16]

Eventually, the infantry regiments were reduced to 500 rank and file as an economic measure and to approximate their actual strength. The daily wastage of deaths, debilitating injuries, and desertions continually drained army manpower. Though the Congressional Resolves of August 7, 1782, that reduced the size and number of the infantry regiments was to take effect on January 1, 1783, Washington implemented the reorganization in the beginning of November 1782. The reform immediately took effect in the Massachusetts Line, reducing its regiments from ten to eight and the Connecticut Line from five to three. The rest of the northern army was left intact in order to give those states time to recruit their forces up to their required strength. Many officers became "deranged," or excess, when their regiments were disbanded. They had to either find a vacancy in a regiment selected to continue or leave the service. Whether they quit the field or stayed in hopes of finding a vacancy, they would be "entitled to full pay and subsistence up to the first of January."[17]

Washington had to reduce the number of regiments before the construction of the huts. At New Windsor Cantonment there is no evidence to determine where the initial tent camps were in relation to the huts. The temporary cloth structures would have been as close as possible to the worksites without interfering with hut construction. Marching to their encampment sites under the direction of the quartermasters and camp colormen, the soldiers set up tents and added fieldstone chimneys. The camp colormen laid out the encampment site with string guidelines and then used a small flag, called a camp color, to mark the location for their respective companies to pitch their tents. The flag

Detail of Continental Army encampment from the portrait of Colonel Walter Stewart by Charles Willson Peale, c. 1781 (Yale University Art Gallery). Soldiers cook in a circular field kitchen. Individual hearths were cut out of the earth radiating in a circle around the mounds. Messes, groups that normally cooked together, prepared their meals away from the encampment area. The common tents usually held four or five soldiers. Note the musket racks in front. At the New Windsor Cantonment, fieldstone fireplaces and chimneys were added to the tents while the huts were under construction.

was mounted to a pole carried inside the musket barrel, so bayonets were not issued to these men. Had there been one, the blade would have possibly ripped the colors.[18]

Plate VIII, from the *Regulations for the Order and Discipline of the Troops of the United States*, by Major General von Steuben, shows the typical arrangement of an American regimental camp. The eight companies were arranged in three lines. The first two lines were composed of enlisted soldiers, with company officers in the third line and the major, lieutenant colonel, and colonel behind them. Even if there was no enemy in the vicinity, the camps were still laid out in battle formation. "The infantry will on all occasions encamp by battalions, as they are formed in order of battle." At this encampment, Pickering had to depart from this regulation and shorten the distance between the two ranks of enlisted tents to fit everyone into the landscape.[19] When the camps were struck, one servant from every company remained behind to load the tents and other gear into the wagons. Even though officers had greater allocations of the limited transportation space, a number still abused this privilege. Washington finally put a stop to the excess and ordered the quartermasters to throw away any officer baggage loaded onto wagons intended for the soldiers' tents.[20]

While released from the burden of carrying their tents, the men, when separated from their wagons, had to either sleep outside, make improvised shelters out of trees or brush, or use structures and outbuildings, both public and private. Within the infantry brigades the common tent was the most prevalent, followed by lesser numbers of the larger French horsemen's tent. Made from canvas, a tightly woven heavy linen also used for making sails, these wedge-shaped tents were water-resistant, not waterproof. Having no floors, they provided scant protection. Veterans, however, learned to combine the issued bundles of straw with grass and leaves to make comfortable bedding. Soldiers slept in a row, parallel to the tent opening. An English common tent normally held five. Despite Steuben's recommendation to put half a dozen in a common tent, they were "generally too small for 6 men." The horsemen's tent was only "10 inches longer in the ridge & as much more in length," so it could not "contain more than six men." Cartridge pouches, knapsacks, and other individual soldier equipment were usually stored inside. Some of the officers used the more elaborate marquee tent, which had a high roof and removable sides. Due to the shortage of tent cord, they were "obliged to substitute the Cod line which came from Boston last year," though it was too thin. Secured to stakes, the cord made the spare framework sturdier. There are descriptions from other encampments where soldiers built up their tents to keep out moisture and the cold. This was probably done at New Windsor as well. Lieutenant Benjamin Gilbert when he was a sergeant raised his tent "two foot from [the] Ground and made the Walls with flags(tone)." The soldiers were permitted to construct fieldstone chimneys opposite the opening, taking care to stack the stones high enough to prevent the linen from catching fire. In October 1780, Ensign Jeremiah Greenman and fellow officers of the 2nd Rhode Island Regiment moved their "Marques under the Lee of fort Clinton, [at West Point], where we built fireplaces and sealed it within with boards which made it very comfortable." Manning the lines as the troops arrived in New Windsor, Gilbert's light infantry company also constructed chimneys for their tents, and because the following day was rainy, Gilbert "built a bunk to sleep on."[21] Ideally, muskets were not brought into the tents and were either stacked upright, using the bayonets to lock them together, laid on wooden racks, or, when available, stored in their own shelter. Stacking arms was not generally done for extended periods of time because of their vulnerability to being knocked over and the difficulty of removing muskets without taking apart the entire pile. Made from two wooden stakes and a horizontal crosspiece, about a foot off the ground, the wooden racks provided easy access to individual weapons but still exposed the muskets to the elements. Upside-down cone-shaped bell tents, supported by a central pole from which posts projected, were the best means to stack arms in camp but only if the tents were properly used. Officers were warned to ensure that their men disposed of their arms properly in the bell tents and did not let them lean against the canvas, which wore out the tents and facilitated seepage.[22]

Large circular field kitchens with about a dozen places for cooking were typically situated behind the tents. Made of earth piled in a mound, each mess, normally the occupants of a single tent, cooked in square-shaped kitchens cut into the pile. Sutlers, licensed purveyors of sundries and food who traveled with the army, camped between the kitchens. If present, the supply wagons were located behind the kitchens so that in case of attack they could be quickly withdrawn. The draft teams of oxen or horses were placed to the rear of the wagons. The necessaries or vaults for human waste were located

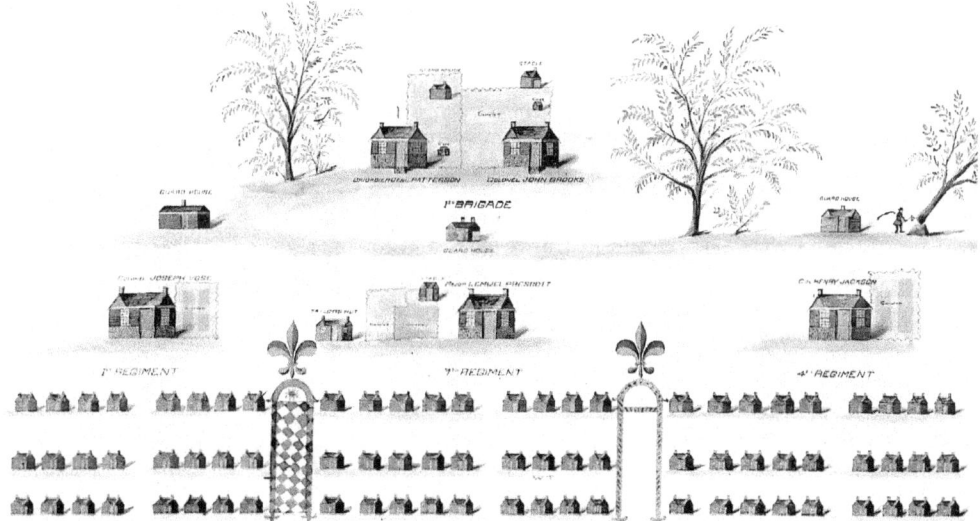

The 1st Massachusetts Brigade from the drawing of the Massachusetts Line at the New Windsor Cantonment after the sketch done by Private William Tarbell of the 7th Massachusetts Regiment. Caldwell and Garrison Civil Engineers Newburgh, New York, 1890. The engineer version is close but not an exact copy. Arrayed in battle order facing a notional enemy advancing from the bottom of the picture, there were two rows of huts for the 1st Massachusetts Brigade's noncommissioned officers and privates, and the third hut was for the company officers. All three regimental commander huts behind those lines had gardens. In the middle was a stable for these huts and the brigade tailor's hut. Three regimental guardhouses lined the opposite side of the road. Co-located, the huts of brigade commander Brigadier General John Paterson and Colonel John Brooks of the 7th Massachusetts, farther up the slope, also had a garden, a stable, and their kitchens are depicted as well. The brigade guardhouse was directly behind the brigade commander's hut. Except for the distinctive arches between the regiments and rendered with slightly less detail, the other two brigades in the drawing are basically the same as the 1st Brigade. Private William Tarbell's hut is in the middle row of the 7th Massachusetts Regiment, third from the right and designated with his initials "W.T." (courtesy Washington's Headquarters State Historic Site Collection, New York State Office of Parks, Recreation and Historic Preservation).

away from the main camp area. Sentinels from the camp and quarter guards were posted in the vicinity to provide early warning in case of alarm. Drums were stacked in front of the adjutant's tent, and the regimental colors or flags were "planted before them."[23]

The drawing of the Massachusetts Line, executed at New Windsor by William Tarbell, a private in that state's 7th Regiment, is the best period representation of the New Windsor Cantonment. Three orderly rows of huts faced the brigade parade grounds, with soldiers in the first two rows and company officers in the third row. Tarbell's hut is marked by his initials "W.T." Field officer huts, brigade commander huts, guard huts, a soldier-constructed meeting hall called the Temple of Virtue, a stand to display fireworks and various other outbuildings were behind the company officer huts. Though contiguous in the drawing, the 2nd Massachusetts Brigade was approximately three-quarters of a mile to the east, near the Clove Road. For the 1st and 3rd Massachusetts Brigades, the gap between the regimental commander huts and the line of guard huts is the location of the road. Encamped on the western side of Beaver Dam Stream, the layout of the New Hampshire, New Jersey, and New York brigades mirrored that of the 1st and 3rd Massachusetts Brigades.

Much speculation has gone into the accuracy of the Tarbell drawing as to whether he took artistic license and engaged in great flights of fancy or was to the best of his abilities a faithful illustrator. Though naive in its composition and above all its scale, some of the imagery is from Masonry. The Masonic order's symbols in his drawing are unmistakable. They were allegories used to assist new members in understanding the beliefs of the society. The large rising sun in the center is a common 18th-century motif and Masonic symbol; taverns were named after it, and decorative arts were covered with it, including one on the top rail of famous presiding chair of the Constitutional Convention, that

Detail from Pierre L'Enfant's drawing of the Continental Army encampment at Verplanck's Point in the fall of 1782 showing a bower with fouled anchor marking the entrance to the Rhode Island Regiment campsite (Museum of the American Revolution).

Benjamin Franklin wondered whether it was a rising or setting sun. This rising sun, with its 13 interlocking rings, was a firework set off during the peace celebration on April 19.[24]

Arches marking the intervals between the regiments and entrances into the camp are similar in shape to the formal entryway of the Temple of Virtue. One of them has an alternating black and white painted square walkway that might ornament a bridge over a low area. Another has an hourglass design. Between the 2nd and 8th Massachusetts Regiments, beyond the entryway, there was a semicircular alternating black and white walkway, just below a tree. In a very poorly drained area, these decorative elements might show platforms built to provide a dry alternative to the spongy morass. Fleurs-de-lis decorated the top of each passage that are so exact that they must have been drawn with a stencil. On top of the arch between the 8th and 5th Massachusetts there are branches with leaves.

The huts took a considerable amount of time to build, but the soldiers did not begin work immediately. They were distressed because their masons and carpenters were not with them to oversee the construction. Soldiers possessing these skills were sometimes detached from their regiments when there were building projects to augment the permanent corps of blacksmiths, carpenters, masons, wheelwrights, leather workers, and other skilled craftsmen called artificers. Washington ordered them to travel to New Windsor as soon as they completed their current work.[25] Though construction of the huts was not finished, soldiers from the Massachusetts Line were ordered to build a jail or provost guardhouse, and officers' guardroom (later called a guardhouse), and a hut for the provost martial. General St. Clair's men built the court-martial room and the hut for the judge advocate general. Initially, the quarters of judge advocate general Lieutenant Thomas Edwards was designated for courts-martial. Assigned the "public building raised by Genl. Knox by Mr. John Ellisons," the hut formerly occupied by Lieutenant Colonel Ebenezer Stevens, commander of the 1780–81 New Windsor artillery encampment, Edwards had to dispossess Joseph King, a retired paymaster of the Artillery Artificer Regiment. Remaining behind as the artillerymen left in the summer of 1781, King and his family moved into Stevens's lodging, which had a "large hall in it for dancing," a "room proper for the courts to sit in." Left out of the new arrangement for his unit and forced to retire from the service that year, King, wounded and taken prisoner in 1777 at the Battle of Short Hills, New Jersey, tried to enter the Invalid Corps during his stay in New Windsor but was unsuccessful.[26]

In January, a detail went to West Point to collect the prisoners and move them to New Windsor. In April 1783, they represented practically every command in the Highlands including the artillery and dragoons. There was even a soldier from Colonel Marinus Willet's regiment of New York state troops. The prisoners were not limited to the American army. In a skirmish between royalist and American militia, John Paulding, one of Major John André's captors, was captured. While General Washington did not approve of "the excursions of these people," primarily undertaken to plunder, he was willing, however, in recognition of his prior exploit, to exchange Paulding. There were four men seized by these roving bands of irregulars during an earlier expedition in the army jail. Whether it was abuse by the prisoners or normal maintenance, there were at least two fatigues in the spring to repair the provost and officer guardhouse. The quartermasters had to supply the fatigue parties with not only tools but also cooking implements for the prisoners. On January 22, 1783, Lieutenant Gilbert led a fatigue "at the Provost Guardhouse." Intended to last three days, it took only two for his men to accomplish the work.[27]

Regimental guard huts separated this function from the sleeping quarters. To preclude having to search through hundreds of soldiers, the sentries were segregated in their own building located behind their commander's hut complex. Not to be confused with the overall camp guard provided by an entire regiment, the quarter guard secured the immediate area around the encampment. With each brigade ordered to conduct these patrols, the 1st New York Regiment performed the quarter guard duty every other day, so they more than likely shared a guard hut with the 2nd New York. The New Jersey Brigade probably also had only one guard hut, but instead of assigning the duty to a single unit, the brigade drew a composite guard from both of its regiments and the 3rd Maryland Battalion.[28] Officers assigned to this responsibility coordinated their actions with the units on their left and right and with the regiment that guarded the entire encampment. Manned continually, the guard huts were the depository of the regimental colors, the rallying point in battle, and physical personification of the unit's honor and were also the jail for prisoners awaiting trial by regimental court-martial. Every guard had a drummer who beat the various calls throughout the day and sounded the alarm. He was sometimes assisted by other musicians, especially for reveille, the morning wake-up call.

Despite the best efforts of the guards and patrols, soldiers continued to plunder, harass, and aggrieve the residents of this camp and local inhabitants. John Abel, John Cogdon, and Philip King, of the 1st New York Regiment, killed an ox during the night of November 11, 1782. They received 100 lashes on their naked backs. Though they evaded the charge of killing a cow and making off with some fowls, 10 soldiers from the 1st Massachusetts Regiment light infantry company were still convicted of "stealing eleven Geese" on Christmas Eve 1782. For unknown reasons, three received 100 lashes, while the remainder only received 75. All, however, had their pay stopped until Mr. Jonas Williams was compensated $15 for the loss. Sergeant John Blaisdell, from the New Hampshire Regiment, was convicted of stealing shoes and boots from the clothier's store in Newburgh. His codefendant, a sentinel on guard duty in the vicinity of the clothier's store, was acquitted. Broken down to private, Blaisdell also received 100 lashes, 25 in each of the lines at this camp, for four consecutive days as a deterrent to others. Soldiers from the 1st Massachusetts Regiment were acquitted of breaking into the house of James Munnell, "insulting and abusing the Inhabitants," attempting to kill two captains from the New Hampshire Line, and stealing one of their hats.[29]

The log huts were arranged in the same orderly three rows as the tent camps. Directing that "regularity, convenience, and even some degree of elegance" guide construction, Washington expected that the buildings and layout of this camp model the discipline of its inhabitants.[30] Soldiers of a regiment lived in 18 huts. Half of the company lived in a hut in the first row, and the other half lived in a hut in the second row. Pickering specified the size and design. The Massachusetts and New York huts were to originally have been 18' wide and 39' long, but the length was reduced a few days later to only 35'. Divided in half by a solid log wall, the soldier huts had a window opening, a door, a fieldstone fireplace, and bunk beds on each side. The beds were made from planks provided by the quartermaster. Six feet long and four feet across, they incidentally corresponded to the size of some of the issued blankets. The hut doorways faced the brigade parade grounds. Clearly, if only boards were provided for beds, the doors, windows, and floors would have to be sawn or riven out of standing timber. Doors and covering for the window openings were a necessity, but floors were not as critical. In the few enlisted hut sites examined by archaeologists, there was no evidence of any wooden floors. Shutters made either of the two ways covered the window openings. A private in the 2nd Massachusetts Regiment was convicted of breaking the windows in the hut of a lieutenant in his regiment.[31] If a lowly lieutenant had glass in his hut, the rest of the officers must have been similarly provided. There was a glasshouse in New Windsor near the river that probably provided the windowpanes used in this encampment. Instead of glass, shutters covered the window openings in the enlisted men's huts. For better access and to protect the muskets, the 1st New York built arms racks. Other regiments more than likely did so as well. Any builders who did not conform with the specifications furnished by Pickering would have to take their hut down and start over. There is no record of any soldiers having to rebuild, and most accounts laud the appearance of this encampment. Washington wrote to Major General John Armstrong of Pennsylvania, the father of Gates's aide, that "we … built the most comfortable Barracks in the vicinity of this place that the Troops have ever yet been in."[32] Most of the huts were finished around the middle of December.

French travel writer Major General François Jean de Beauvoir, Chevalier de Chastellux, visited New Windsor in early December and "stopped long enough to make a courtesy call" at Gates's headquarters. In viewing the nearly completed huts, Chastellux found them "spacious, healthy, and well built … containing two rooms, each inhabited by eight soldiers when full." He probably saw the Massachusetts huts because the New York huts were too far removed from the nearest road. Chastellux apparently counted the four bunk beds per side and assumed single occupancy. Two men, however, shared most of the beds, so the Massachusetts and New York huts could accommodate up to 32 soldiers. Two men in a bed may seem strange, but there was no expectation of privacy for most people in the 18th century. With fewer soldiers, the New Jersey Brigade, which included the detachment from the 3rd Maryland, was initially ordered to build huts 16' wide and 27' long.

Re-created huts of the Massachusetts Line on the historic parkland owned by the Town of New Windsor, New York (author's collection).

The Last Encampment, 1782–1783, 1983, original art by John F. Gould (1906–1996). From Temple Hill, General Washington, along with a party of mounted officers, observe the huts of the 1st and 3rd Massachusetts Brigades immediately to their front and those of the Maryland, New Hampshire, New Jersey, and New York Lines below the distant ridgeline.

Anticipating the arrival of promised recruits, Lieutenant Colonel Barber from the 2nd New Jersey was given permission for his brigade to expand the width of their huts to 18'. Smaller than the Massachusetts and New York ones, the New Jersey huts were probably intended to contain three bunk beds per side, so they were capable of housing up to 24 soldiers. Depending on how the interior was configured, the huts could fit one more bunk if necessary. Still in the environs of Albany when the camp was laid out, there are no references regarding the huts of the New Hampshire Line. Mustering nearly the same numbers as the New Jersey Brigade, the New Hampshire Line possibly followed that brigade's plan for hutting. The battalion companies of the regiments built two huts in the position of highest honor, at the extreme right of their line, for the elite light infantry companies that would rejoin them for the winter encampment. This picked unit manned the advanced outposts south of West Point until the huts at New Windsor were completed.[33]

Smaller than the enlisted ones, the company officer huts of the third line were 22' long and 16' wide. These cabins housed a captain, a lieutenant, and an ensign unless they took advantage of Pickering's recommendation to share quarters with the officers from the other companies in their regiment. They would then have to build only five huts, thereby "lessening the labor, destruction of timber, and consumption of fuel." The quartermaster general "strongly recommended" the lesser number of huts. At least in the Massachusetts Line there was a separate hut for the officers of every company.

The colonel, lieutenant colonel, and major huts, farther back, were slightly smaller than the enlisted ones as well. They could either share or separate into two or three huts.[34] Regardless of how many huts the officers decided to build, there was enough room for everyone to have his own sleeping arrangement, which was either easily portable camp beds or bedsteads, complete with frame, mattress, and linens. More prevalent among the higher ranks, the bedsteads were retrieved from storage at the end of the campaign season. Called back into active service with little prior notice, General Gates arrived without a bed, so Pickering ordered carpenters from the army's corps of manufacturing workmen, called artificers, to make him one. When word got out about Gates's bed, Director General John Cochran contacted the quartermaster to get one for himself. Not wanting to set a dangerous precedent that would inundate the artificers with untold numbers of additional requests, Pickering refused, explaining that he had "but two artificers in wood, ... [who were] wheelwrights with more public work on hand than they ... [could] perform."[35] The officers without a bed would have to either procure one on their own or make one out of boards as the soldiers did. Some of the officers had separate kitchens, gardens, and stables. Tarbell only shows these features in his own brigade and in Colonel Tupper's hut in the 3rd Massachusetts Brigade. There is the assumption that similar officer support structures would have been constructed in all the brigades, including those not from Massachusetts. In September 1783, there were numerous huts sold at auction along with their "appendages," so Tarbell did not account for every structure that was on the landscape.[36] Once the huts were habitable, the tents were turned over to the quartermaster. After several requests, he had to threaten to stop the pay of the officers, who neglected to give back their marquees.[37]

Those officers and soldiers with families could build huts out of the main lines. The enlisted men were warned, however, that "should there be any gambling or carousing in them ... the hut ... shall be immediately pulled down, and the offender removed into the line."[38] Containing only one fireplace, the huts used by the families were a single room. Within the New Jersey Brigade, which included the Maryland Detachment, there were five huts built for the women and children. The New Hampshire Line had 12 of these, and the 1st and 3rd Massachusetts Brigades had 10. There is no return from the 2nd Massachusetts Brigade, but its family huts probably numbered around five.[39] With many people uprooted by the British occupation of large portions of their state, the New York Brigade, while comprising only one-seventh of the army at New Windsor, had one-third of the women and children. Though far in excess of the one woman for every 15 soldiers authorized by Congress to receive a food ration, Washington explained to Superintendent of Finance Robert Morris that "I was obliged to give Provisions to the extra Women in these Regiments, or loose by Desertion, perhaps to the Enemy, some of the oldest and best Soldiers in the service." There were 20 soldier huts located out of the line because of their disproportionate number of family members. A similar indulgence was granted to New York's artillery regiment, the 2nd Continental, provided as at New Windsor, it was not extended "to Women who on the prospect of it, have since been brought into Camp."[40] Unique also to the New York Brigade, four officer huts were built out of the line because some of their families were displaced by the British occupation. Though Martha Washington made the journey to camp, Katherine Hand was there with her husband Edward, and General Gates made pitiful pleas for his wife to do the same. The other officers were apparently content to hope for a leave of absence, called a furlough, and visit their families at home.

The hutting areas were spread out so that the soldiers were not competing for the same trees. Though huts constructed at the major encampments at Valley Forge, Pennsylvania, in 1777–78 and Morristown, New Jersey, in 1779–80 were made of stacked undressed logs, there are inferences to suggest that at New Windsor, the logs were hewn. There was no time for such frippery at these earlier encampments. With troops arriving at their hutting grounds in December, getting the men under shelter was critical. At the Pennsylvania encampment there was no clear plan of how to construct the huts, just basic guidelines on size, height, and alignment. The buildings varied considerably, some dug into the ground rather than raising the walls to the desired height of six and a half feet. Made of several improvised materials, the roofs were poor and did not keep out the elements. Causing continual smoke and being susceptible to catching fire, the chimneys were unhealthy and often dangerous. Two years later and more experienced and adept, the soldiers at Morristown constructed a much-improved log city. As the huts were far more uniform and precise in their layout and standards for individual structures, the winter would have been quite comfortable had it not had the worst weather in living memory.[41]

Hewing is the process of shaping a tree for use as a building material. Once the tree was felled, vertical cuts of a few inches' depth were made with a felling ax on one side of the log approximately six inches apart. Then, starting with the end of the log, horizontal cuts were made with a broadax to split off the chunks of wood. The process was then repeated for the remaining three sides. Possibly, this treatment of logs was what Washington was referring to in his desire that the huts be built with "some degree of elegance." The specifications for the Temple Building, the soldier-built church at New Windsor, called for hewn logs. Company officers of the 1st New York Regiment were ordered in mid–January to "send in Exact returns of the Broad & Narrow Axes now on hand."[42] Though done to determine the status of the tools required to complete their quota of the materials for the Temple, the presence of broadaxes within the companies demonstrated that the regiments possessed the capability to dress the hut logs. Moreover, the approximate month needed to build a hut is strong evidence that the logs were dressed rather than left round. Small pieces of wood plastered over with clay or mud filled the gaps between the timbers.

Shingles for the roof were riven or sliced out of stumps by a sharp cutting tool called a froe. Logs were chopped or sawn into sections and then split into pieces with a wedge. After standing the one-quarter–size piece of wood up vertically, the soldier used a heavy wooden club, called a maul, to drive the froe through it, riving out a shingle in the process. Split along the natural grain of the wood, riven timber was far less likely to warp or crack than that which was sawn. Though Chastellux wrote that "it will appear surprising in Europe, that these barracks should be built without a bit of iron, not even nails which would render the work tedious and difficult were not the Americans very expert in working with wood," the shingles at least were held in place by nails. When he visited the camp on December 7, 1782, the huts were still not finished, so he missed seeing the finishing ironwork. In fact, there was a blacksmith shop operating in every brigade. Private Thomas Foster of the 7th Massachusetts wrote "all hands to Work for the Brigade a making Nails." The fireplace chimneys were made from the abundant fieldstone in this area. Archaeologist John H. Mead discovered that the stones were dressed by masons "to allow a closer fit" and that there was only a back wall. Pickering specified a jambless fireplace, one without sides. In that style, much of the stone chimney weight rested on a horizontal beam five feet high that was secured into the front and back walls of the hut, so sides were not necessary. The back stone wall of the fireplace was the only section that was supported by the ground. Clay served as mortar.[43]

CHAPTER 3

"Our God and Soldier we like adore"
The Diverse Residents of the Camp

> Our God and Soldier we alike adore
> Just at Brink of danger not before
> After deliverance they're alike requited
> our God forsaken and our Soldier Slited[1]

The overwhelming majority of 18th-century men were employed as farmers. In New England, the yeoman worked his own fields and sold the surplus in the local community or nearby town. New York too had many freeholds, but others rented parcels from the descendants of the original Dutch patroons or from the proprietors of the large manorial estates granted during later English rule. In the South, in addition to small market agriculture, there were plantations worked by enslaved people. America boasted a well-developed iron industry as well. Blacksmiths, woodworkers, and a myriad of other trades people fashioned the products of everyday life. Along the coast and navigable inland waterways, the maritime trade employed a significant number. This diverse background provided a reservoir of expertise that could be drawn upon when necessary. Many were tasked with doing duty in their trade at times, which in a few instances was the difference between disaster and survival. American soldier-mariners manned the boats that rescued the trapped thousands in Brooklyn in the summer of 1776 and at the end of that year ferried Washington across the Delaware, enabling the cause-saving victory at Trenton. Far less dramatic but still important were the artificers, military tradesmen who repaired and made cannon carriages, wagons, and accoutrements. Builders oversaw the construction of barracks, magazines, and temporary shelters, such as the huts of winter encampments. Tailors carefully laid out their patterns to maximize the number of uniform pieces and properly fitted the clothing. Bakers made bread, blacksmiths forged iron fittings and tools, and colliers burned wood for charcoal.

While vocation provides some insight into the life of an individual, it does not reveal consciousness, the experiences, attitudes, aspirations, fears, and prejudices. With long-dead people, the only avenue to discover their mindset is the written word. Dominating every aspect of operations, General George Washington's correspondence provides the framework for any study of the Continental Army, and the *Journals of the Continental Congress* documents the troubled civil-military relations. The letters of George Clinton, New York governor and Continental Army brigadier general, ground the reader in the setting of the main American base for most of the war. Though Horatio Gates's papers and the writings of Quartermaster General Timothy Pickering and his assistants contain valuable details about how the army functioned, some of their letters reveal their innermost thoughts. The same cannot be said of Washington. Guarded in nearly all his communications, he never revealed his true self to anyone other than Martha. The depth of his fears, doubts, vindictiveness, and anger will never be known, because as keeper of his legacy, Martha destroyed their personal correspondence. With increasing emphasis in the modern era of social history, the story of everyday people has far more relevance than the tired whitewashed accounts of social elites. In these relatively unknown historical actors, they see themselves and question why these stories have remained untold. It is difficult, however, to get an accurate assessment of the typical Continental soldier, because only one ever wrote a book about his experiences. Born in Massachusetts, but raised in Connecticut, everyman soldier, the impudent Joseph Plumb Martin penned his classic memoir *Private Yankee Doodle* nearly 50 years after the war and did so anonymously. Exalting the common soldier for his loyalty and fortitude in the face of incredible suffering, he pointed out to his readers that "Alexander never could have conquered the world without private soldiers."[2] There are journals and letters that provide a window into the thoughts of a select few, but the great majority of people are lost to history. Official correspondence and orderly books mention certain individuals tasked to do various details or those sentenced to punishment. What little we do know about the individual soldiers, mostly comes from the requirement to record the "Name, Age, size, trade or profession, place of nativity, place of residence, time of inlistment, draft, term of Service, bounty in money clothing &ca." of every recruit.[3] In the absence of actual writings, the best source for details are the pension applications, but most of these are stark lists of commanders, dates, and service locations. In this encampment of more than 7,000 people, only 3—Lieutenant Benjamin Gilbert, Private Thomas Foster, and New York Line family member Sarah Osborn—wrote much about their time in the Continental Army. The diary and letters of Gilbert, a hard-drinking, whoring, soldier-turned-officer of the 5th Massachusetts Regiment, contain some of the best observations of Continental Army life.

Consequently, nearly every Revolutionary War soldier appears as a phantom in the historic record: a shadowy glimpse and they are gone. Henry Kneeland is such a figure. But from these spectral visages it is still possible to reconstruct some of his life. He was a godsend to Thaddeus Dean from the town of Bedford, Massachusetts. The chairman for Class III of the town, Dean was responsible for obtaining a recruit for the army to satisfy the congressional resolution that the states fill their Continental lines.[4] When there was a requirement to provide recruits, officials divided the town into sections based on the number needed. In 1781, Bedford was required to provide seven men, so the town was divided into that many classes. The size of the classes varied based on the household wealth of the citizens, so the heaviest burden fell on those with the greatest means. Kneeland enlisted on March 3, 1781, for three years. At the completion of his service, he was promised a bounty of "Twenty head of cattle, three years old."[5] Each new soldier received the same amount but sometimes in different means of exchange. By promising commodities, the town could divide the burden of providing these cattle among the citizens as a tax in the future. Bedford is a little over 15 miles northwest of Boston.[6]

At 27 years old, Henry Kneeland was of prime recruiting age. He was entered on the rolls by Joseph Hosmer, superior for Middlesex County. Hosmer was careful to denote Kneeland's physical appearance. This description would have proved invaluable in recovering Kneeland if he chose to desert. Kneeland had a light complexion, brown hair, and blue eyes and stood between 5'9½" and 5'11". His occupation was listed as farmer or laborer. He was born in Germany. There were several other Kneelands who served in the war, but he was not related to any of them. In fact, Henry Kneeland was not even his real name. He was Heinrich Kickeland. The clerk of Bedford noted in the town book that "Henry Kneeland [was] one of Bergoines troops & defected from Winterhill."[7] This statement is the only contemporary reference to his service in the British Army during the Saratoga Campaign and his subsequent desertion from the prisoner of war camp, outside of Boston, to the American side. As early as August 1776, the Continental Congress tried to seduce the British German auxiliaries by promising them the rights of citizens and 50 acres of land if they deserted. There is no way of knowing why he assumed the name Henry Kneeland. Both sides did execute deserters captured while serving with the enemy. While changing his name would have helped him from being discovered, there was also a more cynical reason. By 1781, enemy deserters were not eligible to enlist in the Continental Army, and it was illegal to knowingly recruit them.[8] Too many had joined, only to go back to the enemy at the first opportunity. The residence on Kneeland's enlistment papers was Dartmouth, Massachusetts, just south of New Bedford. Why would he have traveled all the way to Bedford, 75 miles away, unless it was to find a town that would enlist him even though he was an enemy deserter if his residence was Dartmouth? Considering that Bedford officials covered up his past to hide their complicity in illegally enlisting him, it is possible that they also might have picked Dartmouth to record on his enlistment papers to give themselves plausible deniability if his true origins were ever discovered. Another reason could be that he searched until he found the town that offered the best enlistment bonus.

By May 1781 Heinrich Kickeland, now Henry Kneeland, was an infantry private assigned to Captain Eliphalet Thorp's company of the 7th Massachusetts Regiment, commanded by Lieutenant Colonel John Brooks. From October 1781 to January 1782, Kneeland was at the "York Hutts" near West Point. Kneeland was on the lines from October to November 1781 and in January 1783.[9] The only other excitement he experienced while in the American army was the November 12–16, 1781, raid into Westchester County, south of the lines, to secure foodstuffs for the army and forage for the animals. Sweeping south through North Castle, White Plains, Eastchester, Mamaroneck, and Wrights' Mills, they killed one enemy and returned with two prisoners, corn, hay and approximately 40 hogs.[10] Tedious drill, fatigue duty, and boredom filled the remainder of his time. Consolation was often found in the bottle. Drunkenness was the root cause behind many of the disciplinary problems. Kneeland appeared twice before a court-martial. Whether alcohol had anything to do with his actions is not known, but in July 1781 he was convicted of "abusing a sergeant [and was] sentenced to receive 60 lashes." Kneeland, however, did manage to escape punishment. He was later pardoned, possibly by the general amnesty Washington extended to all offenders following the victory at Yorktown, Virginia, in October 1781. At the end of October 1782, Kneeland was among the 7,000-plus soldiers who marched into New Windsor, New York.[11]

Private Thomas Foster was also a soldier in the 7th Massachusetts, but his background was far different. A hearty man nearing his 50th year, he was of old Puritan stock from Middleborough, outside of Plymouth. The *Mayflower* passenger descendant witnessed the surrender of John Burgoyne at Saratoga, endured Valley Forge, and fought in the Battle of Monmouth. For the next several years Foster languished in the Highlands, clinging to any rumor of impending peace. Promoted to sergeant in 1780, he did not hold this rank for very long. Allowed to go home on leave the following winter, he overstayed his time by two and a half months. Just 40 days, the furlough gave Foster only a few weeks at home with his wife Mary and with his four children, who ranged in age from seven to 19. The rest of his time was spent traveling the more than 200 miles and back. It was a welcomed respite, and the infrequency of these trips and the short duration made it very easy to put off returning to army life. Going back in June, he was court-martialed and reduced to private. Behaving himself thereafter, he was granted leave again the following year. As he had been back two winters in a row, his son was very upset that he did not return during the New Windsor encampment. Although more time was given, this did not eliminate late returns. Allowed 60 days leave, in December 1782 Ephraim Bailey, also from the 7th Massachusetts, overstayed by one day. Beney Baker, another soldier from that regiment, received 54 days in February 1783 and returned four days late.[12] Pensive about the pending return to army life, they possibly pushed their luck and waited too long to start their journey back.

With so much excitement in the beginning of his service, the subsequent long period of inactivity that followed probably had much to do with Foster's court-martial. Danger or adversity intensely focused the individual on surviving or overcoming the threat, while idleness engendered apathy and disciplinary problems. Having nothing to do was truly "the times that tried men's souls" and character. Officers did everything within their power to keep the soldiers busy with useful activities to combat the ennui, but it was essentially up to the individual to entertain oneself. Drinking was nearly universal, and promiscuous soldiers engaged their mind with the quest for sexual partners.

A surprising number of Americans could read. To rise above the rank of private, a soldier had to be able to write as well. Granted, their spelling might be atrocious, but this would not preclude a promotion. Typical of his writing, Foster recorded on May 11, 1783, that "our famous Tempel of Vertue & Libberty was yesterday almost Washed Down with a Sevear Storm." While not bad by contemporary standards, he wrote in a somewhat antiquated style influenced by the King James version of the Bible. Foster spent much of his time reading about, listening to sermons on, and reflecting on his faith. On January 12, 1783, he perused Reverend James Hervey's *Theron and Aspasio: or, a Series of Dialogues and Letters,* an allegory of the minister's moderate Calvinist views.[13] Regardless of individual spiritually, religion impacted the lives of everyone. Originally in New England, Puritan law pervaded every facet of life. Based on the morality of the most powerful statutory source, the Bible, included among the moral offenses were drinking and Sunday travel and work. Time and the immigration of ever-increasing numbers of nonvisible saints, however, loosened the Puritan grip but not their hold over the mores of society.

Like the United States, the various Protestant denominations dominated this encampment. The typical New Englander was a member of a congregational church that was independent of any central governing body, further reinforcing parochialism. The country had Anglicans, Presbyterians, Baptists, Quakers, German and Dutch Reformed Church members, Lutherans, Methodists, Mennonites, Catholics, and small numbers of other religious groups. A new sect arrived from Great Britain just before the war, led by Ann Lee. Derisively called Shakers because of their frenzied dancing to purge sin, they settled near Albany, New York, and sent out missionaries warning people of the imminent second coming of Jesus Christ. Among some of the learned there was deism, the doctrine of Godly indifference to the fate of his creation, which contributed to the American Revolution, with its unfettered beliefs in freedom and toleration. Many read the Bible or if illiterate gratefully listened to others recounting the stories in it and believed in the Christian God but did not belong to an established church. Lieutenant Samuel Benjamin, of the 8th Massachusetts Regiment, is the only known Jew living in this encampment. Some of the African American soldiers still held traditions from their native land, possibly including the practices of Islam. Though Christian, the Wampanoag Isaac Wickhams of the 10th Massachusetts and later of that state's 2nd Brigade, retained many tribal customs. Enlisting at Pembroke in Plymouth County, he lived at the native "praying town" of Mashpee, on Cape Cod, following the war.[14]

Regularly scheduled divine services served to reinforce the religiosity inherent in most of the soldiers' lives, thereby elevating sagging spirits and curbing the influence of vice because the idleness of a winter camp offered numerous opportunities for drunkenness and other temptations that undermined army discipline. Regardless of beliefs, Americans found comfort and reassurance in their faith, but few other subjects were so potentially divisive. Moreover, spirituality was a powerful weapon, something to be exploited. Though not overly devout, in keeping with his carefully cultivated reserve, Washington fully appreciated the restraining effect that religion had on the conduct of man, so you can imagine his shock in February 1783 at finding that most of the chaplains were gone. Thinking that there was not much for them to do, nearly all the ministers decided to spend the winter at home. Ordering the brigade commanders to immediately recall them to camp, Washington would in future allow only one-third of them to be absent at any one time. He also reserved to his headquarters the authority to grant them furloughs. With the Sabbath, February 16, 1783, the next day and with the soldier-built meetinghouse, the Temple Building, ready for use, he directed the chaplains to work out with their commanders the schedule for divine services. He also pointed out that the chaplains would attract the favorable notice of the soldiers if they regularly attended to the sick in the hospitals as well. Suitably impressed by the response, he believed that the solemnity of the Sunday services would raise morale and improve army conduct.[15] Foster noted that the Sabbath was the first in a long time that bore any semblance to one. In his opinion, the soldiers were better behaved, at least on Sundays, with this emphasis on religious observance. There were still too many instances, however, of profanity and blaspheming for his liking. Having the day off by policy beginning on March 22, the break from duty went a long way to ease the mind as well. The chaplains carefully selected the verses of scripture that had immediacy, often extolling the virtue of the soldiers' patient suffering and trust in the ultimate justice of their fellow citizens. Those who thought otherwise were confronted by Chaplain John Gano on May 11 with his sermon taken from the book of Matthew: "What is a Man profited if he Should Gain the whole World & Loose his Own Soul."[16]

Chaplains Israel Evans of the New Hampshire Brigade; Andrew Hunter of the New Jersey Brigade; John Gano of the New York Brigade; and Joel Barlow, John Barnett, and William Lockwood of the three Massachusetts brigades inspired and even upset Foster with their moving discourses. Sometimes Reverend John Close from the Presbyterian church in New Windsor joined them. He was also the pastor at the First Presbyterian Church of Newburgh and the Bethlehem Meeting House.[17] Attending services in the Temple in mid–March, Foster was "Agreeably Entertained by the Revd. Mr. Evens from ye 2d Timothy 4 Chapt. and 8th verse." Going faithfully every week, Foster noted who preached and sometimes summarized the talks. Thinking that Hunter was "a Very pretty preacher" and enjoying the others, Foster was in awe of Gano. Believing that Gano was Heaven sent, the pious Massachusetts man hoped that God would let the chaplain stay here as long as possible before summoning him back home. Much older than the other chaplains, the studied eloquence and dignity of that Baptist cleric inspired as well as scared Foster. Appealing and damning at the same time, one of Gano's sermons made Foster confess that his "Wicked hart Was full of Cavils and Scrupels and Redy to Goyn the Adversery of precious Souls in the Rejecting the Gospel Offer of Salvation by Christ."[18] Taking upon himself the power to proclaim free grace—the Lord's love, forgiveness, and promise of His kingdom for eternity—Gano made Foster doubt his worthiness for salvation, a terrifying prospect. A challenge to Calvinist predestination theology, this "amazing grace" was available to all who accepted Christ as their personal savior. Continuing the emotional spiritualism and evangelism arising from the Great Awakening of the 1730s and 1740s, free grace theologians preached the power that people possessed to save themselves. Empowering the individual, the democracy of this conviction helped prepare the American people for the independence movement.

Others were not as easily intimidated as Foster and did not find solace in religion or take observations seriously, especially individuals whose alleged conduct was contrary and even damned by scripture. Former aide and rumored lover of General Friedrich von Steuben, Lieutenant Colonel Benjamin Walker in the first sentence of his reply to a query about officer pay gave the snarky quip that "the puritanical Souls are gone to church and have left me to finish the letter they had began in answer to yours respecting the money." Despite chastisement every Sunday, the young people of America enjoyed a very active sex life. "Though this freedom prevails among all ranks, it is particularly striking among the middling classes and common people." Given the high infant mortality rate, people married early to "lose no time in completing the great object, the population of the country." Bundling introduced the betrothed pair to the marriage bed. Fully clothed, the couple spent the night together. Once night fell, however, the practice allowed the most intimate contact in the cloaking darkness. In some areas, even excessive public displays of affection were not stopped by the parental chaperones.[19] Combined with the innumerable liaisons in barns, fields, woods, and other clandestine places of rendezvous, it was not surprising, then, that significant numbers of women went to the altar pregnant.

One man from the promiscuous lower classes, 5th Massachusetts Regiment lieutenant Benjamin Gilbert of Brookfield, impregnated at least one woman and had sex with many other women. He rose from the ranks. One unique aspect of the Continental Army was the relative ease with which sergeants could become junior officers. Many promising noncommissioned officers made this transition. Most officers in professional armies were aristocrats or those who received the patronage of influential persons in the government, so there was a wide social, economic, and psychological gap between them and the enlisted men. Some European merchants found spots for their sons as well. In some instances in the expansion to a wartime footing, the British did promote sergeants to junior officer positions. They, however, would normally be the first to be retired on half-pay at the end of a conflict. Americans by the thousands dropped plows, stored fishing nets, put down their tools, and set out to defend their homes. Out of necessity, some from the meanest walks of life were commissioned. Though they were deemed gentlemen by acts of Congress and the states, government could not legislate away gross deficiencies in education and the most rudimentary social graces. Many of these officers continued the same base behavior they exhibited while they were enlisted soldiers, but they had to be more circumspect and confine their intimates to fellow members of the officer corps.

Serving at Bunker Hill and in the battles for New York City, Saratoga, and Yorktown, Gilbert spent most of his time, however, in the Hudson Highlands, waiting. Heavy drinking and the pursuit of female companionship eased the boredom. Then a quartermaster sergeant, he was left behind in Danbury, Connecticut, from October 1778 to March 1779 because he was far too ill to travel with his regiment to the Highlands. Eli Hoyt, a local militia officer, looked after him during his lengthy recovery. Gilbert went to town every week to see the military doctors and obtain his sick rations and medicine. His condition was so bad that his father traveled more than 100 miles from Brookfield, Massachusetts, to visit him. Daniel Gilbert brought presents of "a Chese and Two pair of Cotton stocking[s]." Gilbert was able to draw rations on a regular basis, and the consistent availability of food went a long way in facilitating his recovery. Time and again, Joseph Plumb Martin stated that it was prolonged hunger that disabled many soldiers, not disease. After six months, Continental Army medical authorities certified that Gilbert was sufficiently recovered to return to his regiment and discharged him from their care.[20] Escaping for most of 1781, he marched in the beginning of the year as part of the force sent to quell the uprising of the New Jersey Line at Pompton, New Jersey, and in February he accompanied Lafayette on the expedition to oppose the British raids in Tidewater Virginia. He did not return until after the Battle of Yorktown.

In his journal and letters, Gilbert faithfully recorded all his dalliances and frequent bouts with the bottle. The escapades of this libertine show an American Continental, warts and all, an officer with no pretense of being a gentleman. During the march to Virginia, Gilbert found southern women so tractable that "any man given to concupience may have his fill." In his defense, when the French encamped at Alexandria, Virginia, in August 1782 on their way north to the Hudson River, they stripped down to their threadbare shirts on a hot day before dancing with the local women, which did not cause "the least embarrassment to the ladies, many of whom were of highly polished manners, and the most exquisite delicacy; or to their friends or parents." Though he believed that the southern ladies were not as beautiful as those from the North, some of the men still took full advantage of any amorous opportunity.[21] Gilbert's promiscuity would eventually cause an unwanted pregnancy. In the ironically named Patience Converse, the daughter of prominent Brookfield, Massachusetts, resident Colonel James Converse, Gilbert found a willing sexual partner. He visited her during his several furloughs. Word of the pregnancy, sent in a letter from her father, was "very mortifying and foreign to … [his] wishes." Pressured to consent to a "matrimonial coalescence," Gilbert sought another way out. In his reply, he all but admitted that he was the father. He bought time by using his military duties as an excuse for not returning right away to settle the matter. Pinning his hopes on the possibility that he was not the father of the child, Gilbert in his subsequent letters was more noncommittal. Though he never admitted paternity, Gilbert eventually paid 30 pounds to receive "a full acquittal from the father and Daughter."[22]

Once bitten, twice shy did not apply to Gilbert. Amid the pregnancy crisis, he established a seraglio near camp, "Vulgalarly called Wyoma," with fellow 5th Massachusetts Regiment hellions Lieutenant John Warren, Lieutenant Park Holland, and Ensign Jonathan Wing. A phonetic spelling of "wame," meaning "womb," "Wyoma" was one of their sardonic names for the female reproductive organ. Whether he appreciated the hypocrisy, Gilbert attended divine service and then sometimes spent the remainder of the day and night at Wyoma. Fifth Massachusetts regimental surgeon James Burr Finley and Ensign Wing frequently accompanied him. The fun lasted as long as Gilbert's money. In August Gilbert received a letter, probably telling him not to return to Wyoma until he paid his bills.[23] Without the financial assistance of officers who had recently left the diminished army, he no longer was able to pay for the ladies' lodging, upkeep, or services.

The most famous enlisted man at New Windsor was not a man at all. Deborah Sampson or Samson, seeking to cast aside "the soft habiliment of ... [her] sex," enlisted in the 4th Massachusetts Regiment in May 1782 under the name Robert Shurtliff.[24] Posted to the elite light infantry, she was wounded a few months later during a skirmish in Westchester County, New York. Subsequently chosen to serve as waiter to General John Paterson, she accompanied him to Pennsylvania in June 1783 as part of the force sent to quell the uprising of that state's Continental Line. In Philadelphia, she became violently ill. Able to hide her secret until she was wounded, she was in no condition to continue the deception. Discovered by tending doctors, Deborah, upon her recovery, was honorably discharged. Had it not been for her sickness in the capital, she would have left the army shortly, with thousands of others, and been lost to history. Instead, the *Independent Gazette or, The New York Journal Revised* published a glowing article, in 1784 about the anonymous female soldier who was "a remarkable heroine, and warmly attached to the cause of her country, in the service of which, it must be acknowledged, she gained reputation." The article also called upon historians to give proper attention to this remarkable woman in writing the history of "our grand revolution."[25] She married Benjamin Gannett of Sharon, Massachusetts, in 1785 and had three children. Her husband did his best to support the family, but his efforts fell short. Disabled by the chronic pain of her wound, Deborah applied for an invalid veteran pension in 1797, but nothing came of the petition. It took a letter from Paul Revere to his congressman in 1804 before she was finally awarded, the following year, a pension of $4 a month. A decade after her death, Benjamin Gannett petitioned Congress for a pension as the widower of a Revolutionary War veteran, but it took more than a year. He died in the interim, but eventually $80 was allotted annually "for the relief of the heirs of Deborah Sampson Gannett."[26]

Several thousand Black men fought alongside white soldiers in the Continental forces. African Americans would not serve again in integrated units until the Korean War. There were many Black soldiers in this camp. Discovering these men in the historic record is sometimes difficult, because there are not always period descriptions such as "negro" or "black" to aid in discerning them. Private Oliver Cromwell from the 2nd New Jersey Regiment, born in Black Horse, now Columbus, New Jersey, fought at Trenton, Princeton, Monmouth, and Yorktown, where "he saw the last man killed." At Princeton, he recalled how they "knocked the British about lively." Living for a century because he did not smoke or chew tobacco or drink alcohol, Cromwell was one of the few soldiers who remained of the Revolutionary army. Despite his service beside white men, he was still denied his rightful place in America's military pantheon. A reporter from the *Burlington Gazette* lamented, "Had he been of a little lighter complexion (he was just half white), every newspaper in the land would have been eloquent in praise of his many virtues."[27]

Inured by hardship, another long-lived resident of the camp, Sarah Osborn, born in nearby Blooming Grove, owed her longevity to a resolute mindset that enabled her to overcome or survive a century's worth of adversity. Raised in northeastern

Pennsylvania, a howling wilderness traversed by dangerous animals and unpredictable parties of Indians, she developed a resilience that only the frontier could impart. After marrying Aaron Osborn, of the 3rd New York Regiment, at Albany in 1780, she followed him to the Hudson Valley and a year later traveled all the way to Yorktown, Virginia, and back. Her first husband, John Read, also a soldier, died in battle a few years before. Among the colorful figures of Osborn's regiment, raised locally in Ulster County, was his company commander Captain James Gregg, who was scalped in the fall of 1777 while on a hunting excursion outside of Fort Stanwix. Located in central New York, this frontier outpost guarded the land route between the Mohawk River and Wood Creek. Suffering periodic bouts of mental illness from this attack, during these episodes he "would frequently say …'Sarah, did you ever see where I was scalped?' showing his head at the same time." Gregg was at this encampment and retired when most of the army was furloughed in June 1783. During this phase of the war, the New York Line spent most of its time in the Hudson Valley and was stationed at West Point when Major General Benedict Arnold escaped to the British. Another New Windsor Cantonment resident until his regiment was disbanded at the end of 1782, 9th Massachusetts surgeon James Thacher treated Gregg after he was evacuated to the army hospital in Albany.

Captain Gregg and Sarah were part of the expedition to Virginia. For the approximately 450-mile journey to Yorktown, Sarah traveled mainly on horseback, in a wagon, or aboard a ship. So as not to unnecessarily encumber the wagons, women needed the permission of a general officer to ride in them. Moving over from the James River, Sarah viewed a melancholy scene on the outskirts of town. On the plain separating the two contending armies were many dead slaves driven out of the village by their erstwhile British protectors to starve or die of disease. Soon after the arrival of the French and American armies, all the allied soldiers, including her husband, toiled away on the siege lines surrounding the British position. Exhausted and famished by their labor, she "carried in beef, and bread, and coffee (in a gallon pot)" to her grateful husband and his messmates. She was one of the few women, at least in her regiment, to make the trip. Her presence in the line of fire attracted the attention of Washington, who asked her why she "was not afraid of the cannonballs." With tongue in cheek she claimed to have replied, "No, the bullets would not cheat the gallows…. It would not do for the men to fight and starve too." While this is possibly embellished, the rest of her narrative is for the most part believable, so this exchange could have happened. She watched the enemy march out to lay down their arms, noting that as the British commander at the surrender General Charles O'Hara passed, "tears rolled down his cheeks."[28]

Washington then returned with his contingent to their former stations, and Sarah spent that winter in northwestern New Jersey. After an uneventful summer, the New York Line and most of the Continentals established the winter encampment at New Windsor. In Aaron and Sarah's hut, built on the outskirts of the main line, Phebe Osborn was born on February 20, 1783. Sarah was among the approximately 250 women at New Windsor, and daughter Phebe was among about 250 children in camp. Considering the amount of families reasonable, given the unique circumstances of this war, Washington was incredulous when Robert Morris informed him in early 1783 that Congress, without consulting him, enacted legislation allowing no more than one woman for every 15 soldiers. With so many dispossessed of their homes especially in New York, it was not wise to strictly enforce a fixed fractional limit to the number of families allowed per regiment to travel with the army. Believing it was his inherent right as a commander to make the determination, he "was obliged to give Provisions to the extra Women in these Regiments, or loose by Desertion, perhaps to the Enemy, some of the oldest and best Soldiers in the Service…. The Cries of these Women; the sufferings of their Children, and the complaints of the Husbands would admit of no alternative." Granting a similar indulgence to the 2nd Continental Artillery at West Point, recruited largely from New York, he warned, however, that it was not to include family members who appeared at the post after hearing about the dispensation. Despite the large number of women anxious to attend the army, the life was hard, with only dire necessity to recommend it. While family was a source of comfort and constant reminder of ultimately what they were fighting for, the soldiers had to worry not only about the safety of their families but also whether they complied with the rules. The women's and children's conduct was strictly controlled. Company sergeants were entrusted with passing on to them any orders and ensuring their compliance. Following the military was a privilege, not a right. Throughout the Continental Army's existence, numbers of thieving, disobedient, and unruly women were thrown out of camp. But good behavior alone was not enough. Though there was the expectation that the women would do the soldiers' laundry in exchange for a small fee and use these proceeds to pay for their food, neither the officers nor soldiers consistently had the money.[29]

Chapter 4

"The service is much impeded, desertion vastly encreased, and the disposition of the Troops extremely soured, by the frequent want of Provisions"

The Failure of the Country to Provide for the Army and the Effect on Soldier Health

When the huts were sufficiently advanced, the soldiers cooked in them. The officers could have kitchens inside their huts, provided there was no difference in the "external appearances from [the] others" or ones "detached eight feet in the rear." The detached kitchens were centered behind the huts. Those of the company officers were 12 feet by 12 feet, while the field officers were 14 feet squared. Kitchens for the brigadier generals were larger still, measuring 16 feet by 16 feet. Officers had soldiers detailed to cook their food and generally answer their wants. Called servants or waiters, they probably lived in the kitchens. Captain Jeremiah Ballard of the 2nd New Jersey Regiment sold a "Negro Boy" servant, who challenged the officer's right to dispose of him as a slave. Washington ordered an immediate investigation to determine whether this young man was free or enslaved.[1]

Fairly generous initially, the ration by the end of the war was still substantial, but procurement, transportation, and other difficulties sometimes forced the army to do without. There were times when the food ration was not delivered, but for the most part the Continental Army was fed. Washington was very involved in monitoring the quality of the food, knowing its effect on soldier efficiency and morale. It is far easier to provide for a force operating in the same area for an extended period than one moving away from its normal supply lines, and the Highlands was such an established position that eventually civilian firms were hired as ration contractors. Taking over this responsibility from military officials, they had "use of all Commissarys storehouses, Scales and weights belonging to the public in this department." This arrangement replaced requisitioning specific supplies directly from the individual states, which did not work. Intended by the superintendent of finance to decrease costs through competitive bidding, the cost per ration, however, remained high. Awarded the contract by Congress in early April 1782, Comfort Sands & Company faced difficulty complying with its conditions. Washington dipped his pen in acid and fired off this piece of vitriol to the contractor at the end of May: "Why Sir are the Troops without Provisions? Why are the deposits which have so often, and so long ago been required by General Heath, and pressed by myself, neglected? Why do you so pertinaciously adhere to all those parts of the Contracts as are promotive of your own Interest and convenience ... you cannot be justified by, and at the same time disregard the most essential claims of the public; thereby hazarding the dissolution of the Army and risking the loss of the most important Post in America?"[2]

While Washington's anger was certainly justified, Sands and his agents needed time to perfect their processes, which until that happened the men unfortunately suffered in the breach. Sands's biggest challenge was that there never was a reliable stream of payments from Superintendent of Finance Robert Morris for him to get ahead of immediate demands. Without this cash, Sands was not given the time to seek out the best possible prices, so he continued expensive short-term purchasing. Agreeing to arbitration of the complaints, Comfort Sands & Company at the meeting held on July 9, 1782, promised to issue until the end of December 1782 the following:

> 1 pound of bread or flour at the option of the contractors
> 1 pound of beef or ¾ pound of pork
> 1 gill of whiskey or "Country Rum" (A gill is 4 ounces. The secretary at war could "order vegetables or other articles instead of rum or whiskey")
> 1 quart of salt to every 100 rations
> 2 quarts of vinegar to every 100 rations (If vinegar was not available, "the value to be drawn in any Article the ... [soldiers] may choose.")
> 8 pounds of soap and 3 pounds of candles for every 700 rations[3]

Shortly after the army arrived in New Windsor, a detail of 10 men, led by a sergeant, built a slaughterhouse and pen at Newburgh to facilitate the issuance of the meat ration.[4] Vinegar, made from fermented hard apple cider, was filled with nutrients, including vitamin C, which prevented scurvy, a breakdown of the soft tissue of the body, causing gum disease and the loosening of teeth. Unaware of vitamins and other nutritional properties, 18th-century people only knew that the ingestion of vinegar improved their health. Salted provisions and hard bread, made of just flour and water, were carried by traveling soldiers or drawn out of magazines along the route of march. The hospitals received additionally West Indian rum, Madeira wine, port wine, muscovado (raw) sugar, coffee, bohea tea, and Indian meal, for the comfort of the sick. Strength reports, not only important for giving Washington an accurate assessment of his potential battlefield numbers, also determined the number of rations.[5]

Despite the arbitration meeting, Sands continued to "impose upon the Army and thereby serve his own Interest, with Impunity."[6] Due to the superintendent of finance's inability to provide him with timely payments according to their agreement so he could plan his purchases, Sands relinquished the contract, ending the issue of rations in mid–October. Wadsworth & Carter stepped in for the short term. Former commissary general of purchases Jeremiah Wadsworth knew how to sustain an army. Provisioner for the French army as well, Washington informed his ally that this arrangement would not interfere with their own supplies. Charging more per ration but giving three months' credit, Wadsworth & Carter agreed to supply the army until the end of the year.[7] They were able to extend credit because their coffers were flush with silver and gold coins. The French during that time "punctually paid their expenses in hard money, which made them acceptable guests wherever they passed. And, in fact, the large quantity of solid coin which they brought into the United States, is to be considered as of infinite importance."[8]

Continually embarrassed by the states' tardiness in paying their taxes, Morris resorted to a circular letter to every governor and receiver of taxes, despite Washington's concern that the British perhaps were contemplating a withdrawal from the country and might reconsider if the extent of the nation's financial weakness was disclosed. Pointedly, the superintendent told the collectors that he did not care whether the people voted for or against taxes; the collectors must draw out the allocations. "In a Country full of supplies," American subsistence remained precarious due to the shortage of money.[9]

William Duer and Daniel Parker assumed the responsibility for feeding the army in the Hudson Valley in January 1783. Though spoken of favorably by Jeremiah Wadsworth, Duer had difficulty complying with the provisions of his last army contract. Having subsisted the troops around Albany previously, the former quartermaster agent faced the same problems there that Comfort Sands faced to the south. Without settlement of his accounts on a regular basis, he was "no longer master of the price of any article, and scarcely in a situation to furnish the Supplies from day to day." In desperation, he threatened to relinquish the contract, but he did complete his agreement. Though his firm was to take over at the beginning of the year, Washington was surprised in mid–December that he had not seen Duer or any of his representatives yet. Only supplied with enough rations to last until the end of the month, Washington expected that the contractors would have acted by now to replenish the supply before the Hudson River was obstructed by ice and the roads were impassable.[10]

The ration was boiled in thin sheet iron camp kettles rather than cast iron ones that were too heavy, especially for the infantry to carry. Light weight and portability, however, came with a price. There were plenty of kettles on hand, but the majority were "burnt through at the bottom" because users let the water boil out, placed them directly on the fire, or used them as frying pans. They only lasted about a year.[11] Generally, kettles were issued one to every six soldiers, who would mess together. This group of intimates usually shared a tent as well and were referred to as messmates. Wooden bowls as well as iron, horn, wooden, or pewter spoons and tin or horn cups were typical eating utensils. Shortages forced messmates to share their implements, and in some cases they had to eat directly out of the camp kettles. With meals prepared by their servants, junior officers dined somewhat better than the enlisted men, while many of their superiors had china services, boxed liquors, and other fine tableware. The number of officer rations increased with rank so they could entertain at a level commensurate with their station. Besides feeding guests, the extra rations allowed them to eat well, even to excess. Whimsically inquiring about their mutual friend Colonel Henry Jackson, Nathanael Greene asked Henry Knox if the 4th Massachusetts commander "was as fat as ever, and … [could] still eat down a plate of fish he can't see over." To amuse themselves, several officers goaded their fellows onto probably the contractors' scales at West Point in August 1783. At 280 pounds General Knox was the heaviest, followed by Colonel Michael Jackson of the 8th Massachusetts, at 252 pounds. Possibly a distant relation, Henry Jackson was only 14 pounds lighter, while Washington, on the other hand, at six feet, two inches and weighing 209 pounds, was an imposing figure who looked every inch the commander in chief.[12] In the meeting with the contractors, held at Major General Robert Howe's quarters at the Deacon Brewster house on December 29, 1782, it was agreed that officers would draw their rations from their designated commissaries on Tuesday, Thursday, and Saturday afternoons. For special occasions they would make exceptions to this schedule. Having to pay for their food, the officers received a subsistence allowance. Lieutenant Gilbert on February 4 "Received a months subsistence in Hillegas Notes," pay certificates issued from the Continental Loan Office by U.S. treasurer Michael Hillegas.[13]

Lack of food or just a desire for something different was the reason behind the nighttime raids of local farms. Hungry soldiers grew increasingly angry and obsessed over how to get something more to eat. Boredom also fueled this obsession. They would try just about anything to add to their meager diet. Hunting was forbidden because it was a waste of government ammunition and a hazard for camp inhabitants. Inspections were ordered to see if cartridges were missing or if powder had been taken out of them.[14] Considering that one-third of the soldiers at New Windsor were wearing brown coats with white underclothes, this certainly added to the danger. Fishing in nearby ponds or streams was safer, and the Hudson River was only two miles away. Lieutenants Benjamin Gilbert and Zibeon Hooker of the 5th Massachusetts fished in a pond north of General Heath's quarters at the Squire Belknap house on May 13. Accompanied by Ensign Daniel McCay, they returned on May 24. A fish spear was found in one of the 4th Massachusetts Regiment's soldier hut sites.[15] With the approach of spring, there were orders for trusted soldiers to go into the countryside to procure seeds for planting regimental gardens. Shortly thereafter the order to advertise for seeds was rescinded because the camp was soon to be abandoned; however, the Tarbell drawing shows gardens among a few of the officers' huts.[16]

Whenever the army established itself at a location, merchants and individuals flocked to the encampment to peddle their foodstuffs and wares. The sutlers, store operators, were chosen by the brigade commanders and licensed by the quartermaster department. They were governed by strict regulations. Uncontrolled sales of alcohol caused drunkenness, which led to disciplinary problems, so any sutler presuming to sell liquors without a license would have his stock impounded and his shop knocked down.[17] When the "country people" brought their goods to the huts they were sometimes abused and robbed by the soldiers. Chagrined by their behavior, Washington told Pickering to designate places for the sale of produce, meat, butter, cheese, milk, bread, pies, and other comestibles, ensuring that a guard detail, supervised by an officer, was present to maintain order. The presence of sentinels also prevented soldiers from trading their clothing and other gear for food. These guards were expected to act. Corporal John McLean of the 1st New York Regiment allowed "a Markett man to be plundered in his presence" and was demoted to private.[18] Besides putting the army in a bad light, further misconduct would put an end to the willingness of people to bring goods into camp. The quartermaster chose one location between the New Jersey and New York Lines, another between the 1st and 3rd Massachusetts Brigades, and the last one on the road between the hospital and the 2nd Massachusetts Brigade. Still too numerous to properly control, the two Massachusetts Line locations were combined and moved to a location by the Temple Building. Only Wednesdays and Saturdays were designated as market days, with advertisements posted to that effect. The first ad ran in the February 20 edition of the *New York Packet and the American Advertiser*, published in Fishkill, New York, by Samuel Loudon. Two weeks later, Pickering posted another announcement with the amended locations and days of the week. In March, sutlers were reduced to one per brigade. Brigade commanders designated officers to inspect the prices and quality of the merchandise on at least a weekly basis. Commanding officers had to certify any soldier obligation to a merchant or individual, before regimental paymasters satisfied the debt.[19]

Officers with money could buy food outside of camp. Gilbert with several other officers from the 5th Massachusetts went to New Windsor on May 12 and enjoyed a fine repast of oysters and punch.[20]

There were always concerns with alcohol. In the 18th century, young men, like their fathers, drank heavily. Easing the boredom, drinking was the universal entertainment. Moreover, collective intoxication was a source of amusement and a bonding experience unless individuals could not hold their liquor and became mean or insubordinate drunks. "Teagues," Irish "St. Partrick's Men … in a high frollick," on March 17 killed two of their number and wounded several others. "St. Partricks Day Called and So Kept by the Teagues for his heroic Act in Driving out of Iroland Snaks toads & Other Vermine; and if he behaved as the Teagues have this Day it is Not a taul to be Wondered at that they Left that Kingdom."[21] Soldiers were issued rum or whiskey as part of the daily ration, but Washington was always apprehensive that this intended restorative was being abused. He did not want to see the alcohol consumed all at once and instead wanted it distributed, mixed with water, at intervals throughout the day. Those guilty of intemperance were to be struck off the liquor rolls and issued vegetables or other articles. As the decline in discipline at the end of this encampment was attributed to the ready availability of alcohol, sutlers and the visiting public were forbidden to sell liquor to the soldiers without the written authorization of an officer.[22] Under no restriction as long as it did not interfere with their duties, officers were free to imbibe. Lieutenant Gilbert too often was in an alcohol-fueled haze, "which operated to the disadvantage of the said Gilbert." He had plenty of company. In December, all the 5th Massachusetts officers drank grog, alcohol mixed with water, usually rum, with their commander Colonel Rufus Putnam. In a customary practice, Lieutenant Nathaniel Thatcher of that regiment at the end of December celebrated his promotion by serving grog to his fellow officers.[23]

All this drinking had an adverse effect on the soldiers' health. Combined with their poor diet and the conditions under which food was stored and prepared, they were susceptible to several diseases. They were continually exposed to the elements as well, which also took a toll on their bodies. Typical 18th-century people lived in a building, slept through the night, stopped and rested when they were exhausted, did not go out in bad weather, stayed in bed when they were sick, ate an adequate selection of well-prepared food, and drank potable water and, except for the small fraction of the population who lived in the coastal cities, were not exposed to large groups of people and their diseases. Often in the military none of these comforts were available, which was quite a shock to those not used to such conditions. War is a discriminator. In every conflict there was the great culling of the weak during the first sustained period of hardship. The very young and old were the most susceptible. Diseases of civilization such as typhoid from contaminated water and communicable diseases such as measles and smallpox decimated bodies already run down from unaccustomed prolonged exertion and not enough food. Only the toughest were fit enough for sustained service, but desperate for men, recruiters accepted nearly everyone, and nature took its course.

Terms of service also had a huge impact. Adopting the militiamen in the beginning of the war, the Continental Congress requested that they serve until the end of the year. Enough agreed to stay and became the Continental Army. After that relatively short period, individuals could go home. For everyone in poor condition, this was their best opportunity to leave. The next term was for double that time, an entire year. This was more detrimental for soldier health and still precarious for the cause. Amid the

Trenton-Princeton miracle, where Washington in a bold military gamble rescued the cause, his soldiers' enlistments expired at the end of the year, forcing him to bribe many of them into staying until the campaign was complete. It was insufferable for the army to attempt to regenerate so frequently, and Congress finally acceded to Washington's request to make the terms three years or for the duration of the war. There would be no more hanging on until the end of their enlistment and going home to recover.

But life in the military was far simpler than at home. Soldiers concerned themselves with their health, food, drink, rest, and personal comfort. The Continental Army, however, challenged every one of these personal aspirations, especially in adverse weather.[24] After marching and countermarching during the summer and fall of 1777 in the unsuccessful effort to keep the British out of Philadelphia, the American army moved northwest of the city to Valley Forge, Pennsylvania. They were the first to winter over in a camp built out of a forest. Standing on the cold ground of those bleak hills, malnourished and without adequate clothing, they cut down the trees and fashioned rude huts. At this Golgotha, over 2,000 soldiers died from sickness and exposure, and many others were irreparably harmed by the dreadful conditions. Well over 1,000 deserted. Fortunately, the weather was not that bad, or who knows whether the army would have held together. Shedding the weak in body and spirit, the remaining stalwarts formed the enduring core of the force that won our independence. At the 1779–80 encampment at Morristown, New Jersey, the worst winter in memory, fewer than 100 died.[25]

The increasing professionalism of the Continental Army also spread to the staff departments, including medical care. Initially providing for a hospital department in the beginning of the war, Congress in 1777 divided the country into four separate districts. The districts were managed by a director general operating out of the district "between [the] Hudson and Potowmack Rivers," who was assisted by deputies in New England and northern New York. One was not initially appointed for the South because there was little fighting there at that time. As much as possible in consultation with his deputies, he ordered and distributed supplies, monitored practices, and compiled monthly reports and forwarded them to Congress. The directors provided "medicines, instruments, dressings, bedding and other necessary furniture, proper diet, and everything requisite for the sick and wounded soldiers." Based on the needs of the military commanders in their districts, the directors located stationary hospitals and supported the personnel assigned to the ones traveling with the mobile armies. Forced to devote much of his time to running his own district, a director could not effectively superintend the whole medical effort, so a year later Congress authorized a deputy for his region.[26]

Under the director's or his deputies' auspices were physicians, surgeons, surgeon's mates, apothecaries, stewards, matrons, nurses, and a support staff. Physicians were doctors trained to diagnose illness, examine injuries, and determine cures. They understood the properties of every medicine and the recommended dosage and could prescribe a course of treatment. Invariably, the prominent and best-trained ones were chosen for the highest-level positions. Doctors Joseph Warren, Hugh Mercer, and Edward Hand shunned their calling altogether and became generals. Only a handful were professionally trained in the medical colleges in Philadelphia or in Edinburgh, London, or the rest of Europe. Most were apprentices with a certificate of proficiency from their physician master. Surgeons performed operations with their medical kit of cutting tools and probes. Physicians, however, did do operations, and surgeons diagnosed patients and administered medicine. Both healers were normally called "doctor." Referring collectively to American practitioners as doctors in the English mode, French general Chastellux believed that "the distinction between surgeon and physician is as little known in the army of Washington as in that of Agamemnon."[27] The best European physicians administered to a wealthy clientele and generally did not lay their hands on patients. When cutting was necessary, the physician guided the surgeon during an operation. Americans did not have the luxury of strict specialization, and anyway, they did not think it was proper to do so "without manifest injury to each." Dr. John Jones, professor of surgery at King's College in New York City, recommended that doctors administer to as many patients as possible and treat a multitude of complaints.[28]

Essentially a mobile city, the Continental Army gave doctors the opportunity to see countless numbers of individuals, with the added benefit of having other medical professionals to consult. Apothecaries gathered, ground, and mixed the various powders, potions, and serums. Symbolic of their craft to this day, the ingredients were ground in a bowl, called a mortar, with a pestle, a rounded club. Equivalent to a high-ranking noncommissioned officer, the hospital steward supervised the facility, ordered and dispensed supplies and food, assisted the doctors and other workers, and filled out forms and reports. The matron oversaw the nurses and guided them in maintaining order and cleanliness. Both male and female nurses delivered the care. Guards were assigned to the hospitals to keep the soldiers from abusing their attendants or roaming about and disturbing the local inhabitants and to arrange for the delivery of the recovered back to their commands. The guards also kept out visitors who might bring in contagion or food and alcohol detrimental to the course of treatment.

Established in 1781 on the Clove Road in the huts formerly occupied by the artillery, over the winter of 1780–81 the general hospital treated everything from fevers to casual injuries and lameness and occasionally gunshot wounds. In the New Windsor facility, you would have seen a variety of patients. Military members traveling through the area and unable to continue with their unit would be left here. This hospital attended soldier families as well. Occasionally, civilians received treatment. Inoculating local people against smallpox prevented the spread of that highly contagious and deadliest of diseases and kept the army from the notoriety of being a bearer of pestilence. Soldiers earned a little extra money by cutting wood for the medical personnel and patients. The New Windsor hospital was under the direction of superintendent Captain Selah Benton of the 5th Connecticut Regiment when the main army arrived, but he was soon replaced by Lieutenant Joseph Crook from the 10th Massachusetts. The "Arrangement of the Hospital at New Windsor Huts" dated June 24, 1783, lists surgeons William Eustis and Samuel Adams, mates William Cogswell and Joseph Prescott, Steward John Brown, Ward Master Daniel Hendry, and Matron Mary Lake. All other personnel were furloughed by that point.[29] Not everyone, however, went to a hospital. The regimental surgeon and his mate first assessed maladies and if possible treated them. Often viewed with contempt, these lowly practitioners' diagnoses were many times questionable, especially when the soldiers realized that instead of harsh medicines all they really "needed was a bellyful of victuals." Depending on the severity and nature of the illness or injury, the individual might warrant evacuation to a medical facility. A place of last resort, hospitals housed people too sick or injured to adequately take care of themselves.[30] New soldiers often suffered from nostalgia or homesickness. They refused to eat and experienced stomach disorders or other hypochondria. On lengthy voyages people gave up and died as a result.

Daily routines of drill and fatigues kept the men busy, so they had little time to think about what they had left behind. The gibes of veterans also made recruits realize that they needed to quickly accept their new condition.[31]

With little understanding of the causes of most diseases, doctors could not always correctly diagnose the malady. Smallpox, with its serum-filled pustules, and the rash associated with measles made them easy to recognize, but what about the host of fevers and chills without such clear symptoms? Well beyond the understanding of 18th-century physicians, contaminated microorganisms in human waste spread typhoid. Bacteria was also present in tainted water, causing dysentery. Because vector-borne diseases such as malaria, yellow fever, and typhus were attributed largely to other causes, those patients might share a ward with sufferers of communicable diseases, such as influenza and diphtheria. Typhus sufferers were not contagious, but the infected body louse that made them sick was. Breeding in unclean clothes and bedding, the hungry lice wasted no time in seeking out other hosts, facilitated by the close quarters. If body waste spread to the water supply, typhoid, malignant bilious fever, might occur, further ravaging the body. Not lost on patients was Dr. Benjamin Rush's observation that "hospitals are the sinks [toilets] of human life in an army. They robbed the United States of more citizens than the sword."[32]

For convenience of operation the large hospitals were best, but the crowded conditions spread disease. Smaller facilities were the easiest to keep clean and isolate contagion. The buildings of the artillery encampment were ideally suited for reuse as a hospital. Officer huts measuring 26 feet long and 20 feet wide, a few slightly longer, and the 20-foot-square soldier huts were available. Tearing down some of their structures for firewood in the spring of 1781, the artillerymen left behind 32 huts.[33] Unlike wards in homes and other requisitioned spaces, the clay chinking between the logs could be removed to increase airflow. Taking in a steady flow of fresh air pushed out any inhaled contaminants. The mosquito-borne disease malaria was attributed to miasmas, noxious odors emanating from marshes; "*mala*" and "*aria*" are the Latin words for "bad" and "air," respectively. Foul smelling air was thought to cause putrid fever. Considering the stench of closely packed bodies, excrement, urine, and other effluvia of sickness, air circulation was considered critical. Some doctors went so far as to suggest the use of tents despite the weather.

Getting soldiers moving and out of the hospital as soon as possible was the immediate goal. The longer a patient languished, the more his condition worsened, but some ailments made standing and walking excruciating. Chronic inflammatory joint diseases such as arthritis and rheumatism sidelined many, including several high-ranking officers. After a while, Washington knew which officers were physically capable of rigorous field duty and which ones were not. Still observing strict decorum in offering commands by seniority, he allowed his generals the courtesy of making the determination themselves as to whether they were healthy enough to accept an assignment. There were less taxing garrison positions, such as West Point and the command of the small northern department, based out of Albany, New York. Often recovering at home, generals and senior officers were not always prompt in updating headquarters on their condition, especially if they perceived that there was not much going on. Washington on several occasions had to reach out to them for their status. Allowing every soldier and junior officer to go home when they were sick, even if distance made it practical, would dissolve the army, but in some cases they were placed in the care of civilians.[34]

Derisively called "the sick, the lame and the lazy," some soldiers did not get better and were eventually examined by a specially appointed board of officers and doctors to determine whether their condition warranted a medical discharge or transfer to the Invalid Corps, modeled after a similar formation in the British Army.[35] Proposed by former British officer Colonel Lewis Nicola, who was appointed commander of that regiment, these sick and injured soldiers guarded facilities such as West Point or did other nonstrenuous tasks, freeing up able-bodied men. While utilizing them to the utmost of their capabilities, it was also an act of humanity to allow them to stay in the service. On December 12, 1782, at 11:00 a.m., a board convened at the hospital huts to inspect patients and the invalids of the Massachusetts Line. The next day, they met at the New York huts to see the unfit soldiers living on the ridge to the west of Beaver Dam Stream. Director General of the Hospital of the United States Dr. John Cochran, Lieutenant Colonel Robert Cochran of the 2nd New York, commander of the New Hampshire Battalion Major William Scott, commander of Washington's guard Captain Caleb Gibbs, and a hospital surgeon composed the inspection board held at the Temple Building in early April 1783. A surgeon or mate accompanied the men from their unit. The results were recorded in the regimental orderly books. If the condition was permanent and prevented the soldier from performing normal duties, the board could recommend a discharge, a release with disability payments, or transfer to the Invalid Corps, whose members still received full pay and benefits. Discharged soldiers entitled to payments received "five dollars per month, in lieu of all pay and emoluments." Worrying that the public might judge these actions as the discarding of disabled public servants, Congress required all invalids who requested a discharge to prove that they could provide for themselves and not become a burden to society.[36]

Eighteenth-century medical practitioners treated the symptoms of the disease, attempting to lessen its severity thereby giving patients the best chance for their natural constitution to overcome digestive disorders such as upset stomachs and dysentery as well as fevers, chills, and respiratory illnesses, such as colds, influenza, pleurisy, and other lung infections. Reducing pain was thought to lessen the severity of swelling, which lessened the recovery time. On the most simplistic level, illness altered the balance of the body, and the physicians sought to intervene to restore the health of the individual. There were many explanations for disease. Still with its adherents during this time, the ancient Greek humors theory put forth that it was an imbalance in the elements of blood, phlegm, black bile, and yellow bile that caused sickness. Increasingly popular and simpler still, the latest theory of nerve stimulation to the muscles and blood vessels took numerous symptoms and reduced them to a formula of irritability or debility. An overactive and irritated body was feverous, chilled, and otherwise responsive. Conversely, a lethargic person suffered from a lack of energy. Regardless of which beliefs the doctor held about the cause of ailments, there was little difference in the treatments. A body that was excessively warm suffered from too much blood according to the humor theory and too much activity according to the nerve stimulation hypothesis. The solution was to liberally draw blood using a cutting tool known as a lancet. The amount was measured by collecting the contents in a bowl. As the blood left the body, the surface cooled, producing the desired effect. Continued fever brought additional rounds of bleeding. The patient either recovered despite the efforts of the physician or was hastened to his grave by the practice. Blood was also exorcised through cupping, heated containers of metal or glass placed on the skin. Blistering with irritants or a heated iron also brought liquid to the surface.

A panacea for too much activity was the bark derived from the Cinchona tree in western South America introduced to Spanish missionaries by native people in the early 17th century. Known variously as Peruvian or Jesuit's bark, its active ingredient, quinine, lessened the fevers and chills associated with malaria and from other causes as well. Weak patients required invigoration through a few mediums: alcohol, soup, anise, pepper, cinnamon, or other stimulants. Whether enervated or overactive, they required purging either orally with the root's jalap, ipecac, tartar emetic, mercury-based calomel, or the metal antimony or through enemas via a clyster pipe syringe.[37] Laxatives such as Glauber's Salt, hydrate of sodium sulfate, castor oil, and olive oil cleansed the bowels.

Doctors carried a small portable chest that held medicine wrapped in paper packets tied with a string and in glass and ceramic containers, scales to measure dosages, and mortar and pestle to prepare those still in raw form. Remedies were taken internally or applied to the skin. External applications required a means to spread the curative. For impetigo, a contagious bacteriological infection of the skin also known as "the itch," sulfur mixed with lard was rubbed into the afflicted area. Conditions permitting, bathing in water mixed with sulfur cleansed the skin and open sores. Scabies, eruptions from mites burrowing into the skin to lay eggs, also created an intense itchy rash. The natural reaction was to scratch the afflicted areas, which created oozing, encrusted scabs. These unclean wounds fostered bacteria that sometimes turned into impetigo. Zinc-based calamine lotion soothed the skin exposed to sunburn, rashes, poisonous plants, and insect bites; served as an antiseptic; and dried oozing skin eruptions.

Smallpox was the only communicable disease that the Continental Army could prevent, provided inoculation was done properly. Healthy subjects were isolated from their fellows because they were contagious during treatment. Doctors collected serum from donors and introduced this liquid with a quill or lancet into a small scratch or cut in the upper arm. The body's immune system attacked this localized infection, producing antibodies that prevented the patient from ever contracting the disease. Finally admitting the futility of trying to avoid smallpox, Washington initiated the first large-scale inoculation of his army at Morristown, New Jersey, in February 1777. Writing to Governor Patrick Henry that spring regarding recruits from his state, Washington strongly urged him to change the laws in Virginia to permit inoculation, stating that smallpox was "more destructive to an Army in the Natural way, than the Enemy's Sword" and that he shuddered when he reflected on the difficulties of preventing its transmission.[38] While legal in most states, the exigencies of the war determined when inoculation was acceptable. The local committee of safety in Newburgh, New York, allowed a few families to undergo the procedure in February 1778 when a carrier of that disease arrived in town. Continental Army brigadier general James Clinton had tried to prevent this for fear of exposing the troops, but he did get them to agree to not let anyone else do it. The committee members were not able to keep this promise. Shortly thereafter, the general was informed that the prominent and influential Ellison family was going to inoculate, and everyone in New Windsor would follow their lead. Writing to his brother George, the governor, for an opinion or positive orders, he asked whether it was advisable to take into custody the offending doctor, Moses Higby, to prevent him from inoculating any more people.[39] With a constant stream of recruits entering the American ranks, inoculations continued throughout the war. Without this wise precaution, every move of the army potentially exposed the unprotected to this infection. Returning to New York following the siege of Yorktown, soldiers carried back smallpox. By January 1782, nine soldiers had already died and the disease was spreading, so nearly 2,000 were inoculated near West Point. Though several died, this effort was successful.[40] At West Point, surgeon James Thacher of the 9th Massachusetts inoculated the women and children traveling with the army during this time. In his regiment alone, 187 went through the process. Unable to delay the inoculation of family members in poor health, the death toll was higher than it might have been had they had the time to wait for a more auspicious occasion. At the 1780–81 artillery encampment at New Windsor, 3rd Artillery surgeon Samuel Adams inoculated military families as well as civilians in the vicinity.[41] Smallpox did not discriminate.

While no battles took place here, there were still large numbers of men with loaded guns. Thomas Foster noted on February 7, 1783, "that a man was shot in the thigh by one of the camp guards."[42] To mend these broken bodies, the doctor surgeons only possessed cutting tools, probes, retractors, tourniquets to stem the flow of blood, and bandages to support and cover the wounds. Time permitting, medicine and bleeding were prescribed to reduce inflammation, which put the patient in the best possible condition for treatment. Sometimes all a physician had available was compassion. As today, some injuries were so grievous that all doctors could do was to make those patients as comfortable as possible until death ended their suffering. Uncomplicated punctures of the skin were simply covered. Stitches were used to join separated pieces of tissue. The discharge of "laudable pus" was believed to be the surest sign that the body was successfully healing. Hesitant to do much in the trunk of the body, fearing that they would just cause further damage, doctors did, however, drain punctured lungs and stomach cavities, return dislocated intestines, and gingerly probe for gun shot, a finger often being the most eligible searching tool. They avoided, however, making any major incisions.

Limbs were a different story. Doctors were comfortable working on them. Depending on the progress of the recovery, a badly damaged arm or leg could always be amputated, which a stabilized person had a good chance of surviving. Simple fractures were carefully manipulated back into place and secured in their proper position by "eighteen tailed bandages."[43] Splints of wood or pasteboard reinforced the bandages and provided a measure of protection to healing bones. Slings supported arms, and crutches enabled a patient to move without putting weight on the injured leg. Compound fractures, where the bone is forced through the skin, were far more dangerous. The extent of the dislocation and the number of splintered bone pieces determined the treatment. Some doctors advocated immediate amputation before the fatal onset of gangrene claimed the life of the patient. Location of the afflicted was a factor. In the poorly ventilated large city and military hospitals, the prognosis for compound fractures was not good. It was not putrid air but rather infecting bacteria that thrived in the close quarters and unsanitary conditions that caused the tissue-destroying disease. Small facilities and tents were the superior environment. Surgeons first had to determine whether the patient was likely to survive the attempt to save the limb.[44] Once having made the determination that it was safe to try, the first step was to remove as many loose bone fragments as practical and then carefully manipulate the injury back into position. During this process, it was sometimes necessary to cut away some of the damaged pieces of bone. The wound was watched for signs of activity, such as the desired discharge of "laudable pus" and the feared appearance and smell of decay. Arresting gangrene before it spread to the trunk of the body was the only way to save the individual. That is why some physicians advocated amputating right away before gangrene had a chance to appear. Amputation was a straightforward operation. Positioned around the firm operating surface, assistants helped the doctor with his work and steadied and if necessary held the patient down. Padding was then put in place to cushion the location of the tourniquet or ligature. Wrapping either one of those constricting bands around the limb, the surgeon then tightened them to stem the flow of blood. Using a long curved knife, he cut through the skin and muscles all the way around to the bone. Taking up the saw, he cut off the bone. With crooked needles and thread or a C-shaped thin tool mounted into a wooden handle, called a tenaculum, the surgeon tied off the principal arteries. Finally, he bandaged the stump. An African American soldier at the New Windsor encampment was jeered at for his awkward gait in the spring of 1783. Having lost all his toes to frostbite and amputation in the failed attack on the fort at Oswego, New York, earlier that year, he, brandishing a bayonet, chased his tormentor, a saucy young fifer named Nicholas Stoner, who fled into the hut of Lieutenant Colonel Robert Cochran of the 2nd New York Regiment. While protecting the boy from physical assault, Cochran, amused by the incident, upbraided him for his callous treatment of a comrade, who deserved his compassion rather than ridicule.[45]

Cuts to the scalp were sutured just like any other wound, but punctures might require dilation to facilitate drainage and relieve pressure. New Windsor Cantonment resident Captain James Gregg, of the 1st New York Regiment, was shot and scalped in 1777 by native warriors outside of Fort Schuyler in present-day Rome, New York. He was then a member of the 3rd New York, which was disbanded in 1781. Doctors stitched up his wounds, and Gregg was "well satisfied in having his scalp restored to him, though uncovered with hair." After a lengthy recovery, he returned to duty but experienced sporadic mental breakdowns from the trauma.[46] Gregg's commander, Goose Van Schaick, spent the first few months of 1783 in Philadelphia "to have the cancer cut out of his face." He returned at the end of April. He had been bashed in the cheek by a musket butt in the attack on Fort Ticonderoga, New York, in 1758, and this old wound turned cancerous.[47] Injuries, swelling and internal bleeding force the brain against the skull, compromising the tissue. Once lost, brain tissue does not regenerate. From time immemorial, man relieved this swelling by cutting a hole in the head. Pierced by flint tools, a few healed prehistoric skulls survive to bear mute testimony to the success of this action by our early ancestors. In stable nondepressed fractures, 18th-century surgeons employed a serrated circular cutting tool, with projecting spike that fixed the instrument in place, called a trephine, to burrow through the bone. With large depressed fractures, cracked or splintered bones were best removed because the benefits of relieving the pressure on the brain more than offset the loss of a portion of the skull. In concussions with no apparent indication of the parts of the brain affected, the person was bled to reduce the fluid pressing up against the swollen injured tissue and was given anodynes for pain. Depending on the patient's response, an incision might be necessary to discharge matter. As with other therapies, the decision as to whether to open the skull was based on the experience and judgment of the surgeon. Above all, Dr. John Jones exhorted his fellow medical practitioners "to peruse the sixth commandment, which is 'Thou shalt not kill.'"[48]

The most common affliction of the head was a toothache. Not normally life-threatening but very painful nonetheless, it was usually cured by removing the tooth. The principal instrument was the tooth key, an approximately six-inch-long iron post affixed to a horizontal wooden handle, with a curved pivoting lever on one end shaped to fit around a tooth. Hooking it with the lever, the practitioner rotated the implement to loosen and draw out the tooth. Gums were invariably damaged as were surrounding teeth during the removal. Sometimes the tooth broke, and in more difficult extractions patients' jaws were fractured; all these procedures were done without the benefit of anesthesia to numb the pain.

Guiding the care in the Hudson Valley and elsewhere was the fourth and final director general of the medical department of the Continental Army, Dr. John Cochran, appointed in January 1781. Apprenticed to a Lancaster, Pennsylvania, physician, Cochran followed up this training with five years of service as a surgeon's mate in the French and Indian War. Establishing a practice in New Brunswick, New Jersey, a few years later, he strongly advocated resistance to Parliament's oppressive measures but took no part in the war until the British coursed through his adopted state after the final defeat of American forces around New York City. Joining Washington as a volunteer during his retreat across New Jersey in December 1776, Cochran proved himself an able practitioner. Recognizing the reports of his merits, Congress appointed him physician and surgeon general of the army in the Middle Department in April 1777. Serving at the Morristown, New Jersey, encampment, over the winter of 1779–80, known for dreadful snow and cold, he returned to the Highlands, where except for an occasional sojourn he spent the remainder of the war.

Cochran stayed at the John Ellison house for a short time at the end of 1780. Liking the charming country estate and unaware that the army intended to camp in the vicinity over the winter of 1782–83, he arranged to again stay with the Ellison family, writing to the quartermaster to that effect. Incensed by Pickering's reply that he had improperly denied Gates, the senior general, second only to Washington, that fine house, Cochran exploded in a scathing letter detailing Pickering's failures and partialities and concluded with an offer to fight a duel. Cochran was angry to begin with, because just prior to this altercation the quartermaster general refused to make a bed for him as he had done for Gates. Justifying the construction on the basis that Gates, with little notice, was summoned back to active service, Pickering did not want to establish a precedent of making them for all the officers. Sleeping on "three very small [stools]," Cochran caught a cold and contracted a fever, which further inflamed his invectives. Pickering ignored the challenge, but Gates got his quarters. That general had refused to accept the much less refined nearby Edmonston house, so Cochran indicated his willingness to stay at the De Peyster family home, on the eastern side of the Hudson. Washington quickly gave his assent, ending the dispute.[49]

Since its opening in the summer of 1781, the New Windsor hospital cared for anywhere from 100 to as many as 250 soldiers and their families at a time. Wives and children sometimes made up nearly 20 percent of the patients. Surviving monthly returns record various fevers, dysentery, diarrhea, rheumatism, ulcers, and a small number who were wounded. Every month there were soldiers going through treatment for venereal disease, usually with mercury, in some form, with its side effects of loose teeth, ulcers, and neurological disorders. Too much mercury caused death. The medicine was not the only source of pain. In his estimates of needed implements in August 1781, Cochran included "6 Dozen penis syringes" to inject doses directly into the urethra. Due to the stigma of "leus venerea," Congress sanctioned every afflicted officer $10 and soldiers $4, the proceeds earmarked to pay for blankets and shirts for the hospitals.[50]

Inevitably, there were deaths in this camp. The most famous was that of Colonel Francis Barber, commander of the 2nd New Jersey Regiment. Having distinguished himself in several battles and been wounded three times, he was killed by a falling tree on February 11, 1783. "Two soldiers were cutting down a tree, at the instant he came riding by it was falling, he did not observe till they desired him to take care, but the suprize was so sudden, and embarrassed his ideas so much, that he reined his horse to the unfortunate spot where the tree fell, which tore his body in a shocking manner, and put an immediate period to his existence in this life." The same fate befell Private Joseph Lovekins, of Ipswich, who was only 17 or 18 years old when he died on November 26, 1782. For Barber, there was a funeral procession that led from his quarters at the Denniston house on February 13 to the Goodwill Church Cemetery in Montgomery, New York, 10 miles away. While there is no documentation, Washington and other general officers might have attended the ceremony. Captain Aaron Ogden of the 1st New Jersey, brother of Barber's deceased wife Mary, was certainly there as well as most of the rest of the officers from that state. Elder brother Matthias, commander of Aaron's regiment, was still in Philadelphia with the army's committee to Congress. Barber was given full military honors, and as was customary, a cortege of officers wearing black mourning bands and a column of soldiers marched with arms reversed accompanied the slowly ambling wagon carrying the colonel to his final resting place, while dirges played on muffled drums covered in black crepe added to the solemnity of the occasion.[51] Though his horse also died in the accident, another one fully caparisoned and carrying Barber's boots placed backward in the stirrups, followed the bier. His sword, in the collection of Washington's Headquarters State Historic Site and currently on exhibit at the New Windsor Cantonment visitor center, was probably placed on top of the coffin along with other arms to form a martial display. After the arrival at the burial ground, sergeants from Barber's regiment bore him to the gravesite, while officers commensurate in rank with the deceased carried a black cloth over the coffin called a pall. Finally, Barber's men fired a final salute. The funeral party departed, and then a burial detail completed the grim task of internment.

But where did Lovekins end up? We do not know the location of his internment or that of any of the approximately 70 soldiers who died here besides Colonel Barber. At least another 68 people died at the New Windsor hospital huts between July 1781 and December 1782. The October 1781 return was lost in the period, the October 1782 return was never filled in besides the heading, and there are no surviving ones for 1783, so undoubtedly there were more deaths at the medical facility. Even after subtracting the 12 deaths in the hospital for November and December 1782 as possible duplicates from the overall Continental Army monthly returns for the New Windsor encampment, there remained over 50 individuals who died there.[52] They were probably interred near the hospital. Elijah Beals, from Lieutenant Gilbert's 2nd Company of the 5th Massachusetts Regiment, "died very suddenly" on April 8, 1783. He was buried the next day, but the spot was not recorded. More than likely following British military tradition, Beals and the other soldiers who died in this camp were "buried at the head of the colours, (it being the most honourable part of an Encampment)," in the front of their parade grounds.[53] Accompanied by his friends and other interested parties, the deceased was carried to his grave by soldiers of the same rank. Over the years people claimed to see gravesites, but none of the burials at this encampment have ever been located.

CHAPTER 5

"A tolerably decent appearance"
Clothing, Gear, Flags, and Identity

Wearing their endured hardships as a badge of honor, embodied in their threadbare but well-maintained uniforms, soldiers considered themselves a distinct society forced to struggle against not only an implacable military foe but also selfish civilians who denied them adequate subsistence, shelter, and clothing. The professional appearance of the troops at the final winter encampment of the Continental Army in New Windsor, New York, in 1782–83 belies the modern perception that American soldiers during the Revolutionary War were dressed in homespun. There were shortages, but the efforts to meet the clothing needs of more than 7,000 men were nothing short of extraordinary. Imported French clothing and cloth was incredibly important, but redyed captured British coats supplied one-third of the soldiers. Completing this international procurement was linen from Holland. The linen arrived in September 1782, but there were no funds to pay for making it into shirts. Washington prevailed upon patriotic Philadelphia ladies to make up shirts "gratuitously for their brave Countrymen."[1]

Though constituted to confront external threats, the Continental Army increasingly focused inward, obsessing about military regalia and professional conduct and ominously realizing the promised pay and perquisites of their service. Engendering pride, their habiliments was also source of jealousy. Distinctions that made soldiers and officers stand out from civilians was grist for the army's detractors. Every effort by the officers to distinguish themselves and their soldiers was viewed by equally ambitious civilians and government officials to be steps toward military ascendancy. In 1781, the Continental Congress forbade the use of elaborate braid on uniforms without Washington's or Congress's consent, citing the expense, but this was more of an effort to reign in perceived conceit.[2] The greatest source of jealousy was the hereditary officer benevolent organization, the Society of the Cincinnati, symbolized by an eagle suspended from a blue and white ribbon worn on the breast. This was the closest America ever came to realizing the worst fears of republicans: a military aristocracy.

The commander in chief observed on February 5, 1783, that he had "the satisfaction of seeing the Troops better coverd, better clothed and better fed, than they have ever been in any former Winter Quarters." Colonel Philip Van Cortlandt, commanding the 2nd New York Regiment, was not as sanguine, however, as he complained that "the month of January 1783, found us in Hutts of our own making as comfortable as Troops could expect without pay, scarcity of provisions at times, and also in Want of Sufficient Clothing however better than we had formerly experienced." Washington wrote to Secretary at War Lincoln the previous November that "the coats of some corps will be entirely worn out in the course of the winter and none will be fit for service at the time which the Army may be expected to take the field." In February, he told Lincoln that "the Officers are making every possible exertion, to put the old Cloathing into as good a state as it will admit, to give it a tolerably decent appearance."[3] There were shortages most notably in shirts, but they were not in rags, too often their condition in the past. Opportunities had been lost because so many soldiers were unfit for duty due to the lack of clothing, officer and common soldier alike.

When the army entered New Windsor, it was clothed as much as possible according to the 1779 specifications, which called for white-faced blue coats for the New England troops and buff-faced blue for New York and New Jersey troops, with the Maryland detachment in red-faced blue.[4] The ground for the regimentals was blue wool that was imported in large quantities from France. Regulations and actual practice, however, were often quite different. A case in point was the use of captured British regimentals to outfit the New Hampshire, New York, and New Jersey Lines and the 10th Massachusetts Regiment. French Expeditionary Force commander the Comte de Rochambeau wrote in his memoirs on September 14, 1782, that he was greeted at Verplanck's Point, New York, by American troops outfitted in French clothing and uniforms taken at the surrender of Yorktown, Virginia, the previous year. Actually, most of the British clothing had been part of the cargo of more than 50 ships of an East and West Indian merchant convoy that was captured in the Atlantic Ocean by a French and Spanish fleet in 1780 between the Azores and Madeira islands off the coast of Spain. Some of those soldiers who had been at Yorktown might have still been wearing the vests and overalls that they received from the stores surrendered by Cornwallis's army, but the preponderance of this clothing was from the seized enemy transports.[5]

Besides the promise of a $150,000 loan payable in three years, this clothing, a gift from the Bourbon courts, was all that John Jay, the unrecognized American minister to Spain, had to show for more than two frustrating and disappointing years in Madrid. Between March and April 1781, Richard Harrison, the Continental agent at Cadiz, Spain, shipped to Boston on four vessels 123 bales, 56 casks, and a trunk containing coats, shirts, waistcoats, breeches, hats, shoes, stockings, and other material, enough to supply about 3,000 men.[6] Gathering the forces for a possible move against New York City, Washington in June ordered that 1,000 of these suits be sent on immediately with a proportion of sergeant coats, hats, waistcoats, and breeches. Reminded of the quantities of clothing that were too small, he wanted them divided into small, medium, and large sizes. Anxiously waiting for the large shipment of clothing and other military stores aboard the transport *Marquis de Lafayette*, he urged General Heath, commander in the Highlands at that time, to expedite the transportation of this clothing to camp. While this was first thought of as a timely windfall, Washington was pained to discover that these coats were red. A further blow was the news that the *Lafayette* had been captured.[7] Despite the presence of Royal Navy cruisers and enemy privateers in all the sea-lanes, most of the shipments, did make it through. Most galling was that more than enough cloth arrived in private ships, but due to "the miserable state of continental Credit, … [the country could not] command a yard of it."[8]

A few months after Yorktown, Heath proposed issuing the British clothing to the 10th Massachusetts Regiment, the New Hampshire, New Jersey, and New York Lines. Lamenting that the coats were the wrong color, there was no other option to achieve uniformity except for the facings, which were several different colors. To compensate "for the real & imaginary defect in colour and quality" of these coats, captured hats and breeches were issued gratuitously to those Continental lines. While the rest of the Massachusetts Line refused the British coats, almost entirely now dyed brown but otherwise unchanged, the 10th Massachusetts could not afford to be particular. Ordered to spend the winter in the remote outposts to the north and west of Albany with the New Hampshire Line, it would be some time before they would get another chance to draw clothing. A notice in the *Boston Gazette* on May 27, 1782, described a deserter from the 10th Massachusetts who wore a "dark brown coat [with] British worsted laced facings." When the regiment was disbanded at the end of 1782 and distributed among the rest of the Massachusetts Line, Washington ordered that for parades and reviews those soldiers needed to form together or have their clothing transferred, because the regiments of the 2nd Massachusetts Brigade had a "disagreeable and speckled appearance." Buttons from the "5th, 15th, 27th, 35th, [40th], 46th, 55th and 60th" British regiments have been found at the hut sites of the New Hampshire, New Jersey, and New York troops. All of these regiments were in the West Indies in 1780.[9]

Washington's order of January 26, 1783, that the New Hampshire Line was to receive new clothing was a relief to Major William Scott, who was admonished for the poor showing of his brigade two days before. First to receive the dyed British coats and recently returned from a year on the northern and western frontier of New York, they were some of if not the most backward

Sketch presumably by French officer Jean-Baptiste Antoine de Verger, a lieutenant in the Royal Deux-Pont Regiment, of an American soldier wearing one of the dyed British coats. Anne S.K. Brown Military Collection, Brown University Library. He is a non-commissioned officer because he has a sword. There are two versions of the drawing, one with no description inserted in de Verger's journal and another tipped into the journal of fellow Royal Deux-Pont regiment officer Count von Closen with the designation "New Jersey." The whereabouts of this second drawing are currently unknown. Based on button discoveries in the vicinity of the New Jersey encampment at New Windsor and the reddish-orange color of the facings, the coat is probably from the 35th Foot. Don Troiani & James L. Kochan, *Insignia of Independence: Military Buttons, Accoutrement Plates, & Gorgets of the American Revolution* (Gettysburg, Pennsylvania, 2012), 192, and 233–234 (Anne S.K. Brown Military Collection, Brown University Library).

troops at New Windsor. More than likely, the principal reason for their poor state was not their posting on the frontier but instead that they had been far removed from the watchful eye of von Steuben and his inspectors and the most discerning judge of them all, General Washington. The New Hampshire Line was told to sort the clothing to maximize the issue, and the new underclothes and white-faced blue coats should have given the troops a decent look, but nothing was "well fitted, nor set off to advantage."[10] While regimental tailors could cut and fit the clothing that was too large, there was not much they could do with clothing that was undersized. There were enough ready-made garments that were made too small without adding to that worthless supply by failing to properly size the clothing.

The most efficient way to dress the soldiers was to ship cloth to camp and have the regimental tailors fit each one. There were specially built huts for this purpose with large glass windows to let in light. Ready-made clothing always had a generous seam allowance for fitting and would include some pieces that were too small to wear; besides, the tailors could make uniform outfits for their regiments. Uniformity was so essential to the discipline of the army that it was even portrayed on paper. Replicating a notional battle line, the September and October 1782 returns of the Continental Army in New York show the brown-coated New Jersey and New York troops composing the left flank; the blue-coated Connecticut, Rhode Island, and Massachusetts Lines in the center; and the brown-coated 10th Massachusetts and New Hampshire men covering the right. By placing the Canadian Regiment in distant Lancaster, Pennsylvania, guarding prisoners, on the extreme right, this suggests that they were also issued the captured British uniforms. Except for the Canadians, "the general order of Encampment [at Verplanck's Point], and the order of Battle for the Main army this Campaign," replicates those returns despite the 10th Massachusetts being stationed at West Point and the New Hampshire Line being stationed at Albany.[11]

Commenting at Verplanck's Point in September 1782 that during a review the light infantry were "dressed in brown coats with green revers and cuffs," French officer Jean-Baptiste Antoine de Verger certainly could have seen some of those picked soldiers dressed in this manner, but it is possible that he could have mistaken the New Jersey and New York Lines and the 10th Massachusetts Regiment arrayed on the flanks for light infantry. In the 1780 captured British convoy there were coats from three regiments with green facings, so at most there would have been three companies, totaling about 150 light infantry dressed this way, as opposed to approximately 1,000 regular infantry wearing the remainder of the coats with that color combination. There were no New Hampshire or Canadian Regiment troops present during this maneuver. The only ones in the dyed British coats were the New Jersey Line, the 1st New York Regiment, the 10th Massachusetts, the units' light infantry companies, and the light company of the 2nd New York. The Jersey and York Lines led the advance, and the 10th Massachusetts probably brought up the trail of the infantry regiments. Taking their place in the position of honor, on the right, the light infantry was predominantly in blue coats faced with white, with lesser numbers in the brown regimentals.[12]

The New York and New Jersey Lines were not so fortunate as the New Hampshire Line, because in January 1783 they turned their coats. Through this process, the coats were taken apart, turned so the worn outside pieces were facing inside, and then resewed. At the end of February, assistant inspector Major William Barber was favorably impressed with at least two of the regiments' efforts: "The coats of the First New

Jersey and Second New York Regiments have been neatly turned and repaired.... The military appearance and economy of those two regiments in every respect are highly commendable, and without exception exemplary to every other in the Army." Colonel Walter Stewart, inspector of the northern army, would write by the end of March, however, that the British coats were not going to last much longer. The cloth had suffered in the overdyeing and was in use for about a year.[13]

Secretary at War Lincoln in December 1782 informed Washington that the cavalry and infantry of the Continental Army were to now wear a red-faced blue coat lined with white, but only a portion of the coats were ever altered to conform with the new regulations. It was not until the middle of April that the regiments that had not mended their coats could draw lots for the first shipment of red cloth. When the scarlet cloth was being distributed in April 1783, Washington hoped there would be enough for "Cuffs, Capes and perhaps half facings."[14] Because the light infantry functioned as a separate corps in the field, uniformity with their regiments was less important than among the battalion companies, so they were ordered to remain in their white-faced blue coats.[15] Presumably, the light infantry, still in the dyed British coats, retained this uniform.

Smallest of the lines at New Windsor, the 3rd Maryland was the only unit that would not have to change its facings, but there was so much else that needed to be altered about this detachment. It was never a good way to start off an inspection when the commanding general could find "Dirt and Trash ... so liberally strewed ... that it was difficult to avoid the filth." Comparing the favorable impression made by the regiment on his left, the 1st New Jersey, with the reprehensible appearance of his Marylanders, Washington pointed out to the detachment commander, Major Thomas Lansdale, that his clothing was only issued six months earlier, while those of the New Jersey men had been worn for nearly a year. Told to thoroughly instruct his command in von Steuben's manual, *Regulations for the Order and Discipline of the Troops of the United States*, Lansdale, owing to the newness of his unit, escaped censure this time, but the commander in chief expected a marked correction. He would not be disappointed. In the next review, it was with pleasure that Washington noted the improved appearance of the Marylanders. Like any good father, he felt as much joy in seeing this transformation as he had pain in delivering the rebuke.[16]

Even among the old corps, there were regiments that were found to be wanting. During a review in February 1783, both the 5th and 8th Massachusetts Regiments of the 2nd Brigade, whose troops should have cut a fine figure in their regulation white-faced blue coats, did not make the "elegant appearance ... which was expected." In confidential letters addressed to the officer in charge of each regiment, Washington told them to put their commands in order or be publicly reprimanded in general orders next time. In keeping with their status as select troops, Washington, "in justice to the [8th Massachusetts] Lt Compy[,] ... thought very few, if any, in the Line made a more soldier-like figure." This reproach probably prompted the commander of the 8th Massachusetts, Colonel Michael Jackson, to order at the end of the month the retailoring of both the regiment's blue coats and remaining dyed British ones.[17] Whether the presence of 2nd Brigade commander Brigadier General John Greaton would have made any difference will never be known, but Washington lamented the absence of so many officers. Only two of the six brigade commanders were present; one of those present had requested to go on leave but was refused.

A committee of officers met in January 1781 to decide on the uniform for the Massachusetts Line. They met again two years later at General Paterson's marquee at New

Windsor to make another determination, but this description has not come to light.[18] With plenty of time to perfect their military appearance and discipline because they had been essentially sedentary in the Hudson Highlands since 1779, the Massachusetts Line had no excuse for deficiencies. Besides, its state was the most active in providing clothing. Not willing to see its soldiers suffer because of the deficiencies of the Continental clothiers, the Massachusetts legislature gave General Washington notice in January 1782 that it would undertake the outfitting of its soldiers. Washington forwarded this message to the president of Congress for a determination as to whether this act was acceptable to the national governing body.[19] Expected to deposit the clothing they procured into the Continental store so it could be equally distributed throughout the entire army, Massachusetts officials, not surprisingly, refused to do so. Unscathed by the war since 1776, the state possessed the capability to cloth its troops when Congress could not. In the spring of 1782, state clothier Ezra Lunt issued 2,000 uniform coats to those soldiers of the Massachusetts Line in need of them. He also provided the first shipment of state-manufactured buff wool breeches, enough to cloth four regiments.[20]

Going through a series of clothier generals, Congress alternated between insisting on dressing the army and foisting the responsibility back on the states. Dangerous dissension could erupt, however, if the individual states were given sole responsibility for outfitting their troops. The soldiers from states with the greatest resources would be amply supplied, while those from the others of lesser means would suffer. Moreover, few other measures would contribute more to the perception that the Continental Line was a coalition of 13 separate armies. As it was, the different sections of the country tended to look disapprovingly at each other. Disparities in the clothing issue only served to further fuel these rivalries. Waiting to pick up his baggage at the tail end of a marching column of soldiers in 1780, Yankee Joseph Plumb Martin watched as soldiers "of the middle states passed ... [and how] it was truly amusing to see the number and habiliments of those attending it; of all specimens of human beings, this group capped the whole." A caravan of wild beasts could bear no comparison with it. There was "Tag, Rag and Bobtail," with "some in rags and some in jags" but none "in velvet gowns."[21] Equally distributing the large number of supplies, shipped mainly from France, was not enough. Much of that material was cloth or partially assembled garments that needed to be put together or at least fitted. Some states would find it very difficult to pay the tailors, provided you could get the material to them. In those regions, partially or in a few instances almost entirely occupied by the enemy, officials were in no position to arrange the manufacture of clothing. Far preferable was to complete the garments in places of safety and transport them overland directly to the armies in the field. To improve the supply of clothing, Washington recommended that "the Country Taylors take the Articles to their Homes to make, under such restrictions as will prevent their embezzlement or loss to the Public." Eager to get the clothing made up, he even arranged for the army ration contractor Comfort Sands to provide the tailors with food.[22]

While it was never proposed to make all the uniforms the same way, the New Hampshire Brigade commander was pained to observe "that notwithstanding All the Efforts that have been used to Perserve uniformity in the troops many of them lost to all sence of honor—and reguardless of their own reputation or that of their Officers appearin upon the parade the Last Inspection with such Alterations in their uniforms as their own foolish fancies dictated and could not have been thought of." The 2nd New Hampshire Regiment set the precedent with its unnecessary alterations of the captured clothing. Redoing the cuffs, collars, and facings of the overdyed brown British coats in white wool cloth, which they bound on the raw edge with white wool tape, they additionally added blue diamonds, bound in white tape, where the tails of the skirt hooked back. To the breast, they added a white star. The next guidance from headquarters was far more pointed. Washington stated that officers were to determine the style of their corps' uniform and ensure that soldiers complied with the decision. With coats wearing the most at the bottom, he recommended shorter tails. Easier to tailor, the contracted tails allowed for the cutting back of frayed areas and provided patching materials. Regardless of the chosen style, turning and repairing the coats was the priority.[23]

Concerned with visually delineating the hierarchy, the commander in chief desired that tailors use better material than that used for the privates as well as superior finishing in their manufacture of sergeants' coats.[24] Besides being of a finer cloth, all the dyed British sergeant coats had plain white lace trim. Musicians wore the opposite colors of their regiments: Massachusetts blue-faced white, Maryland blue-faced red, and among the regiments in British coats a rich palette of greens, yellows, buff, and orange faced in red. The only departure from this convention was in the royal regiments. Dressed in blue-faced red coats, they were decorated with royal lace instead of the distinctive cloth tape specified for each regiment. Buttons of one royal regiment, the 60th Regiment of Foot, have been recovered at the hut sites of the New York, New Jersey, and New Hampshire Lines.[25] There were nine companies in an infantry regiment. Eight of those companies fought in a two-rank battle line standing shoulder to shoulder. They were often called battalion companies. A regiment was divided into two battalions, each containing four companies. The last company was designated light infantry. Working in small groups or massed together with other companies into light infantry battalions, they were given the most dangerous missions. Composed of the best and most vigorous in each regiment, the light infantry were elite shock troops who carried Stony Point, New York, in 1779 and Redoubt Number 10 at Yorktown, Virginia, in 1781, at the point of the bayonet. Light infantry troops were expected to move fast and strike hard, so their coats were cut short to improve mobility. Deborah Sampson, who posed as a soldier in the light company of the 4th Massachusetts Regiment in 1782–83, told her biographer many years later that she received "a blue coat lined with white, with white wings on the shoulders and cords on the arms and pockets." Seriously wounded, she paid a high price to be counted among the worthies chosen to wear that special coat. The lingering effects of these injuries would compel Deborah years later to again don a uniform. In need of continual medical treatment, she eventually agreed to go on the lecture circuit dressed as a Continental soldier to promote a book about her life.[26]

For the officers who paid for their clothing, financier Robert Morris worked out an arrangement in February 1782 to enable the penurious to acquire new uniforms. The ship *Marquis de Lafayette*, filled with among other necessary articles officer clothing, was captured during the passage to America. Unable to provide for the officers from the public magazines, Morris worked out a deal with Comfort Sands & Company, which agreed to accept at face value government-issued notes redeemable in six months. Morris planned to redeem those notes with the year's projected tax revenues. The value of the notes would be deducted from future officer pay. Subalterns, ensigns, and lieutenants received a note for three months' pay, while captains and above received notes for two months's pay. Officers were not obligated to take those notes or patronize that business, but the ones who did were satisfied with the cost.[27] There were also stores in the neighborhood. Lieutenant

Gilbert in February purchased from merchant John Currie a pen knife used to cut the quills used in writing and a drinking vessel or dinnerware made of Britannia, a smooth pewter-like alloy. Currie advertised for sale in the *New York Packet and the American Advertiser* on December 26, 1782, "a General Assortment of Goods, suitable for the season, at the house of MR. WILLIAM ELLISON, in New Windsor." This Ellison brother managed a packet boat, a dock, a warehouse, and a store along the waterfront, while John directed the operation of the Gates's headquarters property. Trying to attract some of the over 7,000 potential customers encamped at the Continental Army cantonment at New Windsor, Currie's notice at the end of February 1783, boasted of "Dry goods, suitable for both army and country," that were recently imported from France and the Dutch Republic. Of interest to the officers, the consignment contained "superfine scarlet, blue, white, [and] buff.... Cloths.... Black, white and coloured Ostrich Feathers and Plumes [and] Best Philadelphia manufactured Beaver and Castor Hats" in addition to a large supply of thread and material for linings and pockets. In this money-strapped economy, he accepted "Cash, Bank Notes, Honourable Robert Morris's Notes, Contractor's due Bills, Subsistence Notes, or any kind of country produce"[28] Though the "lowest Grades of Officers must appear equally well dressed with their Colonels," limits, were set on any embellishments, so they had to scrutinize their purchases of any decorations. Legislators acted in 1781 to prevent the wealthy, such as Colonel Walter Stewart, from outfitting themselves so lavishly as to excite jealousy and agitation by other officers for an increased clothing allowance in order to compete with the fashion trendsetters. Unless approved by Congress or Washington, an officer was not to "wear on his cloaths any gold or silver lace embroidery or vellum, on pain of being cashiered."[29] Lieutenant Gilbert, however, did have military clothing of various quality. Stating that he "dressed for to attend a court martial" on January 6, 1783, shows that he put on his best for official functions.[30]

Tangible proof of the Continental Army's pursuit of military perfection is the thousands of elaborately designed buttons made in the camps and found in the archaeological record. Infantry soldiers wore pewter buttons, an alloy of tin and lead. The buttons had a pewter eye or shank through which thread, cloth tape, or a leather thong held it to the coat. Ranging from plain to rather ornate, a wide variety of buttons was used by the Americans. Officer buttons were often repoussé. In this process, a thin copper alloy or white metal shell was stamped from behind to create a raised design. Plated in white metal, the shell was then crimped around a bone or wooden back already sewn to the coat through deadeye holes. In several sizes, the common raised interlocking letters of the USA button symbolized a united people, but the states still clung tenaciously to their individual identities. The Massachusetts Line arranged for the manufacture of distinctive regimental buttons. Talented soldiers carved the molds and cast the buttons. Numbers of these molds were found in the camps on the east side of the Hudson River opposite West Point. This task was far easier when officer buttons, made by a Massachusetts firm, arrived in the Highlands beginning in the summer of 1781. Using these quality repoussé ones as masters, new molds were made, producing a more refined button than the previous issue. A 6th Massachusetts matrix made from these superior examples was recovered at the New Windsor Cantonment. The state also purchased large numbers of French pewter buttons that had an Arabic number outlined by two concentric circles. New Hampshire and New Jersey soldiers made very limited runs of crude distinctive buttons. With only a few ever discovered and only in small size, these might have been intended just for hats.[31]

Epaulettes of silver or gold bullion thread, with fringe extending down from the shoulder, usually covered by larger coils for officers and worsted with wool fringe for noncommissioned officers, and worn on top of the shoulders clearly identified these leaders to those less than discerning soldiers, who might miss the finer cloth and superior finishing of the uniforms worn by their betters. Due to the shortage of insignia, the clothier general in the spring of 1782 was ordered to obtain worsted shoulder knots (looped cording) for the noncommissioned officers to wear until epaulettes were obtained. Infantry sergeants wore a worsted white epaulette on both shoulders, and corporals wore one epaulette on the right shoulder.[32] Subaltern infantry officers, ensigns, and lieutenants had a single silver epaulette on the left shoulder, while captains an epaulette on the right shoulder. Field-grade officers—majors, lieutenant colonels, and colonels—sported a pair of silver epaulettes. Brigadier generals wore two gold epaulettes with a single silver star on both, while major generals had two stars. General Washington's epaulettes had three stars, but he preferred a well-made but unadorned one for everyday wear. Finally getting his long-coveted promotion to brigadier, Lieutenant Gilbert received "a present of a silver appelet" in January from General Putnam because he no longer needed it.[33]

Additionally, the brigadiers wore a single white feather and major generals a black-tipped white one in their hats, extending vertically from a black and white cockade. To differentiate staff functions, Washington also ordered those sections to wear different-colored feathers: blue for inspectors, red and green for the adjutant general and assistants, and green and white for his aides-de-camp. Aides-de-camp of the other generals had just a single green feather. Feathers were all the rage at that time. Most of the army would eventually wear them. Privates and corporals in the 4th Massachusetts Regiment wore a white feather in the same fashion as a brigadier general. Musicians and sergeants of that regiment put a black feather behind the white one.[34] Major James Keith, of the 8th Massachusetts Regiment, sent his soldiers, who were stationed at West Point, to gather feathers for their hats. He would, however, not be around to receive accolades for his regiment's new plumage. Court-martialed in September 1782 for abandoning his defensive positions in the pursuit of these feathers and for providing a guard for merchandise illegally brought from enemy territory into American lines, Keith was acquitted of the first charge, but his conviction of the second resulted in his dismissal from the service.[35]

Commanders were urged to "be extremely attentive to give them [hats] a military and Uniform appearance by cutting, cocking or adding such other decorations as they think proper." Hats worn by infantry soldiers were round black felt tied up on three sides, with the edges bound in white tape. Cords were often wrapped around the base of the hat to tighten or loosen it. Tassels, the knotted fringe ends of the cord, dangled just below the sides of the hat. In the 4th Massachusetts, however, only the sergeants had a tassel on both the right and left of the hat. The musicians and soldiers suspended both tassels from the right corner. In the 2nd Massachusetts, sergeants could remove the white tape from their hats and give it to one of their men. Soldiers in the 1st New York used flour to clean the bindings of their hats. Embarrassed by the rebuke from Washington over the appearance of his regiment at the review on February 6, Gilbert two weeks later recut and bound the hats of his company.[36] Constructed of leather or made from an existing hat, caps had a semicircular body and an inverted shield-shaped front and visor. Deborah Sampson described her light infantry cap as having a black and white cockade, a red-tipped black plume, and a white cloth band wrapped around the base.[37] Ornate caps were another way to distinguish elite troops. General Rochambeau was the first to make the visible gesture of the alliance by ordering his army to add a black relief to their cockades. Washington in July 1780 reciprocated by ordering his officers to incorporate the white cockade of the House of Bourbon with black, the color adopted from British tradition. Eventually, the order to wear the black and white cockade was extended to all American soldiers.[38] For cleanliness, hair was recommended worn short or tied in the back, but the powdering for inspections included the nonhygienic practices of coating it with tallow, followed by the dusting with flour. For the February muster, the 1st New York spent an entire day cleaning themselves, polishing muskets, whitening and blackening their leather gear, and putting everything else in the best possible condition. Lieutenant Colonel Ebenezer Sproat, commanding officer of the 2nd Massachusetts Regiment, observed that many of his soldiers were filthy. Though they were allowed to charge for this service, which was expected of them, he wondered why the women and children were not apparently doing the laundry.[39]

For fatigue duty during periods of warm weather or in the absence of a coat, the soldiers had a linen hunting shirt, with fringed water-shedding capes. A uniquely American garment, the hunting shirt took on legendary status when riflemen from the Pennsylvania, Maryland, and Virginia frontier clad in them arrived in the American camp outside of Boston in the beginning of the war. Amazing the Yankees with the accuracy of their fire, these marksmen struck terror in every enemy heart, especially the officers, whom they purposely targeted. Because of the importance of the regimental coats and the tenuous prospects of timely resupply, the soldiers were ordered during mild conditions to wear them only for inspections and guard duty. During the winter months, they were expected to wear hunting shirts over their regimentals while on work parties, but 1st New York soldiers were seen in February 1783 carrying firewood against their coats.[40] The hunting shirt, worn over the regimental, however, was no substitute for a warm overcoat. Forced to stand their post in all kinds of weather, most of the sentries were fortunate enough to have thick woolen watch coats with capes. With only a small number of watch coats per company, they were only issued to soldiers on guard duty.[41]

Shirts were in such short supply in the summer of 1782 that some soldiers did not have one.[42] Fortuitously, a ship loaded with linen as well as other supplies for the army arrived in September. The odyssey of this linen, purchased in Amsterdam the previous year, was not unique. Loaned six million livres by Louis XVI's government, Washington aide-de-camp Lieutenant Colonel John Laurens was talked into buying the material in the Dutch Republic by fellow South Carolinian commodore Alexander Gillon, "a measure highly offensive to the French court." Desperate to get back to America as quickly as possible so he did not miss the 1781 campaign, Laurens left the shipping arrangements to the ship captain. Initially loading the cargo on his frigate, Gillon, several months later, transferred it to two Dutch vessels. Leasing this large commerce raider that he named *South Carolina* from the Prince of Luxembourg for three years in exchange for a percentage of his prizes or large fee in the event of its loss or his failure to capture enough enemy shipping, Gillon did not want to waste time carrying cargo. He was supposed to escort those ships to America but never returned, so in October the shipment was offloaded at significant cost in Amsterdam. The shirts were intended for that winter, but the army had to wait another year to receive this supply. Condemned upon his return to the United States for the quixotic odyssey of the *South Carolina*, Gillon was not the only ship captain censured for neglect.[43] John Paul Jones and a number of others were also blamed for the delay or loss of imported military stores. Given the catch-as-catch-can way that the Americans relied on to transport their imported articles, the captains were not totally to blame. In December 1780, Washington vented to General Lincoln that 10,000 uniforms were delayed in France because American agents argued over shipping the consignment and that there was clothing destined for the Continental Army languishing in the West Indies for more than a year and a half. "Scandalous neglect or inattention" was not limited to American agents overseas. Forgotten and wasting away, 80 wagonloads of clothing, enough to outfit the entire army, had sat in Springfield, Massachusetts, through much of 1780 for lack of transportation. Most of it had been there almost two years. Large quantities of rotten shoes had to be thrown away.[44]

Washington wanted soldiers to receive at least two shirts, because without a spare the one would "soon be rotted off their backs. Despite the heroic efforts, of the ladies of Philadelphia, to make shirts out of the linen shipment, they were thousands short of this goal. Though loath to make partial issues, the demand for shirts was so great that the regiments drew lots for the available supply."[45] In addition to the regimental coat, hunting shirt, and shirts, the typical Continental soldier at New Windsor Cantonment had a pair of breeches, a pair of overalls, one or two waistcoats, stockings, a pair of shoes and buckles, garters, a hat, and neck stock. Overalls or gaitered trousers had a distinctive tongue at the bottom that covered the instep, shedding water, mud, and other debris. At least in the 1st New York Regiment, the soldiers preferred breeches, which ended just below the knee. But their commander, Colonel Goose Van Schaick, wanted to preserve this more formal garment and advocated greater use of the overalls.[46] Ideally, wool breeches, overalls, and waistcoats were used in the cold months, and the linen ones were worn in warmer weather. In February 1783, Van Schaick ordered his company commanders to make black wool half-gaiters. Turning the shoe into a boot without the discomfort of leather, these spatterdashes extended to the calf and served the same purpose as the gaitered portion of the overalls. Considered stylish as well for reviews and maneuvers, the light infantry, in green-faced brown coats, fastened gaiters over their overalls in September 1782 to impress General Rochambeau and other dignitaries from the French Army.[47] As previously suggested, this unit might have been instead infantry battalion companies in the captured dyed British coats.

The death of Major General William Alexander, Lord Stirling, in Albany, New York, on January 15, 1783, prompted some of the general officers and others to don black ribbons or other devices symbolizing grief and go into mourning for a month.[48] Looking for ways to reward his soldiers at no cost to the country, Washington in August 1782 borrowed an idea from Massachusetts general John Paterson, who had conferred on his brigade herringbone-shaped strips of white cloth worn three inches from the top seam of the left shoulder for every four years of reputable service. Paterson copied this inverted V-shaped decoration from the French *galons d'ancienneté* (seniority braid), also known as brisures. The commander in chief changed the time requirement to three years and shortly thereafter ordered that the strips of cloth match the facing color. He expected that "those gallant men who are thus designated will on all occasions be treated with particular confidence and consideration." The award was not automatic. Regimental boards of varying strictness selected worthy candidates who met the time in service criteria. Washington tried to introduce some equity to the process by forming a board of officers to determine criteria to guide the selections. Awards for service longevity were

Badge of Military Merit (courtesy New Windsor Cantonment State Historic Site, New York State Office of Parks, Recreation and Historic Preservation).

not something that could not be taken away. Offending soldiers had their Honorary Badge of Distinction torn off in front of their assembled regiments.[49]

For those soldiers who really distinguished themselves, they were "permitted to wear on ... [their] facings over the left breast, the figure of a heart in purple cloth, or silk, edged with narrow lace or binding." The Badge of Merit or Badge of Military Merit, later called the Purple Heart after its modern successor, was the Revolutionary War equivalent of the Medal of Honor. The army was not always consistent in its use of terminology. On the bottom of discharges at the end of the war was printed "[blank] has been honored with the Badge of Merit for [blank] Years faithful Service." This discrepancy has led some to the erroneous conclusion that far more purple-colored heart decorations were awarded. A powerful symbol of faith, fidelity, and ultimately love, the heart kindled strong feelings in the 18th century and still does today. The hearts were placed on the tails of many regimental coats as a sign of loyalty, and it was not a far stretch to use a heart to recognize consummate devotion: bravery in combat or steadfast service. Though this award was established at the same time as the Honorary Badge of Distinction, a selection board met for the first and apparently only time in April 1783. Choosing two soldiers, one whose last name began with a "B," Sergeant William Brown, formerly of the 5th Connecticut Regiment, and the other a "C," Sergeant Elijah Churchill of the 2nd Light Dragoons, from depositions submitted by recommending officers, the board was ordered to meet again, but there is no record that it ever did, which begs the question as to whether the stack was in alphabetical order and other deserving candidates missed out. The other recipient, Sergeant Daniel Bissell, was chosen directly by the commander in chief. In an age, however, when officers received the lion's share of rewards, though only three of these badges were given out, "the road to glory in a patriot army and a free country ... [was] thus open[ed] to all."⁵⁰

Officers need not worry that they were not eligible for Honorary Badges of Distinction or the Badge of Military Merit. There were several other ways to recognize their bravery and faithful service. Some of them had started out as soldiers and had risen through the ranks to the officer corps, an infrequent occurrence in European armies. Their commissions were government securities, which entitled them to receive half of their pay for life if they served to the close of the war. Forced to enact this legislation in 1780 to stem the torrent of officer resignations, Congress at the end of the conflict no longer needed the officers and looked for ways to renege on this promise. During the ensuing war of words between Congress and the military leadership, known as the Newburgh Conspiracy, which fortunately, for "the fate of unborn millions," remained only that, the writer of the two inflammatory letters setting in motion the showdown challenged officers to not sit idly by to "grow old in poverty, wretchedness and contempt."⁵¹ Possibly more disturbing to some than a life of penury was the loss of the power and prestige they enjoyed while wearing the uniform. Colonel Walter Stewart wrote to

Detail from "West Point, New York" by Pierre L'Enfant showing the Continental Army in the summer of 1783 (Library of Congress Photographs and Prints Division). After most of the army was furloughed at New Windsor in June 1783, the remainder moved to West Point. The soldier next to the officer pointing with his sword has a herringbone-shaped Badge of Honorary Distinction on his left arm.

General Gates in the middle of June 1783 stating that "the poor, deluded crowd must return home [to] the ridicule of their neighbors, and when their present plumage is lost, they must return to labor" and insignificance. Obtaining a leave of absence at the very end of the war, Colonel Matthias Ogden, of the 1st New Jersey Regiment, showing incredible naivete, had intended to wear his uniform while conducting business in France until Washington pointed out to him that in Europe, decorum prohibited military officers from engaging in mercantile pursuits.[52]

This longing for continuous recognition gave rise to the Society of the Cincinnati. At a meeting presided over by von Steuben in the Temple on May 10, Generals Knox, Hand, and Huntington considered suggestions for governing the proposed officer association. Though the idea was often attributed to the status-seeking former Prussian officer, Knox was chiefly behind the formation of this organization. Recording secretary and Knox aide Major Samuel Shaw prepared the authorizing document. Founded at the Verplanck house, the headquarters of the inspector general, a few days later, this benevolent fraternity realized the long-held wish of many: "to render permanent the cordial affection subsisting among the officers." They took their inspiration from the example set by Lucius Quintus Cincinnatus, who led the Roman army to victory and then quietly returned to his farm. Moreover, the choice of that historical figure justified in their own minds their plowing of their fields, just like their former privates. Each officer contributed a month's pay for a relief fund. The interest on this sum was made available for the unfortunate.[53] While it was not written in any bylaws, the society also intended to act as a powerful lobby to exact veteran benefits from the states and the federal government.

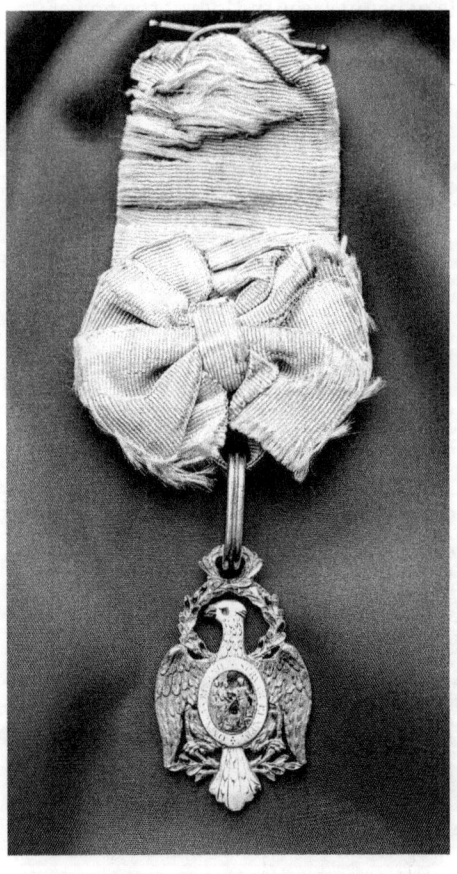

Washington aide-de-camp Lieutenant Colonel Tench Tilghman, Society of the Cincinnati Eagle & Ribbon (The Society of the Cincinnati, Washington, DC).

The eagle badges, adopted as the symbol of the order, were certainly not in keeping with Cincinnatus's humble return to obscurity, but the members certainly offended American sensibilities when they made their association hereditary. Of "such stuff ... [kings] are made on." With stars in his eyes, those worn on a brigadier's epaulettes, Colonel Lewis Nicola, commander of the Invalid Corps, just a year before wrote a letter to curry favor with Washington. In the fawning document, Nicola recommended that America adopt a monarchy, with the commander in chief as the first king. Incredulous that anyone in his army held such thoughts, Washington told Nicola to never again make this suggestion. Washington, however, did accept his nomination as first president general of the Society of the Cincinnati. He was chosen by his remaining officers in a meeting held in the Temple on June 19,

1783. Citing the press of personal business, he did try to resign the office a few years later after his gravitas helped the membership weather the fervent objections to their organization, but he yielded to their entreaties for him to continue, holding the position for the rest of his life.[54]

Inspired as much or more so by jealousy than concern for the organization's long-term effect on the liberties of the country, John Adams, Samuel Adams, John Jay, and many others within and without the government bitterly denounced this military aristocracy. Thomas Jefferson felt that for the sake of the republic, the group needed to "distribute their funds, renounce their existence [and] melt up their eagles." Succumbing to the outcry, the members agreed to wear the medals only at their own gatherings and at funerals. Writing from his baronial estate Monticello, the Virginia ideologue gloated that the officers were forced to stop offending the public with their pretentious exhibitions. The most virulent response to the Society of the Cincinnati did not come, however, from the American people; it came instead from the citizens of Paris. During the Reign of Terror, a Jacobin rode through the streets of the French capital leading a horse whose neck was covered with crosses of St. Louis and Society of Cincinnati eagles, stripped from nobles at the guillotine. Approving of the benevolent aim of this organization, General Heath from the beginning was opposed to this chivalric order and its regalia, which was more in keeping with European aristocracy than a republican people. Finally relenting, he joined. But a decade later with the backlash against the symbols of rank and privilege during the French Revolution, Heath withdrew his membership, the only officer to do so.[55]

Further distinguishing a soldier was the tools of his trade: his arms and equipment. When the Continental Army marched into the New Windsor Cantonment, the enlisted men carried a musket with attached bayonet and sling, a cartridge box, a knapsack, a haversack, and a canteen. Significantly absent was a belt worn over the right shoulder that extended to the left side, which held the scabbard for the bayonet. Shortages of leather to make these carriages forced Washington in August 1780 to order that bayonets stay constantly fixed on the end of the musket. More than just a measure to address a deficiency, the arrangement sent a message to the troops that they were expected to close with the enemy. Changing the weight and balance of the firearm, the continued carriage of the more than a foot-long, three-sided iron stabbing weapon gave soldiers time to get accustomed to the new configuration until it was second nature. All privates turned in their bayonet belts. Symbolic of their authority, corporals and sergeants, however, were required to have sidearms, so they kept the belts and placed their bayonets in the scabbards when they were on duty and not carrying muskets. Noncommissioned officers with swords wore them instead of a bayonet. Two weeks later enough swords arrived to provide one each to the regimental quartermaster sergeants and every first sergeant.[56] There was a wide variety of short swords issued to walking soldiers. They were often called hangers because they hung on the left side on a waist or from an over-the-shoulder belt and were both locally made and captured, but it is not possible to determine which specific sword was used by individuals. Some of the light infantry sergeants had waistbelts fastened by cast brass "USA" buckles that carried scabbards containing brass hilted swords with the same "USA" designation. These accoutrements were presented by Lafayette when he commanded their division. The then quarter master sergeant Benjamin Gilbert at the end of August 1778 drew a "Hushing Cutlash, [Hessian Cutlass], presumably from the stock of weapons surrendered by the German troops at Saratoga, the previous year."[57]

Swords also distinguished the officers, and they were required to procure their own. After his promotion to officer, Gilbert had to turn his enlisted sword in. Though costing 90 pounds, his new hanger was probably a very basic model, paling in comparison to the one mounted in silver found in November or early December 1782 between Fishkill and Fishkill Landing.[58] Inflation made everything very expensive. Dismounted ensigns and lieutenants at the platoon level carried a large foot-long large spear called a spontoon mounted on a wooden pole six and a half feet long as another distinguisher of their rank.[59] Earlier in the war many officers carried firearms, but the extensive maintenance required for this type of weapon took too much time away from their primary duty of commanding their troops. Functional as well as decorative, the spontoon made it easier for soldiers to find their commanders. While the spontoon was useful for hand-to-hand fighting, the opposing sides did not normally get that close. At least one officer, sergeant, or corporal availed himself of an over-the-shoulder bayonet carriage from the British stores surrendered at Yorktown. Fastened by a square brass plate with "REV" cast into it, this buckle was from the 80th Regiment of Foot, the Royal Edinburgh Volunteers. This clasp was lost or discarded at the hut sites of the New Hampshire light infantry, New Jersey, and New York Lines, all of which were at Yorktown. Another British buckle was found in camp. Made of square brass with a lion's head projecting out of it, this plate is not marked, so without further information it is not possible to determine its origin.[60]

Joseph Plumb Martin observed that the government neglected feeding and clothing the Continental Army but always managed to provide arms, accoutrements, and ammunition.[61] Both British and French muskets were used in this camp. American-made guns were all but gone, having given way to ones made by European manufactories. French muskets eventually prevailed in the Continental Army. In just one shipment from France, Colonel John Laurens in February 1782 brought back "nine or ten thousand stand of arms." A stand of arms was a weapon complete with ramrod and bayonet. Stamped "US" or a variant on the barrel, lock, and sometimes stock to prevent embezzlement, they were produced at the arsenals of St. Etienne, Mauberge, and Charleville, France, the latter predominating.[62] Muskets were plentiful, but there was a small shortage of bayonets. Soldier were required to have a flint secured in the jaws of the musket cock to ignite the gunpowder and a spare in their cartridge pouch. There were also muskets missing stoppers, a wooden plug inserted in the barrel to keep out rain and snow. One of the sources for lubricating the musket locks was offal, the internal organs of slaughtered animals.[63] Thinking of the future and postwar supply, Washington was anxious that recruits were not issued new muskets when serviceable older ones were available. He also forbade the exchange of repairable guns with the new arms. There were always large quantities of muskets that only required minor repairs, so the commander in chief accepted the recommendation of General Knox in September 1782 to investigate employing qualified German prisoners as armorers. Forwarding the idea to Secretary at War Lincoln, Washington also proposed the alternative of contracting out the work. The secretary replied that he was sending for the Germans. Overall, the arms, accoutrements, and ammunition at the New Windsor winter encampment were in good condition. This state was an improvement from the previous summer, where in a June 1782 review numbers of muskets failed to fire. When the trigger was pulled, the notched tumbler disengaged, releasing the flint-holding cock. Forcefully propelled forward by the main spring, the flint struck against the firm surface of the hammer, creating sparks and opening the pan. The sparks dropped down into the reservoir in the lock, called the pan, igniting the gunpowder placed there in the first step of the loading process. A flame then shot through a small hole in the side of the gun barrel, called the vent or touchhole, and set off the charge, propelling the musket ball. In that military parade, the issue was that the hammers required hardening because they were too soft to provide the needed resistance to consistently produce sparks.[64]

There is no mention of hammer stalls, leather sheaths to cover the hammer to prevent accidental discharges if the cock was accidentally disengaged in loaded weapons. In *Cuthbertson's System for the Complete Interior Management and Oeconomy of a Battalion of Infantry* by British Army captain Bennett, a revision of his original 1768 work, he recommended them on campaign.[65] With misfires, the soldiers first took remedial action by tightening and repositioning the flint or replacing it with the spare in their cartridge pouches. They would have to borrow a musket tool from one of the noncommissioned officers to make these adjustments. Not usually available in enough quantities to issue to everyone, this tool was used to disassemble the arms. Blockage or restriction of the vent resulted in a flash in the pan; the priming charge went off, but the main charge did not. To rectify this issue, touchholes were enlarged in some of the new muskets.[66] Still, thick residue built up from firing, sometimes clogging the vent. Suspended from a chain often affixed to the cartridge box strap was a small pick that was inserted into the vent to clear the obstruction, and a horsehair brush was used to whisk away the greasy deposit. Flints were only good for a certain number of shots, depending on the power of the mainspring and hardness of the hammer. When it was worn or broken, the soldier swapped it out for the extra carried in his cartridge pouch. French flints were amber in color, and British ones were black.

There were no rifles in this camp. Imitating fletching, the line of feathers spaced around the end of the shaft that gives the stabilizing spin to an arrow, rifling grooves, cut into a barrel, spun the ball. "Towards the end of the war little use was made of them, as it was found that the difficulty of reloading the rifles more than offset the advantages derived from their accurate aim."[67] Used to advantage on many occasions, the rifle, however, was very slow to load. Rather than quickly ramming the ball home as with the musket, the rifleman, after pouring in the propelling charge, had to first place the ball inside a greased cloth patch before putting it into the end of the barrel. With the grease serving as a lubricant, he pushed the ball all the way down to the bottom of the barrel, following the grooves. He then primed, usually with a finer grade of powder from a horn container. Very vulnerable during this lengthy process, the Americans learned to place them among musket-armed soldiers for protection. Not normally fitted for bayonets, rifles were at a distinct disadvantage in hand-to-hand fighting. During a masterful British bayonet attack on the night of September 20–21, 1777, on Pennsylvania troops encamped outside of Philadelphia at Paoli, one of the regiments, armed mostly with rifles, was overrun. Also made individually of nonstandard calibers, every rifle had its own mold. Periodically, the rifleman had to melt lead in a pot and pour it into the mold to make more ammunition. Musket balls, on the other hand, with generally only two sizes left by the middle of the war, were mass-produced.

Pistols were normally only used by mounted men. In the infantry, just the generals and some of the field-grade officers carried them. General Paterson, commander of the 1st Massachusetts Brigade, lost a fine British pistol, manufactured by the private contractor Wilson, somewhere on the Albany Post Road between Peekskill, New York, and the large American campground on the Beverly Robinson farm.[68] Intended for personal protection, the pistol was not easily loaded while mounted, so officers generally did not carry an ammunition holder. They put the powder and balls in saddlebags or portmanteaus on their saddles. Expected to fire many rounds during an engagement, the infantry needed better access. Various holders, including pockets, were used. Nonstandard cartridge containers or lack altogether of them was a serious liability for the Continental Army. In the so-called Battle of the Clouds on September 16, 1777, during the campaign to defend Philadelphia, a terrific rainstorm damaged the poorly protected American cartridges. This was one of the factors that prevented Washington from making another stand to defend the capital. By the middle of the war, the army began to replace all its ammunition carriers with new ones made to carry 29 cartridges. New Windsor Cantonment has one of these cartridge pouches. Produced by leather workers at the depot in Springfield, Massachusetts, this box was inspected by artificer officer Captain William Hawes, director of that "public factory." Certifying acceptance, his stamp "W. Hawes" was placed at a 45-degree angle on the inside bottom of the outer cartridge box flap. An exact copy of a popular British pouch, it has a wooden block with drilled holes to hold the individual cartridges, a thick leather outer flap and a thin leather inner flap to protect the ammunition from the elements, and an over-the-shoulder carrying strap. In the tin under the block, soldiers carried an extra musket flint, cleaning rags, and sometimes spare cartridges. Except when soldiers were on detached service away from their ammunition wagons, they were ordered not to carry individual cartridges or packets of them in their "pockets or in the bottom of their Cartridge boxes." Thick rounded leather gussets on the sides of cartridge pouches created a seal with the outer flap, and "United States" was stamped into them at the top to signify government ownership.[69]

Anything made by hand by multiple people always varied in quality and durability. Assistant inspector Major William Barber reported in February 1783 that many of "the cartridge boxes are of a bad kind and getting out of repair." He recommended exchanging them, but there were none on hand. Secretary Lincoln assured Washington that the old boxes were being repaired and new ones were being made, but this supply probably did not arrive before the disbandment of most of the army a few months later.[70] The weight of the ammunition broke the stitching and separated the gussets, and the cold and wet cracked and split the leather. To further waterproof and strengthen the leather, black ball, a substance made of hard wax and lamp black, was worked into the surface. Many surviving examples still have this thick coating. Black ball was also used to polish shoes and boots. A distribution of pipe clay was made in the spring, enough to provide each man with about a pound.[71] This substance was used to whiten belts and cover stains on clothing.

Ammunition was a one-ounce lead musket ball. British muskets had a .75-caliber barrel, while the French ones had a .69-caliber barrel. This means that both balls had a diameter of around three-fourths of an inch. The musket balls were slightly smaller than the barrel to compensate for the buildup of black powder residue. There must have been some safeguard to prevent the issue of incorrectly sized ammunition. Three-quarter-inch musket balls were too big for the .69-caliber barrels, and the French musket balls would be less accurate fired from the larger bore of the British muskets. To increase their firepower, they added three pea-sized balls of buckshot to every load.[72] Washington made sure to point out to the newly constituted Board of War overseeing the Continental Army on behalf of Congress that any contracts for making ammunition needed to include buckshot. Making a cartridge was simple. A musket ball was wrapped in a paper tube, three buckshot were dropped inside, gunpowder was poured on top, and then the end was folded over and secured. During loading, a soldier pulled a cartridge out of his pouch, tore away the paper at the top with his teeth, poured a small amount of powder into the pan, brought the charge up to the barrel and inverted it so the remaining powder poured down the barrel, placed the cartridge into the opening, and rammed it home.[73]

As with nearly everything the Continental Army did, its processes improved over time. Premade cartridges were a vast improvement over the powder horn. Cartridges, made under the supervision of specialists, were better still. Initially recommending to General Knox in January 1778 to continue the practice at Valley Forge of regiments making cartridges, Washington two months later ordered a detail of poorly clothed soldiers to report to the specially prepared workshop, called a laboratory, to perform this task.[74] Outside of the controlled space of the laboratory, soldiers were not a reliable source of ammunition production, which was rarely done in ideal conditions or locations. Unsteady hands dropped the gunpowder, and other forms of carelessness resulted in considerable waste. The quartermaster department did employ civilians to make ammunition. In April 1781, John Beaks received payment for working 26 days in March in the laboratory in Philadelphia and for the 1,000 musket cartridges made by his wife. She probably made them in their home. William Davis also worked that month in the laboratory and made another 500 musket cartridges at his residence.[75]

In addition to fighting gear, the soldiers carried camp equipage to sustain them in the field. Linen knapsacks contained spare clothing and personal items. Blankets were strapped to the top. Vertical leather straps, supported by a horizontal crosspiece, distributed the weight of the load. The back was painted to provide a measure of protection from moisture and in some cases had to be augmented to compensate for the inferiority of the materials used in its construction. Made from poorly woven and thin cloth, some of the knapsacks required gesso, a mixture of plaster and glue, to stiffen their backflaps before the paint was applied.[76] Linen haversacks, cloth bags that held the food ration, were carried on the left side of the body, suspended by a strap of the same material worn over the right shoulder. Round wooden canteens were also slung over the right shoulder and rested on top of the haversack.

Making the men take care of their uniforms and equipment, procured at great expense and effort, was a constant challenge. In the British Army, stoppages were taken from the soldiers' pay for missing clothing and gear unless it was "lost in action, or unavoidable accident." Von Steuben in his manual prescribed the amount of the deductions, but no regulations existed to enforce this provision. Washington ordered Pickering on January 1, 1781, to formulate a proposal for holding soldiers' accountable for missing or abused issued articles. Finally, more than two years later a standing order prescribed that before any noncommissioned officers or privates received pay, leaders had to inspect all their property, issued by the army, and make stoppages for any deficiencies.[77]

An essential part of military pageantry, the approximately five-foot-high and six-foot-long infantry regimental color or colors marked the center of the unit's line, provided the unit was furnished with them. Carried in turn by the ensigns, the lowest-ranking officers, the flags made it easier for commanders to discern which regiments were present and served as a highly visible rallying point. Moreover, a disgrace to lose to the enemy, this cloth symbol embodying the honor of the regiment made soldiers stand and fight in their defense, whereas otherwise they might give way. Commissary General of Military Stores Samuel Hodgdon submitted to Secretary at War Lincoln an estimate in June 1782 for the cost of 100 silk flags: "The name of the State & the number of the Regiment to be done in a garter of blue with pure gold leaf. Two silk Tassels to each standard & the ends of the staff mounted with brass." This number was subsequently reduced to 50. Told about the purchase, Washington wrote to Lincoln in August that the army needed these flags to make a truly professional showing and that Lincoln should hurry them to camp.[78] Still waiting in February, Washington wrote to the secretary that he wanted them forwarded. Lincoln promised to send them but "wish[ed] they were better than they are." Finding out in the second week of March that the colors arrived a while earlier, Washington demanded an explanation from Pickering. The quartermaster general explained that the field commissary of military stores, Richard Frothingham, received them in a box with other articles in camp at the store, one of the rooms in the Temple Building, and distributed everything else but them. Quite annoyed that a letter from the secretary at war was the first information he had of their arrival, Washington ordered on March 14 that the regiments without flags draw them from Frothingham.[79] Presumably conforming to the June 1782 estimate, these flags were devoid of any designation, leaving it up to the regiments to paint their number and state.

Doing far more than just cover the soldiers' nakedness, military clothing made a bold statement of style, tradition, and discipline. Though sometimes incorporating French influences, the American uniform was mostly a legacy of the British Isles. It was not pure chance that Washington adopted a buff-faced blue coat. Traditionally, those colors were associated with England's liberal Whig Party, America's staunchest defenders in Parliament. In 1780, he ordered all general officers to follow his example. The commander in chief and his officers and soldiers took great pride in their appearance bordering on obsession. By the time of the New Windsor Cantonment, the Continental Army was outfitted like European regulars and expected the nation to maintain it in this fashion. Gone were Ralph Waldo Emerson's "embattled farmers," and in their stead stood military professionals with all the promise and terror of a standing army. So great was the army's vanity that it was only necessary to threaten offenders with the "disgrace of being held up to public view in a disagreeable manner" to shame them into making an immediate correction. While solicitous of accolades from its fellows, the American people, allies, and the grudging respect of its enemies, the Continental Army ultimately had its eyes on posterity, as indicated in a verse from an undated poem in an orderly book of the 2nd New York Regiment:

> The riseing world shall sing us a thousand years to Come
> And tell our Childrens Children the Wonders we have Done &c[80]

Whether procured in the aftermath of great sea battles, imported from Europe, or manufactured in America, every garment and accoutrement delineated social hierarchy and served as a visible statement of the army's discipline. Most importantly, the uniform came to define who the soldiers of the Continental Army were.

CHAPTER 6

"So usefull a Scheme"
The Temple of Virtue

The huts were completed by the end of December 1782, but there was no rest for the soldiers. Over the past few months their only day off was Thursday, November 28, a day of thanksgiving proclaimed by Congress. Though a traditional day of rest, a Sunday was regarded as any other day by military authorities until the construction of the camp was further along. Chaplains prepared sermons befitting the occasion, and the men were refreshed with an additional ration of West Indian rum. On this cold day, Thomas Foster went to the Presbyterian church in New Windsor, where Israel Evans gave the discourse. Impressed by the solemnity of the occasion, Foster could not remember a better thanksgiving. Accompanying the service, a band played in the front gallery while vocalists sang from two side galleries. General Washington and his guard were among the attendees.[1]

The relatively mild weather made the winter less taxing, but the favorable conditions gave soldiers little respite. Except for some cold days and a storm on December 17, when snow fell nearly two feet deep in the shortest time Foster had ever seen, the weather during the first two months at the cantonment was pleasant.[2] Though there were few opportunities, the troops did take advantage of a January snowfall to lay up magazines of firewood. That night, another storm dumped about a foot of additional snow. Applauding their efforts, Washington felt that the use of sleds diminished the labor and the wear of their clothing. He urged the men to take advantage of every snowfall to amass a wood supply that would carry them through April or even May. Having to pay landowners for the value of the timber felled, enterprising soldiers, who transported wood on sleds to sell in New Windsor, were prohibited from continuing the practice. The men cutting wood for the hospital, however, did receive "six pence, or half a ration per cord," from the quartermaster. By the middle of April, the army was forbidden to cut down any more trees unless it had written permission from Pickering. There was a sufficient supply already in the vicinity of the cantonment. Despite repeated warnings of severe punishment, soldiers still burned many wooden fences as well.[3]

It was a shame that Washington would get little use out of his own beautifully fashioned sleigh that the artificers at West Point had made for him in less than a month to replace his old one, which the quartermaster general had left behind in Philadelphia.[4] The new sled arrived during the mid–January snowstorm or slightly thereafter, so there were only about 10 to 15 days left in the season where there was enough snow to warrant the use of a sleigh. A week after the mid–January storm it rained, and the ground was slushy. A week after that, the snow was almost all gone. February 2, 1783, in Thomas

Foster's estimation, was the coldest day in 16 years, but three days later it was warm and rainy. On February 7, 1783, Lieutenants Benjamin Gilbert, Moses Carlton, and Pelathiah Everett from the 5th Massachusetts Regiment walked to Newburgh and then traveled in a sleigh on the Hudson River back to New Windsor. Foster continued remarking on the weather until the end of the encampment. Snow fell for much of the day on February 9, but on February 18 it was "Remarkably Warm and the Froogs … [were] heard to sing Merriyly." Though there was no snow, March 10 had one of the lowest temperatures of the winter and possibly was the coldest day in camp. There was a little bit of everything on March 23, when there was "hale Snow & Some Thunder." Changing from rain, the last snow fell on April 12. Just six days later, the weather was hot and dry. Not acclimated to this dramatic temperature change, Foster was nearly overwhelmed by the heat. Except for a few frigid nights during the first week of May and a very cold day on May 19, the weather ranged from mild to warm.[5]

Without the extreme deprivations experienced at Valley Forge, Pennsylvania, over the winter of 1777–78 and during the horrific weather of the 1779–80 Morristown, New Jersey, encampment, soldiers at the New Windsor Cantonment had no excuses to avoid work. Guard details, military drills, fatigue duty, and several building projects filled the rest of their days at New Windsor. Idleness gave the men too much time to ruminate over their ill usage. There were, however, some sources of amusement and opportunities to leave for a while. Besides the occasional distraction, life in a winter camp was quite boring. This feeling was shared by both officers and the enlisted men. While soldiers were restricted to camp unless they had a pass or were accompanied by an officer or noncommissioned officer, officers came and went as they pleased when off duty except for the requirement to attend roll calls. Except for extended absences such as furloughs, they just needed to inform their superiors, who usually consented if there was nothing going on. Officer activities were restricted only by their next duty assignment and purse. At the sign of the Confederation tavern in New Windsor, Abraham Van Duerzen offered "a Five Alley, a Nine Pin Alley, Bindy-Wicket, Cricket, Chess, etc." and other sorts of entertainment, but this tavern was at best a minor diversion.[6]

For the literate, reading and writing letters was a way to connect with distant loved ones. Creating anticipation, writers eagerly awaited replies and were disappointed at not receiving them. Given that the regular post was prohibitively expensive for the impecunious soldiery, it is noteworthy that a steady stream of correspondence traveled between home and camp. All you had to do was find someone going in the right direction. In the summer of 1782, Foster sent a letter to his family, carried by Lieutenant Richard Bagnell of his regiment. During the New Windsor encampment, 2nd Massachusetts sergeant major Jonathan Farnam delivered a letter to his wife. In January 1783, 4th Massachusetts sergeant Melatiah Cobb of Kingston carried a letter to Foster's neighbor and another to his wife, along with a book. Three years before Foster prevailed upon Toby, an African American soldier from Raynham, the next town over from his own. A letter from Foster's wife dated August 30, 1782, was not delivered until on October 16, one and a half months later. A direct trip was much quicker, but there is no way to know how long the letter waited for a deliveryman, the circuitousness of its route, or the number of hands through which it passed. On May 17, 1783, Peter Oliver, a young Black soldier, carried a letter from Lieutenant Gilbert, marked 9. Not knowing whether his correspondence would arrive in chronological order or at all, Gilbert numbered his letters to his father.[7]

The military did carry mail, but the service was irregular and only traversed routes used by the army. Official correspondence was franked, traveling free of postage, but Congress enacted legislation to prevent abuse of this privilege. In late January 1783 John D. Alvey, deputy postmaster of the main army, placed an advertisement in the *New York Packet and the American Advertiser* listing the mail at the Continental Army post office, in Newburgh, by Washington's headquarters. Among numerous ones addressed to Continental Army officers, such as General Knox and doctors John Cochran and David Townsend were letters to a number of civilians including Daniel Birdsall of Peekskill, Daniel Elmer of Goshen, Gilbert Roberts of Little Britain, and John Currie, the merchant selling from the William Ellison property along the Hudson River in New Windsor.[8]

Gossip and speculation about national and world events were often intriguing. Returning from furlough in mid–December just prior to his promotion to general, Colonel Putnam brought the heinous story of a Connecticut man who killed his wife and four children and himself. Putnam also expressed his opinion that the British would not be able to relieve their defenders of Gibraltar. The Royal Navy, however, was able to break through to the fortress. Only the preliminary peace articles lifted the blockade. At the end of August 1782, the 100-gun first-rate ship of the line HMS *Royal George* sank while having a leak repaired at Spithead, off Portsmouth Harbor. The mighty ship went down with around 900 people, including Admiral Richard Kempenfelt and over 300 visiting women and children.[9] Visiting friends at West Point was easier with the return of passenger service on the Hudson River. Beginning on March 23, a packet sailed between Newburgh and the fort, leaving at 10:00 a.m. and returning at 4:00 p.m. This courtesy precluded the need for individual barge crews. For the convenience of the officers in this camp, a stop in New Windsor was added. The boat left the Continental dock at Newburgh at 9:30 a.m., arriving at New Windsor half an hour later. Established nearly a month later, West Point's packet boat left at 10:00 a.m. for Newburgh and returned at 5:00 p.m.[10]

Regardless of money and freedom to travel, there was little to do in the Hudson Highlands, so officers and soldiers alike were anxious for furloughs home or somewhere else. Having prevailed upon Congress earlier in the war to limit granting authority to himself and commanders of separate armies, Washington strictly controlled the number of soldiers and officers allowed to leave camp. Originally, regimental commanders could grant furloughs, a privilege that was continually abused. Though he had given up on his plans to winter at Mount Vernon, the commander in chief was solicitous to see his officers granted this indulgence, provided enough remained to ensure discipline and soldier welfare. As the officers were entrusted with enforcing personal hygiene, the proper preparation of rations, and sanitation around the camp, Washington expected them to take a paternalistic interest in their men, a charge that was not possible from afar. Having been absent during the entire 1782 campaign, General Rufus Putnam, being only in camp for a few weeks, had, to Washington's amazement, asked for another furlough. With his troops suffering from his absence, Putnam was shamed into withdrawing the request.[11] Discovered visiting his family when another field officer was on furlough, Colonel Matthias Ogden, commander of the 1st New Jersey, petitioned Washington for leave to travel to Europe. Pressing business concerns and disgust over the officers' negotiations with Congress over back pay and the pension led to his unauthorized absence. After obtaining permission from Congress, Ogden headed overseas at the end of April and never returned to the army.[12] By the time Robert Howe requested leave in

February, the commander in chief was in no mood to brook any more general officer absences without a pressing reason. General St. Clair was already on furlough in Pennsylvania. Gates's wife was in such declining health that he would probably have to depart shortly for Virginia to visit her. Only two of the six brigadier generals were in camp, and one of them was requesting a furlough. After making Howe feel as guilty as he could, Washington consented to the absence.[13] Clearly, many of the officers had moved on in their minds and were preparing for their transition back to civilian life. Even within his own military family, he found it difficult to make the furlough process work. After conceiving an equitable plan, he had to guilt one of his aides-de-camp, Major Hodijah Baylies, into returning. Having already let Lieutenant Colonels David Cobb, Jonathan Trumbull, and Tench Tilghman leave, Washington had only two aides left. Sharing the workload, the commander in chief was confined indoors more than he wished. Dissuading Baylies of the notion that there was little to do in a winter camp, Washington pointed out that the administrative requirements of his headquarters did not diminish during that season.[14]

In a regiment, only one field officer and one staff officer could be absent at any one time, provided they found someone else to do their duty. The individual companies were limited to one officer and one noncommissioned officer and two privates. New to his company, Gilbert could not get a furlough because his commander, Captain Nathan Goodale, and the other officer, Lieutenant Joseph Smith, had priority.[15] Officers were threatened with arrest if they exceeded the authorized number of furloughs or issued passes in lieu of them. Washington desired that soldiers with Honorary Badges of Distinction receive preference in the selections. At New Windsor, only General Gates could authorize officer furloughs. The time frame was logged in at the orderly office. Noncommissioned officers and privates carried a printed form filled in with the terms of their absence. This information was also recorded in the regimental books. By April 15, 1783, all officers and soldiers had to be back in camp.[16] Depending on the distance from home, many days were consumed in travel. Normally, only trustworthy soldiers were given furloughs. Despite this faith, the temptation not to return was very strong. Enlisted soldiers were beset by the pleas of long-suffering family members, while others were just tired of military service. Soldiers who did not return were treated as deserters. Latecomers were still punished. Private Thomas Foster of the 7th Massachusetts Regiment had been a sergeant until he overstayed his furlough. Not every homecoming was joyous. The embittered wife of the drum major in Joseph Plumb Martin's regiment, told him that when her husband came home in late 1778 or early 1779, he took all her money, infected everyone with impetigo, and then left. Reasoning that she could find out from someone else, Martin thought better of telling her of his liaisons with other women.[17]

Unable to obtain a furlough, Lieutenant Gilbert did his best to entertain himself. At the Temple in March, he watched music inspector Lieutenant John Hiwell display his singing talent. Gilbert bought a ticket for a concert on April 8 and attended another one on the evening of April 17, the day on which the cessation of hostilities was announced to the officers at the noon levee.[18] Other times Gilbert drank, often to excess, and sought out the companionship of young women. Along with Lieutenants William Eysandeau, Park Holland, and John Warren and Surgeon's Mate William Lawton, Gilbert went to Newburgh on the evening of January 8 for a dance at "Captain Colman's." Another time, a man brought his wife and three daughters into camp, ostensibly to do sewing. Gilbert drank tea with them at the quarters of Lieutenant Eysandeau and then invited them back to his quarters, where they "moved a number of Country Dances." Possibly trying to find officer husbands for his daughters, "Mr. Homes" should have looked more into the character of the men to whom he was parading his girls. In March, Gilbert went to "Mr. Waggoner's" in Newburgh and "had a gentile Dance with the Ladies of that place." There were many other small dances conducted at the quarters of various officers, with the local young women apparently eager and willing to enter camp. They were probably flattered by all this attention. Numerous other times, Gilbert with a friend or two went in the evening to the brothel Wyoma, where he "fared exceeding well." He returned sometimes early in the morning.[19]

Everyone who stayed in camp that winter focused on the construction of the Temple of Virtue. A church, the building was also a monument to themselves, destined to last in American memory, though it stood for less than a year. Proposed by Israel Evans, chaplain to the New Hampshire Brigade, the Temple, reminiscent of a New England meetinghouse, served a variety of functions. Evans knew Washington very well. While standing next to the commander in chief at Yorktown, a cannonball or shell struck close enough to throw sand on Evans's hat. Observing the minister's agitation, Washington calmly told him to take his souvenir of the battle back north and show his family.[20] Thinking highly of Evans's suggestion, Washington requested that the officers who were "desirious of promoting so usefull a Scheme" meet at General Gates's quarters the following day, December 26, 1782. Bad weather, however, forced the postponement of the meeting until the 27th at 11:00 a.m.[21] Unlike previous winter encampments, the huts at New Windsor were completed relatively early, so Washington welcomed the distraction. Except for glass and other finishing material, the Temple was built out of local timber and fieldstone.

The Temple was known variously as the Temple of Virtue, the "Temple of Virtue & Libberty," the "Temple Building," the "New Building," the "Public Building," and the "New Public Building," and practically every soldier in camp eventually worked on the large structure. Benson Lossing in his mid–19th-century *Pictorial Fieldbook of the American Revolution* claimed that "Virtue" was dropped from the name after the inaugural celebration devolved into a drunken party. Though this contention is unsubstantiated, the dour and unpopular Colonel Pickering did lament "how little will it deserve the name, for how little virtue is there among mankind."[22] "Temple" was the convenient short name for the building, along with all the other titles. Casting his judgment on the moral failures of himself and others in the camp, Thomas Foster used "Temple" frequently in his journal, but in mid–May he reused the term "Tempel of Vertue & Libberty."[23] Had there been a change of the name in response to any improper behavior, moralist Foster would have faithfully recorded this fact.

Much speculation has gone into the reason for the name "Temple of Virtue." James Fordyce in 1757 published his brother David's work *The Temple of Virtue a Dream*. In this morality play, a pilgrim in his sleep goes on a fanciful journey in search of the "Abode of Happiness." Encountering suffering born of vice everywhere along the way, he traveled to an eminence crowned by a rectangular "sacred mansion" of a plain but dignified appearance.

> The area of the Temple was filled with a glorious "multitude, which no man could number" collected out of all tribes and nations, who lived in holy union, and conversed together with perfect efteem and confidence. Stationed near the Throne, was a diftinguished company, on whom the GODDESS fmiled with correfpondent fatisfaction. My Guide informed me they

were a set of illuftrious Worthies, who had approved themfelves patterns of every excellence, the promoters of TRUTH, the defenders of Liberty, the benefactors of mankind, the very lights of the world.[24]

In its second printing at the start of the American Revolution, the contents of this allegory were well known to ministers on both sides of the Atlantic. Such idyllic allusions would have struck a chord with American preachers, who viewed the war not only as a political struggle but also as a battle between New World virtue and the vice of the Old World. But from what classical example did Fordyce base his story. Supported by two rows of the simplest form of column, the Doric, "in a quadrangular form" and crowned with a large dome, his example was borrowed from antiquity, more specifically ancient Rome. In the Temple of Honor and Virtue near the Porta Capena in the eternal city, those qualities were worshipped as deities. Throughout much of Roman history, various cults and shrines were centered around those attributes.

Colonel Benjamin Tupper from the 6th Massachusetts Regiment, with the assistance of engineer Major de Rochefontaine and Lieutenant Henry Nelson from the 3rd Massachusetts Regiment, supervised the construction. Responsibility for preparing the materials was divided among the regiments in camp. The building was 110 feet long and 30 feet wide. Materials included 5,120 feet of hewn timber for the exterior and interior walls, 3,000 laths for affixing the interior plaster, 21,000 roof shingles, 1,000 split ribs for the internal framework, and stones for chimneys and the underpinning of walls. The soldiers received extra rations of food and rum for performing this fatigue.[25] General Gates trusted that he would not hear any complaints or objections to the work. Having nothing left to lose after his reduction from sergeant to private, two years before for overstaying his furlough, Private Foster knew to "Obay or have the Strip[e]s," a flogging. He confided in his journal that the officers were driving them in the freezing cold to complete a structure, the purpose of which they had no idea.[26] Gates could hardly have expected that the little extra food and drink would be perceived as fair compensation for the tremendous amount of hard labor involved. Under pressure to get the building in usable condition for the festivities planned for February 6, the anniversary of the French alliance, Colonel Tupper reported to Gates that the 2nd Massachusetts did not supply its quota of finished wood. In relaying this dereliction of duty to headquarters in Newburgh, Gates added that he regretted that the unit was far too anxious to rid themselves of the axes. First apologizing to Gates for delaying the project, Major Robert Oliver then went on to blame Tupper for not letting him know, as agreed, how many timbers and shingles were expected each day so he could assign the correct number of men. With the weather conducive for making shingles, Gates called for carpenters, skilled in this task, to meet the next day, January 27. Needing every able hand and determined to redeem themselves from their previous reproach, the 2nd Massachusetts went after soldiers who claimed that they could not help due to sickness or lameness without first being examined by the regimental surgeon. They also expressly forbade the hiring of others to perform their share of the work.[27]

Having less than a week left, Tupper again appealed to Gates to push commanders. this time for the nails requested, so he could complete shingling the building. They were given this order in the middle of the month.[28] Really feeling the pressure and in a fit of self-pity, Tupper cried out to Gates that the lack of nails "has thrown our flowing sails aback and should I fail of compleating what is expected by the 6 of February, those who are deficient in those matters ought to be answerable and not poor me, who am in this case only a servant." The 1st Massachusetts and New Jersey Brigades, despite several directives, neglected to comply. Promptness in the delivery of their share of nails only got the 2nd Massachusetts Brigade more work, as they were called upon to make up for the deficiency of others. Tupper could have gotten even more assistance from that brigade if its armorers, who claimed exemption from doing anything but arms repair, were ordered to make nails. Carpenters, masons, and blacksmiths were working up to the 11th hour trying to complete as much as possible before the big day. After a last-minute request on February 4 for five benches from each regiment, needed by 10:00 a.m. on the 6th, Tupper could do no more. He was out of time. Totally worn down physically and mentally, he stayed long enough to receive accolades for his accomplishment and then went on furlough. During his absence, Lieutenant Nelson assumed primary responsibility for directing the work.[29]

Everyone did get a break of sorts on February 6. Instead of laboring on the incomplete building, they prepared for a noon inspection on their respective parade grounds, with all the preening that engendered. Following the review, the army formed in a single line below the Temple and on the rise behind the Maryland, New Hampshire, New Jersey, and New York Lines to the west, the last great gathering of the army. At the signal, the soldiers began a "feu de joye," a celebratory sequential firing of blank musket cartridges in honor of the occasion. Rolling gunfire echoed through the valley, and smoke filled the air, making a spectacular display. A snowfall that day added to the sublimity. Near the Temple, hundreds of people from the army and the surrounding community assembled to watch the spectacle. After finishing the exhibition, the men returned to their encampment areas and were rewarded with a gill of rum, four ounces. Hosted by the commander in chief and Martha, the officers assembled inside the Temple Building for a "cold Collation," an unheated selection of refreshments often displayed in an artful manner. Sot Lieutenant Gilbert noted the food as well as the large amounts of wine. As it was a cold day, hopefully the windows and doors were in place, but the inside was still only bare logs and lathe strips. Besides the Washingtons, Henry Knox and Lucy, Edward Hand and Katherine, and practically every other officer was in attendance, but Gates was sick in bed at his headquarters. Writing to his wife that day, he said that it was just as well that she did not make the trip north from Virginia, because the hardships of the journey and the cold weather might have proved fatal. Over 500 ladies and gentlemen attended, and they were delighted by the events of the day.[30] The mood of the commanders of the 5th and 8th Massachusetts Regiments changed, however, when afterward they received confidential letters from Washington informing them that he was displeased with the condition of their units at the review.[31] Serving doubly as the dedication ceremony for the still unfinished structure as well as the celebration to mark the anniversary of the alliance with France, Reverend Evans, the building's originator, gave an oration to inaugurate the festivities. The melancholy Pickering always had something to say about everything, usually negative. Deprecating most of the attendees as being unworthy of the lofty morality envisioned by Chaplain Evans, Pickering also thought that the preacher's sermon "fell vastly short of ... [his] expectations."[32]

Waiting for warmer weather, a lime kiln was erected on the land of Abel Belknap in March. Changing the chemical composition of the lime by heat, this stone oven was sufficient to burn the approximately 300 bushels needed. Lime, sand, and water made the plaster for finishing the interior. Fragments of this plaster greatly aided the archaeologists in locating and confirming the identity of the site. By the end of the month, the best masons and carpenters in camp were striving to complete the building.³³ General Heath, who replaced General Gates as cantonment commander, described the completed Temple:

> Upon an eminence, the troops erected a building handsomely finished, with a spacious hall, sufficient to contain a brigade of troops on Lord's days, for public worship, with an orchestra at one end; the vault of the hall was arched; at each end of the hall were two rooms, conveniently situated for the issuing of the general orders, for the sitting of Boards of Officers, Courts Martial &c. and an office and store for the Quarter-Master and Commissary departments. On the top was a cupola and flag-staff, on which a flag was hoisted occasionally for signals, &c.

There are two divergent views regarding the appearance of the Temple of Virtue. The building reconstructed on the actual footprint of the original by the National Temple Hill Association between 1962 and 1964 was taken from historical documents and the description and drawing of it in Benson Lossing's *Pictorial Field-Book of the Revolution*. Based on his visits to Revolutionary War sites in the mid–19th century, he sought to document "the remaining physical vestiges of that struggle." Invaluable in detailing the appearance of locations and buildings that have long since been altered or destroyed since that time, the book is for the most part accurate, but subsequent research has proven that some of the information is incorrect. Sometimes forced to rely on the testimony of witnesses recalling events from more than 60 years earlier, he was not to blame if memory proved a treacherous ally. At the end of October 1850, longtime resident of nearby Little Britain "Major" Robert Burnet described the Temple Building to Lossing.

Benson Lossing drawing of the Temple, based on the description of Robert Burnet. Benson J. Lossing, *Pictorial Field-Book of the Revolution*, 2 vols. [New York, 1855] 1:685 (Clipart from the Florida Center for Instructional Technology).

Temple of Virtue and detail of the Massachusetts Line encampment from the 1890 copy of the Private William Tarbell drawing (courtesy Washington's Headquarters State Historic Site Collection, New York State Office of Parks, Recreation and Historic Preservation).

Burnet recalled that it was a single-story rectangular structure made of squared timbers, with a wide roof, a door in the center, and many windows. The window openings, not fitted with glass, were about the size of a gunport on a war vessel. A lieutenant in the 2nd Continental Artillery during the last two years of the war, Burnet was never stationed at this camp, but he claimed to have been present in the Temple during Washington's speech to his officers on March 15, 1783.[34]

The other image of the Temple of Virtue is in the drawing of Private William Tarbell. Believed to have been done while he was at New Windsor, the structure depicted is far more refined than the one described by Burnet. A large gable end bisected the roof on the western side, creating a portico that was flanked by freestanding classical columns. In this projection was a single staircase or symmetrical pair that led to a platform above the entryway. Above the doorway was a transom protected by an arch-vaulted overhang, surmounted by a triangular gable end with circular window in its center. Contemporaneous New England meetinghouses with the same style of portico often had a corresponding pulpit window placed into the opposite wall to provide light for the minister. Tarbell shows five large windows eight to 10 panes high and four panes across to the right of the doorway and four windows on the left. Flat rectangular cornices decorated with two rows of seven black and white squares protected the top of each window.

A wooden walkway of alternating black and white painted squares led to the entrance, and a flagpole protruded from the top of the gable end.

While there is no evidence that Masonic rituals were ever held in the Temple, the signs of that secret society are in the Tarbell drawing. Considering that many Continental Army officers were also Masons, it is hard to believe that the symbols of that order in the architectural elements were mere coincidence. While the ached-vaulted ceiling in the portico and another one in the main hall of the Temple seem an overcomplicated and unnecessary exercise in pretentiousness for a temporary structure, there were deeper meanings in these features. In the book of Job, the biblical prophet "compares Heaven to an arch supported by pillars. This is, of course, allegorical, even as is the name 'Holy Royal Arch' degree in Masonry. The pillars which support the arch are emblematical of Wisdom and Strength; the former denoting the wisdom of the Supreme Architect, and the latter the stability of the universe." The gable end, with a circular window divided by cross-shaped muntins into four quarter panes, might represent the Eye of Providence, or the all-seeing eye of God. Not generally recognized as a Masonic symbol until 1797, this iconic representation of divine providence dates to the ancient Egyptians. Beginning in the Renaissance, Christians sometimes enclosed the eye in a triangle to represent the trinity.

In drawing the Temple, Tarbell probably first did the outline and the portico and then the windows. To fit five windows on the southern side, he had to make them

Rocky Hill Meeting House in Amesbury, Massachusetts, constructed in 1785. Though only a single story, the portico of the Temple Building was like the one in this church (Historic New England).

Chapter 6. "So usefull a Scheme"

Rocky Hill Meeting House interior showing the staircase in the portico (Historic New England).

narrower than the four corresponding ones on the northern side. These thinner windows appear to show four panes across and 10 panes high, a unique configuration that could easily be dismissed as an expedient employed by an amateur artist, but the numbers 4 and 5 are important to Masons and are replete throughout the Bible, as is the number 40: for 40 days and nights the rain fell to cleanse the world in the great flood;

waiting 40 days after the ark came to rest on top of Mount Ararat, Noah opened the window to send out a raven and then a dove; Moses twice spent 40 days on Mount Sinai; the Israelites spent 40 years in the wilderness, one year for each day their spies spent in the promised land; and Jesus fasted for 40 days in the wilderness and was seen for 40 days after his crucifixion. For these and other biblical examples, 40 is considered sacred. The four windows, on the northern side, are wider and look like four panes across and eight panes high, a very common form. Quickly delineating the panes by hand, Tarbell was not very careful in rendering them.

The Temple of Virtue had nine windows on its eastern and western sides, four north of the doorway, and five south of it. Believed by Masons to be a place of darkness, the north symbolically is less bright, so that is possibly the reason for the lesser number of windows on that side. Significant in themselves to Masons, four and five add up to nine, represented by the sides of three equilateral triangles. The "Equilateral Triangle is the symbol of Deity, so the Triple Triangle composed of three Equilateral Triangles is the symbol of the Triple Essence of Deity or, to the Christian, the Mystery of the Trinity."[35] Two rows of seven alternating black and white squares adorned the window cornices. The Bible is filled with references to seven or multiples of that number: Noah received the warning seven days before the flood and loaded seven of each clean animal into the Ark, Solomon took seven years to build his temple, and Jesus spoke seven last words and told his apostle Peter to forgive a transgressor 70 times seven and hundreds more.

Part of the creation myth adopted by the founders of Masonry in the early 18th century was that the Masonic Order descended in an unbroken line from Hiram of Tyre and Hiram Abif, the builders of Solomon's Temple and the first grand masters. Masonry certainly existed before the 18th century, but the practices began to be codified with the founding of the first Grand Lodge in Great Britain in 1717. Flanking the entrance to Solomon's Temple were two pillars. Historians disagree whether they were freestanding or held up the porch roof. According to Masonic tradition, the mosaic floor was made of alternating black and white stones, a metaphor to show the contrast between good and evil. The Temple of Virtue's walkway and window cornices were painted in black and white alternating squares. Moreover, the walkway gives perspective to the drawing, a simple device commonly used in 17th-century Dutch genre paintings. "And the house which king Solomon built for the LORD, the length thereof was threescore cubits, and the breadth thereof twenty cubits, and the height thereof thirty cubits." Converting the Hebrew long cubit of 20.4 inches to modern measurements gives the size of Solomon's Temple as approximately 102 feet long, 34 feet wide, and 51 feet high. A single-story building, the Temple of Virtue was no way near as high but with the length 110 feet long and 30 feet wide, it was somewhat close in its footprint. After learning the purpose of its construction, the devoutly religious Thomas Foster softened his opinion and observed that the "Building Which is Converted to Many Uses ... Makes me think of Sinagoge(s) of Old."[36]

Reverend Elwood A. Corning, founder and first president of the National Temple Hill Association, defined the object of the organization: "To Restore the Temple where the Republic was Spiritually Re-Born." Formed on March 15, 1933, at General Knox's headquarters in Vails Gate on the 150th anniversary of Washington's speech denouncing the Newburgh Conspiracy, the association sought to establish a historic site and then petition for its acquisition by the National Park Service.[37] Finding the location of the original Temple of Virtue and building a replica of it on top of the site took another three decades. When they were ready to build, there was much debate over what drawing to use as the basis for the reconstruction. Both the Lossing sketch and the Tarbell drawing were well known to the leadership of this organization. In the late 19th century, the trustees of Washington's headquarters in Newburgh, New York, learned about the existence of Tarbell's rendering of the Massachusetts encampments at New Windsor. West Point historian Major Edward C. Boynton obtained permission from William's grandson, Luther Tarbell, to borrow the drawing in order to make a copy of it. In 1890, Boynton commissioned Caldwell and Garrison, a Newburgh civil engineering firm, to make the facsimile. In the collections of Washington's Headquarters State Historic Site, the engineer drawing is not an exact copy but rather an interpretation of the original. After examining the Tarbell drawing, many historians at that time were convinced that Lieutenant Robert Burnet did not describe the Temple of Virtue to Benson Lossing but instead described Starkeans Hall, the Masonic lodge at West Point.[38] Despite this resolute belief, the National Temple Hill Association chose the Lossing version.

Finding the site was not easy. Any aboveground traces of the building had long since vanished, but recognizable vestiges of it did survive for years. In 1824, I. Finch, a travel writer, visited the New Windsor encampment, guided by a Continental Army officer who had been an adjutant during the war. Ascending the hill, they were drawn to a prominent man-made stone feature 100' × 40', delineated by 3-foot-high foundation walls.[39] Benson Lossing in the late 1840s explored the remains of the huts and causeway. In the field owned by William McGill at the top of a hill, Lossing identified an 80' × 40' stone foundation as the site of the Temple of Virtue. Another long rectangular pattern of stones with fireplace openings, however, was just to the north. Believed by some to be the site of the Temple Building, Lossing dismissed the location as a foundation for a Massachusetts "barracks."[40] No troops were encamped on top of Temple Hill, so what did he see? Though short in his estimation of the length by 30 feet, he might have correctly located the site of the Temple. His calculations could have been off, or the missing portion might have been carted away. But the other nearby extended foundation does raise doubt about his assertion. In that vicinity were also the provost guardhouse, the officers' guardhouse, and the court-martial room. The confusing jumble of rock footings, some compromised by the hand of man and the elements, would have made it very difficult for him to be certain. By the time the National Temple Hill Association began to look for the Temple site in the late 1950s, the aboveground foundation stones had been incorporated into the numerous stone walls in the vicinity or the large stone monument erected in 1891 to commemorate that building. Except for an 18-foot continuous section of the east wall extending from the northeast corner, the rest of the foundation was 2-foot-square stone footings. The archaeologist found charcoal around the perimeter. As the Temple was built in the coldest months of the year, he theorized that was from the fires used to thaw the ground for excavation. But even if the foundation was dug in warmer weather, getting down 2.5 feet for the entire length of the perimeter would have been very difficult if not impossible, given the technology available to the Continental Army in 1783. There are far too many large rocks in this mountainous region, so it was far easier to build on piers

Fifteen feet in from both the northern and southern sides of the building, there was evidence of a wall. These sections were further divided in half, creating two 15-foot square rooms. All the inside corners of the four rooms contained a fireplace. Sharing the same chimney as the two on the northern side, an approximately 6-foot-wide fireplace faced the main hall.⁴¹ Two of these rooms were used for meetings, courts-martial, and the issuance of orders. Offices for the quartermaster department and the field commissary of military stores, a commissary store, and storage space for replacement arms, equipment, soldier gear, and other articles were in the two spaces on the other end. On March 6, Lieutenant Gilbert purchased items for himself and fellow officers sharing his cooking arrangements from the commissary store.⁴²

Finding plaster and small nails with a handful of other nonarchitectural artifacts, the archaeologist was troubled about not finding any window glass. Dismissing the large windows, he believed Tabell's version of the Temple of Virtue would have required most of the available glass between Philadelphia and Boston.⁴³ Hardly a precious commodity, glass was readily available. Including so many details, Tarbell could only have executed his drawing during this encampment. The Temple of Virtue was sold at the September 2, 1783, auction to local merchant and highway master for the New Windsor district James Latta for 15 pounds, eight shillings. The main value of the structure was not in its wooden walls or framing but rather in the finishing materials. Though constructed of approximately the same amount of wood as three or four huts of Massachusetts and New York design, it realized far more money. The windows were the most valuable part of the building, followed by the doors and finishing woodwork. Latta would have carefully dismounted the windows, making sure not to break the panes. Rushed during his search of the interior, the archaeologist did not find any evidence of a floor, but it was methodically removed by the quartermasters prior to the auction. Boards intended for the brigade hospitals were diverted for that purpose.⁴⁴ The orchestra would have had value as well. Military musicians and vocalists performed during church services and conducted concerts at other times from this semicircular platform. During a moment of reflection, the elderly warrior accompanying I. Finch nostalgically recalled, "In this building I listened to the most delightful music I ever heard." Foster's account of "a Gallery for the Musick" implies a balustrade or decorative railing.⁴⁵

Heath recorded in his journal that the Temple was "sufficient to contain a brigade of troops on Lord's days." Brigades at New Windsor, however, ranged in size from approximately 800 to 1,600 men, far beyond the capacity of the 80- × 30-foot main hall. But the chaplains did take turns at the pulpit throughout the day, typically conducting a total of four services. With several brigades, the army prescribed a procedure that allowed the most interested soldiers to attend regularly. Thomas Foster went to meeting every week and summarized the sermons in his journal. For the service conducted at 11 o'clock on February 23, the New York Brigade was authorized to send just a battalion about half, from each of its regiments, consisting of 12 files drawn from every platoon. A file was two soldiers. There were two platoons in a company and four companies in a battalion, so the maximum allocation for each regiment was 192,384 total. Based on this example multiplied by four, a brigade or equivalent of soldiers could attend divine worship every Sunday. The 2nd Massachusetts Brigade on February 23 did not properly account for the building's limited capacity, so its 5th Regiment had to go back to camp. In warmer weather the building was able to reach larger numbers of celebrants, and 1,200 gathered inside and on the Grand Parade at the end of May.⁴⁶ On April 19, 1783, eight years to the day after the war started, the declaration of peace was "to be Read in the tarret of the Temple." Formed by the gable in the Tarbell drawing, the turret, the term used by Foster to describe the portico, was Heath's cupola. A staircase on one or both sides led to a dais above the main doorway. By opening the circular window in the gable end, a speaker could address the audience inside and the people gathered outside. Lieutenant Colonel David Cobb, one of Washington's aides-de-camp, while not present, repeated the story of another aide, Lieutenant Colonel Jonathan Trumbull: "the General took his station in the desk or pulpit" in his speech to the officers on March 15, 1783.[47] With no mention of the portico, Washington probably was in the main hall. Every regiment was ordered on February 4 to make five benches, about 8.5 feet long. The 11 regiments present in camp would have made 55 benches, and if the three battalions made three a piece, there would have been a total of 64. Absent on the lines during this order, the 1st New York Regiment was ordered on February 28 to make one bench per company, another eight or nine.[48] These additional seats raised the total to around 73. With approximately six per bench, the Temple had seating for nearly 450 people.

Along with the work on the Temple, a passage across the low ground west of the building was under construction. While the valley between the 1st and 3rd Massachusetts brigades and the Maryland, New Hampshire, New York, and New Jersey Lines is normally a wetland, it was not the case in 1782 because the region was suffering through the most extreme drought in memory. Shriveled from the lack of water, much of the wheat crop in surrounding areas was only fit for feeding livestock. Authorized to draw Colonel Charles Armand's legion of cavalry and infantry back to the northern army, Washington elected to keep them in Virginia. The lack of rainfall caused such a forage shortage that feeding the existing horses was difficult enough without adding to their numbers.[49] The ground was so dry that soldiers were cautioned about the accidental spread of fire. Snowmelt and the return of normal precipitation necessitated the construction of a raised causeway to maintain communication with the regiments on the western side of Beaver Dam Steam. Otherwise, these soldiers had to walk half a mile through the woods to reach a road. Had the officers searching for a winter encampment site seen the normal condition of the Beaver Dam Stream valley, it is very unlikely that they would have recommended New Windsor.

After one unsuccessful attempt, brigade commanders decided to make the causeway pass in a straight line from the space separating the 1st and 3rd Massachusetts Brigades to the gap between the New Jersey and New York Brigades. Responsibility for making the saucissons, the bundles of sticks necessary to raise the roadbed above the water level, was apportioned among the different brigades. Once staked down, the saucissons were covered with the saturated mud dug from the ditches on either side. Hook-billed fascine knives were used to cut the sticks. Chains or rope was used to compress the bundles for tying. Because two layers were necessary, "the upper covering the intervals between the lower" meant that over 4,000 were made, along with two five-foot-long stakes to secure each stack. By the middle of March, the materials were ready to span the 1,440-foot length.[50] Once completed, this embankment suffered damage during every appreciable rainfall and required constant repair and maintenance. The causeway's hard-packed earthen course is still visible on the eastern side of the stream. On both sides of the watercourse, the reinforced rock approaches remain, as does the pile of stones in the streambed that supported the saucissons.

Chapter 7

"Had this day been wanting, the world has never seen the last stage of perfection to which human nature is capable of attaining"

The Newburgh Conspiracy

In the spring of 1782, Washington complained in a private letter to Secretary at War Lincoln that his quartermaster general, gone from headquarters for some time, had been so uncommunicative that it was as if he did not have one. The consequence of Pickering's absence and the failure to keep him informed was that he had no idea of the supply situation or whether the army could mount a campaign that year. A Virginia gentleman used to deferential treatment, the commander in chief did not order but expressed his desire that the quartermaster return as soon as possible to address all the complaints. Lincoln replied that on the advice of Robert Morris, Pickering was hiding at his residence near Philadelphia until he had funds for his department to function and was not likely to soon return without Washington's urging. The quartermaster general explained to the commander in chief that he left instructions for his deputies to make the necessary arrangements for the upcoming campaign. Promising to bring back the funds to pay for these expenditures, he was detained waiting for this cash but was disappointed. He went on to say that he could no longer abuse the public creditors with the deception of purchasing supplies without any prospect of obtaining the funds to pay for them. Fairly soon, no one would sell the army anything on credit. In taking the field, commanders had to plan for not only supplies, transportation, the terrain, weather, time, and the enemy but also for the inordinate contingency costs of campaigning in this country "where each individual neither gives his house nor his field to incamp in without being paid for it in hand."[1]

The animal fodder situation was especially bad. All the generals, field-grade officers, and staff were authorized one or more riding horses, but this total did not exceed 200. Based on his limited capability to obtain forage, Pickering specified the minimal number necessary for the officers to function over the winter. His agents would send any excess animals away from the area or the officers could pay for the feed themselves and get reimbursed. Despite the quartermaster's plan, the situation in camp deteriorated by the end of December. Washington's own horses had not eaten in days, and General Gates "for want of five pounds worth of forage ... [had] lost a public Team of Horses worth more than L100." Officers required to do duty on horseback could not because their famished mounts were too weak from not eating to carry them. The light dragoon dispatch riders could no longer carry the mail. Pickering was ordered to relay the situation to Superintendent of Finance Robert Morris and immediately return to camp to address the supply issues. Granted leave in mid–November to go to Philadelphia to attend to his wife, who was critically ill, Pickering did warn Washington that everything was well in hand during his absence except forage. Pessimistic about obtaining any money to purchase more, he could not promise that there would be enough.[2] The poor conditions of the officers' mounts might have lessened the enjoyment of their fox hunt scheduled for December 23. Inviting ladies and gentlemen from both Ulster and Orange counties to gather at Samuel Wood's Tavern, they promised merriment and a sumptuous affair.[3]

No one envied Pickering. Besides the continued dearth of resources, balancing accounts was extremely difficult, especially when several subordinates were acting in your name. Forage Master Samuel Evans was tried for fabricating accounts of issue, falsifying returns, and forging receipts. He was found guilty of all charges, but the court was aware of the difficulties he faced. Rather than his actions being intentional, he was just careless at times in following procedures. Though the court recommended he forfeit his pay for three months, the commander in chief remitted the sentence because of the favorable representations made on Evans's behalf. Bartholomew Fisher, another forage master, was charged with defrauding the officers in their grain allowance for April 1783. The charges against Evans were not supported, so he was acquitted.[4] Often inadequately provided with forms and paper to document their activities and pressed for time, the purveyors of supplies were blamed for systemic shortfalls.

Unbeknownst to Pickering, his absence also enabled him to avoid for a time dealing with the October 26, 1782, arrest warrant issued on behalf of Melancthon L. Woolsey for trespass and a bill of 3,000 pounds. The Ulster County sheriff was commanded to "take Timothy Pickering Esqr. If he shall be found in your Bailiwick and him safely keep, so that you may have his body" before the New York Supreme Court on January 24, 1783. Speculating in quartermaster certificates, Woolsey bought them from holders at a substantial discount and then sued the quartermaster general for the full amount. Though Congress recommended to the states to pass legislation protecting government officials who incurred debts on behalf of the public, New York took no such action. Upon his return to headquarters in early January Pickering was taken into custody. He posted bail to gain his release and vowed "to defend the suit to the last extremity." Thanking God that he had no private property in this state, Pickering would go to jail rather than satisfy the obligation to the "vexatious suitor." It did not come to that. New York finally enacted a law to prevent civil suits against agents making purchases for the confederation.[5]

The disappointments all had to do with money, or the lack thereof. More specifically, who would levy and collect taxes and how aggressively, the same issue that started the conflict? British efforts to infringe on colonial autonomy by trying to raise revenue through taxation ended in revolution, and this zealously guarded self-rule prevented a coordinated American war effort. Never able to effectively marshal all its resources because the states would not totally comply with the allocations made on them by Congress for supplies or money and would not empower the national government to tax its citizens, the United States financially limped along. The "powers of congress are only recommendatory; while one State yields obedience, and another refuses it; while a third mutilates and adopts the measure in part only, and … the willing States are almost ruined by their exertions, distrust and jealousy succeeds to it; hence proceed neglect and ill-timed compliances (one state waiting to see what another will do)." Thus, the Continental Army lived hand to mouth, never having the resources to make long-range plans, which unnecessarily prolonged the war. The need for funds was paramount. In January 1781, Colonel John Laurens was sent on a mission to request succor from the French court. In his instructions, Washington told his young aide that if he was given the choice between the king sending a second division to augment Rochambeau or receiving instead the equivalent in money, he was to take the cash. Money would energize the entire American war effort by attracting men into the ranks and drawing out supplies. National pride demanded that the United States not sit back and let a foreign power secure its independence. The American people were laggard enough without additional French troops to further rationalize their torpor. Moreover, patriotism had long since faded away, few new recruits were willing to join without a substantial bounty, and the people expected full market value for their produce sold to the Continental Army. While dispatching a superior fleet to maintain control of the eastern seaboard was important, French financial aid would place the American forces in a better position to take advantage of that contingency or any other development. Wages were often months in arrears, and no one in uniform was paid in 1782. Congress made no effort to address the issue and would not let the states do it. No state settlements were allowed past August 1780, and their securities from the first nine months of that year were discounted nearly by half. The military held many of these bonds in the form of pay or depreciation certificates. Morris in May 1782 asserted in a circular letter to the state governors that if they did not remit their taxes, the country was going to economically founder.[6] All the available cash, such as it was, had to go for sustaining the army in the field. Salaries were a priority only to the officers and soldiers. Sarcastically summarizing state indifference, Washington reported that officials believed "that the Army had contracted such a habit of encountering distress and difficulties, and of living without money, that it would be impolitic and injurious to introduce other customs in it."[7]

Despite ever-increasing numbers of coins pouring into the country from enemy lines, allied armies and navies, and foreign loans, there were never enough to come close to meeting demands. The private Bank of North America, chartered by Congress in 1781 to assist in financing the war, tenaciously held onto its coins, preferring to issue notes instead. Many individuals also withheld their coins from circulation. Far more welcome than government paper, even coins could not be trusted due to the number of counterfeit, debased, clipped, and short-weight ones. Not having a scale to check their weight, Washington had to exchange five gold coins sent to his spymaster Major Benjamin Tallmadge that were too light. The British in New York City circulated gold coins, reduced along the edges or holed through by a punch. Derisively called "Robertson's" by Americans, after the corrupt governor of that garrison, General James Robertson, the enemy quartermaster staff made enormous profits from the residue of all the coins that passed through their hands. Every hole or cut was not done with fraudulent intent but rather to bring a coin to a standard weight. After drawing gold coins for their worth as bullion from the Bank of North America, Pickering was sent a letter on December 23, 1782, from assistant quartermaster in Philadelphia and commissary of military stores Samuel Hodgdon informing him that they were too heavy according to the current valuation. Advising him to turn in his French guineas, both overweight and underweight, Hodgdon told Pickering that he needed to clip the rest in secret; otherwise, the army might accuse him of malfeasance. "Tis shameful business," the exasperated quartermaster general replied, but still he requested Hodgdon to send him clippers, hole punches, and a small lead anvil. Pickering was not sure whether he would ever again draw any more bank gold.[8] Silver coins were cut into "half, quarter and eighth parts, to make change[;] … this arbitrary division of the money [made] great frauds … inevitable." With mints producing three or four times as many as other nations, Spanish coins predominated. The proliferation of hard money, however, was a mixed blessing. Though indispensable in drawing out the resources of the country, too often these materials were diverted to the enemy. With Continental currency not negotiable beyond American lines, the anonymity and universal acceptance of specie fueled this illicit traffic. Increasingly disbursing more silver and gold, U.S. officials further exacerbated this problem. Provisions still streamed into New York, and with more people possessing cash, ever-increasing amounts of merchandise came out in exchange, helping the British military and financial condition. "Men of all description … [were] indiscriminately engaging in it, Whig, Tory, [and] Speculator." There were other reasons than payment in specie and the higher amounts offered that made trade with the enemy more attractive. With policies formulated to try to prevent engrossers from buying large quantities of necessary articles to drive up prices, attempts at price fixing, which included the set amounts given for commodities impressed and embargoes preventing sales out of state, some sellers put profit before patriotism.[9]

Paper currency, known as bills of credit, were a promise to pay the individual, usually in Spanish dollars, English shillings, or the value in silver or gold. There were, however, nowhere near enough silver coins or bullion to back all the paper money. Shortly after the fighting started, people responded to the proliferation of bills of credit by withdrawing their hard money from circulation.[10] Paper money had been used extensively in colonial America, usually in time of war, to provide a circulating medium. Strictly controlled as to the amount of issue, the notes paid interest until they were finally redeemed and retired. Though the increasing quantities of bills made their value decline, officials had no other option to address the mounting war expenses. Also, homegrown forgers and those counterfeiters operating at the behest of British officials flooded the American economy with phony currency, further undermining its worth. Since their inception in Massachusetts in the late 17th century, these notes were extensively faked, prompting authorities to sometimes order printers to include on them "Tis Death to counterfeit" or a variant of that warning. The states and Congress resorted to the printing house as the panacea for all their financial woes. By the fall of 1779 when there was about $200 million in circulation, national legislators temporarily stopped the presses. In March 1780, they worked out a scheme whereby the depreciated notes would be redeemed at 40/1 for a new emission, thereby reducing the debt to a more manageable $5 million. New notes would be limited to $10 million. Then, this currency would be taxed out of circulation, retiring the debt. What no one took into consideration was that there were also millions of dollars of commissary and quartermaster certificates issued for supplies and services purchased from individuals, and it was next to impossible to get an idea of how many of them existed. Officials had to allow the payment of taxes with these securities as well as paper money. Specific supplies for forage and feeding the army were levied upon the states according to their size. The intent was that they would use the taxes raised by the new emission to pay for their share. With not enough people turning in the old bills, the states could not exchange them for the new ones and were unable to pay for their portion of the provisions. George Grieve, translator of Chastellux's work, waxed perhaps a bit too poetically of the paper emissions, observing that most people lost money in proportion to their net worth, which served the same purpose as direct taxation.[11]

Assuming office in early 1781, Superintendent of Finance Robert Morris ably brought some order out of the chaotic financial situation. In an age when conflicts of interest were common, he was allowed to continue his business pursuits while in office. Privy to the most intimate government secrets, he profited extensively from his position. Engaging in privateering and foreign trade, he was sometimes allowed to continue his shipments despite embargoes, which earned him exorbitant returns.[12] His first act was to propose that Congress grant a charter to the private Bank of North America. This institution would provide a reliable source of national credit and reassure investors of the creditworthiness of the country. Though capitalized by foreign loans and the fees from stock subscriptions, he still needed the states to deposit the tax proceeds, allocated to them by Congress, to complete the funding. Morris issued his own notes in anticipation of future revenue, backed by this repository. Making an ostentatious show of the specie on hand, the bank issued notes exceeding that amount up to the level of risk they were willing to accept, anticipating or, in other words, gambling that they would have enough money to redeem them when due. If the institution loaned too much, it could fail. Increasing efficiency with competitive bidding and holding government agents strictly accountable for all disbursements, the sagacious moneyman pressured the states to contribute, but they still lagged far behind in their appropriations. They had to either aggressively assess and collect taxes from their citizens or let Congress do it for them. Increasingly like-minded nationalist politicians agreed that vesting the central government with the power to raise revenue was the solution. The first step in this process was the ratification of the 1781 Impost, a 5 percent tariff on imports. Fearing the power of the other states and the country, Rhode Island held out knowing that this tariff would only fund, not satisfy, the nation's debts. Once the precedent for national taxing authority was established, there would be no limit to the number of new levies, undermining the sovereignty of the individual states. In December 1782, the Virginia legislature rescinded its approval of the Impost, all but killing the measure.[13] Desperate to force the states to provide the means for the government to function, nationalists made common cause with the army. They found a willing coconspirator in General Gates. Dismissed after the Battle of Camden pending a court of inquiry, he waited almost two years before Congress repealed the call for an investigation and reinstated him. Given command of that

Major John Armstrong (1758–1843) by Rembrandt Peale, from life, c. 1808 (INDE 14025) (Courtesy Independence National Historical Park).

part of the Continental Army moving into cantonment at New Windsor, Gates established his headquarters at the elegant home of merchant John Ellison. By that point, the British garrisons in the South were being withdrawn so they could send further troops to the Caribbean, but they still held on to New York and a few other locations. Helping their allies by forcing the enemy to maintain such a large garrison to defend their positions around the city, the army in the Hudson Valley waited on news of the peace negotiations. Gates was joined by aides-de-camp Major John Armstrong and Major Christopher Richmond.

Armstrong, educated at the College of New Jersey, later Princeton, entered the army as a volunteer in 1776. General Hugh Mercer took the young man into his military family as an aide with the rank of major. Mercer served with his father, John Armstrong Sr., during the French and Indian War. Riding into battle beside his chief at Princeton, New Jersey, Armstrong Jr. narrowly escaped death, but Mercer was mortally wounded. Unemployed, Armstrong entered into the service of Gates and served with him during the Saratoga Campaign. Following Gates to a quiet post in New England, Armstrong tagged along on the unsuccessful Massachusetts expedition in 1779 against the British in Maine. Appointed deputy adjutant general in 1780 with the brevet rank of lieutenant colonel, he was struck down with illness on his way to join Gates, who had taken command of the southern army. Armstrong missed the Battle of Camden but accompanied his commander to Philadelphia that fall, where his general demanded a court of inquiry into his conduct during that engagement. Refusing to take the field before the onus of Camden was removed, Gates waited two years before Congress assured him that there was never any censure and that a trial was unnecessary. Having become fast friends, Armstrong joined Gates at New Windsor. With the encouragement of Gates and others, Armstrong wrote the two anonymous letters that set in motion the Newburgh Conspiracy, which incited the passions of every officer in the army. Despite his authorship of those treasonable broadsides, he went on to a distinguished career in politics and the military. He was a state senator and later ambassador to France. At the beginning of the War of 1812, Armstrong was appointed brigadier general and a short time later was named secretary at war.

Christopher Richmond first appears on the muster rolls in January 1776 as a clerk to William Smallwood, the colonel of the 1st Maryland Regiment. Richmond was paymaster on January 1, 1777, and was promoted to lieutenant on May 27, 1778. He later transferred to the 2nd Maryland Regiment. The Maryland Line was one of the best in the Continental service, fighting bravely at Long Island, Brandywine, Germantown, and Monmouth and then in the South. Richmond was present at some of the hardest fought and most desperate actions of the war. Promoted to captain shortly after the Camden disaster, he ended the war as an aide to General Gates. Though signing his correspondence as a major, this was a staff promotion that did nothing to advance Richmond's rank in the line.[14]

In December, Gates complained that for the past two weeks neither himself nor his aides received any feed for their horses. The shortage of forage necessitated the removal of most of the horses from camp, but the ones that remained did not fare very well. Gates wrote to the unresponsive Pickering that he had placed the animals in the care of William Edmonston to keep them from starving. There were still enough mounts, however, for the officers to organize a fox hunt for December 23. Taking back possession of his horses, Gates wanted to buy some corn, at a very high price, from his host John Ellison in January and wanted to know how much Pickering would allow for the purchase in his forage accounts. A stable was erected for Gates and his military family. Major Richmond also arranged with Edmonston to supply the headquarters with firewood.[15] At the end of the month, Gates was joined by a headquarters guard of a sergeant, a corporal, and six men from the Massachusetts Line and a man from the rest of the regiments, making a total of 14. Just a detachment, the Marylanders were excused from this duty. Gates wanted dependable men so he would not have to replace any. A guard hut was built to lessen the wear on the soldier's shoes from having to march back and forth to their encampment sites. Two heavy woolen watch coats were requested in January for the use of the soldiers at their guard posts, indicating the number who were on duty at any given time. Washington aide Humphreys replied that a general issue of watch coats would happen shortly. The commander in chief's comment that the regiments providing guards will send their soldiers dressed in watch coats indicated that either he did not know that Gates intended to keep the same one until the weather improved or a reversion to the original rotating schedule.[16] With his immediate personal needs satisfied, he dedicated his time to organizing the construction of the Temple of Virtue. Besides this project, the soldiers were busy constructing and repairing roads to facilitate movement around the encampment area.[17] Suffering from an illness at the end of January, Gates wrote to his wife Betsy more than a week before inquiring why she had not come to camp and why had she not written since October. She also had been ill.[18] The celebration on the anniversary of the French alliance on February 6 and the visit of Secretary at War Lincoln in the middle of the month broke the monotony, but excitement was not long in coming.[19]

In January, legislators received the memorial from Major General Alexander McDougall, Colonel Matthias Ogden, and Lieutenant Colonel John Brooks, the army's committee to Congress. Though expressed in respectful terms, it was an indictment charging that American independence was based on the ruin of the citizens comprising the military. Having "borne all that men can bear," they wanted money sent to camp as soon as possible. "The uneasiness of the soldiers for want of pay, is great and dangerous; and further experiments on their patience may have fatal effects." They also wanted Congress to determine the nature of the officer pension.[20] Typical, their request resulted in the designation of committees to study the matter and debate but not much else. Unlike soldiers who enlisted for a length of time or for the duration of the war, the officers could quit the service at any time simply by resigning. Faced with adversity and economic hardship, many officers either resigned or threatened to do so. To prevent the wholesale loss of the entire officer corps, Congress in 1780 approved a pension based on the British model. Officers who served until the end of the war would receive half-pay for the rest of their lives. This measure replaced the 1778 act, which granted only seven years of half-pay. Though feeling that the officers had lost all patriotic virtue and aghast that they had to be bribed to continue in the service, national legislators acceded to the blackmail. But with the promising peace negotiations following the Battle of Yorktown seriously undermining their bargaining power, the officers' service was not so vital, so the country chose to ignore their request to find the means to pay for this legislation.

Having taken advantage of the military's power to compel obedience by force, congressmen, snug within their self-righteous collective irresponsibility, the greatest defect of large decision-making bodies, always placed the welfare of the officers and men very low in their priorities. But with "Congress weak as water and impotent as old age" and "the states obdurate and forgetful," the representatives were not entirely at fault. Not caring where the chief blame lay, the officers were determined to end the perfidy. They threatened that a mutiny was inevitable if the unmovable legislators failed to act, which they would not suppress with the energy of the past.[21] Pinning all of their hopes on Robert Morris to broker a deal, General Gates wrote to his friend and former colleague from the Board of War, Pennsylvania congressman Richard Peters, in February that "the political pot in Philadelphia Boils so furiously" and closed the letter with the imploring avowal that "the Financier has the prayers of the Army." Brooks and Ogden consulted with Morris on January 21. There are no details of their discussion, but subsequent events showed that they must have decided on a bold if not reckless gambit. All three of the army delegation met with Morris on February 4. Making the first move, Morris added drama and weight to the officers' appeal by tendering his resignation, to take effect at the end of May, if Congress failed to establish a general fund. He declared that it was deceitful to continue spending when the outlook for repayment was so bleak. Shocked and despaired of finding anyone approaching his capabilities to replace him, the legislative body decided not to publicly disclose the financier's threat. Ominously, Gouverneur Morris, assistant to Robert Morris, wrote to John Jay, one of the peace commissioners in Paris, that unlike all other national creditors, "the army have swords in their hands." Whether they would use them against their own government remained to be seen. While the army suffered with wages that were months in arrears, government officials were always paid promptly.[22] The defense for regularly remitting civilian salaries was that they had to pay for the necessities of life, unlike the military, where though it might be substandard or insufficient, food, shelter, and clothing were provided. Though the officers continued to send memorials to Congress in deferential language, they were infuriated by this inequity. Taking advantage of the army's coercive power, legislators continued in the belief that they could impose upon the troops with impunity. Needing to contain this resentment, Washington gave up any thoughts of spending the winter of 1782–83 at Mount Vernon. He had to "stick very close to the Troops this Winter and to try like a careful physician to prevent if possible the disorders getting to an incurable height."[23]

Washington expressed his apprehension to Alexander Hamilton. While admitting that the continued neglect was a major concern, Washington still expected to maintain order and disband the army without incident. Worried they would be turned out of service without their back pay and other promised emoluments of service, both officers and men were anxious about the impending peace. Questioning Hamilton's warning and motives in pointing out that dangerous combinations were forming in the officer corps, Washington postulated "the source of which may be easily traced as the old leven [Gates], *it is said*, for I have no proof of it, is again, beginning to work, under a mask of the most perfect dissimulation, and apparent cordiality." Intriguingly, David Head argues in his *A Crisis of Peace: George Washington, the Newburgh Conspiracy, and the Fate of the American Revolution*, that "old leven" is not a reference to Gates but instead is "more likely the old slander of indecision and not a specific person" and that the term was "a colloquialism drawn from a Bible verse (1Corinthians 5:7) warning against old prejudices irrationally retained." Head contends that Douglas Southall Freeman, in his epic biography of Washington, made this determination and that all subsequent authors accepted his conclusion. Thomas Fleming in his *The Perils of Peace: America's Struggle for Survival after Yorktown*; William M. Fowler, Jr., in *American Crisis: George Washington and the Dangerous Two Years after Yorktown, 1781–1783*; and Dave Richards in

Swords in Their Hands: George Washington and the Newburgh Conspiracy also decided that "old leven" was a reference to Gates. Countering Head's argument is that these ideas had to come from somewhere and would carry the most weight expressed by Gates. In a letter to General Washington on April 8, 1783, Alexander Hamilton used the term "old leaven" in reference to commissioners to France Silas Deane and Arthur Lee, whose recriminations against each other earlier in the war were a national scandal. "Old leven" refers to individuals or a group who were a bane to someone. Not one to call out his enemies in writing and preferring oblique references, Washington expected this kind of behavior from this known intriguer. He had no way of knowing that Gates was just a facilitator, not a leader, in these maneuvers. Based on their previous history, the commander in chief was predisposed to think the worst of him. As a subordinate, Gates had to dissimulate and be false and respectful even though he could not stand Washington. Conveniently, however, they stayed three miles apart, so the two could avoid contact. Quite unusual in the very social Continental Army, they did not make any visits to each other's headquarters. It is quite possible that Gates feigned sickness on the anniversary of the French alliance so he did not have to be around Washington. Presiding over the March 15 meeting in the Temple, Gates was surprised by the commanding general's unexpected appearance. If not Gates, who could it be? Washington had disposed of all his adversaries in the army by this point except Gates. Still with his adherents, Gates delighted in playing the demagogue and hoped to reap some benefit for his efforts. With his known icy relationship and host of reasons to question the leadership, conduct, and decisions of the commander in chief, he was the most likely to agree to taking drastic steps to further the agenda of the army and the nationalist faction. Moreover, in one of the biggest crises of the Continental Army, it is telling that there is no indication that Washington made any effort to reach out to his deputy and commander of his army at New Windsor for assistance. The man the commander in chief trusted the least was in control of thousands of troops, an authority Washington deemed necessary to cripple at the height of the crisis.[24]

Using his former aide as a harbinger, Washington wanted the schemers to know that he was aware of their intrigue. Trusting that Hamilton's "prudence will direct what should be done with this," he knew that this information would eventually reach his intended audience. In their evolving relationship, the commander in chief used the language of a colleague soliciting the assistance of a peer rather than a superior making demands of a subordinate. Since that heated exchange two years before on the staircase at the Thomas Ellison house, just a mile south of his current headquarters, Washington tried to atone for losing his temper over Hamilton's delay in responding to his summons. Knowing that his sensitive young military secretary was brilliant and an indispensable member of his staff, Washington should have known better than to treat him as a lackey. Tired of incessant paperwork and intimately aware of the commander in chief's faults, Hamilton made the most of the altercation to escape from Washington's orbit and used this affront to exact whatever preferment he could from him. Wanting to lead soldiers in battle for some time, there is the distinct possibility that Hamilton purposely overreacted to this minor indignity to force the breakup. At Yorktown, Washington, bypassing far more deserving officers, gave him command of the light infantry assault against Redoubt Number 10, a key enemy installation. Though only a colonel at the end of the Revolution, Hamilton parlayed his unique affiliation with Washington to attain the third most senior position in the army assembled to put down the Whiskey Rebellion in 1794 and position himself as de facto commander during the Quasi-War with France at the end of the decade. Moreover, he owed his position as secretary of the treasury to his former military chief.

When Colonel Walter Stewart, army inspector and former Gates aide, arrived in camp, he explained that Congress was impotent. Sent by nationalists who were trying to strengthen the power of the central government, Stewart immediately caused a furor in camp. In this context, the term "nationalist" refers not to an organized party or movement but instead to like-minded individuals discussing in one-on-one conversations or in small groups the necessity for a more effective country legislature. With no designated leaders, specific agenda, and course of action, a desperate and militant clique within this school of thought fomented unrest in the Continental Army to achieve its political ends.

More appropriately termed the "New Windsor Conspiracy," because the plot unfolded in the army encampment located southwest of Newburgh, a coterie of army officers gathered at John Ellison's the next day, choosing Gates's aide John Armstrong to frame their call for action. Specifically, they wanted their back salaries, the payment of their subsistence and allowances, and action on servicing the pension promised in 1780. With the American war effort at its nadir that year, officers were resigning in large numbers. To slow the losses, Congress agreed to grant half-pay for life to any of them who served until the end of the conflict.[25] Armstrong wrote an appeal for the officers to meet on March 11 to discuss their next move and followed with a second letter a few days later. Circulated anonymously, the letters urged the officers to threaten representatives in the Continental Congress with military force to compel them to redress the officers' long-standing grievances.

In a room of Gates's headquarters, the general's aides-de-camp Majors Armstrong and Richmond and Stewart and his assistant Major William Barber gathered. Armstrong later claimed that there were around a dozen officers present, adding to the aforementioned list: "Surgeon William Eustis, Lieutenant Colonel James Miles Hughes [of the New York Levies], Major T. Stewart, a Major Moore [possibly William Moore from

Major General Alexander McDougall (1732–1786), 1786, by John Ramage, miniature on ivory, 1⅝ × 1¼ inches. Purchase, The Louis Durr Fund, New-York Historical Society, 1953.318 (© New-York Historical Society).

Lieutenant Colonel John Brooks when governor of Massachusetts, by Gilbert Stuart, c. 1820 (Collection of the Honolulu Museum of Art. Gift of Mrs. Edward T. Harrison, in memory of her husband, Edward T. Harrison, 1965 [3370.1]).

the 4th Massachusetts] and three or four subalterns of the line." In an interview with historian Nicholas Sparks, Armstrong stated that Major Nicholas Fish of the 2nd New York Regiment was there as well. Convalescing during this time in the eastern parlor of the John Ellison house from a wound received while defending American ships from British gunboats in the Hudson River off Tarrytown, New York, in July 1781, Captain George Hurlbut of the 2nd Continental Light Dragoons must have at least observed the conclave.[26] Gates, undoubtedly aware of their intent, gave the attendees some guidance and left them to do the staff work. It stretches credulity to think that those letters left the Ellison house without his review. In the appendix of George Bancroft's *History of the Formation of the Constitution of the United States of America* is an excerpt from a letter sent by Gates to Armstrong in June specifying the role everyone at his headquarters played, thereby acknowledging his total complicity in the affair: "That Stewart was a kind of agent from our friends in congress and in the administration, with no object, however, beyond that of getting the army to co-operate with the civil creditors, as the way most likely for both to obtain justice; and that the letters were written in my quarters by you, copied by Richmond and circulated by Barber." Robert Morris had already weaponized the private holders of government debt. Bullying the feckless officials frustrating his financial reform efforts, he contemptuously informed state governors in January 1782 that his suspension of interest payments "produced much clamor among the public creditors" and that his expectation was "that it will occasion much more."[27]

Despite the decisive victory at Yorktown, Virginia, in October 1781, which ultimately forced Great Britain to sue for peace with the recognition of American independence, little had changed for the American people or the confederation's soldiers. Deprivation and suffering were still their lot in life. Most of their spleen was vented at Congress, the ineffective rump of that confident body that had declared independence just seven years before. With a penchant for mob violence, the masses took to the streets. The wealthy also felt the ineffectiveness of Congress, most importantly its inability to raise revenue to pay for the operation of government. Representing the interests of the country's creditors, Alexander Hamilton, Superintendent of Finance Robert Morris, Morris's assistant, the transplanted New Yorker Gouverneur Morris, and other nationalists agitated for a strong central government that had the power to tax. They abhorred

Colonel Walter Stewart, by Charles Willson Peale, c. 1781 (Yale University Art Gallery).

the mob, but the army on the other hand, if properly directed by well-disposed officers, could menace Congress without fear of causing social upheaval. With pay months or even a year or more in arrears and Congress's inability to agree on a plan to pay the promised pension to the officers, the nation's governing body had few friends in the military. Capitalizing on this enmity, the nationalists turned to the inspector of the northern army, Colonel Walter Stewart, to carry with him to New Windsor their guidance, if not outright instructions, on how to provoke the officers of the army encampment. Son-in-law of the powerful Philadelphia merchant Blair McClenachan who, like his father-in-law, held large quantities of government debt, Stewart was ideally situated to broker an alliance between the private and public creditors.[28] Enough pressure might coax the parsimonious states into finally passing the Impost, a 5 percent duty on imports. Nationalists believed that military intimidation would force the states to vest the central government with the power to raise the revenue needed to satisfy all the country's obligations. Amid the tumult, news of the preliminary peace articles arrived in camp, further fueling the ardor of the hotheads.

Money is power and a source of great jealousy. Moreover, following it is often revealing. Far too coincidental was the timing of the delivery of the specie in camp to pay just the enlisted men. The heavily laden wagons plodded north from Philadelphia to Pompton, New Jersey, where General Moses Hazen's men relieved the escort and conducted the shipment to Ringwood. A detail of a captain with 50 men went down to accompany the wagons the rest of the way. The three kegs, containing $10,000 in coins, was not enough, however, to accomplish the intent of providing a month's pay. Lieutenant Colonel John Brooks probably accompanied this train, because he was "carrying an additional consignment from the pay Office of $5,000 in cash and $6,266$^{60/90}$ in drafts on Washington." Since the pay would be primarily expended in this state, Washington requested every possible assistance from Governor Clinton and New York legislators to encourage moneyed men to exchange the bills of credit that accompanied the specie for coins. The payments started on March 6, just two days before the nationalist emissary arrived in camp. Drawn by Deputy Paymaster Hezekiah Wetmore, regimental paymasters received instructions on what paperwork to submit in order to receive the weekly pay of about "half a Crown per Man" for the noncommissioned officers and soldiers. The weekly soldier pay, of around $.50 and $.75 for the noncommissioned officers, was to continue in the same amount as long as the money lasted, which Lieutenant Gilbert understood to be 13 weeks. During this time, a sergeant in the Corps of Sappers and Miners stationed at West Point, assault engineer Joseph Plumb Martin, received his second cash payment, refuting his claim that the only time he was ever paid in coin since the first years of his service was on the way to Yorktown in 1781. Initially intending to wait until enough coins were available to complete an entire month's pay, Washington decided to give the order to start doling out the money because of the anxiousness of the men. Rather than risk the premature exhaustion of the specie, soldiers had the option to instead choose to receive $2 in cash and the rest in merchandise from the firm Duer & Parker. This mode of payment also had the gratuitous effect of precluding them from expending the entire amount on liquor. Vast quantities of goods were sent to camp, earning the contractors a hefty profit. In early April, Lieutenant Gilbert accompanied men of his company to New Windsor, where he helped them buy merchandise using their pay orders.[29]

"The Officers get no pay as yet, and very little prospects of getting any period." Buoyed by the news from Lieutenant Colonel Brooks at the end of January that there were prospects that a month's pay in Morris Notes for the entire army was possibly forthcoming, Lieutenant Gilbert was very disappointed when this did happen. While the specie payment was in contemplation, Morris worked out a plan to pay the officers. Also timed for effect, his unexpected largesse to them was to earn their support for his political agenda. They would receive wages for one month, redeemable after two months. Because they received a month's pay in coins during the Yorktown Campaign, the officers who served in Virginia were excluded from this disbursement. Traveling south to the Tidewater with Lafayette in early 1781, Gilbert was not eligible for this payment. Though they too received a month's pay in hard money, the noncommissioned officers and soldiers who served in Virginia were still allowed to collect the weekly payments. Delaying the issue of the certificates until enough money was available so that most of the officers could start receiving them, Morris, in early April, ordered $10,000 a week forwarded until the payment was completed.[30] Having done so well from a previous commission and probably being overstocked, contractor Daniel Parker in March proposed to Washington advancing a month's pay in merchandise to the enlisted men, but Robert Morris could not give his assent, replying that "the State of the Finances will by no Means admit of it." A month later, Parker proposed advancing three months' pay to the army. He traveled to Philadelphia to discuss the matter with Morris, but the superintendent did not accept this offer either.[31]

Stewart was the spark who ignited the Newburgh Conspiracy, but Gates's receptiveness to the ploy enabled the events to go as far as they did. Prone to flattery, Gates was assuredly full of himself that the nationalists approached him. Gates was an opportunist in constant search of influential friends, and his susceptibilities made him putty in the hands of smarter men. His ambition, negotiable principles, and pliability made him ideally suited for a leadership role in this plot. In dissecting this crisis, it is important to understand the deterioration of the relationship between Washington and Gates. At the beginning of the American Revolution, Gates was made a brigadier general and appointed adjutant general of the Continental Army. A very capable administrator held

Left: **Alexander Hamilton (1755–1804), by Charles Willson Peale, from life, c. 1790–1795 [MYR1](INDE 11877) (courtesy Independence National Historical Park).** *Right:* **Robert Morris (1734–1806), by Charles Willson Peale, from life, c. 1782 (INDE 14112) (courtesy Independence National Historical Park).**

Gouverneur Morris by Thomas Sully, 1808 (Collection of the Historical Society of Pennsylvania).

in the highest esteem by the commander in chief, Gates possessed great organizational skills and, most importantly, knew how an army should operate. Though Washington despaired of running the army without him, Gates, recently promoted to major general, left for the Champlain Valley in June 1776 to restore order in the forces of the Canadian expedition. Consolidating the units at Fort Ticonderoga, he dramatically improved their health and morale, instilled discipline, and renewed their ardor. Revived, they contested General Carlton's advance up Lake Champlain until cold weather forced him to withdraw to Canada. Gates then returned to the main army, but by the following March he was back at Ticonderoga, where he forced a showdown with Major General Philip Schuyler over who would direct the operations of the northern army. When Congress reaffirmed the New Yorker, Gates, a man on the make with no patrimony or decades of political influence, had to make his own opportunities and revealed how ruthless he could be in the pursuit of preferment. Shamelessly promoting himself, he harangued his supporters in Congress to push for his appointment to sole commander in the north. While Gates undermined him in the capital, Schuyler tried to stop another British army. By August 1777, American forces were just outside of Albany, the British objective, and 100 miles to the west, Fort Stanwix was besieged. Fort Ticonderoga had fallen, and though skillfully slowed by Schuyler's men, the enemy commander General John Burgoyne was still advancing. The loss of this bastion and the constant withdrawals gave the Gates faction what it needed to finally force Schuyler's removal. Triumphant, Gates assumed command in the middle of August and, with characteristic efficiency, prepared the northern army to rejoin the fight. Advancing to prepared positions, he fought two battles at this location, breaking the British momentum. Pursuing the defeated enemy, he forced their capitulation at Saratoga.

In the afterglow of his victory against Burgoyne, Gates was brought down by suspicions that he sought to supplant Washington. Jealous of Gates's victory at Saratoga, the commander in chief chose to find deeper meaning in every slight, eventually concluding that there was a conspiracy against him, the so-called Conway Cabal. The controversy started when Major General William Alexander, Lord Stirling, revealed to Washington that his aide was told the contents of a private letter sent to Gates by Brigadier General Thomas Conway, a French officer in the American service. Carrying the news of the British surrender at Saratoga to Congress, Gates's aide Lieutenant Colonel James Wilkinson on the way spouted off the ridicule heaped on Washington and the American military leadership by Conway in that document: "Heaven has been determined to save your country; or a weak General and bad Councellors would have ruined it."[32] While the exact wording of the sentence cannot be confirmed because the offending letter no longer exists, the tone is quite clear. Gates was discombobulated by the accusatory manner taken by Washington in disclosing that he knew the contents of the Conway letter, and his awkward response made it appear that he was involved in a treacherous correspondence. Panicking after the discovery, he ineffectually denied that he shared Conway's views and made himself look ridiculous in the attempt. He was already suspect for perceived flaunts to Washington's authority, especially reporting his Saratoga victory only to the president of Congress. The commander in chief, however, chose to forget that he demurred when asked by that body to name a successor to Schuyler, so the legislators directly chose Gates. Washington's only responsibility in this decision was to notify him of his appointment. Assuming Conway's letter was only a part of greater machinations, Washington felt confirmed in his suspicions when Gates was appointed president of the Board of War, Congress's council for army affairs. Besides a gold medal and a sword, this appointment was intended to reward him for Saratoga and put him in a position where he could employ his organizational skills throughout the country. With such a wide and nebulous mandate, Gates inevitably found himself in conflict with headquarters. Intended to perform only administrative functions, the board members, under his leadership, took it upon themselves to plan military operations without first consulting Washington. Obsessed with the conquest of Canada, Gates proposed an expedition into the former French possession headed by Lafayette and seconded by the duplicitous Conway. Concluding that this scheme was intended to embarrass and separate himself from his young protégé, Washington ruthlessly went after Gates and used his sense of betrayal to spur his defenders to confront all his critics, masterfully making his detractors seriously consider ever disparaging him again. From then on, Gates had to bear not only the transparent enmity of the commander in chief but also the disdain of Washington's multitude of supporters. Questioning Gates's complicity in the supposed cabal, Washington was cool to him thereafter. Gates never recovered from these implications, inventions of the commanding general's sensitive psyche, and avoided from then on when possible directly serving alongside his former friend.

Leaving the Board of War in the spring of 1778, Gates held a few assignments in quiet areas before retiring to his Virginia estate at the end of 1779. Recalled following the loss of Charleston and most of the southern army in May 1780, he assembled the scattered commands at Hillsborough, North Carolina. Finding few soldiers and virtually no supplies, he rashly led his men into South Carolina to seize provisions from the well-stocked British outposts. Apparently forgetting that at Saratoga he faced a desperate overextended enemy with an army firmly entrenched on Bemis Heights that was waxing daily, an overconfident Gates went on the offensive. He wanted to silence his critics that he stole the triumph from Schuyler and prove that he could maneuver an army and then lead it to victory on the battlefield. Facing in the open a foe flush with success deep in royalist-dominated territory, however, was a far cry from the ideal conditions at Saratoga. Also, besides being greatly dispirited by the fall of Charleston, the Americans were in poor physical condition due to inadequate shelter, food stores, and other material. Self-assured despite his falling out with Washington, Gates discovered that knowing martial theory paled in comparison to comprehending the capabilities of the men he commanded. His intent was to take up a strong defensive position just beyond the enemy's works outside of Camden, South Carolina, and make them attack him.

To arrive undiscovered, Gates resorted to a night movement, an unusual occurrence and a difficult task for inexperienced troops. Unexpectedly blundering in the darkness into General Cornwallis' army, Gates had no choice but to fight in the morning and not on his desired terrain. Had he pushed out his cavalry far enough, he would have discovered the British movement in time. Preparing for battle on the morning of August 16, Gates, anchoring his line between two swamps, arrayed his best troops on the right, the Continentals, in accordance with traditional European doctrine. He faced an enemy similarly deployed. Predictably, the best of the British force quickly routed all the American militia on the left and in the center and then joined in with the other units on the other flank to break the unsupported Continentals. Gates's broken ranks were then driven from the battleground. Fleeing the field in a futile attempt to rally the militia, in whom he had placed too much faith, and then to avoid capture, he left the rest of his men to their fate. But in the aftermath of this total defeat, he created yet another army, cobbling it together from the debris of this most recent catastrophe. Had he been more cautious and bided his time, he would have had a formidable host eventually to face down Cornwallis.

Staying above the fray, Washington often let proxies do his dirty work. Alexander Hamilton, with obvious delight, lampooned the downfall of his general's rival. Refusing to return to service without exoneration for his defeat at Camden, Gates waited two years before Congress repealed their resolution for an investigation. Arriving in the Highlands just before the New Windsor winter encampment, he was greeted by Washington, who was polite but distant. With no respect for his aloof commander and his handling of the army, Gates, having all the makings of a demagogue, would take care of the men, accomplishing what Washington either could not or would not.

Writing at the Ellison House, Major Armstrong appealed to the basest instincts of resentment and ingratitude:

> When those very swords, the instruments and companions of your glory, shall be taken from your sides, and no remaining mark of military distinction left but your wants, infirmities and scars! Can then, consent to be the only sufferers by this resolution, and retiring from the field, grow old in poverty, wretchedness and contempt? Can you then consent to wade through the vile mire of dependency, and owe miserable remnant of that life to charity which has hitherto

been spent in honor? If you can, go, and carry with you the jest of tories, and the scorn of whigs—the ridicule, and what is worse, the pity of the world; go starve and be forgotten. But, if your spirit sufficient to oppose tyranny, under whatever garb it may assume, whether it be the plain coat republicanism or the splendid robes of royalty; if you have not yet learned to discriminate between a people and a cause-between men and principles-awake-attend to your situation, and redress yourselves. If the present moment be lost, every future effort is in vain. Your threats then will be as empty as your entreaties now. I would advise you, therefore, to come to some final opinion of what you can bear and what you will suffer. If your determination be in any proportion to your wrongs, carry your appeal from the justice to the fears of government; change the milk and water style of your last memorial; assume a bolder tone, decent but lively, spirited and determined, and suspect the man who advise to more moderation and longer forbearance.

This letter, distributed to the officers in camp on March 10, stirred long-harbored bitterness by reminding readers of the numerous instances of ill treatment by an ungrateful nation and emphasized that their power to obtain justice would end with the army's disbandment and dispersal. Armstrong closed with a call to meet the next day and prepare a final memorial to Congress, which was in effect an ultimatum to redress their long-standing grievances or else.[33]

In his office in the Hasbrouck house in Newburgh, General Washington contemplated the best way to manage the crisis. Regardless of whether this threat was real or just an elaborate bluff, the implications of the letter shocked him. Throughout its long-troubled history, the officers had kept the Continental Army together despite dreadful conditions, bitter defeats, and soldier mutinies. If the officer corps turned against the country, who could prevent the military from dictating to its civilian masters? One of the considerations for concentrating the army was that in case of a revolt by one of the Continental lines, loyal troops were close by to put it down. On the other hand, the mass gatherings also invited collusion and the quick spread of mutiny. Presciently, Washington had warned Secretary at War Lincoln the previous October that the patience of the army was at an end and that unless something was done to assuage their resentment, he was concerned about the possible consequences. During that time, the contrived pageantry to impress the officers of the visiting French army engaged the soldiers' attention, but he dreaded the idleness of the forthcoming winter encampment. "It is high time for a Peace," the indignant commander in chief beseeched. Disconcerted that his officers were adding to the unrest, Washington countered the first letter by expressing his "disapprobation of such disorderly proceedings" and directed that they meet instead on March 15 to hear the report of the committee of the army to Congress. Rather than exacerbate the situation with a direct attack on the contents of the letter, he bought time by channeling their anger to "rescue the foot, that stood wavering on the precipice of despair." Washington directed the officers to consider the army committee report and determine a plan to achieve their ends. Wanting to shape their response, he requested that the highest-ranking officer present to him the results of their deliberations. Though the commander in chief plainly stated that he was "fully persuaded that the good sense of the officers would induce them to pay very little attention to this irregular invitation," in the second letter to the officers on March 12 Armstrong argued that Washington, by not banning further meetings, actually supported their tough rhetoric. Writing from the cocoon of headquarters, Washington aide Lieutenant Colonel Benjamin Walker believed that most of the officers did not support the arguments in the Armstrong letters, but the feeling in camp, however, was far more receptive.[34]

While Washington was initially unsure whether the first letter was written in the nation's capital, the appearance of the second one referencing the first so soon erased any doubt about the author being close at hand. But it was still: "generally believ'd the scheme was not only planned, but also digested and matured in Philadelphia." Trying to find out whether his former aide, now a New York delegate in the Continental Congress, knew anything about the intrigue, Washington wrote to Alexander Hamilton about the steps he had taken. Washington also implored him to use his influence with the delinquent members opposing the army's just demands, warning that "they must be answerable to God and their Country for the ineffable horrors which may be occasioned thereby." The letter served its purpose to confirm his suspicion that the agitation originated in the seat of government. Possibly trying to magnify his actual role, Hamilton recounted his efforts to convince fellow delegates of the necessity of bringing to bear the combined pressure of both the public creditors and the army, all but admitting to being part of the faction who initiated the affair. Praising Washington's handling of the letters by not "attempt[ing] to stem a torrent, but divert it," Hamilton reasoned that "the discontents of the army might be turned to good account ... [and that the] earnest, but respectful application for redress ... [would] have a good effect."[35]

Hoping that passions would cool sufficiently in the interim, Washington made sure trusted subordinates would attend the meeting, and he prepared a surprise. Though he sympathized with the army's plight as much as someone from the privileged class could do, he by no means sanctioned the extortion of Congress. A public meeting was far preferable to an unauthorized one held in secret. Shoring up his position before the potentially explosive gathering, "the Genl. Came to camp and sent for the Officers commanding Brigades ... and was happy to find a unanimous determination to support order and ... to Suppress every attempt at disorderly Conduct."[36] Having put out the fire, just smoke remained. Staff officers still schemed and plotted, but without the backing of troops, they were powerless. There is no record that Washington ever met with Gates. This is not surprising. The commander in chief never took him into his confidence after the Conway Cabal in early 1778. Washington also suspected that Gates was somehow involved in the affair and had no doubt, however, about the involvement of "a certain Gentleman from Phila.": Stewart.[37] To demonstrate Congress's good intentions, Washington inserted into the March 13 general order a copy of its resolution addressing the army's memorial in January. While acknowledging the validity of the petition for settling the officer pension and pay, subsistence, and clothing accounts, the legislators continued to equivocate. Robert Morris was directed to liquidate the accounts as soon as the state of the finances allowed. Congress pledged to wrest from the states the means to satisfy all the country's creditors, a feat it heretofore was never able to do. The disclosure of this resolution, which vowed to employ authority that Congress did not possess, might have backfired on Washington. Rather than inspire confidence, the timid promises only confirmed the impotence of the national governing body.[38]

In the Temple of Virtue at the encampment at New Windsor, about 150 officers gathered on March 15, ostensibly to hear the latest report from their committee to Congress. Washington's choice of date was no random act but rather a conscious decision to call the conspirators' attention to another Ides of March, nearly two millennia before, where the course of the western world was decided by the assassination of dictator Julius Caesar. Unlike with that murder and the struggle for power that followed, Washington was determined not to let them "overturn the liberties of ... [the] country ... open the floodgates of civil discord and deluge … [the] rising … [American] empire in blood." Unexpectedly and certainly not welcomed by the plotters, he appeared at the meeting and addressed the esteemed gathering:

> GENTLEMEN,
>
> By an anonymous summons, an attempt has been made to convene you together. How inconsistent with the rules of propriety, how unmilitary and how subversive of all order and discipline let the good sense of the army decide….
>
> The way is plain, says the anonymous addresser. If war continues, remove into the unsettled country, there establish yourselves, and leave an ungrateful country to defend itself…. If peace takes place, never sheath your sword, says he until you have obtained full and ample justice. This dreadful alternative, of deserting our country in the extremest hour of her distress or turning our arms against it (which is the apparent object unless Congress can be compelled into instant compliance) has something so shocking in it that humanity revolts at the idea….
>
> And let me conjure you in the name of our common country, as you value your own sacred honor, as you respect the rights of humanity, as you regard the military and national character of America, to express your utmost horror and detestation of the man who wishes, under any specious pretenses, to overturn the liberties of our country and who wickedly attempts to open the floodgates of civil discord and deluge our rising empire in blood….
>
> You will give one more distinguished proof of unexampled patriotism and patient virtue, rising superior to the pressure of the most complicated sufferings. And you will, by the dignity of your conduct, afford for posterity to say, when speaking of the glorious example you have exhibited to mankind: Had this day been wanting, the world had never seen the last stage of perfection to which human nature is capable of attaining.[39]

Washington poured out his heart to them, but so deep was their resentment that by and large, most of them were still unmoved. Never having given a speech to an assemblage of his officers before, he was first at a loss as to how to respond to their dismissal of his plea. In a fit of desperation, he reached into his pocket and pulled out a private letter from Congressman Joseph Jones, one of the military's staunchest supporters. Washington struggled to read it to them, but his eyesight was failing. His speech, in his own hand, was in large letters, but the Jones letter was written in smaller script, making it very difficult to read. He finally set it down and pulled out his new spectacles. Just a few at headquarters had ever seen him wearing them. This was his first use of them in public. Washington put on his spectacles and, in a self-effacing manner, "begged the indulgence of his audience while he put them on, observing at the same time, that he had grown gray in their service, and now found himself growing blind." While not present at the speech, Lieutenant Colonel David Cobb repeated the story of fellow aide Lieutenant Colonel Jonathan Trumbull about Washington, saying, "Gentlemen, you will permit me to put on my spectacles, for I have not only grown gray, but almost blind, in the service of my country."[40]

Gone for that poignant moment was the iconic great captain on horseback, and in his stead was revealed a fellow sufferer, aged beyond his years. Extremely difficult for such a proud man, this humble admission of human frailty unleashed a tidal wave of emotion. "There was something so natural, so unaffected, in this appeal, as it rendered it superior to the most studied oratory; it forced its way to the heart."[41] Some cried or choked back tears. Others felt the burn as their feelings of shame increased the flow of blood to their faces. The physical embodiment of the American cause turning against the government was an indictment against Washington. Overcome by this you respect the rights of humanity, & as you regard the Military & National character of America, to express your utmost horror & detestation of the Man who wishes, under any specious pretences, to overturn the liberties of our Country, & who wickedly attempts to open the flood Gates of Civil discord, & deluge our rising Empire in blood. —

By thus determining—& thus acting, you will pursue the plain & direct road to the attainment of your wishes. — You will defeat the insidious designs of our Enemies, who are compelled to resort from open force to secret artifice. — You will give one more distinguished proof of unexampled patriotism & patient virtue, rising superior to the pressure of the most complicated sufferings; — And you will, by the dignity of your Conduct, afford occasion for Posterity to say, when speaking of the glorious example you have exhibited to Mankind,—"had this day been wanting, "the World had never seen the last stage "of perfection to which human nature "is capable of attaining"

G:º Washington

compassionate response, Washington finished his speech and left as unceremoniously as he had arrived. According to Pickering, who wrote to his assistant and friend Samuel Hodgdon the following day about the meeting, Washington read the entire Jones letter or at least the pertinent passages. The Virginia legislator recounted the concerted efforts under way to permanently fund Congress and the need for the army to wait just a little while longer. While adding further to their acclaim, their stoicism was the best tack to receive their due. Threats would only harden the intransigence of certain congressmen to national revenue-raising authority. While not mentioning Washington putting on his spectacles, the quartermaster general did believe that the reading of the Jones letter was not planned. Many years later, Pickering still held to his view that it was an impromptu act. He did, however, with the passage of time recognize the significance of Washington donning his spectacles. "The incident, apparently, & I believe really casual, seemed to me to have a happy effect, in producing a sympathetic feeling in the audience." Astutely confirming the support of key leaders and increasingly exerting control over the situation in the days before the officer meeting, Washington must have contemplated responses if his speech fell flat, including playing the martyr.[42]

From his command at West Point, General Knox looked with apprehension at the events unfolding in New Windsor. Though he was one of the most outspoken supporters of the nationalist cause and had helped draft the officers' memorial to Congress, he did not advocate a heavy-handed approach. Counted on by Washington, Knox, after thanking the commander in chief for "his excellent speech," led the assembly in quickly renouncing the base summonses. He then guided the preparation of yet another pleading resolution, but this time it worked to a point.[43] Taking the initiative away from the instigators, General Putnam proposed the formation of a panel, representing all levels of command, to draft the objectives of the assembly. This was seconded by Adjutant General Hand, and the officers accepted and agreed that Knox, Lieutenant Colonel John Brooks, and Captain Howard (probably Captain Benjamin Heyward of the 6th Massachusetts, who would have brought his prior experience as regimental paymaster) would compose the committee. They had half an hour to frame their findings. Testifying before the packed hall immediately afterward, they first stated their "unshaken confidence in the Justice of Congress" and that they viewed "with abhorrence, and reject with disdain, the infamous propositions contained in a late anonymous address to the officers of the army." The group finished with praise for its committee to Congress pursuing since January the following:

1. Present pay
2. A settlement of the Arrearages of Pay and security for what Is due.
3. A commutation of the half pay allowed by different resolutions of Congress for an equivalent in gross.
4. A settlement of the accounts of deficiencies of rations and compensation.
5. A settlement of the accounts of deficiencies of cloathing and compensation.

Packed with Washington loyalists, the committee did as the commander in chief expected. Knox's faithfulness was well known, and Colonel Brooks had already shown

Opposite: **The last page of Washington's speech to his officers. Note the large size of the script. (Collection of the Massachusetts Historical Society).**

his fidelity by revealing that there was a plot to incite the army. The last member of this group, Captain Heyward, one of General Rufus Putnam's officers, was counted on to support the arguments of his brigade commander. Calling for the formation of this panel, Putnam a day or two before wrote a detailed rebuttal to Armstrong's remonstrances, but the rejoinder was never presented to the officers in camp. The question is why. It is quite probable during Washington's appeal to the brigade commanders prior to the March 15 showdown that Putnam disclosed to him his response and that the commanding general asked him to hold off from doing anything with it. Having already decided to deal with the crisis head-on, Washington would not have wanted any other effort to lessen the impact of his surprise direct challenge to the plotters. Additionally, the distribution of Putnam's letter would have invited harangues from others including Armstrong, further muddying an already confusing situation. A copy written by Knox's aide Captain John Lillie is preserved in the artillery general's papers. It is likely that this document was used as a reference during the committee's deliberations.[44]

The storm had passed, ending the last major crisis of the American Revolution. Instead of fomenting unrest among the disgruntled soldiery, the officers would do their utmost to ensure that the men were peacefully dispersed to their homes. The country could look ahead to a bright future where the rule of law, not the passion of designing men, governed. In his dexterous defense of civilian control over the military, Washington made his most important contribution to the democratic experiment in the United States except for his stepping down after two terms as the nation's leader.

While Benson Lossing in his mid–19th-century biography of Philip Schuyler cited a subsequently missing source that placed the New York congressional delegate and former Continental Army major general at this meeting, there are no other accounts that corroborate this information. Schuyler was known to have been at Kingston, about 40 miles away, that morning attending a session of the New York State Senate, but it was still possible for him to have arrived in time for the noon meeting. Plausibly, Washington or someone else could have contacted him or, paying a courtesy call at headquarters, he agreed to accompany the commander in chief to camp. One could imagine Washington saying, "Come Philip, let us surprise our old friend." Besides the commanding general, the last person Gates would have wanted to see was the man he ruthlessly supplanted as commander of the northern army in 1777. Had Schuyler been present, he would have disconcerted Gates, buttressed Washington, and been an influential witness to the proceedings. In his lost letter to Stephen Van Rensselaer written two days later, Schuyler was quoted by Lossing as saying that "the whole assembly were in tears at the conclusion of his address. I rode with General Knox to his quarters in absolute silence, because of the solemn impression on our minds. I have no doubt that posterity will repeat the closing words of his Excellency's speech—'Had this day been wanting, the world would have never seen the last stage of perfection to which human nature is capable of attaining.'"[45]

Not everyone, however, was ready to acquiesce so easily. Colonel Pickering, the beleaguered supply officer who experienced the wrath of everyone including Washington because he lacked the funds to execute the duties of his office, disgustedly related to his wife that "the result of this meeting has given me another instance of the fickleness of popular assemblies; and shows how easily a fluent orator, with plausibility only to support him, may govern them as he will." To Samuel Hodgdon, Pickering dipped his pen in acid and wrote, "Was it wise to adopt a resolution that would brand with infamy the man, the brother officer, whose watchful eye & able pen might discover and save them from the evils which ingratitude & injustice might bring.... And thus the body of officers, in a moment, damned with infamy two publications which during the four preceding days most of them read with admiration & talked of with rapture." Pickering tried to object not to the whole proceedings but instead to the cowardly disavowal of the sentiments expressed in the two letters. No one seconded him. He did not vote for the final resolutions, but he was in the minority.[46]

The specter of military revolt spurred Congress to finally act. On March 22 the officer pension settlement was finally approved, a commutation of the half-pay for life into full pay for five years in cash or in government securities at 6 percent annual interest. For the 2,480 officers eligible for the pension, five years' full pay amounted to approximately $5 million, nearly double the estimate to pay the entire army for 1783. Several state legislatures, however, balked at the measure and received approval for working out an accommodation with their officers to compensate them in a manner acceptable to the public.[47] Pleased by the quick response, Washington wrote to Elias Boudinot, the president of Congress, that the measures would increase army faith in their countryman and convince those who served of the sincerity of the legislators. Officers under his command had until April 25 to take or refuse the lump sum commutation of the half-pay. Wasting little time, the officers of the Massachusetts Line unanimously accepted the offer just a couple of days after the question was presented to them. By the end of April, Washington was able to report to Secretary at War Lincoln that all of his officers except for the distant Rhode Islanders had given their assent to commutation.[48] Guarding the approaches to Albany, the Rhode Island officers shortly thereafter conveyed their approval.

Though Washington unexpectedly attended the March 15 meeting and shamed the officers into denouncing the proceedings of the past week and pledging obeisance to Congress, the crisis was not yet over. Warning Joseph Jones a few days later, Washington stated that he had calmed everything down for now, but Congress had to fulfill the nation's promises to the army or risk another possibly more dangerous disturbance.[49] Learning that Robert Morris was suspected of being behind the intrigue, Washington was incredulous that the people principally responsible for establishing independence were "made use of as mere Puppets to establish Continental funds ... [and] that the Army (considering the irritable state it is in, its sufferings and composition) is a dangerous instrument to play with." He later attributed the plan for inciting the army to achieve the nationalist political agenda mostly to Gouverneur Morris. Both the superintendent of finance and his assistant were involved. No sooner had the legislators consented to lift the "injunction of secrecy" than someone, possibly Robert Morris himself, gave a copy of his resignation letter to printer Eleazer Oswald, who published it on March 1 in his Philadelphia newspaper, the *Independent Gazetteer*. The story was quickly picked up by papers domestically and around the Atlantic world. Morris's silence on the Newburgh Conspiracy in the weeks following the affair speaks volumes. Timed for effect, his request to the president of Congress to make his resignation public at the end of February casts further doubt on Morris's innocence. Not replying to any of Washington's correspondence since early April, Morris on May 29, before addressing the business at hand, spent two pages defending himself from charges of being a "Leader of Sedition."[50] Washington suspected that Hamilton was involved as well, but his former aide was his only channel for getting additional information about the plot. Given his intimate association with the commander in chief and other influential men in the Continental Army, knowledge of the situation in camp, and well-known aspiration for a stronger confederation, Hamilton was quite a trophy for the schemers. Moreover, his soaring intellect and persuasive arguments were handy to have at one's disposal, as was his able poison pen to disarm opponents. Indiscrete and sometimes toxic, Hamilton had a big mouth, which led to the duel in which he was killed by Aaron Burr.

Gates's finances were in a perilous condition by this point. He was heavily in debt to Robert Morris, so if he did not openly push the matter, his interests lay with threatening Congress. In rationalizing the incident in June, Gates asserted that they had only the aim of "getting the army to cooperate with the civil creditors, as the way most likely to obtain justice." At the end of March, Gates had left for his home in Virginia to be with his ailing wife. She died in June. Though far removed from the scene, he lamented to Pickering in May that he felt "the Distresses of the poor fellows who have been our Faithful Companions through the War, as if those Distresses were all my own."[51] During a visit to Philadelphia at the end of April, Colonel Ogden told Major Armstrong that the officers greatly regretted not continuing to aggressively pursue the redress of their grievances and that the opportune moment had passed. Since the announcement of peace, all the soldiers wanted to do was go home, effectively ending their use as a bluff. After obtaining the consent of General Washington, Ogden was in the capital to get Congress's permission to go on a business trip to Europe. Having given up on the frustrating negotiations, he took an unauthorized leave ostensibly to visit his family in New Jersey, but he was also possibly seeking to convince his state's congressmen to change their vote in favor of commutation. When the army delegation first arrived in January, he vowed not to return to camp without an acceptable answer to the memorial. Though commutation was achieved, pay and subsistence payments were still outstanding. Ogden kept his pledge and never went back.[52]

Ogden went on to disclose that a "timid Wretch discovered it to the only man from whom he was to have kept it, and concealed it from those to whom he had expressly engaged to make it known." Entrusted with the same instructions from the nationalists as Colonel Stewart "to prepare ... [the officers'] minds for some manly, vigorous, Association with the other public Creditors," Lieutenant Colonel Brooks instead went to the commander in chief, concluding that Washington would protect him. The conspirators intended to consult Washington but much later in the process. Balancing the committee as a representative from New England, if the Massachusetts lieutenant colonel was selected also as a voice of reason and moderation, this choice backfired. Shrinking before this immense responsibility, he did not have the heart to follow through with the plot. Backed by soldiers with muskets, battlefield heroics was one thing, but Brooks did not possess the courage to singularly challenge both Ogden and, more ominously, the former Sons of Liberty street tough McDougall. It was not that Ogden did not have some impropriety in his past. Stooping to extortion before to get his way, he had no scruples about employing the necessary subterfuge to arouse Congress. In 1779, the officers of his brigade submitted a remonstrance to the New Jersey Assembly demanding their pay, subsistence, and clothing allowances in coin or otherwise calculated to account for depreciation. When nothing was done, Ogden personally went to the legislature and told its members that they had three days to provide relief or else at the end of that time the officers of his regiment would consider themselves out of the army. This was a dangerous precedent that chagrined Washington, and state officials quickly acted to avert the walkout. After recounting to Gates Brooks's betrayal, Armstrong went on to write that he intended to compose another anonymous letter but gave up the idea, as having "seen the impotency of the army and the Assurance of Congress—they see our weakness and laugh at our resentments.... The army look back with horror and regret upon the mistaken step they have taken and like contemptible penitents who have sinned beyond the prospect of salvation, wish to have it to do over again. It is now, however, too late."[53] Accompanying the specie delivery in mid-February, Brooks carried to General Knox, the army's chosen spokesman, the report of the committee to Congress, a letter from Gouverneur Morris, and probably the letter signed with only the pseudonym of Brutus. At the same time, Morris wrote another letter to General Greene promoting the same idea of bringing together the pressure of all national creditors, both public and private, and not dividing the army's effort by resorting to seeking redress separately with their individual states.[54] Those seeking Continental funds opposed any recourse to the states.

Accounting the discouraging meetings with congressional representatives in their report, McDougall and Ogden indicated that Brooks had additional information that they did not want to commit to paper. Presumably, Brooks was to communicate the same course of action recommended by Brutus, the transparent pseudonym of McDougall, in a letter to Knox written in mid-February and in another one at the end of the month that the officers prepare themselves to pressure Congress into agreeing not to disband the army without a final settlement of accounts if they would not do it of their own accord. A decision on this matter was expected shortly, so Knox was told to do nothing until the pleasure of the legislators was known. Taking it upon themselves to make that declaration would "disgrace the national character." Brutus hoped that justice would be done without the threat of violence, but he warned that they needed to ready themselves for any eventuality. Brooks was supposed to importune the officers to support this stratagem. Knox considered "the reputation of the American Army, as one of the most immaculate things upon earth, and that we should even suffer wrongs, and injuries to the utmost verge of toleration, rather than sully it in the least degree." He did, however, conclude this observation ominously: "But there is a point, beyond which, there is no sufferance. I pray sincerely we may not pass it." He was not going to do anything but grumble. After Knox expressed his dread of the army resorting to coercion and Brooks's failure to act, the advocates of a stronger central government turned next to Gates, choosing his former aide Colonel Stewart as their messenger. But forewarned by Brooks of the plot, Washington undoubtedly had already considered potential countermeasures. Adding fuel to the fire was that legislators did not accede to the request to settle the military's accounts before disbandment. A sense of urgency pervaded this intrigue as well due to the pending announcement of peace. Gates was aware of at least some of the machinations afoot, but Knox's leadership of the officers' efforts to petition Congress and the high regard in which he was held by all parties made the artillery general the logical first choice of the nationalist faction. Hamilton shrewdly pointed out to Washington in February that Knox "has the confidence of the army & is a man of sense. I think he may safely be made use of." Having been too long the "representative of fools and Rascals," General McDougall "closed his embassy" to Congress at the end of May and returned to the army enclave in the Hudson Valley.[55]

CHAPTER 8

"Awakening again the spirit of Emulation and love of Military Parade"
Manning the Force and Training for Battle

After years of war, finding acceptable recruits was very difficult. Officials could enlist inhabitants from their own state between the ages of 16 and 50 who were able to withstand the rigors of military service. Individuals on either side of those parameters, however, did slip through. Limiting their authority to recruit only among state residents was intended to prevent individuals from enlisting multiple times and absconding with the bounty. Eventually Continental officers were assigned to oversee the mustering of these new soldiers. When state officials oversaw the screening, the army received "hundreds, of old Men, mere children, disordered and decripid persons." Pressured to produce, recruiting officers could not afford to be too particular. Besides, they received $2 for every man who enlisted for the war.[1] Despite the best efforts to keep out questionable recruits, they continued to enter the service. Tipping the scales at over 250 pounds, 8th Massachusetts commander Colonel Michael Jackson was a dominating presence with boldness to match his voluminous size. Despite the protests of mustering officers and other officials, he took into his regiment in January 1777 all five of his sons, ranging in age from 10 to 18. The youngest three, he insisted, could perform the duty of musicians. By the end of the war, four remained in the Continental Army and were officers at the New Windsor Cantonment.[2]

Attrition seriously impacted the capability of the regiments. Gains no way near made up for losses. With the Continental Army force to periodically consolidate and reorganize, this continual flux prevented the development of the cohesion necessary for units to operate at peak efficiency. During this process officers were "deranged," left out of the new arrangement, and compelled to leave the service. Appointed by the stroke of a pen from Congress or the states, there were always more seekers than officer positions. The same, however, could not be said for the enlisted men. Getting individuals to turn out for emergencies was one thing, but convincing them to sign on for lengthy periods of time or for an undefined term was very difficult. The exhilaration of the initial patriotism died quickly as Americans resigned themselves to a hard and prolonged struggle. In hindsight, all this suffering eventually ground down the British will to continue the conflict but did not encourage enlistments. The reasons for joining were as varied as the individuals. Boredom, the desire to serve with family members or friends, community pressure, and the pay and clothing issue were some of the more common reasons. But it was never easy to attract independent-minded Americans to willingly give up their freedom, so the recruiting of new soldiers was one of the greatest challenges faced by authorities. Many valuable officers were detached to perform this critical service. Though there was a cash bonus and the promise of clothes to entice prospective recruits, few were willing to join. With so many objectionable enlistees being foisted upon the army by less than discerning officers, authorities made an example of Lieutenant Colonel Ezra Badlam of the 8th Massachusetts Regiment. He was charged with enlisting deserters from both the French and British, who were precluded by law, and undersized boys, "an idiot" and "a negroe lame in the ancle." Convicted of conduct unbecoming an officer and neglect of duty, Badlam was found guilty and dismissed from the service. Despite the example made of him, recruiters were still accepting men from the French service. Embarrassed by the entire situation, Washington pledged to Admiral Vaudreuil that he would "prevent in future any Mischiefs of that nature" and return any that are found.[3] While drawing the line on deserters, the Americans were not above enlisting soldiers from among the prisoners of war. At the end of December 1782, 120 or 130 volunteers from Burgoyne's and Cornwallis's armies were sent from their prison camp outside of York, Pennsylvania, to fill out the ranks of the Continental Army in the Hudson Valley.[4] With Black soldiers, there was always the question of whether they were free or enslaved. An enslaved person had to have permission from his master to join. Captain Hobby tried unsuccessfully to retrieve his slave, serving in the ranks of his 3rd Massachusetts Regiment. Washington would not release the man without a replacement.[5]

From the beginning of 1780 to the following spring, the Massachusetts Line had been hemorrhaging men. During that period over 5,000 left the ranks, which amounted to almost three times its size in March 1781. A small number died, deserted, or were taken prisoner, but the overwhelming majority were simply discharged from the service.[6] The Continental Army was ostensibly a volunteer force. Soldiers enlisted for either a set length of time or for the duration of the war. Some were drafted or levied from the state militia to augment the army for short periods of time, usually for a campaign. By the middle of the war, enthusiasm for military service had waned considerably. Desperate to entice recruits, Massachusetts officials started to offer substantial incentives for short-term enlistments. Calculating men saw an opportunity to hire themselves out for the bounty and clothing, do just several months of duty, and then join again for another bonus. This practice was bitterly resented by the soldiers who enlisted for longer periods. To attempt to address this inequity, Massachusetts in early 1781 gave every man who only received "a small bounty" for enlisting for the war a gratuity of $24 in specie to show them that they were "yet the objects of a friendly recollection." "Short inlistments ... [were an] extravagant expence to Towns and Individuals"; were "destructive of Order, Oeconomy and [the] System ... [of] Finances; and were "the chief source of the disappointments, misfortunes and perplexities" and "the great cause of protracting the War." Strategically, the reduction of the American army at the end of every year enabled the enemy to detach large numbers of soldiers for expeditions elsewhere with impunity.[7]

Moreover, recruits required constant training in drill and discipline, which reduced the veteran instructors to "perpetual slaves." They were deficient in not only marching and the manual arms but also obedience, an intangible military necessity. Less altruistic and patriotic, the short-term soldiers were often just interested in the pay and benefits and were a cancer in the ranks. This constant stream of resistant civilian attitudes and opportunism undermined authority and infected the minds of the long-serving soldiers. Disgusted by this servitude, Gilbert, a sergeant at that time, believed that officials could have enlisted the recruits for a longer period at the same price they paid for six months' service. During the enlistees' short term, the regiments pressured them to remain in the ranks, usually unsuccessfully. Explaining the frustration of devoting a considerable amount of time to make the new recruits serviceable only to see them leave shortly thereafter, Washington tried to convince Congress to draft men for the war, but the representatives were unwilling to take such an objectionable step. In October 1780, Congress recommended that the states fill up their lines by drafting men who would serve for at least one year unless they were replaced sooner by a long-term enlistee.[8] This stopgap would give them more time to find men who would agree to sign on for a few years or for the duration.

In 1782, New Hampshire despaired of "raising either Men or Money." Massachusetts voted for 1,500, half the number required. Connecticut also agreed to pay for only half of its deficiency of 1,475, substantial numbers of which would only serve until the end of the year. Rhode Island raised men for nine months, while New York drafted men from its militia who would only serve until January 1783. New Jersey relied only on a small cash bounty to entice recruits, so its prospects of substantial augmentation were quite remote.[9] Grasping at any measure to increase the number of soldiers enlisted for longer durations, Washington wrote to Lieutenant Colonel Frederick Weissenfels of the New York Levies that many of his men would probably join the Continental Line if they were encouraged by him and his officers.[10] With recruits so hard to obtain and his position dependent on maintaining his unit's strength, the financially strapped former Prussian, Dutch, and British officer was not likely to urge any soldiers to leave his command. Washington was so desperate to fill the ranks that he ordered the senior leadership of every state represented in his army to compile rosters of every deserter going back to 1777, giving each deserter's description, location of enlistment, and term of service, to send to their governors for use in retrieving them.[11] Serving in the 15th Massachusetts Regiment at Saratoga, Valley Forge, Monmouth, and Newport, Private Benjamin Parker did not receive a desired furlough in September 1778, so he deserted. Accepting the amnesty offer of Washington and that of the State of Massachusetts enacted on June 5, 1780, he returned on February 4, 1781, and was assigned to the 5th Massachusetts. Seeing little good from these pardons, the commander in chief believed that they encouraged desertion, because the soldiers left the ranks or overstayed an authorized leave at home and then waited "for a proclamation as a thing of course." Completing his original obligation, Parker then served the term of John Bond.[12]

Once a month, the brigades were mustered and inspected. To ensure the integrity of the examination, inspecting officers were from outside of the organization. During the muster, the number of effective and noneffective soldiers was tallied to give commanders an assessment of the available strength of the army. There was quite a difference between the paper count and the actual amount available for duty. Further reducing combat power, there were a number of soldiers used as servants. They were categorized as being with arms or without arms. The servants without arms only had to appear at the monthly inspection. While exempt from regular guard mounts and other camp duties, the ones with arms had to appear when the regiment paraded and whenever the officer on whom they waited had duty, in addition to the monthly inspections. General officers of the line were allowed four servants, while colonels, lieutenant colonels, and majors two servants, and captains, subalterns, surgeons, and mates had one servant. Officers of the staff were similarly provided, but several civilian workers in those departments had them as well when they were not authorized to have any. Washington was astonished to discover that there were also officers who had retired from the service who still retained servants. The civilians and retired officers were ordered to return them to their regiments as soon as possible. A few were lax in ensuring that their servants appeared at the musters when they were close enough to easily attend them. Inspectors were ordered to report the offenders to headquarters.[13] Besides the servants, there were soldiers in the hospital, on furlough, on detached duty, and absent for myriad other reasons. As many as a third of the army might not be available, so getting every possible body at the muster was essential.

With so many absent, military drill and training were far less effective. Repetition instilled in the memory the appropriate response to the practiced maneuvers. Consistency in knowing who is giving commands and what the expectations are, the uniform conduct of the various exercises, and the demonstrated reactions of the soldiers on your right and left, front, or rear made the men understand their role in the line of battle. When soldiers were standing next to dependable friends and comrades, their nerve and resolve were steadied by the resulting esprit de corps. Missing officers and soldiers forced the regiments to reorganize, placing leaders and men in unaccustomed positions and surroundings. While the drill manual did ground the army in the basic practices, certain commanders preferred some maneuvers over others and put their personal interpretation to the regulations. The Continental Army organized and trained for battle, according to the *Regulations for the Order and Discipline of the Troops of the United States*, developed by Major General Friedrich von Steuben at Valley Forge, Pennsylvania, in 1778 and published the following year. Training his model companies personally, he developed a drill that would endure into the War of 1812. A retired officer from the vaunted army of King Frederick the Great of Prussia, von Steuben through his knowledge and zeal earned the position of inspector general, the officer primarily responsible for assessing army adherence to established standards. His manual was a simple and comprehensive methodology for training. Von Steuben's teachings also included the manner to lay out encampments and preserve their order and cleanliness, the conduct of inspections, roll calls, guard duty, drum calls, preservation of arms and ammunition, treatment of the sick, and the responsibilities of every individual position. While devoting some time to the musket drill, he concentrated on forming and maneuvering the various subdivisions of the army. Deploying into a position of advantage quickly and in an organized a manner as possible was the goal, but most important was the capability to withdraw from a dangerous situation in an orderly fashion.

A typical battle formation consisted of brigades in line, with artillery interspersed among them. Brigades consisted of two to five regiments. During the New Windsor Cantonment, the main threat was the British forces in New York City, so all the artillery was left at West Point. Eight companies of the regiment fought in a two-rank battle line, sometimes further divided into two battalions, to ease command and control. Normally the taller soldiers were in the back, with the shortest of both ranks in the center of each line. This disposition was necessary because the front rank did not kneel during firing. The rear rank simply stepped to the right and fired over the shoulder of the soldiers in front of them. During some inspections when Washington was particularly trying to please the reviewer, he wanted "the tallest men ... to be in the front rank." The drummers and fifers were on the flanks unless the regiment was formed into two battalions. In this configuration, one pair of musicians was moved from the flanks to behind the second battalion symmetrical to the drum major and fife major, centered in the back of the first, and another four sets were placed in the middle.[14]

The ninth company, light infantry, served with other chosen men and was organized into battalions. Composed of the best soldiers in a regiment, light infantry were used as shock troops to attack critical enemy positions or acted to guard the front, rear, and flanks of the army. Washington preferred robust men of medium stature. The assistant inspector general was ordered to examine all the light infantry and dismiss anyone who did not have the requisite appearance and discipline. Because of the important duties they performed, it was essential to maintain them at full strength, necessitating periodic drafts from the battalion companies. Sometimes employed in extended order, separated from others by several yards or in small groups where they might go up against individual enemy soldiers, the light infantrymen were reminded to pick out a target to engage and not just fire in the target's general direction.[15]

The battalion companies, formed in two lines, massed their fire with volleys to compensate for musket inaccuracy, so aiming was less critical. Firepower was important, but it was not always the determining factor in battle. Discipline that enabled soldiers to maintain their formations under fire and withstand casualties without fleeing the battlefield was equally crucial. Lining up men also answered the psychological need to bunch together in times of danger and took advantage of the herd mentality, the submission to the influence of peers and authority figures on an emotional rather than rational basis. Appealing to personal pride and obligation to the country, leaders and comrades deftly employed shame, the same moral cudgel wielded against individuals since they were old enough to understand the concept. Fiery preachers threatened the wrath of the Almighty upon whoever did not do what was expected of them. Were it not for higher ideals, reasonable beings would not risk their life for such abstract concepts as loyalty, honor, and duty. Steadied by the example and, when necessary, the coercion of veteran officers and noncommissioned officers, spread throughout and around their ranks, the soldiers, intimidated by the consequences of personal failure, struggled to the limits of their ability and courage to obey. Expected to lead from the front, officers strove to master the art of battlefield maneuvering, because fortitude was not enough; tactical competence and above all judgment were essential. Even with these core capabilities and a numerous well-trained, decently clad, and adequately fed force deployed on favorable ground, they also had to recognize the inherent risks of their decisions, the element of chance, and the maxim that the enemy has a voice and, with the British Army, a stentorian one.

The distance when opposing sides started to fire on one another varied considerably, but normally it was no more than 200 yards. While it is true that the horrific casualties of American Civil War battlefields were due to the Minié ball, fired from the muzzle-loading rifled musket, another significant factor was the engagement distance between opposing lines. Despite the improvements in technology, there were instances when Civil War commanders, trusting in the mettle of their men, led them right into the teeth of the enemy, pitting them in short-range firefights that turned into bitter slogging matches of attrition. With some notable exceptions, this approach was unheard of during the first half of the Revolution, where exchanges of musket fire were generally at greater distances and of short duration. Expecting his men to close with the enemy, Washington advised his officers in the summer of 1780 to watch their soldiers so they did not expend their ammunition at excessive ranges and then plead when their cartridge boxes were empty to leave the field. In the event they ran out, they were to stand their ground with just their muskets and bayonets, making it unlikely they would ever slyly shoot away their cartridges again.[16]

Once the fighting commenced, it was very difficult to get the formations to fire volleys simultaneously. With their voices drowned out by the noise of battle, officers did well to get a company to fire in unison. Commanders had to constantly look to their right and left for cues as to what to do, provided it was possible to see through the white plumes of smoke. In some cases, military maneuvers looked staggered due to the lag time for leaders to recognize the action of other units and then conform to their movements. Redeploying your men based on a misinterpretation of what others were doing or blindly following the lead of someone else could have fatal consequences. Moreover, soldiers were not chess pieces or toys and at times required prodding and manhandling to get them to execute orders. One of the most complicated and important maneuvers was forming a line from a column of platoons. Half of a company, the platoon had approximately 10 to 15 men in each rank. From this base unit in the von Steuben drill, officers formed companies, battalions, regiments, brigades, and divisions. A battalion column was eight platoons following one after the other. With such a narrow frontage, the column could be moved very quickly. To form a two-rank battle line from a column, the base platoon halted at the chosen position, and then the remaining platoons marched to either the left or right of the base platoon or in both directions until all were deployed. A regiment had over 200 soldiers standing shoulder to shoulder in each of these two lines. Stationary or advancing very slowly to maintain order, a battle line was the best formation to use during contact with the enemy. But it was very difficult to maneuver in the face of fences, buildings, and other obstacles. When deployed this way, the maximum number of muskets could be brought to bear, and a wall of steel was presented with the bayonets. It was not common for opposing forces to get close enough to engage in hand-to-hand combat, but in the night attacks on the fortifications of Stony Point, New York, in 1779 and Redoubt Number 10 at Yorktown, Virginia, in 1781, the American light infantry went in with unloaded muskets and fixed bayonets. During the desperate fighting in the South in the latter part of the war, instances of close-quarter fighting increased, the inevitable result when veterans squared off.

Though the column was a very flexible and quick form of maneuver, it was also potentially very dangerous. Solid shot fired from an artillery piece would plow through several lines of soldiers before its momentum was spent. At close range, the artillerists fired tins of small iron balls called case shot that increased in size and diameter with the bore of the gun and also fired canister, musket balls packed into a similar container. Alone or in combination with musketry, the concentrated fire would shatter the head of a column. Conversely, cannonballs fired at a line would at most hit three or four, and the effect of case shot, canister, or musket fire would have far less impact dispersed throughout the length of the formation. Also, soldiers caught in a column can bring to bear only the two rows of muskets in the front. Another very difficult maneuver was turning the linear formations. Swinging the lines like a gate on its hinges either to the right or left, the wheeling line faced the same dangers as a column of platoons if its flank crossed in front of artillery or an enemy battle line. Prone to bowing in the middle when done in line, the wheel was best executed at the platoon level, but von Steuben said it could be done "even [by] a battalion."[17] Far preferable was the oblique step, where the soldiers kept their bodies to the front while stepping off at a 45-degree angle to the right or left. This movement did not expose the flanks to enemy fire.

While hailed as a transformative event in the development of the Continental Army, improvements in discipline had a human cost, evident in the fighting following the loss of Charleston, South Carolina, in May 1780. Emboldened by their experience, training, and pride, the Continentals' maintenance of their positions in the face of approaching enemy battle lines and increasing instances of their intentionally engaging in close-quarter combat took its toll. The core of the armies in the south were small numbers who bore the brunt of the fighting and consequently suffered most of the casualties. These American regulars' inspiring example steadied the militia, and their epic stands also enabled the part-time soldiers to save themselves during battlefield reverses. Except for his disputed claim of victory in the Battle of Eutaw Springs fought in September 1781, General Greene was narrowly defeated in every other encounter. Unflappable, he laconically observed to the commander in chief and a few others in the same vein that "we fight get beat and fight again."[18] With his Continentals to rally around, Greene did just that. This resilience helped win the war.

No matter how many times soldiers maneuvered and performed the manual of arms, there was always room for improvement. Reviews were conducted at every opportunity. The elaborate ceremonies celebrating the juncture of the French and American armies at Verplanck's Point in September 1782 culminated in a large-scale deployment, but that was an anomaly. Typically, maneuvers were conducted at brigade level or below due to space limitations. Washington watched these exercises with a scrutinizing eye. There was little that escaped his attention. He spared no ink in specifying in minute detail any deficiencies. On one occasion, he observed that the soldiers were not only out of step but also did "not step boldly and freely; but short and with bent knees."[19] In an organization where honor was prized above all other personal traits, Washington sought to improve the conduct of the army by appealing to the soldiers where they were most vulnerable: their pride. He based his findings on his own observations and reports received from the inspector general. Von Steuben and his assistants examined every aspect of army operations. By regulations, the senior assistant inspector, the adjutant general, commanded the inspectors and assigned their duties. This was not their responsibility alone. The Prussian wrote in his manual that "the oftener the soldiers are under the inspection of their officers the better."[20] Every morning, officers were to scrutinize the soldiers' clothing and make sure that their hair was combed, their faces and hands were washed, and their accoutrements were in order. Most important was the review of the arms and ammunition.

The parade grounds for the 1st and 3rd Massachusetts Brigades were directly in front of their huts on the eastern side of Beaver Dam Stream. Those of the New York, New Jersey, Maryland, and New Hampshire Lines were in front of their huts on the western side of that watercourse. The 2nd Massachusetts Brigade parade was located between their huts and the Goshen Road. Formations, roll calls, and some maneuvers were conducted on these cleared areas. To ready the ground for use, soldiers took away movable obstructions and dug up any stumps or cut them flush. Washington ordered the brigade commanders at the end of March 1783 to inform him of their selected maneuvering ground, but except for the 2nd Brigade, there were no suitable places other than the limited spaces immediately in front of their huts.[21]

The ability to perform the manual of arms and execute the varied drill maneuvers was a perishable skill, so Washington wanted the soldiers paraded as soon as the weather permitted. He wanted to again awaken the "love of Military Parade and glory, which was conspicuous the last campaign." Equally important was keeping alive the competition between the various corps, appealing to the human desire to outperform others. He also sought to galvanize the general officers commanding brigades. Their visible leadership was so essential that the commander in chief expected "to see the General Officers daily on Horseback at the Head of their Commands, teaching them by precept and example, every thing that is reputable and glorious in the profession of Arms." These considerations were the principal reasons for establishing this large encampment.[22] No matter how well soldiers and individual units were trained, large-size maneuvers were necessary to develop the requisite synergy for the army to act in concert. Bringing them together also ensured the uniform application of rules and regulations. Depending on the personality of the commander, detached units could vary from one extreme to the other in the way they enforced discipline.

CHAPTER 9

"No Military neglects or excesses shall go unpunished"

A Decline in Discipline and Increased Challenges to Authority

Lieutenant Gamaliel Bradford of the 7th Massachusetts Regiment had the misfortune of being observed personally by Washington "marching a Guard in a very irregular and unmilitary manner" on March 8, 1783, at a time when the commander in chief was looking to make an example out of someone to check a perceived slide in discipline. Admonishing the young officer in general orders, Washington warned the rest of the army that "no irregularity" that came to his attention would "pass unnoticed."[1] While General Washington thought on February 10, 1783, "that the hutts in point of convenience, regularity and elegance have equaled, if not surpassed his most sanguine expectations," he put forth several standing regulations on health and discipline. The soldiers were ordered to remove small brush and other rubbish away from their huts and parade grounds, where it was to be burned or otherwise disposed of. Riding with the secretary at war, a week later, Washington was very pleased with their efforts. General Lincoln was impressed by the sanitation and perfect order of the camp. In every brigade, a captain of police was charged with enforcing compliance.[2] Officers of police were to see that the huts were cleaned and swept out on a daily basis and that blankets were aired out on poles in the manner done by the 2nd Massachusetts. This regiment also swept out their fireplace hearths and put green brush in the chimneys. The way meals were cooked, the time they were consumed, and the overall messing arrangements were also scrutinized. With the weather improving, Lieutenant Colonel Ebenezer Sproat ordered his men on April 22 to use only the kitchens at the head of the parade ground. Cooking inside not only made the huts uncomfortable but also threatened the impressive health of the regiment. The month before, he ordered the construction of seven-foot-long forms supported by "firm crotches" for use in cutting and apportioning the meat ration. These structures were placed six feet in front of the poles for airing the blankets. Necessaries, vaults sunk in the ground for human waste, were built away from the hutting area and hidden from view. With the onset of warm weather, they were to be covered over daily with dirt. If fresh straw became available, soldiers would get a new supply every two months for use as bedding. By the middle of March, Colonel Pickering was told to get it to the men as soon as he could.[3] Despite Washington's orders to the contrary, the 3rd, 4th, 5th, and 8th Massachusetts Regiments were admonished in March for the "large quantity of Filth" about their encampments. They were ordered to immediately remove it. Archaeological investigation with ground-penetrating radar in the early 1980s showed that the camp, however, was generally kept clean.[4] Every morning, the captains of police reported to the field officer of the day, who by the spring operated out of a room in the Temple Building. Normally invited to share Washington's table during their tour, the field officers of the day were excused until they were relieved because headquarters was too far away. At the conclusion of their shift they went to Newburgh, where the commander in chief wished to share "the pleasure of their company."[5] In the informal setting of a meal, Washington received their reports and queried them about conditions within the army.

The first acknowledgment of imminent peace, which came at the end of March, further undermined how seriously the army took its military duties.[6] Increasingly petulant, the soldiers were harder to control after this news.

The officers only had themselves to blame for the deteriorating disciplinary situation. Their mutinous threats during the Newburgh Conspiracy infused the same spirit of resistance to lawful authority in their men. Mutiny, the collective resistance to authority, threatened the very existence of the army. No other force in the world would have continued in the face of such hardships. By the middle of the war, however, some of the soldiers were no longer willing to accept their condition. There was no lack of provisions in the country, but the inefficient suppliers could not always gather and, more importantly, transport the rations and other necessities to where they were most urgently needed. Throughout the war, there were several mutinies ignited by this continued neglect. Soldiers vented their frustrations by defiance and in a few instances by assaulting their superiors. Obedience and subordination were the foundations of military society, but disobedience and insubordination were common in the Continental Army. It was difficult to adjust from the familiarity enjoyed before the war with community members who were exalted to leadership positions. Discipline improved with time, however, as the soldiers adjusted to military life and the ranks were eventually filled with increasing numbers of veterans. Responsible for directing the daily lives of the soldiers and implementing military justice, the officers struggled to maintain order. They were guided by precedent, general orders, and the Articles of War, the Continental Congress's authorizing document for adjudicating military offenses. Passed on June 30, 1775, and comprising 69 articles, the army's justice system evolved throughout the war. Intended to be all-inclusive, commanders, however, still found ways to place their own stamp on its implementation.[7]

The systematic issuance of orders was critical to the smooth operation of this encampment. In the middle of April 1783, General Washington reinstated the daily levee. All officers, not otherwise engaged, were expected to attend this meeting, where the general officer of the day made his report and his relief received the daily orders and the passwords needed to enter and reenter the camp: the parole and countersign. Addressing topics important to all leaders, they heard how other officers were dealing with the increasing number of disciplinary problems and received guidance. Every general and head of department had to attend or send a representative. Hosted by the adjutant general, the levee was held at the Temple Building at noon every day. Beginning in the first week of May, the regiment on fatigue duty furnished three men led by a corporal to assist him with running the levees. With the camp in the process of being disbanded, the last levee was held on June 11, 1783.[8]

Officers and soldiers were punished for what they did or failed to do. There were a variety of transgressions. Theft, insubordination, and desertion were the most prevalent.

Serious and all officer offenses were tried before a general court-martial, held under the auspices of the commanding general. All the proceedings were reviewed by the commander in chief, and sometimes he lessened the sanction. In several instances, Washington questioned the lenity of the punishment but still approved the findings of the court. On rare occasions, he disapproved the rulings. The board of officers specially detailed for this business could sentence noncommissioned officers and privates to some form of corporal punishment up to death. Throughout the war, flogging the bare back with a leather whip, called a cat-o'-nine-tails, was the most common castigation. Under the supervision of the regimental drum major, the drummers meted out these beatings. Young soldiers might instead receive the whipping on their backside. Initially set at 39, "40 save one," the number derived from the Bible used by many of the colonies, the maximum number of lashes was eventually increased to 100. With death, the only other option for more severe crimes, Washington asked Congress's approval to leave the number of lashes to the discretion of the court-martial or fix the limit at 500. He was refused. The death sentence had lost its deterrent effect because lesser crimes were punished with vigor, while most of the condemned escaped execution. This inequity only served to encourage the commission of heinous offenses. Without a proper graduation of sentences, Washington warned that officers would be tempted to return to severe arbitrary punishments to maintain discipline.

Though the Articles of War tried to specify the penalty for every conceivable offense, officers sometimes punished as they pleased. Earlier in the war, offenders were forced to run the gauntlet while being pummeled by their comrades or were confined in a dungeon or made to suffer other physical torments, limited only by the imagination of the court. Eventually these unrestrained acts of tyrannical official vengeance were stopped, though there still were opportunities to uniquely shame wrongdoers. Soldiers were also tried at the regimental level, subject to the review of the officer in command. Dealing with minor crimes not involving officers, the regimental courts could not inflict the death penalty. They still could, however, wreak terrible vengeance upon a perpetrator with the effrontery to burglarize the hut of his regimental commander. Convicted of stealing two shirts from Colonel Michael Jackson's quarters, 8th Massachusetts drum major Jeremiah Allen was "reduced to a private. Sentenced to Receive one hundred lashes on his bare back, at four different roll calls, wear a clogg [wood block] on his leg, be pinned and walk with the Sentinel who guards in the intermediate time." Jackson readily approved the sentence. Far more lenient, a regimental court in the 5th Massachusetts on December 28, 1782, sentenced enslaved soldier Humphrey Hubbard to the biblical allotment of 39 lashes for theft.[9] Soldiers were sometimes flogged and then drummed out of the army to the tune of "The Rogue's March": "Poor old soldier, poor old soldier.... Fifty [lashes] I got for selling me coat Fifty for me blankets. If I ever I 'list for a soldier again the devil shall be me sergeant." Sergeants and corporals might escape with only the loss of their rank. Cutting off the herringbone Honorary Badges of Distinction in front of their assembled regiment or some other form of public humiliation was another option. Private Joseph Sharkey of the 8th Massachusetts was sentenced to appear at the next "roll call with the axe tied to his neck and halt in front of each company and say this is the public axe I offered for sail."[10] Sometimes the Articles of War were not specific enough, so orders further defined prohibited activities. Gambling was forbidden as "the foundation of evil," leading to hard feelings and possible fights. Soldiers of the 8th Massachusetts, however, did it anyway by "pitching coppers." In the game, coins were thrown toward a wall or other vertical surface, and the pitcher with the closest one collected all of them. Considering this practice prejudicial to good order, they were told to stop. To reinforce the point, two soldiers subsequently caught were each sentenced to 10 lashes, but one of them was pardoned. There was the same problem in the 2nd Massachusetts. Admonishing his men that it is "a ruination much too low for soldiers," Lieutenant Colonel Ebenezer Sproat threatened to punish anyone caught playing this game in the future. Ingenious at conforming to the letter of the order while clearly violating the spirit of it, they simply substituted buttons, only to be told to stop that "as well as the pitching of dollars or any object that imitates the game."[11] Despite being reduced to private from the rank of sergeant, Thomas Foster believed that the military regulations were fair, but he lamented the inadequacy of their enforcement. Leaders did nothing to stop the widespread use of profanity and the taking of the Lord's name in vain, thereby risking divine retribution for their indifference.[12]

Held to higher standards of conduct, officers were dealt with differently than the noncommissioned officers and privates. Officers were placed under arrest and relieved from duty until the case was presented before a court-martial. Enlisted soldiers were confined pending trial in the camp guardhouse by the provost of the Marechaussee Corps, the military police of the army; in their absence, soldiers were detailed to serve in that capacity. Offenders at the regimental level were held in the unit's guard hut. There were several sentences that the court-martial could select from to determine a condign punishment for an officer. The two mildest judgments, intended only to embarrass, were to reprimand the officer in regimental, brigade, or general orders or order him to ask the offended superior's forgiveness in front of his corps. In some instances, officers were suspended for a specified period. Washington queried a board of generals if these officers still should receive their pay or emoluments and whether they should be placed "under Military restraint."[13] Dismissal ended their service. Besides death, the worst punishment was being cashiered, expulsion from the military in disgrace. Fellow officers were expected to have nothing further to do with the offender. Many were cashiered in absentia for overstaying their leave home, such as Captain Ebenezer Frye of the 1st New Hampshire Regiment and Lieutenant John Meacham from the 3rd Massachusetts.[14] Others were cashiered for drunkenness, fraternization, fraud, insubordination, assault, or cowardice.

In this period, piques between officers were quite common. Sensitive to slights and any disrespect, they went to various lengths to defend their reputation. Though against regulations, duels were fought, normally with pistols. New York civil authorities issued a warrant to arrest Lieutenant Nathaniel Stone of the 1st Massachusetts for the murder of fellow officer Captain Luke Hitchcock of his regiment in a duel at West Point in February 1782. Stone served until June 1784, and there is no indication that he was ever held accountable for the death. Taking care of their personal affairs beforehand, these gentlemen risked death to satisfy points of honor. Others used the military justice system to exact their revenge. Washington, borrowing from Shakespeare's *Henry V,* pleaded in vain in 1778 for officers "to consider themselves as a band of brothers cemented by the Justice of the common cause, that a perfect harmony might subsist among them and that they would settle all personal disputes among themselves in an amicable manner, ever being cautious not to trouble Courts Martial or the General with private dissensions or add papers to the public files which may hereafter reflect disgrace upon themselves and the Army."[15] In an escalating dispute with Lieutenant Crocker Sampson from his regiment, Ensign James Sawyer of the 7th Massachusetts was brought before a court-martial for disorderly conduct, causing a commotion during the night, being absent from his quarters. breaking open Lieutenant Sampson's chest and stealing the contents, and abusing and assaulting him on several occasions. The court did not consider making noise and lodging out of his quarters as ungentlemanly, and Sawyer was also acquitted of the theft. Though found not altogether justified in the attacks, he was not censured by the court because of "the provocation he had received from Lieutenant Sampson." Lieutenant Thomas D. Freeman was accused of acting in concert with Sawyer to assault Sampson and steal from him. With Sampson's reputation sunk by the earlier trial, Freeman was found innocent of all charges.[16] In January 1783, Captain Phineas Bowman, a company commander in the 5th Massachusetts, was convicted of disrespect toward his commanding officer and acting contrary to the expectations for an officer and a gentleman. Sentenced to three months' suspension, he had to also solicit forgiveness from Lieutenant Colonel Ezra Newhall in front of a formation of the entire 2nd Massachusetts Brigade. Officers of that regiment urged Bowman to press his countercharges against Newhall. Lieutenant Gilbert wrote to his company commander Captain Nathan Goodale, who was home on furlough, that he was the primary witness against their commander, and Bowman did not want to proceed until he was present. Newhall was reported as being under arrest in *Massachusetts Soldiers and Sailors of the Revolutionary War* in early May, but there is no record of any trial. Gilbert could not have been that upset with Newhall, because two weeks later he played cards in Newhall's quarters one night. The following evening, Gilbert dined there with Newhall and afterward held a dance with other officers of his regiment.[17]

While suspicious people and strangers might be stopped, questioned, and sometimes detained, there were generally few limits to freedom of movement in the country provided one did not commit trespass. The only major exception to this entitlement during the war was the prohibition against entering and exiting enemy lines. Soldiers, on the other hand, were strictly controlled and could not come and go as they pleased. For the most part, officers when not on duty had fewer limitations on their freedom. Noncommissioned officers and privates were restricted to camp unless they were on authorized business or possessed written permission. After the beating of the tattoo at night, the soldiers were restricted to their huts. In April 1783, the tattoo was changed to 9 p.m., probably an hour later than before.[18] This does not mean, however, that the soldiers did not find ways to leave. During most of these unauthorized absences, they preyed on the fields and larders of the army's neighbors. Embarrassed by the complaints of victimized residents in New Windsor, Washington called upon his officers to discover the culprits who were "committing wanton instances of plunder and outrage" and inflict upon them a swift and appropriate chastisement. Despite the order the marauding continued, so stronger actions were necessary. Advanced outposts of guards, called pickets, were established whose sole purpose was to keep the men in camp. Washington wanted the winter to be as undemanding as possible, but he threatened that the continued untoward behavior would necessitate a manifold increase in the numbers of guards, making their time quite miserable instead.

Very few noncommissioned officers and soldiers were authorized to be out of camp. Only general officers and regimental commanders could give passes, written permission to be away from their units. At least four roll calls were conducted at unstated times in a 24-hour period to ensure compliance. Catch rolls were ordered during the night, forcing the men to form on their parade grounds and answer when their names were called to discover if anyone was missing. Every brigade formed a patrol of 24 men headed by a captain, who was assisted by another officer and two sergeants. Half of this party marched around their designated route to the left and the other to the right, crossing paths at times. Anyone caught by the watch received summary punishment on the spot, which was not to exceed 100 lashes. Soldiers apprehended with plunder would "be tried for their Lives" by a general court-martial. Concerned that marauding was indicative of a breakdown in discipline, Washington wanted it thoroughly suppressed. A patrol picked up two of Lieutenant Gilbert's corporals in January 1783 who were caught out of camp after the tattoo.[19] Unsupervised, the patrols could not be trusted either. Officers were wise to keep them away from residences in the area. If it was necessary to enter a house to check for soldiers, they or their noncommissioned officers had to supervise the search. Initially, relief of the field officers of the day and patrol leaders took place at 10 a.m. at the left of the 3rd Massachusetts Brigade, but the rendezvous was later changed to the Temple Building.[20] With no enemy in the vicinity to threaten the camp, Washington was concerned that the guards were professionally paraded and posted. Prior to assuming this duty, the soldiers labored to perfect their appearance and military bearing. Hair was lightly coated with grease and dusted with flour to give a powdered look, faces were clean-shaven, muskets were burnished, and uniforms were mended. The Grand Parade was established in front of the Temple Building. At noon the regiment, relieving the one on guard, formed for inspection by the general officer of the day and then drilled and maneuvered for him. Following the review, soldiers not immediately on duty repaired to their huts, and that regiment remained under arms until relieved the following day.[21] Operating out of the regimental guardhouses, sergeants of the guard at specified times led the reliefs to their posts from this building. We do not know the length of time spent on station, but the stint was probably shortened in bad weather. Thick woolen watch coats, in numbers enough only for the guards, made the duty tolerable. In the British service, the regimental colors were normally lodged in the guardhouse for safekeeping, and the Americans generally followed this practice. Concerned that the official announcement of peace on April 19 would lead to a further decline in discipline, Washington ordered every brigade to form a camp guard "for the preservation of good order." From the officers' guardroom, the commander of the main camp guard coordinated his efforts with those from the brigades. Before April 16, 1783, a single regiment provided both the guards and the soldiers for fatigue. After that date, one regiment did guard duty while another did the fatigues.[22]

Some soldiers left camp with the intention of never returning. Excluding the Connecticut and Rhode Island regiments, 479 infantrymen deserted from the northern Continental Army between November 1782 and June 1783. In April and May 1783, 42 alone deserted from the Canadian Regiment.[23] The punishment for this uniquely military crime could be execution but was more likely flogging. During desperate times when desertion was rife, courts-martial were more inclined to sentence offenders to death, the gratuitous effect being to deter further instances. Washington, however, always leaned toward mercy. In most instances, the condemned were allowed to agonize over their fate, only to receive a last-minute reprieve. Of the 11 men sentenced to death for quitting the service in May 1780, only one was executed.[24] Multiple offenses or the incorrigible and unrepentant character of the individual might sway the court to pass and follow through with the ultimate judgment. Conversely, those soldiers with past redeeming qualities would be shown leniency. There was one crime, however, that was unforgivable unless there were extenuating circumstances. Individuals who deserted the Continental Army and then joined the British upon capture were tried and in nearly all cases executed. This standing policy threatened to sour the heady news of the Yorktown victory. Washington gave notice in the beginning of the siege that if the place was taken, all American deserters would "be instantly Hanged." Unable to secure a favorable disposition for them during the surrender negotiations, Cornwallis crammed 250 of these desperate souls onto the sloop *Bonetta and* left the few remaining ones to their fate. Not one to back down, Washington, by allowing this ship to depart free of inspection, gave the deserters a way out and saved himself from ignominy. In the trials following the battle, all nine soldiers convicted of "Inlisting with the Enemy and bearing Arms against these United States" at Yorktown were sentenced to hang. But early the following year, amnesty was offered to American deserters in the British ranks to reduce the size of their royalist corps.[25] With the war drawing to a favorable conclusion, no one at New Windsor received a death sentence for desertion, but the courts did order punishment, usually 100 lashes. At least in one case, the flogging was not done all at the same time; instead, the deserter was given "twenty five lashes each morning, [for] four mornings successively."[26] Richard Joel, from the 2nd Massachusetts Regiment, had "his honorary Badges taken off by the Drum Major" in front of his regiment and received 50 lashes. John Edwards and Noah Allen of the 2nd New Hampshire Regiment escaped any punishment. They were fortunate enough to have deserted around the time of the French alliance, which was marked in camp by a large celebration and a general pardon of all prisoners. The commander in chief always believed that the judicious application of mercy was far more effective in maintaining discipline than the harshest of examples.[27] Military justice was intended to correct behavior without being vindictive. Washington did not enjoy seeing his soldiers punished: "The frequent occasions the General takes to pardon, where strict justice would compel him to punish ought to operate on the gratitude of offenders to the improvement of their morals." Besides granting clemency on the anniversary of the French alliance, Washington did so again on June 2 as the army was preparing to leave New Windsor.[28]

The official cessation of hostilities was proclaimed in camp at noon on April 19. The preliminary peace articles arrived in Philadelphia the month before, but legislators had to confirm the information and determine how to proceed, which took time. Receiving Congress's proclamation on April 16, Washington queried his general officers about deferring the announcement, knowing that the soldiers enlisted for the war would demand an immediate discharge "and unless gratified in their Wishes, that the most disagreeable consequences will ensue." Wanting an orderly reduction of the force, he wanted to conform with the withdrawals of the British from American territory. Missing or choosing not to recognize the difference between the cessation of hostilities and the final peace treaty, many shared the views of Private Thomas Foster, whose only ambition was to leave the service and return home,[29] as if such information could be kept secret. Positive signs and optimistic rumors augured this conclusion. At the end of March, Lieutenant Gilbert heard that representatives signed the treaty on January 20, 1783. The following evening, March 27, he received further verification of the news, and the officers of his regiment stayed up late drinking and dancing to celebrate. On March 28 the report was confirmed in General Orders, and the soldiers joined in the revelry. The normally reserved General Washington first brought the information to camp. Unable to contain himself after receiving a letter from the French minister to the United States the Chevalier de La Luzerne announcing that the suspension of hostilities was signed on January 20, 1783, in Paris and was to take effect in America on March 20, Washington rode to the Temple and told a group of officers assembled there for a court-martial on March 26. In no time the word spread. Though he did not have the authority to officially proclaim an end to the war, Washington expressed his assurance of that occurrence. On March 29, Foster and the members of his regiment assembled to hear the letter sent by Elias Boudinot, the president of Congress, describing the peace. Throughout that day, "soldiers continued marching, Huzzaing & drinking." A good omen, the next evening the northern lights made a spectacular show. Magazine keepers were no longer to give out cartridges without orders. On April 8 the British deputy adjutant general, Captain John Stapleton, from the 17th Light Dragoons brought the report to Newburgh of the peace agreement and afterward came to "Camp and frollick[ed] With ... [the] officers." Foster wrote in his journal on April 16 that "the [o]fficial Acct. of the Peace Reached head quarter to the Great Joy Some as Well as the Greaf of Others."

Writing to Captain John Pray on the lines, Washington directed him to immediately release all his prisoners and return everything he captured to British-controlled territory. After the end of hostilities was formally announced, Washington on April 21 told General Knox, commander of West Point, to allow any American ship to sail past his post from either direction. Either ending the prohibition on his own initiative or unable to stop the vessel with no chain in the water, the first ship to sail past New York City since the British capture in 1776, a schooner out of Nantucket, docked in Newburgh on April 18 carrying a cargo of "fish, oil, rum & c."[30] A striking sign of peace, the enormous 60-ton chain at West Point that had been brought out to block the Hudson River every navigation season since 1778 lay rusting and unused. Despite the cessation of hostilities, a regiment continued in the region of the lines to assist with the administration of law. Traversed by lawless banditti, some of whom masked their outrages and depredations under the guise of either British or American partisans, Westchester County required the muskets of the Continental Army to restore order.[31]

After recovering over the winter from a lengthy illness at his Vermont home, Battle of Bennington hero Brigadier General John Stark arrived in camp during this time and assumed command of the combined New Hampshire and Rhode Island Brigade. Recognizing the futility of trying to suppress information that was already common knowledge, Stark first read the peace articles to an assembly of officers in the Temple on April 17.[32] This decision also gave Washington the opportunity to tidily end the fighting eight years to the day it started in 1775 on Lexington Green. The quartermaster general was ordered to hasten the arrangements for printing discharges for the men enlisted for the war, a sure indication that the end was nigh.[33] In anticipation of the army's disbandment, regimental paymasters were given instructions on how to prepare the settlement accounts. The quartermaster department provided the paper, which was always in short supply. Having established an office at the home of William Bedlow along the Hudson between Newburgh and New Windsor at the end of March to settle pay, depreciation, subsistence, paymaster, and recruiting accounts, Paymaster General John Pierce was already in camp to direct the arrangements. Expecting that the paymasters would exercise the utmost care, Washington charged Assistant Clothier General David Brooks with providing the financial records from his department to Pierce.[34] They received credit for any promised clothing item not issued, as it was calculated as part of soldier pay.

At noon on April 19, the announcement of peace was read to the crowd gathered in front of the Temple Building, followed by three cheers of huzzah. Chaplain Gano then made a prayer, and singers performed "Independence" by William Billings, accompanied by musicians. Inside, Washington concluded the ceremony with the toast "Happy and lasting Peace." The day before, Foster believed that "the Dickclaration is to be Read in the tarret of the Temple," out of the circular window of the gable facing the Grand Parade, but Heath said it was done from the door. With little room in the gable, conducting the event by the front door was far easier. Amid the celebrations the woods caught fire, but the blaze was stopped before it spread to the huts by the quick action of the men.[35] That evening the proclamation was read to to every regiment and separate battalion in camp, assembled on their individual parade grounds. Nearly 80 years later, 2nd New Hampshire private Samuel Downing, one of a handful of remaining survivors of the Revolution, recalled that following that formation, they lit 13 candles in their huts.[36] The day culminated with an impressive fireworks display. Everyone interested in viewing the show gathered so they could see the stage, a stand built on the hill a few hundred yards southeast of the Temple. "Erected to display fire works, april, 19, 1783," the stand was a platform and elaborate facade designed to add to the visual wonder of the exhibition and disguise the mechanisms and stagehands employed in the production. Experts in shells and other pyrotechnics, artillerymen prepared the charges and set off the fireworks. Though he received news of his mother's death that day, rustic Thomas Foster was suitably impressed:

> But however, the Curaosity of Many of the Seans Especielly the fire Works are Very Entertaining and More So to Us in this Cuntery as we ware Intirly Ignorant of the Same; to See two Men on horse Back in the Livery of Offecers with Drawn Sword in their hands and See a burd flying in the are With a fire brand or Match in his Mouth and Set fire to the foresaid horses

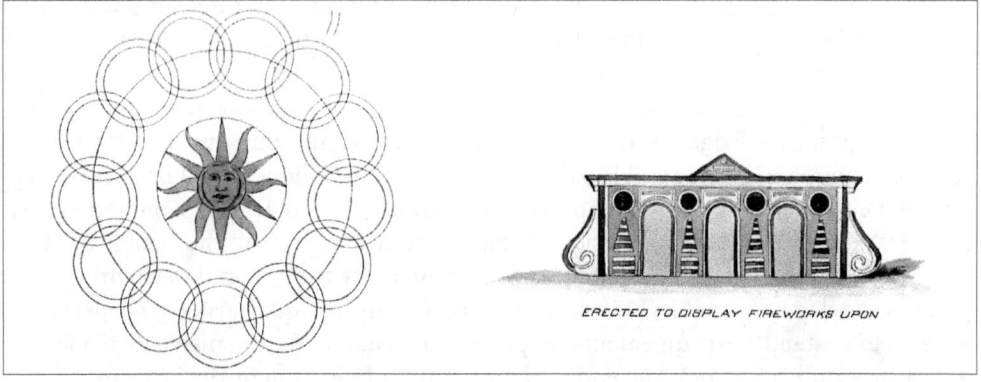

Sun Firework with Ray Halo Surrounded by 13 Interlocking Rings and Stand "Erected to display fire works upon" from the 1890 copy of the Private William Tarbell drawing (courtesy Washington's Headquarters State Historic Site Collection, New York State Office of Parks, Recreation and Historic Preservation). The nearly identical "Fixed Sun, with a transparent Face" is from Denis Diderot and Jean D' Alambert, *Le Encyclopedie, Fabrication Des Canons* (Inter-Livres, 2002 [1762–1772]), Artificier Plate IV, Figure 78. Featured prominently in the top center of the Tarbell drawing, instead of fireworks shooting out in a circle from the center as depicted in the Diderot *Encyclopedia* plate, there were 13 interlocking rings. Presumably, when this display was ignited, rockets made the rings spin. Exposed over the years to too much light, this image in Tarbell's rendering is barely legible.

and See the horses and their Riders Meet Runing on a Rope and Contend with Each Other; is Such a Sean as Would Give the Ignorant World a Very Great Shock. And Many Other Such Like fire Works ware Displayed that I am Not at Leasure heare to Mention for Want of time.[37]

Despite Foster's amazement, displays of this kind had become such standard fare by the time of the New Windsor Cantonment that no one else made any mention of the fireworks. Fairly uniformed in composition by this point, it was probably like the show held in New York City in December 1783 to celebrate the withdrawal of British troops. Broken down into three sets, that exhibition employed many of the same pyrotechnics used in modern fireworks, including the addition of various ingredients to the powder to produce brilliant colors. Starting the show was "a dove descending with the Olive-Branch, which" set "Fire to a Marron Battery." A marron battery was a wooden box containing rockets. Going off at the same time, the missiles rose to a certain height and then burst into smaller charges that cascaded down like a fountain and made crackling noises. Rocket bursts, fixed and whirling fiery wheels on stands, balloons, rising fireworks, and tourbillons, including a rising spiral tourbillon, were interspersed throughout the entire program.

The first set also had a "Pine Tree," a "Flaming Star," a "Grand Volute illuminated, with a projected Wheel in Front," a sheaf of wheat known as a "Gerbe," a "Chinese Fountain," and an "Illuminated Star with Rays." A volute was a whirling spiral shell, creating a pinwheel effect. During the interlude was another marron battery and horsemen fighting. Highlighting the second set was a "Cascade of Fire," a "Gerbe," a "Regulated illuminated spiral Piece, with a projected star Wheel illuminated," "One Moon and Seven Stars," and a "Fire Tree." The next interlude was two ships fighting, a marron battery, and a "fue de Joy" of rockets. A fire of joy was set off one after the other in quick succession. Building to a crescendo, the third set had a "Globe illuminated, with an horizontal Wheel," a "Yew Tree of brilliant Fire," sheaves of wheat, an illuminated chandelier, an illuminated double cone wheel, a "Palm Tree," an "Illuminated Pyramid with Archimedian Screws, a Globe and vertical Sun," a "Projected, Regulated Piece of nine M.[arron] B.[attery] canons," a "Fixed Sun, with a transparent Face," and "7 Bee-Hives." The grand finale was "Fame descending" followed by a "Flight of 100 rockets."[38]

Leaving after the noon ceremony for a meeting with Secretary at War Lincoln in Ringwood, New Jersey, regarding the release of British prisoners of war, Washington expressed in the general orders of the day before his heartfelt thanks to all the officers and soldiers who made the victory possible. He especially singled out for the war the men as deserving of the highest honors. Without their prolonged and steadfast service, he could not have planned and executed operations; there would have been no army for the militia to rally around or recruits to augment. Independence was their achievement. Worthy of the greatest esteem from both the army and the nation, these honored military men would soon retire from the field to a happier existence among family and friends. Washington closed with the admonition for them not to ruin the reputation gained at the expense of so much blood and suffering by committing acts to sully this achievement and to leave the ranks with acclaim. For anyone thinking that the peace announcement ended their duty as soldiers, he vowed to maintain discipline until the very end. Every man received an additional allowance of alcohol "to drink Perpetual Peace, Independence and Happiness to the United States of America." This timely stimulant was fortuitous because it was a very cold day, and with the previous day having been so hot, Foster thought that the drastic change could have been harmful enough to cause fatalities without it. Not placated by this contrived celebration, he was exhausted by all the pageantry. Utterly confused by the army not allowing the men to leave and with no word when that would occur, he just wanted his discharge.[39]

Though anticipating that the final peace treaty would arrive in America shortly, the soldiers were not allowed a period of rest after the festivities. That same day, they were ordered to square their proportion of the timbers necessary for an illumination frame to hang large-size transparencies that projected illusory images through lighting. Artfully configured lanterns and candles provided the incandescence. This decorative display was intended as the culmination of the celebration marking the official end of the war. All the regiments and separate battalions received an initial requirement for providing a number of 7-inch squared beams of various lengths. Additionally, they were to send two carpenters, led by a sergeant, from their brigade skilled in framing wood to assemble at the Temple Building the morning of April 22 to work for the project supervisor, the French engineer Colonel Gouvion. He was assisted by an officer from every brigade. A few days later, each brigade was charged with delivering another 7-inch squared beam, 30 feet long. Finally, in mid–May the last requirement was for a certain number of 7-inch squared 25- and 31-foot-long timbers, allocated throughout the individual units in this encampment. The quartermasters designated the stand of trees to cut. Needing to furnish Gouvion with "600 lbs. of clean rendered tallow, 700 yards of cotton candlewick ... and three gallons of Spirited Turpentine," Pickering asked Daniel Parker to purchase these articles in New York City and send them up by the first ship.[40] With Steuben in overall charge of the preparations, the detail-oriented Prussian planned one of the grandest exhibitions ever executed by the Continental Army. He planned a feu de joie, illumination, and fireworks. Using the Temple as a backdrop, the 80-foot-long illumination frame was 100 yards below the building. The frame was projected to incorporate 1,000 lamps. The program designers did not disclose the contents of the show so as to make people curious, the surest way to boost attendance. To enhance further the visual splendor, fine paintings arrived from the nation's capital, probably from the studio of artist Charles Willson Peale, who hoped that by exhibiting his talent to the army he would earn commissions from officers desirous of commemorating their military service with a miniature or larger portrait of themselves in uniform. A year later, Peale opened the Philadelphia Museum containing 44 portraits of "worthy personages" from the Revolutionary War. Presumably, the paintings sent to New Windsor were a selection from this collection. Washington invited French minister de La Luzerne to the observance but then told him that the celebration was on hold until the receipt of the final treaty. The Treaty of Paris was not signed until September 3, 1783, so this celebration never happened. Expecting this extravaganza to be the final showcase of his military organizational talents and the culmination of his efforts to professionalize the Continental Army, Steuben could not contain his disappointment: "This disbandment of the army ... was so thoroughly comic that you would have laughed yourself sick had you seen it."[41]

The preliminary peace articles spurred rumors and speculation about the date of the army's disbandment, further heightening the impatience, recalcitrance, and angst. "The soldiers are loud and insolent, the officers broken, dis-satisfied and desponding." Both officers and men, who had served for many years, were now faced with trying to reestablish themselves in the civilian world, a worrisome prospect for some. Making the military a career was out of the question for all but a fortunate few, because the United

States intended to maintain a very small peacetime force. Seeing that the end was near, soldiers pushed back against authority. After all, their leaders in a short amount of time would be private citizens again with no hold but that of the traditional deference owed to a superior, even a former one. A month later, Washington gave General Knox the authority to furlough any noncommissioned officers or soldiers whose insubordinate behavior was the result of their desire to leave the service. He reasoned that "we are better off without them."[42] General Jedediah Huntington, commander of the Connecticut Line, was granted the same permission, as trust was placed in his discretion and sense. Especially impatient were his soldiers with families, who were anxious to return home to provide for them. More troubling than the letter describing the restiveness of his men was the petition submitted to Washington on April 22 from Huntington's noncommissioned officers requesting the same retirement payment promised to the officers. Though Washington refused to read the petition because it was not delivered through their chain of command, this appeal demonstrated "the absolute necessity of discharging the *Wars men* as soon as possible." New Jersey soldiers "prayed" for an exemption from paying taxes and wanted this recorded on their discharges.[43] The demands would only grow with time.

Conditions at New Windsor also worsened, but the situation was not as bad as at West Point, because here "the different Corps are Checks one upon another." Willful individuals found to their peril that the military would not and could not let any challenges to authority go unpunished. Individual transgressions at New Windsor ran the gamut from failure to follow orders to assaults against officers. Found guilty of insulting and then striking Lieutenant Josiah Smith of the 6th Massachusetts Regiment, Thomas Stevens, from the 3rd Massachusetts, received a sentence of 100 lashes and the public removal of his Honorary Badge of Distinction. Remarkably, he escaped punishment because of the general amnesty of February 6, 1783. On April 22, Sergeant John Oakley of the 2nd New York incited an uprising against his officers and was whipped 100 times, had the label "mutiny" placed on his back, and then was forcibly escorted out of camp, with the drummer probably playing "The Rogue's March." Earlier in the war, he likely would have faced execution. Probably emboldened too by the official announcement of the peace and impending disbanding of the Continental Army, 7th Massachusetts soldiers George Gamboll and Samuel Giles were convicted of "disobeying, and actually opposing the orders of an officer" on April 20. They also received 100 lashes. Corporal George St. Lawrence, from the 2nd New York, told his officer, Ensign Samuel Dodge, at the end of April "damn your orders sir." Two other corporals from the same regiment were also charged with disobeying Dodge. All three were convicted and reduced to privates, but St. Lawrence received 100 lashes as well for his affront to authority. The same court tried corporals Meadows, Barns, and Birch, from the 8th Massachusetts, for mutinous behavior on April 30. While all three defendants were found guilty and sentenced to 100 lashes, Birch did not lose his rank, unlike the other two.[44]

Sheltered from the burden of controlling soldiers, General Heath's aide, Major Henry Sewall, whiled away the hours reading. From printer Samuel Loudon, Sewall bought Scottish author Henry McKenzie's "Julia de Roubigne, a sentimental novel." He later "read the Man of Feeling—written [also] by H.[enry] McKenzie … [and] 1 vol. of Emma Corbit (Corbett) a modern novel, written by Courtney Milmoth (Melmoth)," the pen name of English author Samuel Jackson Pratt. A few weeks later, Sewall read the second volume. Patronizing Loudon again, Sewall received "a pamphlet on the subject of half pay etc. and the volume of McFingal bound," the epic poem written by John Trumbull the writer, not the more famous Washington aide and artist of the same name.[45] For this reason and many others, staff officers were greatly resented by those in the line.

Adding to the unrest were the clamors about the beef ration. The contractors sensibly requested an outside party to inspect all the cattle in the future. On the recommendation of Daniel Parker, Washington appointed Major Henry Wykoff, "a refugee from New York" living in Fishkill, for this purpose. By the end of May, however, the complaints were "so serious and alarming" that Washington wrote to Duer & Parker to immediately improve the provisions. Brigadier General Elias Dayton informed Major General Heath that the meat was so bad by this point that it was barely edible. General Paterson reported that for the past several weeks the entire ration was of poor quality. A similar letter was sent by Brigadier General John Stark. At the same time, the firm was informed that fresh meet was necessary to treat the patients with measles at West Point. A board of generals and commanding officers met in the first part of June to examine how the contractors executed the agreement. They recommended that the army revert to the original deal negotiated by Robert Morris, which Duer & Parker accepted.[46]

When no discharges were forthcoming, the war men agitated for their release from duty. Foster noted on May 8 the consternation felt by the men entitled to discharges and feared what would happen if they were not soon permitted to decamp. Bewildered by the rumors that they would have to wait until October, these soldier grew angrier by the day, and authorities tempted fate with further delay. The army was a sword of Damocles hanging over the nation's head. On Sunday, May 18, Foster recorded that it was "a Very Warme Day and the During War men are Very Warm that they are Not Dismissed from their Bondage & What the Event Will be is not in My power to Determine." Toward the end of the month, many impatient New Hampshire soldiers refused to wait any longer and slipped out over the course of several nights. Nothing was being done, and no one could understand why. Already overwhelming, the public burden unnecessarily increased each day with the retention of men who were mostly no longer needed. Disappointed time and again, they were quite happy to learn in the beginning of June that they would finally receive their discharges.[47]

Washington depended more than ever on the exertion of his officers to maintain order. Unless for emergencies, he would not allow any of them to leave. Certain officers, however, fueled the discontent rather than kept it in check. Aware of their slipping hold over their men, a few instead of backing down rigorously upheld their prerogative. Lieutenant Thomas Freeman of the 7th Massachusetts had a Sergeant Howard, probably Sergeant William Hayward of Bridgewater, from his regiment severely flogged. Court-martialed a few times before, Hayward refused to let the matter rest. Foster felt it was "high time for to Disband the Armey as thare is a Very Greate Oppesison Arisen between the Officers and the Soldiers of Late; and how it Will Stop & Whare I cant think."[48] In early June just before the army left this encampment, soldiers of that regiment singled out an especially despised officer. One night on the 7th Massachusetts parade ground, they hanged an effigy of Major Lemuel Trescott with a mocking epithet. Leading the mob was probably the man who received 100 lashes for being insolent to the major.[49] The soldiers needed to vent their frustrations somehow.

> This Day [May 31, 1783] a tumult is Began on Acct. of the During War Men having furlows in Sted of the Discharges which they are Justly intitled to by their first Inlistment as that specifyed that We Ware at the End of the Contest to be free & now to Only to furlowd us & Not

to Pay us, is an Od unheard of peac of Injustice [?] and Not to be put up With by Brave Men that have fought & Suffered Everything but Yett the Deselution of Soul & body; for they have Never been paid according to Contract but Been Most Shamefully Deseaved and and baffeled Almost in Every articel of Contract Maid them and Now to be Sent into the Cuntery Naked and Desitute of Money and Almost Everything Elce is what you May Call an Inguery to them to their poor famelys; & an Equall Disgrace to the Continent that they under God have Maid free this is Conduct which With a Wilness [?] aught to be obhored by Every Citttezen.[50]

CHAPTER 10

"Retiring from the field of Glory with Joy in their countenances, but poverty in their pockets"

The Shameful Disbandment of the Continental Army

Furloughs were issued instead of discharges. There was little likelihood for a renewal of the conflict, but officials did not want to place this force beyond recall while the British still occupied American territory. But recovering most of these men and reconstituting the army in a reasonable amount of time would have been very difficult. More immediate was that the country could delay indefinitely the settling of the army's pay accounts. Every debtor with large liabilities sought time to work out a solution or to delay the consequences. Discharges implied a final settlement of accounts. Furloughs pushed that payoff to an indeterminate date in the future. Once the official peace treaty was announced, the furloughs would become formal discharges. Confiding to Lafayette, Washington acknowledged that the cost of maintaining the army impelled Congress to furlough the men enlisted for the war, which for all intents and purposes meant discharge. Expecting to draw at least a part of their pay, the officers were shocked to learn that they would get no cash, only promissory notes.[1] When the decision to furlough was announced on June 2, all the generals and commanding officers hastily met and requested that the commander in chief solicit Congress to ensure that no one was forced to leave without receiving certificates for all their arrearages. This was the same unsuccessful demand they made while brandishing the aggrieved army during the Newburgh Conspiracy. Included along with the other obligations were the five-year salary lump sum payment, in lieu of half-pay for life, for the officers and the $80 promised to every war soldier. They also wanted some money to return home with dignity and as a token of appreciation from the nation. First expressing his appreciation for their faith in his advocacy, Washington explained that as a public servant, he had to comply with the wishes of Congress, whose action was the only way to reduce expenditures in order to make it more feasible for a timely settlement of the army's accounts. The pay notes were expected shortly, and he was "certain every mark of attention will be paid" to their grievances. This was more of his platitudes to quiet them, as Washington knew full well that the national legislative body was not going to act on any of the army complaints. After the officers were selected for the regiments of three-year men and to lead the furloughed soldiers home, the rest could choose to either stay or leave camp. In reply to the queries of Colonel Pickering in September, Washington expressed his opinion that all officers on furlough were still entitled to all pay and perquisites, but to reduce current costs, only those still with the army were to receive any payments at that time.[2]

Lacking funds, the best the government could do was give the officers and soldiers certificates for three months' pay in Morris Notes, redeemable in six months. Even with this distant redemption date, the proposal was fiscally irresponsible and precarious. Morris tried to make them payable at two, four, and six months, but with the states making little effort to collect the levies apportioned to them, they were all at the maximum time. Washington needed to disband most of his army right away because without an immediate reduction in expenses, this measure would soon become impracticable. Very apprehensive about the expenditure for army pay, estimated at $750,000, Morris agreed "to risk a large paper Anticipation" but urged Washington to use his influence with the states to encourage them to raise the taxes to satisfy these notes. With his financial standing riding on the outcome and with him expecting to leave office soon, he was understandably initially hesitant to accede to this suggestion when it was first proposed earlier in the year, being wholly dependent on his successor to "save [him] from Ruin." Morris stayed on until November 1784. His periodic threats to resign were his coping mechanism when the demands of his office became unbearable and attempts to get the dilatory legislators do something to make the execution of his responsibilities easier.[3]

Washington warned the superintendent in April that this payment had to arrive before the army began to disband. Receiving word from Morris in early June that he was expediting the pay, the commander in chief sent a messenger to Philadelphia to find out where it was, expecting the worse from the continued delay. Bemoaning that there were no coins in the shipment, he hoped that the arrival of the Morris Notes would placate his officers and soldiers. Lieutenant Gilbert received his promissory certificate on June 14 after the furloughed men left.[4] They would have to wait until the notes were forwarded. Having to obtain special paper to make them less liable to counterfeiting as with his other financial instruments, take the sheets to the printer, and personally sign 6,000 individual slips, Morris did well to get them to the army by the middle of June. A large counterfeit ring was operating within British lines, forging practically every variety of American monetary documents.[5] Some soldiers did not keep them very long, choosing instead to sell the certificates to speculators at a fraction of their value to obtain a little ready cash. Hearing that opportunists were almost immediately preying on his men, Washington counseled them not to shortsightedly fall victim to these vultures, whose enrichment was contrary to the expectations for making this risky payment. Knowing that holders would receive the full value of the notes in just six months, he implored the army to wait and not let financial adventurers profit from their distress.[6] Morris probably would not have expended so much effort had he known the fate of much of this payment. Incredibly, one of the accused speculators was a captain in the 1st New York Regiment, Henry Tiebout. Initially accepting his advice to wait so they received the full amount, the soldiers asked him again to buy their notes, and he finally relented, giving them two-thirds of the amount redeemable in merchandise from local vendors. Ameliorating the officer's impropriety somewhat was that the sellers indicated that if he did not buy their certificates, they would have sold them to somebody else. In July, Congress appointed former paymaster general John Pierce "Commissioner for settling the accounts of the Army." Both officers and soldiers were eventually forwarded certificates of indebtedness, at 6 percent annual interest, for their remaining arrearages. The officer notes included the commutation of the half-pay, subsistence, forage, and pay, while the enlisted men's papers contained the balances due on their clothing account, pay, and the 80-dollar gratuity promised to all the noncommissioned officers and privates who enlisted for the war and served to the end of the conflict. Eventually, about 90,000 Pierce Certificates were issued.[7] Just like with other army pay documents, many veterans disposed of these notes to speculators at a steep discount before the U.S. Constitution rescued the value of these securities.

On Washington's suggestion, soldiers could keep their muskets, accoutrements, and other issued personal gear as revered relics of the nation's founding. With strong paternal sentiment, he espoused this measure: "These constant companions of their Toils and Dangers, preserved with sacred Care, would be handed down from the present possessors, to their Children, as honorable Badges of Bravery and military Merit; and would probably be bro't forth, on some future Occasion, with Pride and Exultation, to be improved, with the same military Ardor and Emulation, in the Hands of posterity, as they have been used by their forefathers in the present Establishment and foundation of our National Independence and Glory." Some questioned the wisdom of this move. Colonel John Lamb, commander of the 2nd Continental Artillery, warned Governor Clinton that if these embittered armed soldiers were discharged in this state they might perpetrate the worst iniquities and that no adequate force was available to quell them.[8] While Lamb's fears did not come to pass, Congress still had cause to rue this gesture because some of these guns were later turned against authorities in Shays' Rebellion. Musicians tried to take advantage of this provision to get guns for themselves but were only allowed to keep their instruments. Their drum or fife, extra pay, and less strenuous service were considered to "fully Ballance the Gratuity intended by Congress."[9] The furloughed surgeons were not allowed to keep their drugs and implements. They had to "return their Medicine Chests and what Instruments they ... [had] belonging to the United States into the Apothecarys Store at New Windsor."[10] A few officers were accused by Duer & Parker storekeeper Melancton Smith of finagling to extract their own gratuity by requesting him to give them a kickback for encouraging their soldiers to expend their pay certificates at his shop. While other merchants gave a commission for this service, Smith at first refused. Overstocked with goods that were steadily decreasing in value, he finally relented and gave 10 percent. The officers suggested he make up the amount of the commission by charging the soldiers more. A board was appointed to investigate the charges and issued a report, but nothing more was ever done.[11]

Despite all the turmoil, there were still some men enlisted for the war who did not want a furlough, anything to put off deciding about the future. Reminded that they were expected to fully perform their obligations until receipt of the final treaty, these soldiers were given permission to affect an exchange with any three-year man interested in leaving the service.[12] Officers decided among themselves who would remain. With more wanting to stay than there were positions for them, the selections were based on seniority, derived from their date of rank. Dejected that his short time in grade averted his retention, Lieutenant Gilbert was forced out. After paying his debts, which might have included his times at Wyoma, he did not have enough funds left to pay for his passage home. He need not have worried, however, because deranged officers could remain with the army until they determined what to do next. Fortunately, he managed to find a position by wearing down Lieutenant Joseph Smith of his regiment, who finally agreed to switch with him. But this success was only a temporary reprieve from facing the world. Counting on partnering with Captain Goodale and others in the purchase of a fine sequestered royalist estate in Albany County, Gilbert was greatly disappointed when the announcement of peace put an end to the confiscations.[13]

Though there were many hardships, army life was predictable, and necessities were provided by the country. For those whose time in uniform spanned many years, the civilian world was a distant memory, devoid of the security of military service and in many cases much harder. Simply picking up where they left off was not an option for quite a few. Life had moved on without them. Some had nothing to return to. Those who did were not the same people they were when they left home. Broken in body and spirit, Gilbert wanted to work hard, but speaking for many, he knew that his physical condition had deteriorated past the point of ever being able to fully recover. His anguish and sense of betrayal pushed him into a mental situation "little short of a delirium." Questioning whether the American people deserved the freedom brought about by so much suffering, he was incredulous that such little effort was expended to recognize their achievement. Thrown out with nothing, he was almost sad that he was still alive to bear witness to this ingratitude. "Where is the Justice, where is the propriety of the Army's bearing the whole burthen of the war."[14]

Pickering took great satisfaction in writing Samuel Hodgdon about the snub of Washington by the departing men. Thinking the reduction shameful, Pickering blamed Congress and the commander in chief for doing little for the army and said that everyone was indignant. Writing a "manly, elegant, and affectionate address" to von Steuben, the New York Line officers paid no attention to the commanding general. The conservative face and shield of the establishment, Washington never would have strongly advocated for anyone and risk destabilizing the political and social order, so important to propertied men such as himself. Under his leadership, the Continental Army was not a revolutionary force and only embodied people fighting for the limited objective of independence from Great Britain.[15]

Each division marched home under the control of a captain and a lieutenant. Not disbanding the army at New Windsor meant that they could still draw provisions along the way so that this disgruntled multitude would not be available for use en masse as a cat's paw by demagogues. In the place where many of them enlisted all those years ago, the soldiers were released from service. Their furloughs were the legal document authorizing the separation. There was no great ceremony to mark the end of this encampment. Beginning on June 5 with the 3rd Maryland Detachment, which had the farthest to go, units started to leave. Taking enough rations to last to Pompton, New Jersey, they drew the rest along their route at Princeton, Philadelphia, Wilmington, and finally Baltimore. They were to march at an undemanding pace by the best possible routes, taking care not to unduly inconvenience the people along their line of march. The New Jersey Brigade followed and then the New Hampshire, and finally the Massachusetts Line began to leave on June 8.[16]

So numerous were the Massachusetts men that they had to march out in separate divisions over several days so as not to overwhelm the facilities along their routes. To ease their journey, the quartermaster general arranged for a ship to carry the personal effects of the officers living east of Worcester County.[17] Already in their state, the New York Line received its furloughs on June 8 and headed off. Two days before, the light infantry company of the New York Line's 1st Regiment presented its colors and musical instruments to Governor Clinton at his residence in Poughkeepsie. Colonel Philip Van Cortlandt, commander of the 2nd New York, escorted this company and at the same time delivered his own regiment's flags and music. Pickering provided a bateaux, at the request of Lieutenant Colonel David Humphreys, for a few 1st New York soldiers and their families who had no means to get to Albany.[18] Anticipating the removal of the remaining element of the army to West Point, regimental and brigade quartermasters were ordered to turn all their spare ammunition in to the camp magazines so it could be transported to Newburgh for shipment to that fortress.[19]

Brevet Brigadier General Moses Hazen, commanding the Canadian Regiment covering the territory south of West Point all the way into northern New Jersey, sent a return to headquarters on June 7 indicating the number of his men willing to accept the furlough. He also reminded Washington that most of his men were either new to this country or exiled Canadians, totally dependent on the justice of Congress for pay and benefits. They had been promised a reward for joining the American ranks. However, the country was in no position to fulfill that promise. Hazen also harped on what Washington was going to do about the latest charges preferred by him and his officers against Major James Reid of his regiment. The much-reviled Reid was acquitted of charges of disobedience of orders, embezzlement, and conduct unbecoming an officer in a court-martial held on December 30, 1782. More than 40 miles away, this letter took time to arrive at headquarters, so Hazen received a personal request two days later asking him to report how many of his men were willing to accept the furlough so that headquarters could send the correct number of discharges. He was to send the remainder to New Windsor as soon as he could. Receiving 300 discharges at his headquarters in Pompton, New Jersey, a few days later, from Colonel Walter Stewart, Hazen replied that most of his men wanted to leave the service but would not before they received the same payment as the rest of the army. Inquiring about the Morris Notes for three months' pay, he took matters into his own hands by soliciting a merchant who was willing to extend approximately a month's worth of soldier's pay in credit to each of his men. Awaiting the arrival of additional merchandise, he expected to march at the latest at the end of the following week. Not receiving this letter until nearly two weeks after it was written and finding no good reason to brook further delay, Washington desired that he put his remaining men on the road right away and move them to the nearly abandoned winter camp in New Windsor. Quartermaster Pickering had already set aside the New York huts for them. After arriving at that location, Hazen was to form his men into two companies with the requisite number of officers. Like all the others left out of the new arrangement, his excess officers could either stay with the army or take their leave. But Hazen never complied with the order to lead the remnant of his regiment to this encampment. Submitting the Reid affair and the subsequent charges of incompetence against Judge Advocate General Edwards for his failure to convict that man to a board of general officers, who found the whole prosecution vexatious, Washington wrote to Hazen hoping that this determination would put an end to the embarrassing and bothersome episode.[20] Devoid of any drama, the furloughed Rhode Islanders left their positions around Albany and headed home via Litchfield and Hartford, Connecticut.[21]

With the disposition of the army decided, Washington took the time to express his concerns for the future. In a circular letter to the states written in early June, he strongly recommended an irrevocable union headed by a strong federal authority empowered to overcome local prejudices, which hindered the formation and implementation of policies for the common good. Furthermore, the states needed to place their trust in their elected solons to do what is right for them and the country. Unless Congress could exercise the prerogatives listed in the Articles of Confederation, "anarchy and confusion" would ensue and tear the United States apart. More immediate, he implored them to fulfill the requisitions made on them by Congress to satisfy "all the public creditors" to avoid bankruptcy and preserve the country's financial standing among the nations of the world. Near and dear to his heart were the public creditors of the officers and soldiers. Not just another expense, the arrears owed them was "a debt of honour... , the price of their blood and of your Independency." To protect America's shores and frontiers, they needed to contribute toward the maintenance of a small standing army. He closed with an "earnest prayer, that God would have you, and the State over which you preside, in his holy protection, that he would incline the hearts of the Citizens to cultivate a spirit of subordination and obedience to Government, to entertain a brotherly affection and love for one another, for their fellow Citizens of the United States at large, and particularly for their brethren who have served in the Field." Though the message was generally well received, some resented the unsolicited advice. First acknowledging his complete deferral to the commander in chief in all matters relating to the army, Rhode Island congressman David Howell was astounded that Washington had the hubris to assume that he had the right to attempt to meddle in the governance of the country.[22] Smallest of the 13 states, Rhode Island feared a federal authority with expansive powers, believing it would result in their complete domination by the rest of the country.

No one was more relieved than Washington as the soldiers peacefully headed home. A few days after the formal announcement of peace in mid–April, he wished to be rid of most of them except for the men intended to receive the transfer of American territory from the enemy and to garrison the frontier. He questioned how long his officers could keep the soldiers against their will. The force guarding the camp was significantly enlarged to contain the unrest and prevent the abuse of his leaders. An ominous feeling pervaded the scene as the officers tried to avoid conflict while still enforcing discipline and making the soldiers perform their military duties. Expecting the worst, the disbandment of the army, without major incident pleased him to no end.[23] A potential major threat to the liberties and democratic institutions of the country was gone. Sharing the British tradition of fearing large standing armies, the American people would not forget this lesson in determining the future of the military and would maintain a very small permanent force.

Approximately 2,500 soldiers remained. Massachusetts had four regiments, and Connecticut one regiment. New Hampshire retained five companies and Rhode Island retained two, with three companies of artillerists from Massachusetts and two from New York. On June 11, the Massachusetts Line officers met in the Temple to decide who would stay with their three-year men. The other lines made the same determination. Two days later, Massachusetts colonels Michael Jackson, Henry Jackson, and Joseph Vose and Lieutenant Colonel Commandant Ebenezer Sproat organized their new regiments. On June 16, they formed into brigades. General Paterson took charge of the first two regiments, and General Greaton took charge of the other two.[24] While most of the tents were turned in when the huts were completed, the same could not be said for the poles. Pickering's belated attempt to recover the poles, handy for many different purposes, during this time met with limited success. Needing to put the three-year men into tents on the plain at West Point, he solicited General Paterson to send around 100 carpenters from his regiments to make poles. Expecting the army to leave for the fort in a few days, the quartermaster was incredulous that these men showed up without provisions and that he had to send them back. He chided Paterson to have them bring food next time and to send not just men but rather those skilled in working wood.[25]

With the withdrawal of the furloughed men, there was no longer a requirement for a general, a field officer, and a quartermaster of the day, only a single field officer and adjutant. Instead of an entire regiment, just the guards formed on the Grand Parade at 9:00 a.m. Besides covering the posts in this encampment, they also protected Washington because his headquarters guard disbanded.[26] Having proposed the construction of the Temple of Virtue and delivered its inaugural sermon, it was fitting that on June 22, 1783, Chaplain Israel Evans performed the final service held inside the building on the topic of peace. The following day, the army marched over Butter Hill to West Point except for the New Hampshire Battalion, which remained behind "to do the ordinary duties." Every nine days, a new unit assumed this responsibility. Also, a surgeon or mate and orderlies stayed behind for a short time with the sick of their regiment until huts were prepared at the mountain fortress. Presented with a sealed letter by the commander in chief on the afternoon of June 24, later found to contain Washington's heartfelt thanks, General Heath started for Boston, ending his military career.[27]

Numbers of furloughed men headed down to New York City seeking employment on the ships embarking the British Army, royalists, and liberated enslaved people. Finding no immediate work, they roamed the streets getting into fights with the royalist refugees, assisted by the British German auxiliaries. Many of these Germans intended to desert and settle in the country.[28] There was the request of Lieutenant Colonel Benjamin Walker for Pickering to provide a tent for "an old faithful soldier" of his company and his wife and three children until this pitiable man could find other shelter. This act of benevolence would enable him to find employment in Newburgh.[29] Needing time to determine what to do next, a few families and individual furloughed soldiers continued in the huts after the army left, with some of the men doing manual labor for local farmers. By the fall, however, just about all of the huts were taken down and moved, except for the few built out of the line for the soldiers with wives and possibly children. At least one of these families remained for an additional year. One by one, Sarah Osborn bid farewell to the companions of so much shared sacrifice and misery until only her husband Aaron, her children, and a few other soldiers who boarded in their hut were left. Three months after the birth of their second child in August 1784, Osborn's philandering husband left her for another woman. After confirming that he had abandoned the family, Sarah took Phebe and Aaron, Jr., to her birthplace in nearby Blooming Grove, the last residents to depart the New Windsor Cantonment.

Chapter 11

Denouement
The Conclusion

> All the world's a stage,
> And all the men and women merely players.
> They have their exits and their entrances,
> And one man in his time plays many parts,
> His acts being seven ages. At first the infant,
> Mewling and puking in the nurse's arms.
> Then, the whining school-boy, with his satchel
> And shining morning face, creeping like snail
> Unwillingly to school. And then the lover,
> Sighing like furnace, with a woeful ballad
> Made to his mistress' eyebrow. Then, a soldier,
> Full of strange oaths, and bearded like the pard,
> Jealous in honour, sudden and quick in quarrel,
> Seeking the bubble reputation
> Even in the cannon's mouth. And then the justice,
> In fair round belly, with good capon lin'd,
> With eyes severe, and beard of formal cut,
> Full of wise saws, and modern instances,
> And so he plays his part. The sixth age shifts
> Into the lean and slipper'd pantaloon,
> With spectacles on nose, and pouch on side,
> His youthful hose well sav'd, a world too wide
> For his shrunk shank, and his big manly voice,
> Turning again toward childish treble, pipes
> And whistles in his sound. Last scene of all,
> That ends this strange eventful history,
> Is second childishness and mere oblivion,
> Sans teeth, sans eyes, sans taste, sans everything
> —Jaques, *As You Like It*, Scene 2, Act 7.

There was no rest for the remaining soldiers in the army. Soon after they arrived at West Point, most of the Massachusetts regiments and a detachment of artillery were ordered to march as fast as possible to put down another mutiny in the Pennsylvania Line. Experienced from crushing the uprising in the New Jersey Line in 1781, the commander of the Massachusetts men, General Howe, led this force south to Philadelphia. About 500 mutineers surrounded the executive chambers and demanded their back pay. When the Pennsylvania Council could not provide for their safety, the Continental congressmen withdrew to Princeton, New Jersey. The mutiny had ended by the time of his arrival, and Howe received instructions to investigate the incident and if warranted bring the principals to trial by court-martial.¹ Simultaneously, the light infantry and one company from the New Hampshire Battalion, under Lieutenant Colonel William Hull, went down to Westchester County to aid civil authorities in reestablishing law and order.²

With the mutiny in Pennsylvania over, the Americans marked time until the British evacuated New York. Having to complete the arrangements for the resettlement of the royalists and liberated slaves under his protection as well as the embarkation of his army and supplies, Sir Guy Carleton was in no hurry, so Washington went on a tour of Saratoga, Fort Ticonderoga, Crown Point, and the Mohawk Valley. His entourage, sometimes approaching as many as 40, included Governor Clinton, Philip Schuyler, New York Militia general and Albany mayor Abraham Ten Broeck, commander of New York state troops Colonel Marinus Willett with headquarters at Fort Plain, and Italian count Francesco dal Verme and his translator and servant Bordone. Carrying letters of introduction from Congress and distinguished personages in Great Britain and France, the count, wanting to see the New World and General Washington, arrived in the Highlands in mid-July, visiting West Point and the nearly vacated New Windsor encampment. Calling on Washington at the Hasbrouck house, dal Verme was invited to accompany him on his tour to the northward. Presumably, the rest of the entourage included most of Washington's aides, probably General Hand and a few otherwise unengaged officers. Commanding West Point and the army during the commander in chief's absence, General Knox stayed behind.

Going all the way to Lake Otsego, where the governor's brother General James Clinton's men built the dam in the summer of 1779 to raise the water level enough to propel his boats down the Susquehanna River for a junction with General Sullivan at Tioga, Pennsylvania, Washington's party also visited the abandoned Fort Schuyler (Stanwix), Fort Rensselaer (Plain), Fort Dayton, and Fort Herkimer. The commanding general ordered that Fort Herkimer be provisioned for 500 men, the force intended to garrison the British-occupied Great Lake fortifications in U.S. territory. On August 1, they had breakfast with George Herkimer in the home where his brother Nicholas died nearly six years before of complications from the amputation of his leg pierced by a ball in the Battle of Oriskany. On August 4, dal Verme departed Albany for New England, and the commander in chief left for Newburgh, arriving the following day.³ Not exactly on the best of terms with Washington, Pickering was not present. In the second week of September, he set out on his own tour with assistant Peter Anspach, Surgeon William Eustis, and Thomas Cogswell, the wagon master general. Pickering intended to stop at "Saratoga, Ticonderoga, and Crown Point; [and] on … [his] return … Bennington, the capital of Vermont, Schenectady, and possibly Fort Schuyler." Conducting department business along the way, his group was back in Newburgh by the end of September.⁴

Encountering Washington at Fort George at the southern end of Lake George, von Steuben was heading north to arrange the transfer of the western posts, but British governor and commander in Canada General Frederick Haldimand refused to discuss the matter until he received instructions from his home government and a copy of the final treaty. The Prussian general, his aide Captain James Fairlie from the 2nd New York Regiment, and engineer de Villefranche were not even permitted to see the forts. Passing through the Highlands on his way to Princeton to inform Congress and Washington, the Frenchman gave the bad news to Pickering, who suspended the transfer of supplies to Fort Herkimer.[5] After the signed treaty was delivered, British officials found other reasons to delay the cession. Forts Oswegatchie, Oswego, Niagara, Detroit, and Mackinac were not turned over to the United States until the spring of 1796.

There was a flurry of activity in the nearly abandoned encampment at New Windsor. The quartermasters were preparing to settle accounts with local landowners and dispose of excess equipment and the buildings. Pickering wrote to General Gates at his home in Virginia requesting to have a trusted third party appraise the public wagon and horses in his possession. It was not practical or cost-effective to send the team to Newburgh or Philadelphia, so he was requested to either keep or sell them and remit the payment with a copy of the sales receipt.[6] Cutting down trees on Thomas Jones's land since 1776, the army cleared about 1,100 acres. This rocky, now barren, landscape was only suitable for planting grass to graze animals. Encamped by the mouth of Murderer's (Moodna) Creek for less than a week, the Rhode Island Regiment still used 162 cords. Local arbitrators determined the value of all the timber cut down at 6,035 pounds, 18 shillings, and 2.5 pence New York currency. Jones was awarded nearly half of that amount, while William Ellison was awarded almost 1,000 pounds and his brother John 691 pounds, 19 shillings, and two dozen more landowners were awarded the rest. Still waiting in October, Jones pressed for his money. Not expected to return anytime soon, he requested that Pickering remit the sum to his brother John in Philadelphia. The quartermaster wrote to his assistant Samuel Hodgdon to take care of the matter. Claiming to have authority from New York state attorney general Egbert Benson and Thomas Jones, John Ellison was preventing the military from selling any of the felled wood or huts on his land and Jones's land until payment was made and threatened to haul into court anyone who did. Pickering viewed this as a "dishonest trick" to discourage the sale so they could keep the wood and still receive reimbursement for the loss of it. To this end, Ellison and other landowners would not let "a shrub, bush or twig to be cut, to make a road to come at them." Ignoring all the threats, Pickering sold the wood and huts anyway, assuring purchasers that he would reimburse them if the transactions were later invalidated.[7] There were still horses from headquarters and the quartermaster that required pasturage. William Smith, Mrs. Tryntje Hasbrouck, Samuel Wood, and John Ellison were paid for use of their meadows.[8]

So well made, the huts were not abandoned to the elements or scavenging locals. Unable to find quarters at West Point, Colonel Michael Jackson of the old 8th Massachusetts and the new 3rd Regiment requested to purchase his hut and have it moved there. Putting more than $20 out of his own pocket into his hut, including oaken planks for the floor and his stable, nails, and several pairs of hinges, Major Job Sumner of the 3rd Massachusetts Regiment wanted an allowance for all his expenses. Also believing that his reimbursement for the $18 spent on his hut was justifiable, Lieutenant Colonel Hugh Maxwell, from the 8th Massachusetts, sold his right in his hut to a Mr. McCoy. Maxwell requested that Pickering allow the man to purchase the public right in this building.[9]

In September, the New Windsor huts went under the gavel. At the same time, all the wood cut by the soldiers was sold. The August 26, 1783, edition of the *New York Packet and the American Advertiser* ran an ad for the auction, scheduled for September 2 at 2:00 p.m. in the Temple, the last official function in the building. James Latta bought the Temple for 15 pounds, eight shillings, and also bought 12 more huts, along with their appendages from the 3rd Massachusetts Brigade, for an additional 18 pounds. The Temple still realized quite a bit of money, despite being stripped of its planks, boards, and benches at the end of July. There was almost no building to sell. Precariously perched on piers or resting on the bare ground, the Temple was nearly washed away by a severe storm of wind and rain on May 10. During another thunderstorm in June that produced hail two inches in diameter, a lightning bolt hit the flagstaff, damaging the portico and stunning a group of soldiers by the door. Samuel Brewster, Jr., purchased nearly every hut and outbuilding of the 1st Massachusetts Brigade, a total of 86 for 119 pounds, 10 shillings. In July he offered $2 apiece for all the huts of the 1st and 3rd Massachusetts Brigades, but nothing came of the proposal. The rest of the 3rd Brigade huts, 42 in all, went to Jonas Williams and Robert Nesbitt. Robert Boyd, Jr., did, however, manage to win the 3rd Brigade commander General Putnam's hut, along with 12 other detached small ones. More detached huts, including General Paterson's, was bought by Nathan Smith.[10] Sale of the New Hampshire, New Jersey, New York, and 3rd Maryland Detachment huts was made easier by Lieutenant John Furman of the 1st New York Regiment, who in June bought all of them for $252, a dollar apiece. Having paid for the ship *Black Prince* used by the army the previous year, this cost was deducted from the purchase price of the huts.[11] Pickering intended to cut up the 2nd Massachusetts Brigade huts and remaining former artillery ones to provide firewood for West Point. The fort, however, did not realize as much wood as anticipated, because rather than pay for the 1,000 rails burned or otherwise appropriated by the soldiers on Reverend John Close's land, he instructed Joseph Davis to assign workman to split replacements 12 feet long and 400 more 8-foot-long stakes out of these buildings. There were certainly nowhere near enough huts left to replace the rest of the missing rails, exceeding 10,000, on the farms of Deacon Samuel Brewster, his son Samuel, John Ellison, and the widow Dusenberry, occupied by Benjamin and Samuel Westlake, so the army had to pay for the damage.[12]

Pickering intended to move what was left of the hospital to West Point. Still stationed at these huts during this time, hospital mates William Cogswell and Joseph Prescott were each allowed forage for a horse to visit outpatients. Both in poor health and required to go to Newburgh and other distant places, they would not otherwise have been able to perform this service. Henry Miller, formerly a corporal in the 6th Massachusetts Regiment, was still so ill in October that he could not take care of himself. Though recovering from sickness themselves, his daughter and young son did their best to look after their father. Pickering requested that contractors supply the family with appropriate rations to facilitate their recovery. If they had any objections to this compassion, he told them to charge his private account.[13] No detail escaped Pickering's attention. Soldier Benjamin Worthy of the 2nd Massachusetts spotted at Mr. Horr's blacksmith shop, at the Nine Partners on the opposite side of the river east of Poughkeepsie, an anvil stolen in June from an armorer's shop in the New Windsor camp. Pickering told him to give the anvil, bought illegally from a soldier named Wilkins, to Worthy, whose receipt would relieve him of any liability. Horr was lucky that Washington was not successful in getting Governor Clinton to convince the New York legislature to prescribe fines or other penalties for its citizens who purchased or received any public property from the soldiers.[14] Closing down an encampment area was never clean or easy. Though he had been in Philadelphia since the summer, General Howe left his servants and guard behind at the Deacon Brewster house. If this was not bad enough, they were using five fireplaces. It was already mid–November, and unless something was done, this retinue would remain all winter. Pickering appealed to General Knox to speak to Howe's aide, Captain Elnathon Haskell, about moving Howe's baggage elsewhere so the quartermaster could shut down this headquarters. Writing to Haskell the same day to that effect, Pickering would not tolerate such profligacy.[15]

Washington left Newburgh in mid–August for the seat of government in Princeton, New Jersey, Congress having fled there during the mutiny of the Pennsylvania Line in June. Graciously accepting thanks on behalf of the nation, the legislators needed his expertise to determine the structure of the army following the war.[16] In mid–October, the legislators issued a proclamation declaring that the war men's and deranged officers' furloughs were now discharges. Kept waiting at his final headquarters at the Rockingham estate for the definitive agreement ending the war, the commander in chief was gratified on November 1 when he received the news that the Treaty of Paris was signed by American and British representatives on September 3. On the same day at nearby Versailles, French and Spanish envoys signed separate peace accords with Great Britain. During this time, the Dutch Republic concluded a preliminary agreement that was not formalized and signed until the following May. On November 2, 1783, the commander in chief issued his final order and valediction to the troops of the Continental Army. Extending his heartfelt farewell to the men he was honored to command, Washington entreated them to "prove themselves not less virtuous and useful as Citizens, than they have been persevering and victorious as Soldiers." The army was reduced by this point to a single regiment commanded by Colonel Henry Jackson called the "1st American," despite being composed mainly of Massachusetts troops, with artillery mostly from New York. On November 25 this regiment, accompanied by the commander in chief, entered New York City from upper Manhattan on the heels of the slowly retiring British. The triumphal American procession continued all the way to the Battery at the southern tip of the island. On December 4, Washington and his remaining officers parted ways in an emotional final meeting at Samuel Fraunces's tavern in lower Manhattan. Immediately following that gathering, the commander was off to Annapolis; the legislative body had again moved, this time to Maryland. Far humbler, but just as heartfelt, was the scene that unfolded during this same time 200 miles to the northeast in Taunton, Massachusetts. Discharged in early November 1783 after the creation of the 1st American Regiment, African American soldier Peter Adams of the 1st Massachusetts Regiment playfully made his return home known at the beginning of December. His daughter Rachael Talbot recorded the incident more than half a century later in a pension declaration. "I well recollect that on one Winter evening while my mother and my self were at home, my father viz. Peter Adams knocked at our door and mother asked who was there, he answered a friend, friend to whome said my mother [Margaret 'Peggy' nee Harden], he replied a friend to General Washington, and as I was going to the door, I heard him set down his musket on the door step. I then said to my mother father is come, and so it proved to be, he had on white pantaloons a Blue Coat faced with read he had also a musket and a pack with him."

There were joyful homecomings throughout the land, but in one household in Roxbury, just outside of Boston, the happiness was short-lived. Retiring in the beginning of November, former 2nd Massachusetts Brigade commander John Greaton died a month and a half later at age 42.[17]

Washington's reunion with his loved ones had to wait for another three weeks. He arrived at Mount Vernon on Christmas Eve. On December 23, Washington had returned his commission to Congress in a formal ceremony, "bidding an Affectionate farewell to this August body," and took his "leave of all the employments of public life." Praising his astute conduct of the war and wisdom toward civil authority, President Thomas Mifflin assured him that although he has retired from public life, his example would continue to inspire posterity.[18] Washington, of course, would not get off so easy. The country was not through with him. He was the archetype of the national character, and his future included more troubles and travails in the service of the nation on his way to fame everlasting. Assuming the role of overall army commander, Knox by the end of the year discharged more soldiers. In June 1784, Congress decreased the standing force to only 80 men: 25 at Fort Pitt and 55 at West Point to guard military stores. At the same time, Congress proposed the formation of a regiment to station in posts on the western frontier to keep the native people in awe. The states of Connecticut, New Jersey, New York, and Pennsylvania acceded to the request of national legislators to provide men for the First American Regiment, the successor to the Continental Army's 1st American Regiment.[19]

What became of the residents of the New Windsor Cantonment, 8,000 people turned out of camp, ready or not, to fulfill their destiny? In numbers of communities especially in New England, most of the good farming land was already taken, and further subdivision was not advisable. There were, however, opportunities in the West and on the high seas. Lieutenant Gamaliel Bradford of the 7th Massachusetts became a ship's captain. In 1800 during the Quasi-War with France while operating under a letter of marque and reprisal, he defeated four French privateers off Gibraltar. Sustaining a wound during that fight that necessitated the amputation of his leg, he was honored for his bravery when the U.S. Navy launched the destroyer *Bradford* (DD-545) in 1943. Were it not for his actions as the captain of a privateer, he would be remembered for posterity as the officer censured by Washington for "marching a Guard in a very irregular and unmilitary manner" at the New Windsor encampment on March 8, 1783, the vagaries of recorded history.[20]

The national government and most of the state governments offered land bounties to both officers and soldiers, the amount based on rank. But not everyone was willing to pick up and move to these distant places, choosing instead to sell off their claims. Large numbers still, however, poured into the new land. Some would follow their officers to a new life on the frontier or seek them out to lead them again in resistance to perceived injustice. Having presided over the lives of these people for so long, officers found that those rigid hierarchies were not so easily cast aside. Even when their service was a distant memory, subordinates generally still deferred to their military betters. One of the leaders of the Massachusetts agrarian uprising that bore his name, Daniel Shays, was a retired officer of the 5th Massachusetts Regiment and friend of Benjamin Gilbert. At New Windsor on June 16, 1783, General Putnam sent Washington a petition he framed, signed by 287 other officers, for his approval and endorsement to Congress. In this document, they requested that the nation designate Ohio as one of the locations for the land grants promised to both officers and soldiers in the beginning of the war. Putnam argued that by encouraging former officers to develop this territory, with military precision they would survey, delineate, design, build, and guard these new settlements, securing them from both British and Native American attack. Five years later, he led adventurers from the Ohio Company of Associates, many of whom were veterans of the Massachusetts Line, into settlements along the Ohio River. Others bought shares during the effort to capitalize on the venture. An engineer involved in the construction of West Point and a surveyor, Putnam was well qualified for laying out the tracts of land and supervising the construction. He taught surveying to Benjamin Gilbert. His group founded the oldest city in Ohio, Marietta, named after the queen of France. Included in this party were 2nd Massachusetts commander Lieutenant Colonel Ebenezer Sproat; 6th Massachusetts commander and Ohio Company of Associates cofounder Colonel Benjamin Tupper; his son Anselm, a captain in his father's regiment; 1st Massachusetts Brigade major Captain Nathaniel Cushing; Benjamin Gilbert's company commander and friend Captain Nathan Goodale; Major Robert Oliver from the 3rd and then 2nd Massachusetts; Captain Daniel Lunt from the 10th and 1st Massachusetts; and 7th Massachusetts captain Asa Coburn.[21]

Prior to moving to Ohio, Tupper helped defend the Springfield Arsenal during Shays' Rebellion. Tupper served under militia major general William Shepherd, who commanded the 4th Massachusetts Regiment until his resignation in January 1783. New Windsor Cantonment residents were on both sides of this conflict. Insurgent leader Luke Day was a captain in the 7th Massachusetts. He was so heavily in debt after the war that his creditors put him in jail, and he had to sell the cut-and-thrust saber presented to him by the Marquis de Lafayette. The young Frenchman gave swords to the officers and noncommissioned officers of his Light Infantry Division. Moses Sash, an African American of Day's regiment, was also part of the resistance, and so were many other former soldiers. Recognized as one of the most spirited in the uprising, Sash was singled out by authorities and personally indicted for his actions. Joined by community members who too were harmed by the postwar depression, these former Continentals provided direction and discipline to the popular revolt in central and western Massachusetts. Relieved by the peaceful return of the army to their homes following the war, government officials succeeded in dispersing the men, but their anger and sense of betrayal remained, compounded by the disillusionment that all their sacrifice availed them nothing. With conditions steadily declining, certain leaders acted.

Rufus Putnam (1737–1824), by James Sharples Senior, from life, 1796–1797 (INDE 11914) (courtesy Independence National Historical Park).

The roots of the rebellion were the extensive public and private debts amassed during the war. Impacted the most by the poor economic situation, farmers in the middle of the 1780s petitioned the General Court of Massachusetts, the state legislature, for the issuance of additional paper currency and a lawmaking farm produce legal tender. Many merchants were part of the select group that owned much of the public and private debt of the state, which, if paid in paper currency, would seriously compromise their financial situation. Elected officials were also counted among the state's largest creditors, including the new governor, James Bowdoin. Speculating in the state-issued securities, they influenced the General Court to redeem the notes at their value on the date of issuance, not at the current rate of depreciation. The legislature's largess to the affluent was to be borne on the backs of the common people. This was all common knowledge, infuriating the original holders who sold them in most cases at a significant discount. By this point, many of the Continental Army officers and soldiers had already disposed of their pay and depreciation certificates, taking sometimes as little as a quarter of their face value. Others let them go for a mere trifle just to get something. Adding injury upon injury, taxes were increased several folds to pay these wealthy opportunists, who wanted their money as soon as possible. The General Court determined to pay off their debt in specie by 1790, draining the limited coins from circulation. No other state was so friendly to public creditors, so most of them contributed large sums to protect the government from the rebels.

Adjournment of the General Court in August without taking any action on the petitions of the people was the final straw. Exhausting every legal means to seek redress, they prepared to take stronger action. Starting with small bands, the insurrection escalated into a popular uprising, organized along military lines. There was a tradition of frontier communities acting to resist unresponsive and tyrannical distant authorities. Styling themselves after the pre–Revolutionary War frontier settlers in North Carolina, the regulators, who resisted a merchant-dominated government, they prevented the opening of courts in the central and western counties of Massachusetts in the fall of 1786. Like the North Carolinians, the Massachusetts regulators sought to exert control over the legal system to restore equity and empathy to the proceedings. Closing courts to stop the passage of detrimental judgments was not a new phenomenon, as armed mobs had interfered with the judicial system before and during the war. Previously, however, the attacks were isolated incidents. Resisters also tried to shut down courts in New Hampshire and Vermont. Militia loyally turned out to defend the government in both states. The Boston oligarchy, however, did not engender such an endorsement from most of the Massachusetts people.

Disconcerted by the events on the frontier, Governor Bowdoin called out the militia to suppress the uprising and restore civil authority. Units in the east turned out, but the response in the affected area was minimal. The people in the west were not going to support a government whose policies were so detrimental to their well-being. While sympathizing with the rebels, most felt that joining their ranks was a step too far. John Paterson, a Massachusetts militia general by this point, led 1,000 men to defend the court in Berkshire County, but most of these men abandoned him in favor of the opposition. General Shepherd succeeded in protecting the Supreme Judicial Court sitting in Springfield, but no jurors would come forward. The coastal militia was not trained, equipped, or inclined to undertake a lengthy campaign on the frontier, so Governor Bowdoin requested troops from Congress. Legislators approved 1,340 soldiers to put down the rebellion, but the states refused to grant the money to finance the expedition. Former 4th Massachusetts and 1st American Regiment commander Colonel Henry Jackson was tapped by Secretary at War Henry Knox to raise this augmentation to the standing army. With little funds, Jackson succeeded in enlisting only a small portion of the desired numbers. Undaunted by the lack of support from the national government, Bowdoin, without legislative approval, formed his own army, commanded by former secretary at war Major General Benjamin Lincoln. Financed by leading merchants and the governor himself, the eastern army of 2,000 would march to the west to join an anticipated 2,400 from the central and western portions of the state. While the eastern counties met their quotas, only 1,000 of the 2,400 men expected from the interior appeared. As if the Massachusetts tax burden was not onerous enough, the General Court made a large appropriation to fund the expedition.

While the soldiers discharged at the end of the war had muskets, other insurgents needed arms. On January 25, 1787, they marched on the Springfield Arsenal to capture the stores of hand weapons, cannons, and ammunition that would be necessary to defeat Lincoln's army, which had marched for Worcester six days earlier. Waiting for them with loaded artillery, the arsenal garrison, led by General Shepherd, held a fortress that the best Continental troops would have been sorely pressed to capture. Unable to disperse the advancing line of rebels by firing the cannons over their heads, Shepherd ordered the guns leveled. The resulting blasts killed several and wounded a score more, compelling them to flee. Some people never forgave him for giving the order to fire. A band of ruffians intent on revenge broke into his stables, blinding and mutilating his fine horses. Re-forming at Petersham, nearly 50 miles to the northeast, the rebels were scattered beyond recall by Lincoln's men in a surprise assault during a snowstorm on the morning of February 2. The only reason that most of the rebels escaped was that their position was on a steep hill, and the attackers were further slowed by deep snow. After all, despite having some former soldiers, this collection of farmers was a mob, not a military force. Half of them were not even armed. Lincoln's army was not much better; only its size and artillery made it formidable. After Petersham, many insurgents, including Daniel Shays, fled to the neighboring states, from which some continued to conduct raids into Massachusetts. In desperation, Luke Day with another insurgent leader, Eli Parsons, went to Vermont and offered command to Ethan Allen, and a few others journeyed to Quebec to request the assistance of Sir Guy Carleton, Lord Dorchester, the governor. Kidnappings and personal attacks lasted until June 1787, when Lincoln finally reestablished government control of the region. Defiance resulted in the offer of concessions, which were the limited objectives of the insurgents. The Massachusetts General Court cut taxes to a small fraction of what they were previously and passed a moratorium on debts. Suspending payments on the past state debt, which sent the value of the promissory notes plummeting, the General Court righted the egregious advantage formerly given to speculators. Combined with the economic upswing the following year, these measures effectively eliminated the causes of unrest. Eventually, after making a full confession like their men, Daniel Shays, Luke Day, and other principals in the rebellion were pardoned and allowed to take the oath of allegiance.

Though there had been clamors for a stronger central government since the inception of United States, Shays' Rebellion provided the impetus to force the issue. No other single event did more to hasten the formation of the Constitutional Convention. The inability of the Confederation government to raise and finance an army to put down the insurrection in Massachusetts was a major issue in the debates. Though there was little danger that the insurgents would have succeeded in overthrowing the Massachusetts government, it was in the best interest of nationalists to make the rest of the country believe that they almost did. Called to revise the Articles of Confederation, the Philadelphia convention was instead used by the advocates of increased federal power to design a new system of government. Assumption of state debt, a major carrot to the ratification of the U.S. Constitution, promised to rescue securities, giving the wealthy speculators a reason to advocate for the new national government. Defeated militarily, the Shaysites rallied opposition to the federal Constitution. Though losing this battle as well, they did not trust this concentration of government power and still possessed their muskets. Raising units from the same area during the American Revolution took advantage of relationships formed over a lifetime, making the military unit an extension of the community. Living in close quarters day in and day out and the shared hardship of service built upon these bonds, which created an intimacy that endured long after the conflict ended. Fostering a sense of mutual obligation, they considered an attack on one as an attack on all.[22]

Not fit for hard labor after his shoulder wound at the Battle of Bunker Hill, Lieutenant Colonel Hugh Maxwell of the Massachusetts Line tried to earn a living from his long-neglected farm and spent two seasons surveying the boundary between the Phelps and Gorham purchases in western New York between 1788 and 1790. Though considering himself disabled since 1775, he waited nearly two decades before finally soliciting Congress for an invalid pension. Traveling to Philadelphia in December 1794 to press his claim, he met with Secretary at War Knox to seek his assistance. During that session, congressional legislators passed a resolution that any officer placed on the invalid list had to first turn in the commutation of their half-pay, which ended Maxwell's efforts. He either had the worst timing possible or, more than likely, the legislation was a direct response to his petition. Like many other Revolutionary War veterans, Maxwell had sold his government securities long ago at a great discount. More generous than wise, he loaned money to friends, much of which was never paid back, and not one to turn away down-on-their-luck soldiers, he was financially ruined by the time of his death. Sailing from Hartford, Connecticut, in the summer of 1799, to sell horses in the West Indies, he died during the voyage.[23]

As a matter of course, many officers went into politics. Horatio Gates was finally coaxed into running for the New York Legislature in 1800 by his friend and presidential contender Aaron Burr, who was trying to line up supporters for his candidacy. From this position, Gates could oppose the Alexander Hamilton–dominated Federalist Party. Elected, Gates helped select the men who would cast the state's vote in the electoral college for Jefferson and Burr and then resigned. The two Republicans, however, tied in the electoral college. Despising Burr, Hamilton wrote scathing letters about him to Federalist electors, which changed enough votes to decide the contest in favor of the Virginian. Not forgetting this opposition and a host of other wrongs, Burr fought the duel four years later in which he killed his nemesis.

Shortly after Gates returned home from the New Windsor Cantonment, his wife died. A few years later, he married a spinster with a sizable fortune who found their estate on the Virginia frontier too far removed from the centers of society, so they moved to New York. There was another reason as well. In involving himself in any business or land speculation in his adopted state, he stood a good chance of being drawn into the sphere of Washington and his legion of adherents, whose coldness was most disconcerting. Taking up residence at the refined Rose Hill farm in the Bronx, which is now on the grounds of Fordham University, the couple lived in comfortable gentility. While losing more friends in the divisive politics of the new republic, Gates still maintained the esteem of a select number of confidants.

Dying in 1806, Gates was laid to rest in Trinity Churchyard in New York City, where America's royal son Lord Stirling, Major General William Alexander, whose revelation of the Conway letter to Washington gave him so much trouble, was buried. Certainly one of his most mean-spirited detractors, Alexander Hamilton, General Schuyler son-in-law and Washington acolyte, was also there, as were the reinterred remains of Brigadier General Richard Montgomery, whose widow, Janet (Livingston) Montgomery, Gates unsuccessfully courted. Having reached such lofty social heights, though his claim to the Scottish earldom was never confirmed by the House of Lords, Stirling spent far beyond his means, commensurate with his new station, and involved himself in failed speculative ventures. The graves of Stirling, who died penniless, and his wife are simple ground-level vaults with stone slab covering. Hamilton is buried in an impressive neoclassical marble sarcophagus surmounted by a pyramid with four urns set into the corners. Following a congressional resolve, in early 1776 minister to France Benjamin Franklin commissioned French Court sculptor Jean-Jacques Caffieri to fashion a monument to honor Montgomery. Caffieri carved an urn on a classical column surrounded by a panoply of arms, resting on an entablature with memorial plaque. After years of delay, the memorial was placed in the east window of St. Paul's Chapel on the grounds of Trinity Cemetery in the late 1780s. In 1818, Montgomery's remains were brought from Quebec and placed beneath the cenotaph. Despite what occurred later, Gates's Saratoga victory should have inspired similar commemoration, but he lies in an unmarked grave whose exact location is lost. He is remembered only by a small stone marker placed by the Daughters of the American Revolution in 2012.

Lieutenant Colonel John Brooks was governor of Massachusetts from 1816 to 1823. Fellow Bay Stater Colonel Timothy Pickering, the harried and unappreciated quartermaster general, employed his remarkable astuteness and organizational talents as postmaster general, secretary at war, secretary of state, senator, and representative for Massachusetts in Congress. Major General Arthur St. Clair was governor of the Northwest Territory and presided over the worst defeat ever inflicted by the natives on an American army. He was attacked along the Ohio-Indiana border during the early morning hours of November 4, 1791; over 600 were killed out of the 1,000 present. This number does not include the more than 200 family members slain. Of the few hundred who escaped, many did not get away unscathed. Former colonels Henry Dearborn from the New Hampshire Line and William Hull of the Connecticut and then the Massachusetts Line became generals in the War of 1812. Hull became governor of the Michigan Territory in 1805, and Dearborn had been secretary at war during the Jefferson administration. Both would have been better to have stayed out of this conflict, especially Hull, who was sentenced to death for his shameful surrender of Detroit in 1812. President James Madison pardoned the aging veteran, who was not up to independent command. Dearborn was not either, despite some early success. He was eventually shunted off to a less active position to make way for younger and more aggressive leaders. Few of the Revolutionary War generation distinguished themselves in this conflict. Appointed minister to France, poet, politician, land speculator, and Francophile Joel Barlow was summoned by Napoleon for an audience in eastern Europe regarding redress for French seizures of U.S. merchant shipping and cargoes. Caught in the retreat of the Grand Armée from Moscow in 1812, he died of exposure in Poland at the end of that year.

The rest of this multitude returned to obscurity except for possibly being paraded on the Fourth of July and in other patriotic celebrations as venerable icons of long past virtue until their steadily decreasing ranks were no more. Desperate for soldiers, military officials accepted minorities, but the white hegemony quickly forgot their contributions when they were no longer needed. Native and African American soldiers returned to marginalization, segregation, and exclusion from mainstream society. Both free Blacks and slaves enlisted. The enslaved were often emancipated for their service, but for all free African Americans their liberty had its limits and was tenuous as long as color-based slavery existed in the world. Relegated to the least desirable and poorest sections of communities or made to live on the outskirts, they struggled to overcome the racism and prejudice, which kept them from prospering. Earning two Honorary Badges of Distinction for his lengthy service in the 2nd New Hampshire Regiment and an earlier unit, Jude Hall, enslaved during his service, was given his freedom at the end of the conflict. Bestowed the sobriquet "Old Rock" for his determination and steadiness in battle, he needed this stalwart resolve to endure the kidnapping and selling of three of his sons into slavery and the expulsion from his Exeter, New Hampshire, home by town officials in 1817. This ouster was not the first time. His family was warned away from Stratham, New Hampshire, in 1792 and Exeter in 1785 and 1795. He lived for a time by a small body of water in the woods that came to be known as Jude's Pond. A musician from Hall's regiment, Cato Fisk, and 18 other African Americans were warned away from Exeter in 1787. A third 2nd New Hampshire soldier, London Daily, along with Rufus Cutler, the son of Tobias Cutler of his regiment, and others formed a society to benefit the Black community of Exeter. Daily stood need of assistance himself. He was sent to debtors' prison in 1820. Too often heavily in debt and just barely eking out a living, Hall, Fisk, Daily, and so many other veterans received public assistance at times during their life, so the pensions enacted in the first half of the 19th century were long overdue.[24]

With the forced removal and seizure of Indian land institutionalized, America's inexorable expansion to the west and south forced the tribes one by one onto reservations. Long before the Revolution, the New England indigenous people were concentrated into small "praying towns" as homesteaders bought and settled on their former lands. Fearful of attacks by fellow Native Americans and the inevitable retaliation by less than discerning white neighbors, tribal groups in New Jersey and eastern New York, in ever-increasing numbers by the mid–18th century, sought the protection of their kinsman to the west. At the dawn of the 19th century, the Indians of the Northeast were dispossessed of all their land except for small tracts previously set aside for them. While there were limited opportunities in these small towns, they were safe from prejudice and racial violence. Moreover, having a highly developed sense of community, native people preferred a tribal society where individual responsibility and welfare are time-honored concerns. Living in the Mashpee reservation on Cape Cod, Wampanoag Isaac Wickhams received his veteran pension for service in the Massachusetts Line. A light infantryman in 1781, he participated in the attack on Redoubt Number 10 at Yorktown, Virginia, in October. After his successful petition, he assisted others and their widows with their applications, testified to the accuracy of that information, and made arguments for their approval.[25]

In recruiting the new federal army, Secretary at War Henry Knox, the former Continental artillery general, ordered Lieutenant John Pratt in 1788 that "neither Negroes; Mullatoes, or Indians are to be received." This prohibition remained in effect through the American Civil War. Though at least one man managed to get past this injunction during the War of 1812, the U.S. regular army did not authorize the induction of African American soldiers until 1866, and these men served only in the newly formed segregated regiments. A change in the law in 1862, however, did allow the formation of Black volunteer units and the United States Colored Troops. While serving as scouts and auxiliaries, Native Americans did not enter the military in large numbers until World War I.[26]

The last New Windsor Cantonment residents lived to see the American Civil War that threatened to tear apart the country they struggled so hard to found. Wanting to survive long enough to see the country reunited, Alexander Milliner, former drummer in the 1st New York Regiment, at 102 years old encouraged recruits to join the 140th New York Volunteers in September 1862 to "great excitement and enthusiasm." Claiming to have served over six years, he fought at White Plains, Monmouth, where he "received a flesh wound in his thigh," and at Yorktown. Among his faulty recollections were serving in the commander in chief's guard and fighting at Saratoga, the Siege of Fort Stanwix, and Brandywine. Milliner's regiment was in the Mohawk Valley but did not fight at either Saratoga or Fort Stanwix, and being on the outskirts of Philadelphia, Brandywine was too far away. He did, however, spend a significant amount of time stationed at Fort Stanwix, which the Americans called Fort Schuyler. There were more spurious claims of serving aboard USS *Constitution* during the War of 1812 and being captured by the French at sea and being imprisoned in Guadeloupe. Milliner probably spent most of his life as a farmer. He was in declining health by the time of his 104th birthday on March 14, 1864, and died on March 13, 1865, a few weeks before the Union victory. Though claiming to have served at Saratoga, Private Samuel Downing of the 2nd New Hampshire Regiment stated in his 1818 pension application that he enlisted in July 1780, so this was not possible, but he was at Yorktown. Encamped by headquarters, Downing remembered seeing Washington every day during the siege. Also a farmer, Downing showed off to a large crowd assembled at his farm to celebrate his 100th birthday by cutting "down a hemlock tree five feet in circumference and later in the day a wild cherry tree near his house, of half that size." Denouncing the secession of the southern states, he too wished to last until the North was victorious, which was granted. He died in early 1867. From Wrentham, Massachusetts, Eleazer Blake responded to the Lexington Alarm, was in a supporting role during the Battle of Bunker Hill, and fought at Saratoga. He subsequently wintered at Valley Forge, survived the battle and awful heat at Monmouth, and served in the Rhode Island Campaign. Enlisting for the war after completing his initial three-year term in the Continental Army, he was a private and then a sergeant in the 4th Massachusetts Regiment. Spending much of his time in the Hudson Highlands, he was furloughed at New Windsor on June 12, 1783. Living briefly in New York and Stoddard, New Hampshire, before settling permanently in Rindge, New Hampshire, Eleazer raised five children with his wife Jerusha Gerould, from his hometown. A farmer and wheelwright, he was also selected as a deacon of the local Congregational church. The house he built still stands. He died in 1852 when he was 95 years old. The Rindge Historical Society has an extensive collection of Eleazer Blake historical manuscripts and objects, including his promotion certificate to sergeant and his discharge signed by General George Washington.[27]

After marching into New York City with Colonel Henry Jackson's 1st American Regiment, Henry Kneeland, the former German auxiliary, was discharged from the Continental Army on December 31, 1783. He returned to Bedford, where he was listed on the tax rolls for 1785 and 1786. There are no other records in Bedford relating to him. The next information we have is his pension application. On March 18, 1818, Congress passed a resolution granting a pension to the officers and enlisted men of the

Continental Army, the navy, and the marines who were in financial need. Wasting little time, he appeared before Morris S. Miller, first judge of Oneida County, New York, on April 2. In his sworn deposition, he claimed that he was 66 years old and needed financial assistance. Kneeland felt confident enough by this time to sign the instrument as Heinrich Kickeland. He probably saw no further need to hide his real name, but there was no reason for him to test the bureaucracy by also divulging that his Continental Army enlistment had been fraudulent because he had been an enemy deserter. Attached to the papers was the discharge given him by General Knox on December 31, 1783. In none of his pension declarations does Kneeland indicate that he was a formerly in the British service. Accompanying the veteran, local resident William Godfrey vouched for Kneeland's integrity. In May, Miller forwarded the depositions to the secretary of the Department of War, John C. Calhoun. In a supplemental affidavit in October 1818, Heinrich Kickeland swore that he was a "German by birth and ... [was] called <u>Henry Kneeland</u> by the English." In December, Calhoun awarded him $8 per month, commencing from the date of his initial deposition.

Two years later, pensioners were required to produce a list of their assets to assist government officials in confirming whether they needed support. All future applicants would have to submit a list as well. Kickeland stated that he was a farmer, but due to his age and failing vision, he was not capable of providing for himself and his family. Signing his name Henry Kneeland in documents prepared by the Oneida County Court of Common Pleas on September 8, 1820, he stated his assets as one acre of land with a small log home in Whitestown, New York, two cows, four pigs, an old horse, a plow, a harness, farming utensils, and household furniture worth $6. His total assets were valued at $150. By this time he was married to Polly, 21 years his junior. He listed no children of his own, but he was taking care of 11-year-old Rachel Hoffman, Polly's orphan niece. Polly died sometime before 1827. On January 18 of that year Kneeland married Nancy (Spencer) Andrews of Litchfield, New York, in her hometown. This required him to travel nearly 150 miles to the New York–Pennsylvania border at age 72. Heinrich Kickeland died on October 17, 1846, in his 94th year. He is understood by his descendants to be buried in the old North Baptist Church Cemetery in Westmoreland, New York. Less than two years later Nancy married another Revolutionary War veteran, Stephen Moulton, originally from Connecticut. He died on July 1, 1851. On February 3, 1853, all widows of Revolutionary War veterans were authorized a pension. Nancy Moulton, 76 years old by this time, applied for one as the widow of Heinrich Kickeland on March 18, 1853. She was placed on the rolls on September 13, with payments backdated to February 3.[28]

Remaining behind after the army left in June 1783, the Osborn family stayed until the following year. Along with several other soldiers, Aaron worked as a laborer for surrounding farmers. A second child, Aaron Jr., was born on August 9, 1784. Shortly thereafter, Aaron took up with another woman and abandoned his family. Traveling to his habitation about 15 miles north of Newburgh, the home of his new wife Polly Sloat, Sarah confirmed that he had remarried and left the next morning. A couple of weeks later he returned and tried to reconcile with her, but she refused to have anything further to do with him. She never saw Aaron again. With smug satisfaction, she had heard that Polly Sloat "died dead drunk, the liquor running out of her mouth after she was dead." The bigamist was living with a third wife in the Mohawk Valley when he died in 1819.

Moving back to her birthplace, Sarah for the next few years struggled to provide for herself and her children until she met John Benjamin, who had been a soldier in the

1st Regiment of the Orange County Militia. They married in April 1787 and had three children: Helen, Samuel, and Christiana. In 1822 they moved to Mount Pleasant, Wayne County, in the northeast corner of Pennsylvania. John died there four years later. In 1837, Sarah applied for a pension "made by the act of Congress passed July 4, 1836, and the act explanatory of said act, passed March 3, 1837." Beginning in 1832, all Revolutionary War veterans with six months or more of service were declared eligible regardless of physical condition or financial status. Previously, they had to demonstrate either service-related disabilities or financial hardship in conformity with the 1818 act. As a widow married to a soldier during the war, Sarah was now entitled to this gratuity. Over time the payment was eventually extended to widows who married soldiers after the Revolution. Despite her pension, Sarah continued to work hard. She spun yarn by hand in the fashion of colonial days, and her quality workmanship was displayed "at the American Institute, the Crystal Palace Exhibition in London and the World's Fair in New York City." Deservedly proud, Sarah enjoyed regaling family and friends with stories of long ago. Having endured so much, she died peacefully in her sleep at 101 years old.[29]

Little is known about what Thomas Foster did after the war other than that he returned home to Middleborough, Massachusetts, and presumably resumed his trade as a blacksmith. Along with his wife, he either accompanied or joined his son Peter, who moved to Middlebury, Vermont, in 1803. Foster died there three years later. Contrary to what might have been expected of Benjamin Gilbert, there was not a life of continued indulgence and dissipation. With "so many enemies" trying to "destroy" him, he did not stay very long at his boyhood home in Brookfield, Massachusetts. Establishing himself on a farm in Middlefield, near Lake Otsego in central New York outside of Cooperstown, he worked hard to develop this property and used the surveying skills taught to him by General Putnam. Confident enough in his situation, Gilbert reestablished his relationship with the families he met while convalescing in Danbury, Connecticut, over the winter of 1778–79, who were probably unaware of his lechery while in the service. Gilbert was permitted to court Danbury resident Mary Cornwall whom he probably met during a party at her house when she was still a young girl. They married in 1786, and Gilbert took his young bride back to New York. Local citizens thought enough of this former debauchee to elect him to three terms in the New York State Assembly, as sheriff of Otsego County for 11 years, and for other local political offices. When not engaged in public service, he devoted his time to his family, the farm, church, and Freemasonry.[30] New Windsor's prodigal son was lost in the fleshpots of the army but was born again in the responsibilities of civilian life. Gilbert died on January 18, 1828, at the age of 72.

What happened to the abandoned 1782–83 Continental Army city? With the last inhabitants of this encampment gone, New Windsor Cantonment existed only in memory and in the detritus of human habitation. Eventually, nature reclaimed the landscape. For years after the army left, sightseers ventured up to the vicinity of Temple Hill in search of vestiges of the former campground. With all the trees gone, the cleared land was either left alone or used as farmland or pasture. The Temple Hill Creamery and dairy operated here in the late 19th and early 20th centuries. In making the land suitable for other uses, it was often necessary to remove the collapsed fireplace and foundation stones. With walls made out of them and other rocks turned up by the plow, most of the aboveground traces gradually disappeared. On June 22, 1883, several thousand people attended the centennial celebration on Temple Hill, including former New York governor Hamilton Fish and about 100 to 120 veterans from "The Orange Blossoms,"

Temple Hill Monument (author's collection).

the storied 124th New York Volunteer Infantry from the Civil War.[31] Placement of the monument in 1891 by the Historical Society of Newburgh Bay and the Highlands was the realization of a long-held desire by many to commemorate the Continental Army's final winter encampment with a permanent memorial. Living nearby in the late 18th- or early 19th-century house just north of the Temple site, longtime property owner William L. McGill leased the parcel to representatives of the Historical Society of Newburgh Bay and the Highlands, giving "Edmund M. Ruttenber, Joseph M. Dickey, Russell Headley, Arthur A. McLean and Wilbur H. Weston and their survivors the use in perpetuity." In 1916 Mary Smith, daughter of William McGill, graciously donated the property to the historical organization, which two years later conveyed it to New York State.[32]

Later generations visualized a much larger memorial. Ultimately, local supporters wanted the grounds turned into a national park. Part of their effort to instill the importance of the New Windsor encampment into the country's consciousness was the staging of large patriotic celebrations. The most famous was held on May 28, 1932, Temple Hill Day, when 137 World War I veterans were presented the Purple Heart Medal in the first public ceremony to bestow the new award.[33] The Purple Heart was inspired by the Revolutionary War Badge of Military Merit created by Washington at his Newburgh, New York, headquarters on August 7, 1782. Following the ceremony to mark the 150th anniversary of the end of the war a year later, they wanted something more tangible. The placement in 1934 of the Mountainville hut—purportedly removed in 1783 from this encampment, on the hillside near the monument, by the National Temple Hill Association—was the first step in the association's plan to visually represent a portion of the Continental Army's final winter encampment. But the preservation organization's

Chapter 11. Denouement: The Conclusion

White Quartz Masonic star two-thirds of the way up the east side of the Temple Hill Monument. The east was the most important direction to Christians, including Masons, because it pointed toward the prophesied location of the Second Coming of Jesus Christ and the Last Judgment. Afraid of missing the promised resurrection of those dead judged worthy by Jesus Christ, Christians were buried facing the east or, less desirably, north or south. A single white quartz stone is on both the southern and western sides but not on the northern side because that direction is a place of darkness, being the last to receive the light and the first to lose it. By tradition, the northern part of a churchyard was intended for judgment and therefore the least honorable, so people avoided burial on the northern side, and in some instances undesirables were relegated to this ground. This feature was recognized by New York State Office of Parks, Recreation & Historic Preservation restoration specialist James Decker (author's collection).

primary purpose was to re-create the Temple of Virtue to serve as a shrine, a goal the association achieved in the early 1960s. The National Temple Hill Association ran the site as a living history museum until the fall of 1967, but the costs of operation forced the association to transfer the property to New York State.[34] Today, the New York State Office of Parks, Recreation and Historic Preservation operates the New Windsor Cantonment, Knox's Headquarters, and Washington's Headquarters State Historic sites, cooperating often with the dedicated group of local historical enthusiasts who were primarily responsible for preserving the old campground, the National Temple Hill Association.

Appendix 1

Organization of the Continental Army in New York and Northern New Jersey in 1782–83

Commander in Chief—General George Washington
Director General of the Hospital of the United States—Dr. John Cochran
Adjutant General—Brigadier General Edward Hand
Assistant Adjutant General—Captain John Carlisle
Assistant Adjutant General—Captain Simeon Lord (appointed April 1783 but took effect February 1, 1783)
Judge Advocate General—Lieutenant Thomas Edwards
Paymaster General—John Pierce
Deputy Paymaster—Hezekiah Wetmore
Inspector General—Major General Friedrich von Steuben
Inspector for the Northern Army—Colonel Walter Stewart
Assistant Inspector for the Northern Army—Major William Barber
Quartermaster General—Colonel Timothy Pickering
Clothier General—John Moylan
Assistant Clothier General—David Brooks
Geographer of the United States (Continental Army)—Simeon De Witt
Marechaussee (Provost)—Captain Bartholomew von Heer
2nd Continental Dragoons—Colonel Elisha Sheldon
Commander, Corps of Engineers—Major General Louis le Bègue de Presle Duportail
Commander, West Point and Artillery—Major General Henry Knox
2nd Continental Artillery Regiment—Colonel John Lamb
3rd Continental Artillery Regiment—Colonel John Crane
Connecticut Brigade Commander—Brigadier General Jedidiah Huntington
1st Connecticut Regiment—Colonel Zebulon Butler
2nd Connecticut Regiment—Colonel Heman Swift
3rd Connecticut Regiment—Colonel Samuel Blatchley Webb
Commander, Southern New York and Northern New Jersey and the Canadian Regiment—Brigadier General Moses Hazen
Commander, Albany/Mohawk—Major General William Alexander (Lord Stirling) (Died, January 1783)

New Windsor Cantonment

Commander, New Windsor—Major General Horatio Gates
　　　　　　—Major General William Heath (Heath left camp November 5, 1782, and returned April 1783)

Commander, Massachusetts Line—Major General Robert Howe

Commander, Maryland, New Hampshire, New Jersey, New York—Major General Arthur St. Clair
Commander, 1st Massachusetts Brigade—Colonel William Shepard (Acting, because senior colonel, retired January 1783)
    —Brigadier General John Paterson—January 1783
Brigade Major, 1st Massachusetts Brigade—Captain Nathaniel Cushing—January 1783
Commander, 1st Massachusetts Regiment—Colonel Joseph Vose
Commander, 4th Massachusetts Regiment—Colonel William Shepard (Retired January 1783)
    —Colonel Henry Jackson—January 1783
Commander, 7th Massachusetts Regiment—Lieutenant Colonel John Brooks
Commander, 2nd Massachusetts Brigade—Brigadier General John Paterson
    —Brigadier General John Greaton—January 1783
Aide to Brigadier General John Greaton—Lieutenant Samuel Mellish (appointed April 1783 but took effect January 7, 1783)
Brigade Major, 2nd Massachusetts Brigade—Captain Abraham Williams—January 1783
Commander, 2nd Massachusetts Regiment—Lieutenant Colonel Ebenezer Sproat
Commander, 5th Massachusetts Regiment—Colonel Rufus Putnam
    —Lieutenant Colonel David Cobb, January 7, 1783
Commander, 8th Massachusetts Regiment—Colonel Michael Jackson

Commander, 3rd Massachusetts Brigade—Colonel John Greaton (Acting, because senior colonel)
    —Brigadier General Rufus Putnam—January 1783
Aide to General Putnam—Captain John Trotter
Brigade Major, 3rd Massachusetts Brigade—Captain K. Smith—January 1783
Commander, 3rd Massachusetts Regiment—Colonel John Greaton
    —Lieutenant Colonel James Mellen—January–June 1783
    —Colonel Michael Jackson—June–November 1783
Commander, 6th Massachusetts Regiment—Lieutenant Colonel Calvin Smith
    —Colonel Benjamin Tupper—January–June 1783
Commander, 9th Massachusetts Regiment (Disbanded January 1783)—Colonel Henry Jackson
Commander, 10th Massachusetts Regiment (Disbanded January 1783)—Colonel Benjamin Tupper
Commander, New Hampshire Brigade—Lieutenant Colonel George Reid (Acting, because senior lieutenant colonel)
    —Brigadier General John Stark—April 1783
Brigade Major, New Hampshire Brigade—Captain Jeremiah Fogg—January 1783
Commander, 1st New Hampshire Regiment (Called New Hampshire Regiment March 1783)
    —Lieutenant Colonel Henry Dearborn (Retired March 1783)
    —Lieutenant Colonel George Reid

Commander, 2nd New Hampshire Regiment (Reduced to battalion of four companies and called the New Hampshire Battalion—March 1783)—Lieutenant Colonel George Reid
    —Major William Scott
Commander New Hampshire Battalion (Created after furloughing of most of army)—Lieutenant Colonel George Reid
Commander, New Jersey Brigade—Colonel Elias Dayton (Acting, because senior colonel; promoted to brigadier general January 1783 and made actual)
Brigade Major, New Jersey Brigade—Captain Richard Cox
    —Captain Aaron Ogden (March 1783)
Commander, 1st New Jersey Regiment—Colonel Matthias Ogden
(Called the Jersey Regiment—March 1783)

Commander, 2nd New Jersey Regiment (March 1783 reduced to battalion of four companies and called the Jersey Battalion)—Colonel Elias Dayton
        —Colonel Francis Barber January–February 1783 (Died February 1783)
        —Lieutenant Colonel John Cumming
Commander, 3rd Maryland Detachment—Major Thomas Lansdale
Commander, New York Brigade—Colonel Goose Van Schaick (Acting, because senior colonel)
Brigade Major, New York Brigade—Captain Benjamin Hicks

Commander, 1st New York Regiment—Colonel Goose Van Schaick
Commander, 2nd New York Regiment—Colonel Philip Van Cortlandt

Appendix 2

Paying the Continental Army

In Congress, May 27, 1778
I. INFANTRY

Resolved, That each battalion of infantry shall consist of nine companies, one of which shall be of light infantry; the light infantry to be kept complete by drafts from the battalion, and organized during the campaign into corps of light infantry:

That the battalion of infantry consist of

COMMISSIONED			Pay per month
I Colonel and captain,			75 dollars.
I Lieutenant colonel and captain,			60
I Major,			50
6 Captains, each,			40
I Captain lieutenant,			26⅔
8 Lieutenants, each			26⅔
9 Ensigns, each,			20
Pay master, Adjutant, Quarter master,	to be taken from the line.	20 dollars. 13 13	In addition to their pay as officers in the line.
I Surgeon,			60 dollars
I Surgeon's mate,			40
I Serjeant major,			10
I Quarter master serjeant,			10
27 Serjeants, each,			10
I Drum major,			9
I Fife major,			9
18 Drums and fifes, each,			7⅓
27 Corporals, each,			7⅓
477 Privates, each,			6⅔

Each of the field officers to command a company.
The Lieutenant of the colonel's company to have the rank of Captain lieutenant.[1]

IV. PROVOST

Resolved, That a Provost be establish'd to consist of

	Pay per month
I Captain of provosts,	50 dollars
4 Lieutenants, each	33⅓
I Clerk,	33⅓
I Quarter master serjeant	15
2 Trumpeters, each	10
2 Serjeants, each	15
5 Corporals, each	10
43 Provosts or privates, each	8⅓
4 Executioners, each	10

This Corps to be mounted on horseback and arm'd and accoutred as light dragoons.[2]

The September 30, 1780, Act of Congress that established the pay of regimental surgeons and mates was changed on March 19, 1782. Regimental surgeons were allowed $59 per month, three rations per day, and the same forage as before. The mates would receive $42 per month and two rations.[3]

The April 22, 1782, Act of Congress changed the arrangement of the rations and subsistence that an officer would draw above their base pay. The resolution was to take effect in May 1782.[4]

	Rations per day	Dols. Per month
A major general	5	31 60–90
A brigadier general	4	25 30–90
A colonel	2	12 60–90
A lieut. colonel commandant	2	12 60–90
A lieutenant colonel,	1½	11
Major,	1½	8
Chaplain,	1½	8
Captain,	1	6 30–90
Subaltern,	1	3 15–90
Surgeon,	1½	4 60–90
Surgeon's mate	1	3 15–90
Quartermaster General,	4	25 30–90
Deputy quartermaster with southern army,	2	12 60–90
Deputy paymaster with ditto,	1½	11
Deputy cloathier with the army,	1	3 15–90
Deputy postmaster of the army,	1	
Commissary of forage,	1½	11
Field commissary,	1	6 30–90
Ditto, southern Army,	1	6 30–90

Appendix 2

	Rations per day	Dols. Per month
Director general of the hospital	2	
Chief physician and Surgeon,	2	
Hospital surgeon,	1	
Mate,	1	
Steward,	1	
Ward-master,	1	

Note. The aforementioned charts are displayed to show Continental Army pay at the end of the war. The infantry regiments were reorganized again in 1781, which is described in chapter 10.

Appendix 3
Duty for the Lines

"The first Jersey regiment will march for the relief of the Infantry on the lines tomorrow (December 5, 1782); the Commanding officer will please call at Head Quarters for Orders, and apply to the Deputy Quarter Master for boats.

The Infantry companies when relieved will join their respective regiments." General Orders, December 4, 1782, in John C. Fitzpatrick, ed., *The Writings of George Washington from the Original Manuscript Sources, 1745–1799*, 39 vols. (Washington, DC, 1931–44) 25:395 (hereafter *Washington Writings*).

"The first Massachusetts regiment to relieve the first regiment of Jersey on the lines tomorrow (December 18, 1782). The Quarter Master Genl. to furnish boats on application from the Commanding officer." General Orders, December 17, 1782, *Washington Writings*, 25:442.

"The second Jersey regiment will march for the relief of the first Massachusetts on the lines on Thursday the second of January next" (January 2, 1783). General Orders, December 31, 1782, *Washington Writings*, 25:496.

"The seventh Massachusetts regiment will march for the relief of the second Jersey regiment, on the Lines, on thursday the 16th. Instant" (January 16, 1783). General Orders, January 14, 1783, *Washington Writings*, 26:35.

"The first New york regiment will march on thursday next (January 30, 1783) for the relief of the 7th. Massachusetts regimt. on the lines." General Orders, January 28, 1783, *Washington Writings*, 26:74.

"The 4th. Massachusetts Regiment will march thursday next (February 13, 1783) to the relief of the first New York regiment on the Lines." General Orders, February 11, 1783, *Washington Writings*, 26:120.

"The 2d. York regiment will march on thursday next (February 27, 1783) for the relief of the 4th. Massa. Regt. on the Lines." General Orders, February 25, 1783, *Washington Writings*, 26:160.

"The 3d. Massachusetts Regiment will march on thursday next (March 13, 1783) to the relief of the 2nd. York regiment on the Lines." General Orders, March 11, 1783, *Washington Writings*, 26:209.

"The New Hampshire regiment will march on Thursday next (March 27, 1783) to relieve the third Massa. Regimt. on the Lines." General Orders, March 25, 1783, *Washington Writings*, 26:259.

"The sixth Massachusetts regt. to hold itself in *readiness* to relieve the Hampshire regiment on the Lines." General Orders, April 8, 1783, *Washington Writings*, 26:306.

"The 6th. Massachusetts regiment will march tomorrow (April 15, 1783) for the relief of the Hampshire regiment on the Lines; the Commanding officer will call at Head Quarters this evening for orders." General Orders, April 14, 1783, *Washington Writings*, 26:315.

"The Maryland Detachment and Hampshire battalion will march on tuesday next (April 29, 1783) to the relief of the 6th. Massachusetts regt. on the Lines." General Orders, April 27, 1783, *Washington Writings*, 26:363.

"The Light companies of the Jersey, the 2nd. York, 5th. and 8th. Massachusetts regts. will take post on the Lines. They are to be on the Grand parade at 9 o'clock tomorrow morning (May 2, 1783) and put themselves under the orders of Major Fish." General Orders, May 1, 1783, *Washington Writings*, 26:373.

"The 2d. Massachusetts regt. will march on tuesday next (May 13, 1782) to relieve the Maryland Detachment and the Hampshire Battalion on the Lines." General Orders, May 11, 1783, *Washington Writings*, 26:424.

"The 8th. Massachusetts regt. will march on tuesday next (May 27, 1783) to Relieve the 2d. Regt. on the Lines." General Orders, May 25, 1783, *Washington Writings*, 26:453.

Appendix 4
Deaths at the New Windsor Cantonment

3rd Maryland Regiment Detachment
1 death January 1783 *(Deaths with no name are from Charles H. Lesser, ed., *The Sinews of Independence Monthly Strength Reports of the Continental Army* (Chicago, 1976) 238–252.
1 death March 1783
1 death May 1783
    Total: 3

Massachusetts Line
1 death 2nd Massachusetts Regiment, November 1782
3 deaths 4th Massachusetts Regiment, November 1782
Private Joseph Lovekins of Ipswich, Massachusetts, 7th Massachusetts Regiment, killed November 26, 1782, by a tree felled by a woodcutting party, Massachusetts Office of the Secretary of State, Secretary of the Commonwealth, *Massachusetts Soldiers and Sailors of the Revolutionary War: A Compilation from the Archives*, 17 vols. (Boston, 1896–1908), 9:998 (hereafter *Massachusetts Soldiers and Sailors*).

Ensign Dominick Trant of Ireland, 9th Massachusetts Regiment, died on November 7, 1782, after a "lingering illness of eight months." "His remains were decently interred in the garrison at West Point, and were followed to the grave by his Excellency General Washington and a very respectable procession." Since Trant probably never made it to New Windsor, his death is not included in the total for this location. Francis B. Heitman, ed., *Historical Register of Officers of the Continental Army During the War of the Revolution, April 1775 to December 1783, with Addenda by Robert Kirby, 1932* (Baltimore, 1967 [Reprint of the new, revised, and enlarged edition of 1914]), 547; and James Thacher, *Eyewitness to the American Revolution the Battles and Generals as Seen by an Army Surgeon* (Stamford, CT, 1994 [reprint of 1862]), 323.

Private Thomas Staples of Mendon, Massachusetts, 10th Massachusetts Regiment, died November 4, 1782, *Massachusetts Soldiers and Sailors*, 14:850.
1 death 10th Massachusetts Regiment, November 1782
3 deaths 3rd Massachusetts Regiment, December 1782
Private Peter Pero or Peroo, 7th Massachusetts Regiment, died of strangulation on December 2, 1782. *Massachusetts Soldiers and Sailors*, 12:180. Although his cause of death is very cryptic, he might have choked from inflammatory fever, which among other conditions included respiratory ailments such as pneumonia. There were 33 inflammatory fever cases reported in the return for the New Windsor Hospital in the month of December 1782. Morris H. Saffron, *Surgeon to Washington: Dr. John Cochran (1730–1807)* (New York, 1977), 200.

Private Isaac Marten of Berwick, Massachusetts, 7th Massachusetts Regiment, died of fever on December 24, 1782. *Massachusetts Soldiers and Sailors*, 10:274. Marten was an African American soldier.
1 death 4th Massachusetts Regiment, January 1783
2 deaths 5th Massachusetts Regiment, January 1783

Private Silas Tobey of Falmouth, Massachusetts, 6th Massachusetts Regiment, died January 1, 1783, *Massachusetts Soldiers and Sailors*, 15:803.

1 death 4th Massachusetts Regiment, February 1783
1 death 5th Massachusetts Regiment, February 1783
1 death 6th Massachusetts Regiment, February 1783
1 death 7th Massachusetts Regiment, February 1783
1 death 8th Massachusetts Regiment, February 1783
1 death 5th Massachusetts Regiment, March 1783
1 death 2nd Massachusetts Regiment, April 1783
1 death 3rd Massachusetts Regiment, April 1783

Private Elijah Beals of Hingham, Massachusetts, 5th Massachusetts Regiment, "died very suddenly" on April 8, 1783. Benjamin Gilbert Diary, 1782–86, Diaries G372, Manuscript Collection, New York State Historical Association Research Library, Cooperstown, New York, April 8, 1783.

2 deaths 5th Massachusetts Regiment, April 1783

Private Ephraim Warren of Shirley, Massachusetts, 7th Massachusetts Regiment, died in hospital of fever on April 7, 1783, *Massachusetts Soldiers and Sailors*, 16:614.

2 deaths 2nd Massachusetts Regiment, May 1783
2 deaths 5th Massachusetts Regiment, May 1783

Joseph Boswell of Dracut, Massachusetts, 8th Massachusetts Regiment, died May 24, 1783, *Massachusetts Soldiers and Sailors*, II:296.

Total:32

New Hampshire Line

12 deaths 2nd New Hampshire Regiment, December 1782
3 deaths 2nd New Hampshire Regiment, January 1783
1 death New Hampshire Regiment, March 1783

Total:16

New Jersey Line

1 death 1st New Jersey Regiment, November 1782.

Colonel Francis Barber of Elizabethtown, New Jersey, commander of the 2nd New Jersey Regiment, killed on February 11, 1783, by a tree felled by a woodcutting party. He was born in Princeton, New Jersey. *The Pennsylvania Packet or the General Advertiser*, Philadelphia, Pennsylvania, February 27, 1783, *America's Historical Newspapers*.

5 deaths New Jersey Regiment, March 1783
3 deaths New Jersey Battalion, March 1783

"St. Patrick's Men" from the New Jersey Line "in a high frollick" on March 17 killed two of their number, and "Several more [were] Badly Wounded." Robert McDonald, trans., The Revolutionary War Journal of Private Thomas Foster 7th Massachusetts Regiment at West Point, Verplanck's Point and Cantonment New Windsor, May 1782–June 1783, The Huntington Library, San Marino, California, March 18, 1783.

1 death New Jersey Regiment, May 1783

Total:11

New York Line

2 deaths 2nd New York Regiment, November 1782
1 death 1st New York Regiment, December 1782
1 death 1st New York Regiment, February 1783
1 death 1st New York Regiment, March 1783
1 death 2nd New York Regiment, March 1783
1 death 1st New York Regiment, April 1783

Total:7

Total deaths: 69

This number is approximate, because there is a possibility that some of these fatalities might have occurred elsewhere. Also, deaths for the month of October and June are not included in this total.

Appendix 5
The Two Anonymous Letters to the Officers of the Army and General Washington's Response

The First Anonymous Letter

Undated letter circulated March 10, 1783, but written earlier. Probably in draft form or at least sketched out for a few days prior to this date, Armstrong wrote the final version after meeting with Colonel Walter Stewart and receiving the guidance he was carrying from the nationalist faction, in Philadelphia.

To the Officers of the Army:

GENTLEMEN:—A fellow-soldier, whose interest and affections bind him strongly to you; whose past sufferings have been as great, and whose future fortune may be as desperate as yours—would beg leave to address you. Age has its claims, and rank is not without its pretensions to advise; but though unsupported by both, he flatters himself that the plain language of sincerity and experience, will neither be unheard nor unregarded. Like many of you, he loved private life, and left it with regret. He left it, determined to retire from the field with the necessity that called him to it, and not till then; not till the enemies of his country, the slaves of power, and the hirelings of injustice, were compelled to abandon their schemes, and acknowledge America as terrible in arms as she had been humble in remonstrance.

With this object in view, he has long shared in your toils, and mingled in your dangers; he has felt the cold hand of poverty without a murmur, and has seen the insolence of wealth without a sigh. But, too much under the direction of his wishes, and sometimes weal enough to mistake desire for opinion, he has, till lately, very lately, believed in the justice of his country. He hoped, that as the clouds of adversity scattered, and as the sun-shine of peace and better fortune broke in upon us, the coldness and severity of government would relax, and that, more than justice, that gratitude would blaze forth upon those hands which had upheld her in the darkest stages of her passage, from impending servitude to acknowledged independence.

But faith has its limits, as well as temper; and there are points beyond which neither can be stretched, without sinking into cowardice, or plunging into credulity. This, my friends, I conceive to be your situation. Hurried to the very verge of both, another step would ruin you forever. To be tame and unprovoked when injuries press hard upon you, is more than weakness; but to look up for kinder usage, without one manly effort of your own, would fix your character, and show the world how richly you deserve those chains you broke. To guard against this evil, let us take a review of the ground upon which we now stand, and from thence carry our thoughts forward for a moment, into the unexplored field of expedient.

After a pursuit of seven long years, the object for which we set out is at length brought within our reach!—Yes, my friends, that suffering courage of yours, was active once—it has conducted the United States of America through a doubtful and a bloody war! It has placed her in the chair of independency, and peace again returns to bless—whom? A country willing to redress your wrongs, cherish your worth, and reward your services; a country courting your return to private life, with tears of gratitude, and smiles of admiration; longing to divide with you that independency which your gallantry has given, and those riches which your wounds have preserved? Is this the case? Or is it rather, a country that tramples upon your rights, disdains your cries, and insults your distresses? Have you not, more than once, suggested your wishes, and made known your wants to Congress? Wants and wishes which gratitude and policy should have anticipated, rather than evaded. And have you not lately, in the meek language of entreating memorial, begged from their justice, what you would no longer expect from their favour? How have you been answered? Let the letter which you are called to consider to-morrow, make reply.

If this, then, be your treatment, while the swords you wear are necessary for the defence of America, what have you to expect from peace, when your voice shall sink, and your strength dissipate by division?

When these very swords, the instruments and companions of your glory, shall be taken from your sides, and no remaining mark of military distinction left, but your wants, infirmities, and scars! can you then consent to be the only sufferers by this revolution, and retiring from the field, grow old in poverty, wretchedness, and contempt? Can you consent to wade through the vile mire of dependency, and owe the miserable remnant of that life to charity, which has hitherto been spent in honour?—if you can, go—and carry with you the jest of tories, and the scorn of whigs—the ridicule, and what is worse, the pity of the world! Go, starve, and be forgotten!

But if your spirit should revolt at this; if you have sense enough to discover, and spirit enough to oppose tyranny, under whatever garb it may assume; whether it be the plain coat of republicanism, or the splendid robe of royalty; if you have yet learned to discriminate between a people and a cause, between men and principles—awake!—attend to your situation, and redress yourselves. If the present moment be lost, every future effort is in vain; and your threats then will be as empty as your entreaties now.

I would advise you, therefore, to come to some final opinion, upon what you can bear, and what you will suffer. If your determination be in any proportion to your wrongs, carry your appeal from the justice to the fears of government—change the milk and water style of your last memorial; assume a bolder tone, decent, but lively, spirited and determined; and suspect the man who would advise to more moderation and longer forbearance. Let two or three men, who can feel as well as write, be appointed to draw up your last remonstrance; for I would no longer give it the sueing, soft, unsuccessful epithet of memorial. Let it be represented (in language that will neither dishonour you by its rudeness, nor betray you by its fears) what has been promised by Congress, and what has been performed; how long and how patiently you have suffered; how little you have asked, and how much of that little has been denied. Tell them that though you were the first, and would wish to be the last, to encounter danger; though despair itself can never drive you into dishonour, it may drive you from the field; that the wound often irritated, and never healed, may at length become incurable; and that the slightest mark of indignity from Congress now, must operate like the grave, and part you for ever; that in any political event, the army has its alternative. If peace, that nothing shall separate you from your arms but death; if war, that courting the auspices and inviting the directions of your illustrious leader, you will retire to some unsettled country, smile in your turn, and 'mock when their fear cometh on.'

But let it represent also, that should they comply with the request of your late memorial, it would make you more happy, and them more respectable: that while the war should continue, you would follow their standard into the field—and when it came to an end, you would withdraw into the shade of private life, and give the world another subject of wonder and applause—an army victorious over its enemies—victorious over itself.

I am, &c.,

----------- ------------

Appendix 5

The Second Anonymous Letter

March 12, 1783

To the Officers of the Army:

GENTLEMEN: The author of a late Address, anxious to deserve, though he should fail to engage, your esteem, and determined at every risk to unfold your duty and discharge his own, would beg leave to solicit the further indulgence of a few moments' attention. Aware of the coyness with which his last letter was received, he feels himself neither disappointed nor displeased with the caution it has met. He well knew that it spoke a language which, till now, had been only heard in a whisper, and that it contained some sentiments which confidence itself would have breathed with distrust.

But their lives have been short and their observation imperfect, indeed, who have yet to learn that alarms may be false, that the best designs are sometimes obliged to assume the worst aspect, and that however synonymous surprise and disaster may be in military phrase, in moral and political meaning they convey ideas as different as they are distinct. Suspicion, detestable as it is in private life, is the loveliest trait of political character. It prompts you to inquiry. It shuts the door against design, and opens every avenue to truth. It was the first to oppose Tyrant here, and still stands sentinel over the liberties of America; with this belief, it would illy become me to stifle the voice of this honest guardian—a guardian who (authorized by circumstances digested into proof) has herself given birth to the address you have read and now goes forth among you with a request to all that it may be treated fairly; that it may be considered before it is abused, and considered before it be tortured; convinced that, in a search after error, truth will appear; that apathy itself will glow warm in the pursuit, and though it will be the last to adopt her advice, it will be the first to act upon it.

The General Orders of yesterday, which the weak may mistake for disapprobation, and the designing dare to represent as such—wears, in my opinion, a very different complexion, and carries with it a very opposite tendency. Till now—the Commander-in-Chief has regarded the steps you have taken for redress, with good wishes alone. This ostensible silence has authorized your meeting, and his private opinion has sanctified your claims. Had he disliked the object in view—would not the same sense of duty which forbade you from meeting on the third day of the week, have forbidden you from meeting on the seventh? Is not the same subject held up for your discussion, and has it not passed the seal of office and taken the solemnity of an order? This will give system to your proceedings, and stability to your resolves—it will ripen speculation into fact; and while it adds to the unanimity, it cannot possibly lessen the independency of your sentiments. It may be necessary to add upon this subject, that from the injunction with which the General Orders close, every man is at liberty to conclude that the reports to be made to Head-quarters is intended for Congress, hence will arise another motive for that energy which has been recommended. For can you give the lie to the pathetic descriptions of your Representatives and the more alarming productions of our friends? To such as make a want of signature an objection to opinion, I reply that it matters very little who is the author of sentiments which grow out of your feelings and apply to your wants—that in this instance, diffidence suggested what experience enjoins, and that while I continue to move on the high road of argument and advice, which is open to all, I shall continue to be the sole confident of my own secret. But should the time come when it shall be necessary to depart from this general line, and hold up any individual among you as an object of resentment or contempt of the rest, I thus publicly pledge my honor as a soldier, and veracity as a man, that I will then assume a visible existence, and give my name to the army, with as little reserve as I now give my opinion.

I am, your,

-------------- -----------

Washington's Response to Anonymous Letter Writer Delivered in the Temple of Virtue, at the New Windsor Cantonment, on March 15, 1783.

GENTLEMEN: By an anonymous summons, an attempt has been made to convene you together. How inconsistent with the rules of propriety, how unmilitary and how subversive of all order and discipline, let the good sense of the army decide.

In the moment of this summons, another anonymous production was sent into circulation, addressed more to the feelings and passions than to the reason and judgment of the army. The author of the piece is entitled to much credit for, the goodness of his pen; and I could wish he had as much credit for the rectitude of his heart; for, as men see through different optics, and are induced by the reflecting faculties of the mind, to use different means to attain the same end, the author of the address should have had more charity than to mark for suspicion the man who should recommend moderation and longer forbearance, or, in other words, who should not think as he thinks, and act as he advises. But he had another plan in view, in which candor and liberality of sentiment, regard to justice and love of country, have no part; and he was right to insinuate the darkest suspicion to effect the blackest design. That the address is drawn with great art, and is designed to answer the most insidious purposes; that it is calculated to impress the mind with an idea of premeditated injustice in the sovereign power of the United States, and rouse all those resentments which must unavoidably flow from such a belief; that the secret mover of this scheme, whoever he may be, intended to take advantage of the passions, while they were warmed by the recollection of past distresses, without giving time for cool deliberative thinking, and that composure of mind which is so necessary to give dignity and stability to measures, is rendered too obvious, by the mode of conducting the business, to need other proof than a reference to the proceeding.

Thus much, gentlemen, I have thought it incumbent on me to observe to you, to shew upon what principles I opposed the irregular and hasty meeting which was proposed to have been held on Tuesday last, and not because I wanted a disposition to give you every opportunity, consistent with your own honor, and the dignity of the army, to make known your grievances. If my conduct heretofore has not evinced to you that I have been a faithful friend to the army, my declaration of it at this time would be equally unavailing and improper. But as I was among the first who embarked in the cause of our common country; as I have never left your side one moment, but when called from you on public duty; as I have been the constant companion and witness of your distresses, and not among the last to feel and acknowledge your merits; as I have ever considered my own military reputation as inseparably connected with that of the army; as my heart has ever expanded with joy, when I have heard its praises, and my indignation has arisen when the mouth of detraction has been opened against it, it can scarcely be supposed, at this late stage of the war, that I am indifferent to its interests. But how are they to be promoted? The way is plain, says the anonymous addresser. "If war continues, remove into the unsettled country; there establish yourselves and leave an ungrateful country to defend itself."—But who are they to defend? Our wives, our children, our farms and other property which we leave behind us? or, in this state of hostile separation, are we to take the two first (the latter cannot be removed) to perish in a wilderness with hunger, cold and nakedness?

"If peace takes place, never sheath your swords," says he "until you have obtained full and ample justice." This dreadful alternative of either deserting our country in the extremest hour of her distress, or turning our arms against it, which is the apparent object, unless Congress can be compelled into instant compliance, has something so shocking in it, that humanity revolts at the idea. My God! what can this writer have in view, by recommending such measures? Can he be a friend to the army? Can he be a friend to this country? Rather is he not an insidious foe? Some designing emissary, perhaps, from New York, plotting the ruin of both, by sowing the seeds of discord and separation between the civil and military powers of the continent? and what a compliment does he pay to our understandings, when he recommends measures, in either alternative impracticable in their nature? But, here, gentlemen, I will drop the curtain, because it would be as imprudent in me to assign my reasons for this opinion, as it would be insulting to your conception to suppose you stood in need of them. A moment's reflection will convince every dispassionate mind of the physical impossibility of carrying either proposal into execution. There might, gentlemen, be an impropriety in my taking notice, in this address to you, of an anonymous production; but the manner in which that performance has been introduced to the army, the effect it was intended to have, together with some other circumstances, will amply justify my observations on the tendency of that writing.

With respect to the advice given by the author, to suspect the man who shall recommend moderate measures and longer forbearance, I spurn it, as every man who regards that liberty and reveres that justice for which we contend, undoubtedly must; for, if men are to be precluded from offering their sentiments on a matter which may involve the most serious and alarming consequences that can invite the consideration of mankind, reason is of no use to us. The freedom of speech may be taken away, and, dumb and silent, we may be led, like sheep, to the slaughter. I cannot, in justice to my own belief, and what I have great reason to conceive is the intention of Congress, conclude this address, without giving it as my decided opinion, that that honorable body entertain exalted sentiments of the services of the army, and from a full conviction of its merits and sufferings, will do it compleat justice: that their endeavours to discover and establish funds for this purpose have been unwearied, and will not cease till they have succeeded, I have not a doubt.

But, like all other large bodies, where there is a variety of different interests to reconcile, their determinations are slow. Why then should we distrust them, and, in consequence of that distrust, adopt measures which may cast a shade over that glory which has been so justly acquired, and tarnish the reputation of an army which is celebrated through all Europe for its fortitude and patriotism? And for what is this done? To bring the object we seek nearer? No, most certainly, in my opinion it will cast it at a greater distance. For myself, and I take no merit in giving the assurance, being induced to it from principles of gratitude, veracity and justice, a grateful sense of the confidence you have ever placed in me, a recollection of the cheerful assistance and prompt obedience I have experienced from you, under every vicissitude of fortune, and the sincere affection I feel for an army I have so long had the honor to command, will oblige me to declare, in this public and solemn manner, that in the attainment of compleat justice for all your toils and dangers, and in the gratification of every wish, so far as may be done consistently with the great duty I owe my country, and those powers we are bound to respect, you may freely command my services to the utmost extent of my abilities.

While I give you these assurances, and pledge myself in the most unequivocal manner, to exert whatever ability I am possessed of in your favour, let me entreat you, gentlemen, on your part, not to take any measures, which, viewed in the calm light of reason, will lessen the dignity, and sully the glory you have hitherto maintained. Let me request you to rely on the plighted faith of your country, and place a full confidence in the purity of the intentions of Congress; that, previous to your dissolution as an army, they will cause all your accounts to be fairly liquidated, as directed in their resolutions which were published to you two days ago; and that they will adopt the most effectual measures in their power to render ample justice to you for your faithful and meritorious services. And let me conjure you, in the name of our common country, as you value your own sacred honor, as you respect the rights of humanity, and as you regard the military and national character of America, to express your utmost horror and detestation of the man, who wishes, under any specious pretences, to overturn the liberties of our country; and who wickedly attempts to open the flood-gates of civil discord, and deluge our rising empire in blood.

By thus determining, and thus acting, you will pursue the plain and direct road to the attainment of your wishes; you will defeat the insidious designs of our enemies, who are compelled to resort from open force to secret artifice. You will give one more distinguished proof of unexampled patriotism and patient virtue, rising superior to the pressure of the most complicated sufferings: and you will, by the dignity of your conduct, afford occasion for posterity to say, when speaking of the glorious example you have exhibited to mankind—"had this day been wanting, the world had never seen the last stage of perfection to which human nature is capable of attaining."

Appendix 6
The Mountainville Hut

"One of the most important treasures" of the New Windsor encampment, the Mountainville hut, moved to Temple Hill in 1934, was believed to have been occupied by two officers because of "its size, 20 by 28 feet." William T. and E. Augusta Hand donated the hut to the National Temple Hill Association. Actually measuring 29 by 19 feet, the little log cabin was originally six miles away in Mountainville, now part of Cornwall, on the farm purchased by John Sackett in 1770. Upon his death, the farm passed to his son, Nathaniel. On January 9, 1834, Nathaniel sold 93 acres of this property to Elias Hand, the family who occupied the property for the next century. Sometime thereafter, a large two-story Greek Revival–style home was attached. During this time, a porch with flying eaves and other decorative treatments were added to the hut to match the new house. A metal shingle roof, added in 1907, was the last major change to the structure.[1]

South of the Temple Hill Monument, the hillside was bulldozed to prepare the site to receive the log building. A concrete and stone foundation was then put down. On the north end of the footing, a fireplace with a bake oven was made from bricks taken from the nearby Deacon Brewster house and local fieldstone. While still in Mountainville, the hut was stripped of its clapboards, porch, roof, doors, lath, plaster, sink, and plumbing. Prior to disassembly, the walls were numbered with a chisel to aid in the reconstruction. Hardly surprising, when the hut was taken apart, several of the beams had to be replaced, including all the sill timbers and four or five others. This last group came from the Rosie Brown farm in Mountainville. New main and attic floorboards, doors, windows, attic staircase, and shingles had to be put in. The lock on the door, on the western side, was taken from Revolutionary War New York governor and Continental Army brigadier general George Clinton's New Windsor house.[2] Completing the installation was the requisite bronze plaque.

John Sackett "probably bought the hut at public auction in September 1783." A veteran of the 1st Regiment Orange County Militia, he must have done some extended service, because he was eligible for a land bounty at the end of the war. Possibly, he was one of the New York levies who were discharged at the camp in December 1782. The quartermaster records list all the hut purchasers, and none were named Sackett. John's son Nathaniel sold the property to Elias Hand for $5,000 in 1834. The farmstead's log hut was where "two generations of the Hand family had been born." The hut was dedicated with great patriotic and religious zeal on October 7, 1934, with William Hand formally presenting the key to the hut to the National Temple Hill Association. Congressman Hamilton Fish, Jr., was master of ceremonies, and the ubiquitous association president Reverend A. Elwood Corning provided the introductory remarks and composed an original song, "Temple Hill," set to the tune of "America." Speaking with the deepest respect, New York State historian Alexander C. Flick recommended that the hut be "put under glass." Mary Patricia Hunt was baptized on August 28, 1938, by Reverend Corning in "the historic Revolutionary Hut on Temple Hill." Church services were occasionally held in the hut as well. Temple Hill Chapter 1782, of the Military Order of the Purple Heart, was organized in the hut in 1941. Its presiding gavel was the second one Reverend Corning had made from the Denniston house beams, the purported ones from the original Temple of Virtue.[3] In 1962 the Brigade of the American

Appendix 6

The Mountainville Hut (Christmas 1934) (courtesy New Windsor Cantonment State Historic Site, New York State Office of Parks, Recreation and Historic Preservation).

Revolution, the international historical association dedicated to re-creating the life and times of the common soldiers of the American War for Independence, was founded in the hut.

As time passed, however, the view of the hut as the rightful centerpiece of a patriotic shrine started to be called into question. Looking at the history with some skepticism rather than emotion and sentiment, its provenance does not hold up to scrutiny. By 1956, New York State historian Dr. Albert S. Corey "recommended, burning the hut since it was in very bad condition … and 'was not authentic.'"[4] Searching the vicinity surrounding the cantonment for vestiges of the Continental Army log city, local history enthusiasts discovered the hut in Mountainville. With nothing other than its general size, proximity to the encampment, and log construction to recommend it, the building was determined to be a field-grade officer hut and was hailed as "the only such relic in existence." The Hand family did not have any information other than that the log hut was on the property when they bought it from the Sackett family. Throughout the management of the park by the National Temple Hill Association, the building was referred to as the officer's hut, but later interpretation has the building as possibly not an officer hut but instead that of sutler Nathaniel Sackett. Sackett ownership of the property proved fortuitous, because Nathaniel Sackett had been a sutler to the Continental Army around Newburgh. On May 13, 1782, the sometimes military intelligence agent "obtained permission from the Commander in Chief to suttle to the Army until further orders."[5]

Considered by Corning to be incontrovertible proof of the hut's authenticity was the "Revolutionary bullets, soldiers' buttons, and a coin bearing the date 1787" found inside that no longer exist or whose whereabouts are unknown. In an interview with New Windsor Cantonment site manager Donald Fangboner in 1974, John T. Hand, son of William T. Hand, remembered that when the building was taken apart "we found several lead bullets—that size … in between the logs." He further recalled that some officers' buttons were found that had an emblem on them, but he could not recall what it was. He did remember, however, that they had a "gold finish" and that "Mrs. [Mary C.] Weston wore it on a ribbon quite awhile."[6] Except for general officers and nonregimentally affiliated members of their staff, there should not have been any brass buttons in camp except for those on civilian or other nonstandard clothing. Also, general officers and the unaffiliated members of their staff wore plain buttons with no design.

Weighing several hundred pounds apiece, the hut walls had to be completely disassembled prior to their removal from the encampment, so it would have been nearly impossible for any soldier material culture to embed itself in the logs to begin with, let alone stay in place during the trip and reconstruction. Musket balls are a very common find at 18th-century farmsteads whether or not the owner had any association with the military, because hunting was widespread. Without further information about the design of the buttons if they ever existed, they could have been just finely made late 18th- or 19th-century civilian or military ones. All a 1787 coin would show is that it was lost in the hut sometime after that date. The most likely conclusion regarding the Mountainville hut is that it was the original log cabin erected shortly after John Sackett purchased the property in 1770. Regardless of whether or not the hut has a Continental Army pedigree, this venerable structure is a rare survivor from the early days of our country.

Chapter Notes

Epigraph

1. To Major General Nathanael Greene, February 6, 1783, in John C. Fitzpatrick, ed., *The Writings of George Washington from the Original Manuscript Sources, 1745–1799*, 39 vols. (Washington, DC, 1931–1944), 26:104 (hereafter *Washington Writings*).

Chapter 1

1. James Thacher, *Eyewitness to the American Revolution: The Battles and Generals as Seen by an Army Surgeon*, reprint ed. (Stamford, CT, 1994 [1862]), 215 (hereafter *Thacher Journal*).
2. Farewell Address to the People of the United States, September 17, 1796, George Washington Papers, Library of Congress, 1741–1799, Series 2 Letterbooks.
3. Circular to the States, May 4–8, 1782, *Washington Writings*, 24:238.
4. Fearing the future greatness of the new nation, it was not in France's interest to make the United States the masters of nearly the entire eastern half of the continent; and To Colonel Elisha Sheldon, December 10, 1782, *Washington Writings*, 25:413–414.
5. William Heath, *Memoirs of Major-General Heath Containing Anecdotes, Details of Skirmishes, Battles, and Other Military Events, during the American War* (Boston, 1798), 358 (hereafter *Heath Memoirs*); Colonel Timothy Pickering to General George Washington, October 25, 1782, George Washington Papers, Library of Congress, 1741–1799, Series 4: General Correspondence, 1697–1799 (hereafter Washington Papers); and General Orders, October 26, 1782, *Washington Writings*, 26: 300.
6. To the Secretary at War Major General Benjamin Lincoln, October 3, 1782, *Washington Writings*, 25:234; To Major Thomas Lansdale or Officer Commanding the Third Maryland Regiment, October 21, 1782, *Washington Writings*, 25:283–284; To Major Thomas Lansdale, November 1, 1782, *Washington Writings*, 25:316; and General Orders, November 10, 1782, *Washington Writings*, 25:328.
7. To Major General William Heath, June 29, 1780, *Washington Writings*, 19:93; Robert C. Bray and Paul E. Bushnell, eds., *Diary of a Common Soldier in the American Revolution, 1775–1783: An Annotated Edition of the Military Journal of Jeremiah Greenman* (DeKalb, IL, 1978), 260–261 (hereafter *Greenman Journal*); and To Lord Stirling, November 13, 1782, *Washington Writings*, 25:338.
8. William M. Willett, *A Narrative of the Military Actions of Colonel Marinus Willet, Taken Chiefly from His Own Manuscript* (New York, 1969 [1831]), 90–93.
9. Colonel Timothy Pickering to General George Washington, October 15, 1782, Washington Papers; and Colonel Timothy Pickering to Lieutenant Colonel David Cobb, October 3, 1782, Washington Papers.
10. General Orders, February 26, 1783, *Washington Writings*, 26:169; and General Orders, April 20, 1783, *Washington Writings*, 26:343–344.
11. To General George Washington, November 7, 1782, Horatio Gates Papers, New-York Historical Society, Reel 13 (hereafter Gates Papers); Memorandum of Officers Quarters in the Neighbourhood of New Windsor & Newburgh during the winter of 1780–81 & 83 (hereafter Memorandum of Officers Quarters), Photostat of an original memorandum in the research collection at the New Windsor Cantonment State Historic Site, originally in the Adjutant General's Office in the War Department but subsequently transferred to the National Archives; and Major General Arthur St. Clair to Major General Nathanael Greene, December 22, 1782, in Dennis M. Conrad, ed., *The Papers of Nathanael Greene*, 13 vols. (Chapel Hill, NC, 1976–2005), 12:335 (hereafter *Greene Papers*).
12. To Major General Henry Knox, November 1, 1783, Letters of Col. Pickering in the Records of the War Department, The Adjutant General's Office Revolutionary War Records, National Archives Microfilm Publication M853, Roll 28, Vol. 87, RG 93, National Archives, Washington, DC (hereafter Pickering Letters); and Captain William North to Major General Friedrich von Steuben, November 6, 1782, Friedrich von Steuben Papers, New-York Historical Society, Reel 6. Pickering believed that it was not essential for major generals to stay very close to their commands. Major Henry Sewall Journal, October 28, 1782, and April 15, 1783,

Maine State Library, Miscellaneous Manuscripts Collection (hereafter Sewall Journal); and William Heath Papers, Massachusetts Historical Society, Reel 26 (hereafter Heath Papers). Until the army was familiar with the location of his Newburgh headquarters, he wrote "Belknaps House" in the headers of his correspondence. He later just used "Newburgh." Octavius Pickering and Charles Wentworth Upham, *The Life of Timothy Pickering*, 4 vols. (Boston, 1867–1873), I:378 and 396–397 (hereafter *Pickering Life*); and To Major General William Heath, March 6, 1783, Pickering Letters, Vol. 85. Reverend Israel Evans was already billeted at Squire Belknap's house, making Pickering question whether Squire Belknap would consent to the return of Heath and his entourage. Marion M. Mailler and Janet Dempsey, *18th Century Homes in New Windsor and Its Vicinity as Depicted by Simeon De Witt Geographer to the Army on His Map of the Cantonment 1783* (Cornwall, NY, 1968), 25–26.

13. Major General Louis le Bègue de Presle Duportail to General Washington, December 24, 1782, Washington Papers; To Major General Louis le Bègue de Presle Duportail, May 10, 1783, *Washington Writings*, 26:416; Memorandum of Officers Quarters, Samuel Wood Bill for Quartering Officers, October 14, 1783, Colonel Timothy Pickering Papers, Huntington Historical Society, Huntingdon, Long Island, New York; and General Orders, February 12, 1783, *Washington Writings*, 26:129.

14. Washington had recommended that the Massachusetts troops encamp on top of the ridge where the Temple of Virtue was later constructed. The officers of that line objected, however. "Tho' the huts would thereby have a southern exposure, yet the bleak situation of the ridge will render the position as cold and uncomfortable as the western exposure of the ground first proposed." The ridge was covered in brush that would require a great deal of labor to remove and was farther from the water and most of the trees suitable for constructing buildings, and the officers believed that their men "would prefer hutting without any teams on the ground first chosen than take the ridge with a hundred." Brigadier General John Paterson, Colonel John Greaton, Colonel William Shepard and Colonel Timothy Pickering to General George Washington, October 29, 1782, Washington Papers. Except for a promise to 2nd New Jersey Regiment commander Lieutenant Colonel John Cummings from Quartermaster Pickering to "pay the hire of teams employed to haul timber for the huts of his regiment—not exceeding twenty four dollars, reckoning each double team at two dollars a day," the historical record is silent about the public hiring draft animals to haul the logs. There must have been offers to pay for teams for the other regiments, because the other soldiers would have demanded it. Pickering "furnished Colo Henry Jackson with money repeatedly ... to defray all our expences." It is probable that these funds were used to hire log haulers. Colonel Timothy Pickering, Memorandum of Matters to be Attended to by the Gentlemen in My Office, November 1782, Pickering Letters. Lieutenant Colonel Ebenezer Sproat hired his own team, and other officers must have done so as well. Lieutenant Colonel Ebenezer Sproat to Deputy Quartermaster General Peter Anspach, November 18, 1782, Miscellaneous Number Records (The Manuscript File), War Department Collection of Revolutionary War Records, 1775–1790s, National Archives Microfilm Publication M859, Roll 111, RG 93, National Archives, Washington, DC (hereafter Miscellaneous Records); and To Brevet Brigadier General Moses Hazen, December 4–6, 1782, *Washington Writings*, 25:400.

15. To Colonel Matthias Ogden, or the Senior Officer with the First New Jersey Regiment, December 4, 1782, *Washington Writings*, 25:396; To the Secretary at War Major General Benjamin Lincoln, November 6, 1782, *Washington Writings*, 25:322; General Orders, February 8, 1783, *Washington Writings*, 26:109; Instructions to the Officer Commanding on the Croton, January 3, 1783, *Washington Writings*, 26:9–10; To Brigadier General Elias Dayton, March 31, 1783, *Washington Writings*, 26:274; Captain Aaron Ogden, Jr., to General George Washington, April 6, 1783, Washington Papers; and Lieutenant Colonel Jonathan Trumbull, Jr., to Captain Aaron Ogden, Jr., April 12, 1783, Washington Papers.

16. *Heath Memoirs*, 288–289; and To Colonel Matthias Ogden, or the Senior Officer with the First New Jersey Regiment, December 4, 1782, *Washington Writings*, 25:397.

17. General Orders, October 29, 1782, *Washington Writings*, 25:304; General Orders, December 4, 1782, *Washington Writings*, 25:395; and General Orders, January 11, 1783, *Washington Writings*, 26:31.

18. General Orders, January 11, 1783, *Washington Writings*, 26:31; General Orders, January 14, 1783, *Washington Writings*, 26:35; General Orders, February 27, 1783, *Washington Writings*, 26:170; and To Pelatiah Haws, February 27, 1783, *Washington Writings*, 26:171.

19. General Orders, March 30, 1783, *Washington Writings*, 26:278.

20. Major David Smith to General George Washington, October 14, 1782, Washington Papers; Major General Henry Knox to General George Washington, November 12, 1782, Washington Papers; and To Major General Henry Knox, November 13, 1782, *Washington Writings*, 25:338.

Chapter 2

1. Ebenezer Elmer, "Journal of Lieutenant Ebenezer Elmer, 2nd New Jersey Regt," *Proceedings of the New Jersey Historical Society*, Vol. 3, 1848–1849, 101.

2. Lieutenant Colonel Tench Tilghman to John Bingham, November 28, 1782, J. H. S. Fogg Autograph Collection, Maine Historical Society.

3. Joseph B. Riling, *Baron von Steuben and His Regulations Including a Complete Facsimile of the Original Regulations for the Order and Discipline of the Troops of the United States* (Philadelphia, 1966), 77, 90–93 (hereafter *Von Steuben Regulations*).

4. General Orders, April 2, 1783, *Washington Writings*, 26:282; Regimental Orders, January 27, 1783, Orderly Book of Sergeant Peter Gaspar, Captain John C. Ten Broeck's Company, First New York Regiment, January 1, 1783, to April 19, 1783, United States Military Academy Library Special Collections Division, West Point, New York (hereafter 1st NY Orderly Book); and James A. Roberts, *New York in the Revolution as Colony and State*, 2 vols. (Albany, NY, 1904) 1:73 (hereafter *NY in Revolution*).

5. Worthington C. Ford, ed., *Journals of the Continental Congress, 1774–1789*, 34 vols. (Washington DC, 1904–1937), report from Secretary at War Major General Benjamin Lincoln, December 24, 1781, 21:1182–1183 (hereafter *JCC*). "The method hitherto practiced in the Army of inlisting men to serve as fifers and drummers and paying them additional pay is attended with manifest injury to the service for nothing is more common than to see men employed in that duty who are in every respect fit for soldiers, whilst boys hardly able to bear arms are put in the ranks." When music was called for, the musicians were to be taken from their corps only "as often as the good of the service shall make necessary." General Orders, February 16, 1783, *Washington Writings*, 26:138; Inspection Returns of the Music in the Army under the Immediate Command of His Excellency, General George Washington, West Point, Jan 1st & June 1st, 1782, 4th Massachusetts Regiment; and Henry Knox Papers, Massachusetts Historical Society, Roll 8 (hereafter Knox Papers). The June 1782 return lists seven drummers, six fifers, two learning drums, and two learning fifes. The last four soldiers are possibly infantry being taught to play these instruments. Return of the 5th Massachusetts Regiment of Foot commanded by D. Cobb Esqr., 14th Feb 1783, Rufus Putnam, Weekly Returns, 5th Massachusetts Regiment, January 1781–April 1783, United States Military Academy Library Special Collections Division, West Point, New York, Microfilm Archives. To complete their establishment of musicians, this regiment required only two more. Inspection Report from Major William Barber, February 27, 1783, Miscellaneous Records (hereafter Barber Report).

6. General Orders, April 1, 1778, *Washington Writings*, 11:194–195.

7. General Orders, November 22, 1782, *Washington Writings*, 25:367.

8. General Orders, November 5, 1782, *Washington Writings*, 25:319; General Orders, November 10, 1782, *Washington Writings*, 25:328; and General Orders, December 16, 1782, *Washington Writings*, 439–440.

9. General Orders, November 24, 1782, *Washington Writings*, 25:370.

10. General Orders, November 27, 1782, *Washington Writings*, 25:375; To Colonel Benjamin Tupper, November 27, 1782, *Washington Writings*, 25:379–380; and General Orders, December 9, 1782, *Washington Writings*, 25:411.

11. General Orders, January 6, 1783, *Washington Writings*, 26:13.

12. To Major General Marquis de Lafayette, October 30, 1780, *Washington Writings*, 20:266–267.

13. To Lieutenant General Comte de Rochambeau, April 7, 1781, *Washington Writings*, 21:426; To the Committee of Conference, August 21, 1781, *Washington Writings*, 23:30; and To John Parke Custis, February 28, 1781, *Washington Writings*, 21:319.

14. General Orders, December 12, 1782, *Washington Writings*, 25:424; and Charles H. Lesser, ed., *The Sinews of Independence Monthly Strength Reports of the Continental Army* (Chicago, 1976), 240–242 (hereafter *Sinews of Independence*).

15. General Orders, February 19, 1783, *Washington Writings*, 26:147; To the Secretary at War Major General Benjamin Lincoln, October 14, 1782, *Washington Writings*, 25:257; To the Secretary at War Major General Benjamin Lincoln, November 6, 1782, *Washington Writings*, 25:321; To Captain Abel Weyman, December 9, 1782, *Washington Writings*, :411–412; To the Superintendent of Finance Robert Morris, December 11, 1782, *Washington Writings*, 25:419; and Muster of 1st and 2nd Regiments New Jersey Continental Line from January 1782—April 1783, Photostat of an original form in the research collection at the New Windsor Cantonment State Historic Site. Originally in the Adjutant General's Office in the War Department, this record was subsequently transferred to the National Archives.

16. General Orders, November 1, 1780, *Washington Writings*, 20:279.

17. General Orders, October 30, 1782, *Washington Writings*, 25:310–313.

18. Captain George Smith, *An Universal Military Dictionary: A Copious Explanation of the Technical Terms & c. Used in the Equipment, Machinery, Movements, and Military Operations of an Army* (Museum Restoration Service, Ottawa, Ontario, 1969 [reprint of Whitehall, 1779]), 45 (hereafter *Smith's Military Dictionary*); and General Orders, May 24, 1780, *Washington Writings*, 18:407.

19. *Von Steuben Regulations*, 77; and Colonel Timothy Pickering, Ground necessary for an Encampment, probably late October 1782, Timothy Pickering Papers, Reel 56, Military Papers, 1767–1792, Massachusetts Historical Society (hereafter Pickering Military Papers).

20. General Orders, August 22, 1781, *Washington Writings*, 23:38.

21. General Orders, October 13, 1781, *Washington Writings*, 23:217; *Smith's Military Dictionary*, 243; Assistant Quartermaster and Storekeeper Christopher Meng to Colonel Timothy Pickering,

May 25, 1782, Miscellaneous Records, Roll 80; and Rebecca D. Symmes, ed., *A Citizen-Soldier in the American Revolution: The Diary of Benjamin Gilbert in Massachusetts and New York* (Cooperstown, New York, 1980), 53 (hereafter *Gilbert Diary*); General Orders, October 29, *Washington Writings*, 25:304. Soldiers at New Windsor were "allowed to put chimnies to their tents, and make themselves comfortable in them 'till their hutts can be built." General Orders, November 2, 1782, *Washington Writings*, 25:317. The officers were cautioned, however, "to be very attentive in seeing that the tops of the Chimneys are carried above the tents, to prevent their being scorched by the heat or fired by the Sparks." *Greenman Journal*, 184; and *Gilbert Diary*, October 28–28, 1782.

22. General Orders, June 13, 1778, *Washington Writings*, 12:53.

23. *Von Steuben Regulations*, 79.

24. Denis Diderot and Jean D'Alembert, *Le Encyclopedie, Fabrication Des Canons* (Inter-Livres, 2002 [reprint of 1762–1772]), Artificier Plate IV, Figure 78, pictures the exact same stand minus the rings.

25. To Major General Henry Knox, October 28, 1782, *Washington Writings*, 25:303.

26. General Orders, December 4, 1782, *Washington Writings*, 25:396; Colonel Timothy Pickering to Lieutenant Thomas Edwards, October 31, 1782, GLC01450.075, Gilder Lehrman Institute of American History, New York; Heitman, Francis B., ed., *Historical Register of Officers of the Continental Army During the War of the Revolution April 1775, to December 1783 with Addenda by Robert Kirby*, 1932 (Baltimore, 1967 [Reprint of the New, Revised, and Enlarged Edition of 1914]), 333, hereafter *Officer Register*; William A. Ellis, ed., "The Diary of William S. Pennington" (Part 2 of 2), *Proceedings of the New Jersey Historical Society* 64, no. 1 (January 1946): (hereafter Pennington Diary); and Joseph King to Secretary at War Major General Benjamin Lincoln, September 10, 1782, Letters and Reports from Maj. Gen. Benjamin Lincoln, Secretary at War, 1781–83, Papers of the Continental Congress, compiled 1774–1789, 693–694, M247, Roll 162, RG 360, https://www.fold3.com/images/424632 and 424635 (hereafter Continental Congress Papers).

27. General Orders, February 2, 1783, *Washington Writings*, 26:89–90; Provision return for Certain Army prisoners in provost at New Windsor Cantonment, under contract for the states of NY & NJ commencing & ending the 12th of April 1783, Heath Papers, Reel 26; To Lieutenant Colonel William Stephens Smith, February 6, 1783, *Washington Writings*, 26:105; General Orders, March 12, 1783, *Washington Writings*, 26:210; and *Gilbert Diary*, January 22 and 23, 1783.

28. General Orders, November 19, 1782, *Washington Writings*, 25:355; 1st NY Orderly Book; and Jersey Brigade Orderly Book, Regimental Orders for the Jersey Brigade, November 9—December 31, 1782, The Huntington Library (hereafter Jersey Brigade Orderly Book).

29. General Orders, April 16, 1783, *Washington Writings*, 26:327; General Orders, November 23, 1782, *Washington Writings*, 25:368–369; General Orders, January 28, 1783, *Washington Writings*, 26:73–74; and General Orders, March 13, *Washington Writings*, 26:220–221.

30. General Orders, October 28, 1782, *Washington Writings*, 25:303.

31. Regulations for Hutting, November 4, 1782, Pickering Letters, Reel 27, Vol. 85; Colonel Timothy Pickering, Plan & Disposition proposed for the huts of the winter following 1782, early November 1782, Pickering Military Papers; Colonel Timothy Pickering Circular modifying the hut construction plan, November 7, 1782, Pickering Letters, Reel 27, Vol. 85; To Unknown Recipient, October 23, 1782, Pickering Letters, Reel 27, Vol. 84; and Regimental Orders, March 21, 1783, The Papers of William Torrey (Lieutenant & Adjutant), 2nd Massachusetts Regiment Orderly Book, September 6, 1777–May 31, 1783, 24 vols., microfilm edition, 1976, Library of Congress (hereafter 2nd Mass. Orderly Book).

32. Thomas L. Purvis, *Colonial America to 1763* (New York, 1999), 107; Regimental Orders, March 27, 1783, 1st NY Orderly Book; and To Major General John Armstrong, January 10, 1783, *Washington Writings*, 26:27. By the middle of December, "the armey [was] Bussey in Making their Barraks which they have Got in a fine way." Robert McDonald, trans., The Revolutionary War Journal of Private Thomas Foster, 7th Massachusetts Regiment at West Point, Verplanck's Point and Cantonment New Windsor, May 1782–June 1783 (Huntington Library, San Marino, CA), December 18, 1782 (hereafter Foster Journal). Gates concurred with this assessment, writing to von Steuben that "our men are becoming so adroit and perfect in the Art of Hutting, that I think they will be more comfortable and better Lodged, in the Quarters they build for themselves than in Those any City in the Continent would afford them. This mode of covering an Army for the winter is New in the Art of War." Major General Horatio Gates to Major General Friedrich von Steuben, November 22, 1782, Gates Papers, Reel 13. Attributing the precise arrangement of the camp to the professionalism fostered by Steuben, General Howe gushed to the inspector general, "Your children, for so I call our army, have been laboring day and night to build their huts.... I cannot conclude this letter without conveying to you what I am sure your attachment to the army will render pleasing to you, that they universally think and speak of you with love, pleasure, gratitude, and applause." Major General Robert Howe to Major General Friedrich von Steuben, November 1782, quoted in Charles Royster, *A Revolutionary People at War: The Continental Army and American Character, 1775–1783* (New York, 1979), 332 (hereafter *Revolutionary People*).

33. Howard C. Rice, Jr., ed., *Travels in North America in the Years 1780, 1781 and 1782 by the Marquis de Chastellux*, 2 vols. (Chapel Hill, NC,

1963), 2:514–515 and 605 notes (hereafter *Chastellux Travels*). George Grieve, who translated *Chastellux's Travels* into English, made the following observation: "Throughout America, in private houses, as well as inns, several people are crowded together in the same room; and in the latter it very commonly happens, that after you have been some time in bed, a stranger of any condition (For there is little distinction), comes into the room, pulls off his clothes, and places himself, without ceremony, between your sheets." To Lieutenant Colonel Francis Barber, November 5, 1782, Pickering Letters, Reel 27, Vol. 84; and General Orders, November 25, 1782, *Washington Writings*, 25:370.

34. Colonel Timothy Pickering, Circular modifying the hut construction plan, November 7, 1782, Pickering Letters, Reel 27, Vol. 85; and Colonel Timothy Pickering, Return of the number of Huts and their fire places in the Cantonment of the Army in the vicinity of New Windsor—1783, May 1, 1783, Miscellaneous Records, Reel 94 (hereafter Hut and Fireplace Return).

35. To Dr. John Cochran, October 15, 1782, Pickering Letters, Reel 27, Vol. 84.

36. Sales at Auction September 2, 1783, for account of the United States, of the building called the Temple, the Huts late the cantonment of the first and third Massachusetts Brigades, and Sundry detached Huts, in David J. Fowler, *Guide to the Sol Feinstone Collection of the David Library of the American Revolution* (Washington Crossing, PA, 1994), image between 240 and 241 (hereafter Building Auction).

37. General Orders, December 20, 1782, *Washington Writings*, 25:454; and General Orders, January 18, 1783, *Washington Writings,* 26:48.

38. Regimental Orders, December 8, 1782, 2nd Mass. Orderly Book.

39. Hut and Fireplace Return.

40. Jan. 24, 1783, Return of the No. of Women & Children in the several Regts & Corps stationed at and in the vicinity of West Point and New Windsor that drew rations under the late regulations showing also the number of rations allowed for Women and Children by the present system, Peter Force Collection, Transcripts, 1520s–1880s, Series 7D, Library of Congress (hereafter Women & Children Return); To the Superintendent of Finance Robert Morris, January 29, 1783, *Washington Writings*, 26:79; and To Major General Henry Knox, March 8, 1783, *Washington Writings,* 26:199–299.

41. John B.B. Trussell, Jr., *Birthplace of an Army: A Study of the Valley Forge Encampment* (Harrisburg, PA, 1976), 19–21. Lafayette described the huts as "little shanties that are scarcely gayer than dungeon cells." Russell F. Weigley, "A War of Posts" (Washington, DC, 1983), 54–63.

42. General Orders, October 28, 1782, *Washington Writings,* 25:303; Report of Colonel Benjamin Tupper, Major Etienne de Rochefontaine, and Lieutenant Henry Nelson to either Major General Horatio Gates or General George Washington, early January 1783, Washington Papers (hereafter Tupper Report); and Regimental Orders, January 13, 1783, 1st NY Orderly Book.

43. *Chastellux Travels*, 2:514;; Foster Journal, December 31, 1782, and January 27, 1783; and Foster Journal, February 9 and 16, 1783; Foster spent a great deal of time in the shop because there was "Such a call for Work." Very devout, he did not like it when he was forced to work on the Sabbath, so he "Did as Little of it as We Could help for We have ginerley A Nuff to Do in the Weake time." The following week there was no labor, which made it "appeair Like Saboth Day although Meny Notorious Profanations are planly to be Observed in Many hear in the Armey." A month later, fatigue duty, reviews, and inspections were ended on Sundays "except on extra occasions." General Orders, March 22, 1783, *Washington Writings*, 26:250; John H. Mead, Summary of Archaeological Surveys, Excavations, Etc. at the New Windsor Cantonment, Prepared by John H. Mead, November 24, 1980, New Windsor Cantonment State Historic Site Collection; and Joseph Sopko, "Geophysical and Soil Chemical Investigations at New Windsor Cantonment," 1983 Symposium on Archaeology of the Revolutionary War Period Held at New Windsor Cantonment State Historic Site, New Windsor, New York, in Charles L. Fisher, ed., *Northeast Historical Archaeology* 12 (1983): 24–30 (hereafter "Soil Investigations"). Soil chemical investigations at an enlisted men's hut site, also from the 4th Massachusetts, suggest that one fireplace was used more extensively than the other. A possible explanation for this finding was that cooking in one fireplace required less wood and that it could be done by a minimal number of soldiers. Though anxious for the men to have wooden floors like the officers, Pickering could "hardly attempt to procure them at a time when … the public funds [could] … so ill afford the disbursement." He still, however, wrote to his assistant Nicholas Quackenbush to investigate the availability of boards for not only bunks but also doors and windows. Realizing that the minimum cost of the boards would save "much toil and destruction of clothing" and prevent the destruction of "valuable timber" for which the owners would "not presently be paid," Pickering appealed to Robert Morris for funds. To Assistant Deputy Quartermaster General Nicholas Quackenbush, November 4, 1782, Pickering Letters, Reel 27, Vol. 84. The same soil chemical investigation that revealed information about fireplace usage also provided evidence that enlisted soldier huts did not have wooden floors.

Chapter 3

1. To his Father and Stepmother, October 15 [17], 1780, John Shy, ed., *Winding Down the Revolutionary War Letters of Lieutenant Benjamin Gilbert of Massachusetts, 1780-1783* (Ann Arbor, MI, 1989), 26 (hereafter *Gilbert Letters*).

2. George F. Scheer, ed., *Private Yankee Doodle Being a Narrative of Some of the Adventures,*

Dangers and Sufferings of a Revolutionary Soldier by Joseph Plumb Martin (New York, 1988 [1962]), xxiv (hereafter *Private Yankee Doodle*).

3. General Orders, February 5, 1781, *Washington Writings*, 21:185–186.

4. *JCC*, October 3, 1780, 18:897.

That it be recommended to the states to fill up their respective regiments by Inlistments for and during the war; but in case the full quota of any of the states cannot be compleated with such recruits by the first day of December next, that it be recommended to such states or states to supply the deficiency with men engaged to serve for not less than one year, unless sooner relieved by recruits inlisted for the war, which they are requested to exert their utmost endeavors to obtain, as speedily as possible: and in order thereto, it is further recommended that the officers at camp be empowered and directed to use every prudent measure, and improve every favourable opportunity, to inlist, for the continuance of the war, such men belonging to their respective states, as are not engaged for that period, whether now in the field or hereafter, from time to time, joining the army; and that a recruiting officer from each corps be kept in the state to which the regiments respectively belong, to inlist recruits for the war, as well as to relieve those who are engaged for a shorter or limited term as to supply casual deficiencies.

5. Abraham English Brown, *History of the Town of Bedford, Middlesex County, Massachusetts, from Its Earliest Settlement to the Year of Our Lord 1891* (Bedford, MA, 1891), 27 and 67.

6. John Warner, *Historical Collections Being A General Collection of Interesting Facts, Traditions, Biographical Sketches, Anecdotes &c., Relating to the History and Antiquities of Every Town in Massachusetts, with Geographical Descriptions* (Worcester, MA, 1841), 348.

7. Massachusetts Office of the Secretary of State, Secretary of the Commonwealth, *Massachusetts Soldiers and Sailors of the Revolutionary War: A Compilation from the Archives*, 17 vols. (Boston, 1896–1908), 9:338–341 (hereafter *Massachusetts Soldiers and Sailors*). For more information, see Michael S. McGurty, "Henry Kneeland one of Bergoines troops & defected from Winterhill," *Hudson River Valley Review* 30, no. 1 (Autumn 2013, 47–60); and Louise K. Brown, *A Revolutionary Town* (Bedford, MA, 1975), 295.

8. *JCC*, August 14, 1776, 5:653–655; President of Pennsylvania, (Governor) Joseph Reed to the Chevalier de La Luzerne, August 3, 1780, Paul H. Smith et. al., eds., *Letters of Delegates to Congress, 1774–1789*, 25 vols. (Washington, DC, 1976–2000), 15:540 notes (hereafter *Congress Delegates Letters*). French minister to the United States, de La Luzerne was told by the president of Pennsylvania Joseph Reed that he was "perfectly free" to enlist the British German auxiliary deserters because "the recruitment of deserters into the Continental Army was expressly prohibited."

9. *Sinews of Independence*, 204; and *Massachusetts Soldiers and Sailors*, 9:339.

10. George A. Billias, *General John Glover and His Marblehead Mariners* (New York, 1960), 186.

11. *Massachusetts Soldiers and Sailors*, 9:339; General Orders, October 20, 1781, *Washington Writings*, 23:247; *Massachusetts Soldiers and Sailors*, 9:339; and Henry Kneeland Pension Files, Revolutionary War Pension and Bounty-Land Warrant Application Files, National Archives Microfilm Publication M804, Roll 1501, Massachusetts, Records of the Veterans Administration RG15, National Archives, Washington, DC (hereafter Kneeland Pension Files).

12. Foster Journal, February 7, 1783; *Massachusetts Soldiers and Sailors*, 1:451, 469.

13. Foster Journal, May 11, 1783, and January 12, 1783. Reverend James Hervey's *Theron and Aspasio*, first published in London, in 1755, was an allegory for his moderate Calvinist views. James Hervey, *Theron and Aspasio: or, a Series of Dialogues and Letters, Upon the Most Important and Interesting Subjects* (London, 1755).

14. *Chastellux Travels*, 2:603 notes; Simon Wolf and Louis Edward Levy, eds., *The American Jew as Patriot, Soldier and Citizen* (Philadelphia, 1895), 45; and *Massachusetts Soldiers and Sailors*, 17:294. Wickhams served in the Marquis de Lafayette's light infantry during the 1781 campaign in Virginia that ended at Yorktown. Daniel J. Tortora, "Indian Patriots from Eastern Massachusetts: Six Perspectives," *Journal of the American Revolution*, February 4, 2015 (hereafter "Indian Patriots").

15. General Orders, February 15, 1783, *Washington Writings*, 26:135–136.

16. General Orders, March 22, 1783, *Washington Writings*, 26:250; Foster Journal, March (16?), April 6, April 13, and May 25, 1783; Foster Journal, February 16, 1783; and Foster Journal, May 11, 1783.

17. Edward M. Ruttenber, *History of the Town of New Windsor, Orange County, N.Y.* (Newburgh, NY, 1912), 93.

18. Foster Journal, March 16(?), 1783; and Foster Journal, April 13, 1783, "3 Saboth in March (16 or 23) 1783 & This Day 4th Sabth. Marche (23 or 30)." Foster could have been off by one Sunday, because right after "This Day 4th Sabth. Marche" the next entry is "Monday, Tusday & Windsay" (March 31, April 1, and April 2) followed by "Thursday Apriel 3d 1783."

19. Lieutenant Colonel Benjamin Walker to Lieutenant Colonel William Stephens Smith, March 16, 1783, New Windsor Cantonment State Historic Site Collection; and *Chastellux Travels*, 1:288 notes. Walker reported that the terms of the long-anticipated peace treaty had just arrived and then briefly summarized the Newburgh Conspiracy. Both Walker and Smith were aides-de-camp to Washington.

20. *Private Yankee Doodle*, 182; and *Gilbert Diary*, 38–46.

21. To Lieutenant Park Holland, August 1781,

Gilbert Letters, 47; and *Chastellux Travels*, 2:615 notes.

22. To Colonel James Converse, September 30, 1782, *Gilbert Letters*, 69; and *Gilbert Letters*, 95.

23. J.A. Simpson and E.S.C. Weiner, eds., *The Compact Oxford English Dictionary*, 2nd ed. (New York, 2000), 2262; To Captain Jonathan Stone, March 1, 1783, *Gilbert Letters*, 86–87; and *Gilbert Letters*, 98.

24. Deborah Sampson Gannett, *An Address, Delivered with Applause, at the Federal Street Theatre, Boston, Four Successive Nights of the Different Plays, Beginning March 2, 1802; and After, at Other Principal Towns, a Number of Nights Successively at Each Place; By Mrs. Deborah Gannett, the American Heroine, Who Served Three Years with Reputation (Undiscovered as a Female) in the Late American Army* (Dedham, MA, 1802), 12.

25. J. Holt, pub., *The Independent Gazette, or, The New York Journal Revived* (New York, December 13, 1783—March 11, 1784), January 10, 1784, New York Public Library.

26. *Journal of the House of Representatives of the United of States, Being the First Session of the Fifth Congress: Begun and Held at the City of Philadelphia, May 15, 1797, and in the Twenty-First Year of the Independence of the Said States* (Washington, DC, 1826), 3 (November 28, 1797): 990; Paul Revere to his congressman Representative William Eustis, February 20, 1804, Miscellaneous Bound Manuscripts, Massachusetts Historical Society, and Alfred F. Young, *Masquerade The Life and Times of Deborah Sampson, Continental Soldier* (New York, 2004), 229; *Bills and Resolutions, House of Representatives*, 24th Congress, 2nd Session, House Resolution 890, January 31, 1837, A Bill For the relief of Benjamin Gannett, widower of Deborah Gannett, a soldier of the revolution; and *Bills and Resolutions, House of Representatives*, 25th Congress, 2nd Session, House Resolution 184, In Senate of the United States. June 18, 1838, Received, An Act For the relief of the heirs of Deborah Gannett, a soldier of the Revolution, deceased.

27. William C. Nell, *Colored Patriots of the American Revolution* (Boston, 1855), 160–162.

28. John C. Dann, ed., *The Revolution Remembered: Eyewitness Accounts of the War for Independence* (Chicago, 1980), 240–250 (hereafter *Revolution Remembered*); *NY in Revolution*, 1:157; and General Orders, After Orders, July 4, 1777, *Washington Writings*, 8:347; and Richard Eldred, "The Heroine of Yorktown," *Daughters of the American Revolution Magazine* 118 (November 1984), 634, 635, and 698.

29. *Women & Children Return*; To the Superintendent of Finance Robert Morris, January 29, 1783, *Washington Writings*, 26:78–80; To Major General Henry Knox, March 8, 1783, *Washington Writings*, 26:199–200; General Orders, September 8, 1782, *Washington Writings*, 25:139; and To the Superintendent of Finance Robert Morris, January 29, 1783, *Washington Writings*, 26:79.

Chapter 4

1. Regulations for Hutting, November 4, 1782, Pickering Letters, Reel 27, Vol. 84; "Soil Investigations," 24–30; and To Brigadier General Elias Dayton, April 7, 1783, *Washington Writings*, 26:304.

2. To the Superintendent of Finance Robert Morris, July 30, 1782, *Washington Writings*, 24:440–441; General Orders, October 15, 1782, *Washington Writings*, 25:263; *JCC*, April 5, 1782, 22:173; and To Comfort Sands, May 25, 1782, *Washington Writings*, 24:285.

3. Arbitration Papers between the Continental Army and Contractor, July 9, 1782, Washington Papers.

4. General Orders, November 12, 1782, *Washington Writings*, 25:333.

5. To the Board of War, June 21, 1781, *Washington Writings*, 22:246–247; General Orders, March 19, 1783, *Washington Writings*, 26:247; and Arbitration Papers between the Continental Army and Contractor, July 9, 1782, Washington Papers.

6. To the Superintendent of Finance Robert Morris, August 5, 1782, *Washington Writings*, 24:467–468.

7. General Orders, October 15, 1782, *Washington Writings*, 25:263; To James McHenry, October 17, 1782, *Washington Writings*, 25:269; To Major General Benoit Joseph de Tarle, October 7, 1782, *Washington Writings*, 25:244–245; and To James McHenry, October 23, 1782, *Washington Writings*, 25:289.

8. *Thacher Journal*, 266; *Chastellux Travels*, 2:572 notes. "The prodigious quantity of French money brought into America by France's fleets and armies and the loans made to Congress, together with the vast return of dollars from the Havana and the Spanish, Portuguese, and English gold that found its way into the country from the British lines, rendered specie very plentiful toward the conclusion of the war, and the arrival of the army of the Comte de Rochambeau was particularly opportune, as it happened at the very distressing crisis of the death of the paper currency. The French money alone in circulation in 1782 was estimated, after very accurate calculations, at 35 million livres, or nearly a million and a half sterling."

9. To the Superintendent of Finance Robert Morris, September 22, 1782, *Washington Writings*, 25:187–188; Superintendent of Finance Robert Morris to State Governors, October 5, 1782, Washington Papers; Superintendent of Finance Robert Morris to State Receivers, October 5, 1782, Washington Papers; and To Lord Stirling, Major General William Alexander, September 18, 1782, *Washington Writings*, 25:174.

10. To William Duer, April 25, 1782, Washington Papers; William Duer to the Superintendent of Finance Robert Morris, September 6, 1782, Washington Papers; To William Duer, September 18, 1782, *Washington Writings*, 25:175; To the Superintendent of Finance Robert Morris, December 11, 1782, *Washington Writings*, 25:418; and To

William Duer, December 20, 1782, *Washington Writings*, 25:453.

11. Assistant Quartermaster and Storekeeper Christopher Meng to Colonel Timothy Pickering, May 25, 1782, Miscellaneous Records, Reel 80; Colonel Timothy Pickering to Lieutenant Colonel Benjamin Walker, March 22, 1783, Washington Papers; General Orders, June 19, 1781, *Washington Writings*, 22:233; To Colonel Timothy Pickering, February 10, 1781, *Washington Writings*, 21:206; and General Orders, January 9, 1781, *Washington Writings*, 21:73–74. During preparations for the campaign of 1781, Washington ordered that "Every Mess must carry its own Camp Kettle," possibly toted in canvas bags with canvas or leather carrying straps that were proposed to be made from old tents earlier in the year. Kettles in bags, besides making them easier to carry, would "not grease and injure the soldiers cloaths."

12. Major General Nathanael Greene to Brigadier General Henry Knox, September 29, 1781, *Greene Papers*, 9:412; Benson J. Lossing, ed., "The American Historical Record and Repertory of Notes and Queries, Concerning the History and Antiquities of America and Biography of Americans," *Potter's American Monthly: An Illustrated Magazine of History, Literature, Science and Art* 3, no. 29 (May 1874).

13. General Orders, December 31, 1782, *Washington Writings*, 25:495–496; and *Gilbert Diary*, February 4, 1783.

14. General Orders, October 30, 1782, *Washington Writings*, 25:309.

15. *Gilbert Diary*, May 13 and 24, 1783.

16. General Orders, March 24, 1783, *Washington Writings*, 26:257–258; Regimental Orders, March 25, 1783, 1st New York Orderly Book; and Lieutenant Colonel David Humphreys to Colonel Timothy Pickering, April 1, 1783, Miscellaneous Records, Reel 83.

17. General Orders, November 23, 1782, *Washington Writings*, 25:369.

18. General Orders, January 24, 1783, *Washington Writings*, 26:62; and Regimental Orders, January 26, 1783, 1st New York Orderly Book.

19. General Orders, January 31, 1783, *Washington Writings*, 26:87; General Orders, March 2, 1783, *Washington Writings*, 26:175–176; Samuel Loudon, ed., *The New York Packet and the American Advertiser*, 1776–1783, December 12, 1782, Filmed by the New-York Historical Society, University Microfilm, February 20, 1783, and March 6, 1783 (hereafter *NY Packet*).

20. *Gilbert Diary*, May 12, 1783.

21. Foster Journal, March 18, 1783; and Foster Journal, March 17, 1783.

22. General Orders, May 16, 1782, *Washington Writings*, 24:260–261; and General Orders, May 21, 1783, *Washington Writings*, 26:446.

23. *JCC*, November 28, 1782, 23:647; and *Gilbert Diary*, November 28, 1782. On November 28, 1782, "a day of thanksgiving and prayer" set aside by Congress "to thank God for all his mercies," he "drank grogg [alcohol mixed with water, usually rum] with Dr. [Origin] Brigham, drank too freely which opperated to the disadvantage of the said Gilbert, went to bed at Roll call." *Officer Register*, 121 and 537; Dr. Origin Brigham was a surgeon's mate in the 2nd Massachusetts Regiment. *Gilbert Diary*, December 20, 1782; and *Gilbert Diary*, December 27, 1782. Lieutenant Nathaniel Thatcher at the end of December "wet his commission by giving all the officers of the [5th] Regt a drink of grogg." *Gilbert Diary*, February 2, 3, 6, and 28, 1783, March 19 and 20, 1783, and May 12, 17, and 22, 1783. In addition to grog, over the next few months Gilbert also drank cherry (brandy), wine, some "Egg stuff" (eggnog), methiglon (fermented honey), and lemon punch.

24. *Private Yankee Doodle*, 15 and 107. Just wanting: "to take a priming before ... [he] took upon ... the whole coat of paint for a soldier," Joseph Plumb Martin joined a unit of six-month volunteers from the militia, called levies. Serving from July 1776 to the middle of December, he went home and then the following spring made the fateful decision to sign on for the duration of the war. "There was no going home and spending the winter season among friends and procuring a new recruit of strength and spirits. No, it was one constant drill, summer and winter; like an old horse in a mill, it was a continual routine." *Private Yankee Doodle*, 247. "What a soldier of the Revolution valued next to the welfare of his country and his own honor, that is something to eat and being all in good health and having the prospect of a quiet night's rest."

25. *Sinews of Independence*, 54–70 and 144–166.

26. *JCC*, April 4, 1777, 7:231–237; and *JCC*, February 6, 1778, 10:128–131.

27. *Chastellux Travels*, 1:87.

28. John Jones, *Plain Concise Practical Remarks, on the Treatment of Wounds and Fractures; To which is Added, An Appendix, On Camp And Military Hospitals; Principally Designed for the Use of young Military and Naval Surgeons, in North-America* (Philadelphia, 1776), 6–9 (hereafter Jones's *Practical Remarks*).

29. General Orders, November 10, 1782, *Washington Writings*, 25:328; General Orders, November 12, 1782, *Washington Writings*, 25:333; and *Dr. Cochran*, 250–251.

30. *Private Yankee Doodle*, 51. "What is termed going on command is what is generally called going on a scouting party or something similar. I told the sergeant I was sick and could not go. He said I must go to the doctor and if he said I was unfit for duty, he must excuse me. I told the sergeant I was sick and could not go. I saw our surgeon's mate close by, endeavoring to cook his supper, blowing the fire and scratching his eyes. We both stepped up to him and he felt my pulse, at the same time very demurely shutting his eyes while I was laughing in his face. After a minute's consultation with his medical talisman, he very gravely told the sergeant that I was unfit for duty, having a high fever upon me. I was as well as he; all the medicine I needed was a bellyful of victuals."

31. *Thacher Journal*, 203.

32. Benjamin Rush, "The Results of Observations Made upon the Diseases Which Occurred in the Military Hospitals of the United States, during the Late War," In *Medical Inquiries and Observations*, 4 vols., 2nd ed. (Philadelphia, 1805), 1:276.

33. Regimental Orders, December 13, 1780, Lieutenant James G. Giles, Orderly Book: COL. John Lamb's Second Regiment Continental Artillery, Early American Orderly Books 1748-1817, Reel 13, National Archives. Pennington Diary, 32-33; and Return of Huts at the Gen. Hospl at New Windsor with the No. of Fires, Miscellaneous Records, Reel 95.

34. *Private Yankee Doodle*, 182; and *Gilbert Diary*, 38-46. The then quartermaster sergeant, Benjamin Gilbert, was left behind in Danbury, Connecticut, from October 1778 to March 1779 because he was far too ill to travel with his regiment to the Highlands. Eli Hoyt, a local militia officer, looked after him during his lengthy recovery. Gilbert went to town every week to see the military doctors and obtain his sick rations and medicine. His condition was so bad that his father traveled more than 100 miles from Brookfield, Massachusetts, to visit him. Daniel Gilbert brought presents of "a Chese and Two pair of Cotton stocking[s]." Benjamin was able to draw rations on a regular basis, and the consistent availability of food went a long way toward facilitating his recovery. Time and again Joseph Plumb Martin stated that it was prolonged hunger that disabled many soldiers, not disease. "Here was the army starved and naked, and there their country sitting still and expecting the army to do notable things while fainting from sheer starvation." After six months, Continental Army medical authorities certified that Gilbert was sufficiently recovered to return to his regiment and discharged him from their care.

35. *Private Yankee Doodle*, 43.

36. General Orders, December 11, 1782, *Washington Writings*, 25:423; General Orders, April 5, 1783, *Washington Writings*, 26:297; General Orders, January 1, 1783, *Washington Writings*, 26:3; General Orders, August 3, 1782, *Washington Writings*, 24:460; and JCC, April 23, 1782, 22:209-210. Emoluments were rations, clothing, shelter, and other entitlements.

37. *Private Yankee Doodle*, 190-191. Getting a severe stomachache from eating "an old ox's liver," Joseph Plumb Martin was given "a large dose of tartar emetic [antimony potassium tartrate], the usual remedy in the army for all disorders, even sore eyes." Taking half or two-thirds of the medicine without results, he finally swallowed all of it "and discharged the hard chunks of liver like grapeshot from a field-piece."

38. To the President of Congress, February 5, 1777, *Washington Writings*, 7:105; and To Governor Patrick Henry, April 13, 1777, *Washington Writings*, 7:409.

39. Brigadier General James Clinton to Governor George Clinton, February 26, 1778, Hugh Hastings, comp., *Public Papers of George Clinton First Governor of New York War of the Revolution Series*, 8 vols. (Albany, New York, 1899-1904) 2:808-809 (hereafter *Clinton Papers*).

40. *Heath Memoirs*, 326-328.

41. *Thacher Journal*, 257-258; and Dr. Samuel Adams, Samuel Adams's Private Miscellaneous Diary Kept Ann. Dom. 1781, When he was Surgeon to the Massachusetts Regt. Of Artillery Which did duty at the several places of New Windsor, Philipsburgh West-Point ... , February 1, 1781, Samuel Adams Papers, Manuscripts and Archives Division, New York Public Library.

42. Foster Journal, February 7, 1783.

43. Jones's *Practical Remarks*, 38.

44. Jones's *Practical Remarks*, 45.

45. Jeptha R. Simms, *Trappers of New York: or, a Biography of Nicholas Stoner and Nathaniel Foster; Together with Anecdotes of other Celebrated Hunters, and Some Account of Sir William Johnson, and His Style of Living* (Harrison, New York, 1980 [1871], 88-91.

46. *Thacher Journal*, 114-115.

47. T.W. Egly, Jr., *Goose Van Schaick of Albany 1736-1789: The Continental Army's Senior Colonel* (Privately Printed United States, 1992), 106-107; and *Officer Register*, 557. The most senior colonel in the entire army, he might have also taken this opportunity to lobby for promotion to general. If so, he was unsuccessful. He did, however, receive a brevet promotion to that rank in October 1783, which carried the prestige but none of the emoluments.

48. Jones's *Practical Remarks*,12.

49. Dr. John Cochran to Colonel Timothy Pickering, October 23, 1782, Miscellaneous Records, Reel 83; To Dr. John Cochran, November 3, 1782, Pickering Letters, Reel 27, Vol. 85; Dr. John Cochran to Colonel Timothy Pickering, November 4, 1782, quoted in *Dr. Cochran*, 242-244; To Dr. John Cochran, October 15, 1782, Pickering Letters, Reel 27, Vol. 84; Dr. John Cochran to Colonel Timothy Pickering, October 15, 1782, Miscellaneous Records, Reel 83; and *Dr. Cochran*, 76.

50. Quoted in *Dr. Cochran*, 184-200, 135; and JCC, January 6, 1778, 10:23 and 24.

51. *The Pennsylvania Packet or the General Advertiser*, Philadelphia, Pennsylvania, February 27, 1783, America's Historical Newspapers; Foster Journal, November 26, 1782; *Massachusetts Soldiers and Sailors*, 9:1009; General Orders, February 12, 1783, *Washington Writings*, 26:129; and General Orders, April 12, 1778, *Washington Writings*, 11:252.

52. *Sinews of Independence*, 238-254, quoted in *Dr. Cochran*, 184-200.

53. *Gilbert Diary*, April 8 and 9, 1783; and *Massachusetts Soldiers and Sailors*, 1:855. Pickering instructed his subordinates to keep a supply of coffins on hand in various sizes "that the dead may no more be buried in their blankets, to the offence of the army and inhabitants." Colonel Timothy Pickering Memorandum of matters to be attended to by the gentlemen in my office, November 1782, Pickering Letters; Bennett Cuthbertson, *Cuthbertson's System for the Complete Interior Management and*

Oeconomy of a Battalion of Infantry (Bristol, UK, 1776), 160 (hereafter *Cuthbertson's System*); *Newburgh Gazette*, September 1, 1857; Lewis Beach, *Cornwall* (Newburgh, NY, 1873), 143; *Newburgh Daily Journal*, May 14, 1883; Edward M. Ruttenber and Lewis H. Clark, comps., *History of Orange County, New York with Illustrations and Biographical Sketches of Many of the Pioneers and Prominent Men* (Philadelphia, 1881), 226; John J. Nutt, *Newburgh: Her Institutions, Industries and Leading Citizens* (Newburgh, NY, 1891), 33; *Newburgh Daily Journal*, May 14, 1883; and John W. Jordan, comp., "Continental Hospital Returns 1777–1780," *Pennsylvania Magazine of History and Biography*, April 1899, 4 and 10–18. The returns show 134 patients, which reflects the deduction of 1 soldier listed as an orderly, who is presumed not sick but sent to assist in providing care. There are also returns of the sick sent to Dr. Alison not listed specifically as being sent to the New Windsor hospital, so those numbers are not included in the total. All of these admitted soldiers were from the southern states of Maryland, Delaware, Virginia, and North Carolina. Historic Site Manager of New Windsor Cantonment Jane Townsend to Regional Historic Preservation Supervisor Wallace Workmaster, January 25, 1987, Memorandum: The Soldiers' Graves at NWC, New Windsor Cantonment State Historic Site Collection; Donald C. Gordon, President, *The New Windsor Cantonment National Temple Hill Association, Inc., Annual Report 1963*, 14, New Windsor Cantonment State Historic Site Collection; Author not Identified, "Temple Hill and Its Vicinity," *Historical Society of Newburgh Bay and the Highlands*, publication no. 19, 1924, 21 (hereafter "Temple Hill Vicinity"); and Joseph B. Burnet et al., *New Windsor Centennial Temple Hill, June 22, 1883* (Newburgh, NY, 1883), 11 (hereafter *New Windsor Centennial*).

Though none of the burials at this encampment have been located, over the years people have claimed to see gravesites. An article in the September 1, 1857, *Newburgh Gazette* reported that the "causeway across the swamp is comparatively perfect [and] many of the huts occupied by the soldiers are still marked by chimney backs." The "Temple is well ascertained ... and the rude stone marks the head and foot of the sleeping soldier." In 1873, Lewis Beach noted "mounded earth, devoid of head-stone yet speaking in still and silent tones of the patriot dead." A decade later, Joel Headley in the *Newburgh Daily Journal* claimed that there was a "graveyard of the American Army near the 'Temple.'" He was probably just reciting the claim in Edward M. Ruttenber and Lewis H. Clark's *History of Orange County, New York*, published two years earlier that "in the vicinity of ... [the Temple] was also the hospital and bakery, and a short distance east was the burial-ground." Undoubtedly, the graves of those who died at the hospital were nearby. Soldiers encamped at New Windsor, however, possibly retrieved their dead from the hospital and buried them with their comrades in camp.

The most compelling statement in the *History of Orange County, New York,* regarding the New Windsor Cantonment burials is that "the space between the camp and the Temple was partly a swamp, which was crossed by a causeway made of logs. Immediately in front of the camp was the parade-ground. In the graveyard, now overgrown with trees, are still-marked the resting places of the dead." By 18th-century military custom, the dead of this encampment were buried at the head of their respective parade grounds. John J. Nutt in his *Newburgh, Her Institutions, Industries and Leading Citizens*, published in 1891, wrote that "a number of years ago, several graves were found in a strip of woods on the Heron farm." Headley claimed, however, that those graves were not from the Continental Army's last winter encampment but instead were from "three Southern regiments stationed on the eastern slope of Snake Hill far apart from the main army that was encamped on another slope beyond a marsh." The Heron farm was in the environs of the 1780–81 artillery encampment, the 1781–83 hospital, and the 1782–83 hutting grounds of the 2nd Massachusetts Brigade. This vicinity was also possibly where Dr. Frances Alison established his Continental Army hospital in October 1778. Initially receiving the sick from the encampment at the Beverly Robinson farm, opposite West Point on the eastern side of the Hudson River, he cared for nearly 150 patients before the temporary facility was closed in February 1779. Presumably, some of his patients died. Trenches were dug in 1963 by amateur archaeologist Ernest Rodman on the Epiphany College property, located on the old Heron farm, and in October 1986 two mounds were tested by professional archaeologist Edward Lenik, but no remains were discovered in this vicinity. An article titled "Temple Hill & Vicinity" in the *Historical Society of Newburgh Bay and the Highlands* publication for 1924 mentioned a "burying ground" a quarter mile south of a large building around the Maryland, New Hampshire, New Jersey, and New York hut sites. None of these claims were backed by any evidence.

Chapter 5

1. For my initial study of the uniforms at this encampment, see Michael S. McGurty, "'A tolerably decent appearance': The Clothing of the Continental Army at the New Windsor Cantonment, 1782–83," *Military Collector & Historian* 63, no. 2 (Summer 2011): 89–100; To Clothier General John Moylan, September 25, 1782, *Washington Writings*, 25:207.

2. *JCC*, February 28, 1781, 19:206–207.

3. To Major General William Heath, February 5, 1783, *Washington Writings*, 26:97; Jacob Judd, comp. and ed., *The Revolutionary War Memoir and Selected Correspondence of Philip Van Cortlandt*, 2 vols. (Tarrytown, NY, 1976) I, 67–68 (hereafter *Van Cortlandt Memoir*); To the Secretary at War Major General Benjamin Lincoln, November 6, 1782, *Washington Writings*, 25:323; and To the

Secretary at War Major General Benjamin Lincoln, February 24, 1783, *Washington Writings*, 26:158.

4. General Orders, October 2, 1779, *Washington Writings*, 16:388.

5. General Orders, September 13, 1782, *Washington Writings*, 25:157 notes; Lieutenant General Comte de Rochambeau to George Washington, October 23, 1780, Washington Papers; and To the Board of War, November 19, 1781, *Washington Writings*, 23:353–354.

6. Richard Harrison to General George Washington, April 30, 1781, Washington Papers.

7. To the Superintendent of Finance Robert Morris, July 13, 1781, *Washington Writings*, 22:367; and Rhode Island Delegates to Governor William Greene, December 6, 1781, *Congress Delegates Letters*, 18:237–238. "The King (Louis XVI) upon hearing of the Capture of the Transport, the Marquis de la Fayette was apprehensive that our troops would be distressed for want of cloathing, and had given orders to replace all the cloathing and other articles that were taken in that transport."

8. To Major General Benjamin Lincoln, December 11, 1780, *Washington Writings*, 20:462.

9. To Major General William Heath, December 31, 1781, *Washington Writings*, 23:415. The disassembly, dying, and sewing back together of these British coats was overseen by officials operating out of the Continental Army clothier store in Newburgh, New York. The Invalid Corps was filled with soldiers who were injured in battle or debilitated in such a way that they could not withstand the rigors of field service. They were used to garrison forts such as West Point or were given tasks, within their capabilities, to free up able-bodied men. There was little danger of Invalid Corps troops being mistaken for the enemy, so their coats were not dyed. They received the coats of the 5th Foot, possibly at the behest of their commander, Colonel Lewis Nicola, whose first assignment, as a British officer, was in the unit that later became this numbered regiment. Don Troiani and James L. Kochan, *Insignia of Independence: Military Buttons, Accoutrement Plates, & Gorgets of the American Revolution* (Gettysburg, PA, 2012), 192 (hereafter *Insignia of Independence*); and Major General William Heath to General George Washington, November 17, 1781, Washington Papers.

British Regiments in the West Indies, in 1780

Regiment	Facing Colors	Regimental Lace (worsted tape, fashioned into rectangular blocks, sewn around each buttonhole and on top of the back coat vent)
4th Regiment of Foot	blue	white with blue stripe
5th Regiment of Foot	gosling green	white with two red stripes
15th Regiment of Foot	yellow	white with yellow and black worm, red stripe
27th Regiment of Foot	buff	white with one blue and one red stripe
28th Regiment of Foot	bright yellow	white with one yellow and two black stripes
35th Regiment of Foot	orange	white with one yellow stripe
40th Regiment of Foot	buff	white with a red and a black stripe
46th Regiment of Foot	yellow	white with red and purple worms
49th Regiment of Foot	full green	white with two red stripes and one green stripe
55th Regiment of Foot	dark green	white with two green stripes
60th Regiment of Foot	blue	white with two blue stripes

Philip R.N. Katcher, *Encyclopedia of British, Provincial, and German Army Units, 1775–1783* (Harrisburg, PA, 1973); and Hew Strachan, *British Military Uniforms 1768–96: The Dress of the British Army from Official Sources* (London, 1975), 179–181.

As far as it is known, buttons from all but the 4th and 49th Regiments of Foot were found at the hut sites of the New Hampshire, New Jersey, and New York Lines. Since much of that encampment site was covered over by the construction of the Thruway, the missing regimental buttons could be underneath the fill, just have been missed, or they could have been on the coats issued to the Canadian Regiment or the 10th Massachusetts, who were elsewhere.

The 2nd New York received the coats of either the 15th, 28th, or 46th Regiments. "At Hampton in the Jerseys," Sergeant James Selkirk recorded in his memoirs that "in the spring [of 1782] we got complete uniforms from the British clothing that was taken at Yorktown. The facings was taken off and the coats colored brown and made up again with yellow facings." He also received a "white waistcoat and pantaloon [that made] a very good appearance." Even though Selkirk believed that his uniform came from the stores surrendered at Yorktown, it was from the merchant convoy captured by the French and Spanish in 1780. Only one yellow-faced regiment was at Yorktown, the 80th Regiment of Foot, and none of its buttons have been found at the New Hampshire, New Jersey, and New York Lines' hut sites.

The belief that the issue was "the only way of preserving a compleat uniformity in the three Brigades" demonstrates that the principal concern was the body of the coat, not the facing color. With both the 1st and 2nd New York totaling over 500 men after the consolidation of their lines at the end of 1781, they must have received coats from more than one British regiment. They were probably not the only ones. There were six American regiments in the dyed British coats on the western ridge at New Windsor, and buttons were found there from nine different British regiments. Though the discovery of buttons of similar-faced units near each other at the New Hampshire, New Jersey, and New York hut sites at New Windsor suggests that there was an attempt to issue these coats by brigades, there were just not enough of each color combination to do that completely. Anyway, the facings were meant to be distinctive, so this effort would have had limited success.

The discovery of 5th and 55th Regiment of Foot buttons in the vicinity of the New York and New Jersey Lines' encampment at New Windsor do not contradict the possibility that de Verger saw battalion companies, not light infantry. They both had green facings. The New Jersey Line and the 1st New York Regiment were the van during the Verplanck's Point maneuver, a place often accorded to the light infantry. Michael Wolfe, ed., "A Memoir of the Revolutionary War (Sergeant James Selkirk 1756–1820)" (Draft, New York State Library, 1993), 48; *Sinews of Independence*, 214; Don Troiani and James L. Kochan, *Don Troiani's Soldiers of the American Revolution* (Mechanicsburg, PA, 2007), 179; Assistant Clothier General David Brooks to General George Washington, April 1, 1782, Washington Papers; Major General William Heath to General George Washington, December 22, 1781, Washington Papers; and Marko Zlatich, *New England Soldiers of the American Revolution* (Santa Barbara, CA, 1981), 32.

Considering that this soldier's coat still had the regimental lace on it, the assumption is that most of the other ones retained it as well. The Jean-Baptiste Antoine de Verger drawing of the soldier in a dyed British coat, however, does not show any lace, but he probably just omitted this detail. But the 2nd New Hampshire made new white facings, collars, and cuffs, bound with the same-colored tape for these coats. General Orders, March 3, 1783, *Washington Writings*, 26:181.

After being ordered to cut and make the blue coats according to one pattern and the brown ones to another pattern, the "Commanders of Companies (of the 8th Massachusetts) will have the larger button[s] cast and made into Small ones which method will be both nefesary and of a better Appearance," necessary, that is, in order to replace missing buttons and present a better appearance with the smaller facings. Regimental Orders, February 28, 1783, 8th Massachusetts Regiment Orderly Book, The Huntington Library, San Marino, CA (hereafter 8th Mass. Orderly Book). The 8th Massachusetts Regiment was probably one of the regiments that exhibited a "disagreeable and speckled appearance." Don Troiani, *Military Buttons of the American Revolution* (Gettysburg, PA, 2001) 91 (hereafter *American Revolution Buttons*).

In addition to the buttons listed in this book as being found at the New Hampshire, New Jersey, and New York hut sites, Washington's Headquarters State Historic Site has a 40th Regiment of Foot button recovered from there as well. The 40th Regiment of Foot was in the West Indies in 1780. Washington's Headquarters State Historic Site Collection.

10. To Assistant Clothier General David Brooks, January 26, 1783, *Washington Writings*, 26:70; To Major William Scott or Officer Commanding the New Hampshire Brigade, January 24, 1783, *Washington Writings*, 26:63; To David Brooks, January 26, 1783, *Washington Writings*, 26:70; and Inspection Report from Colonel Walter Stewart, March 25, 1783, Miscellaneous Records, Reel 111 (hereafter Stewart Report).

11. *Sinews of Independence*, 234–237; and General Orders, August 29, 1782, *Washington Writings*, 25:84–85.

The "Return of Clothing in Store" on April 4, 1782, at Newburgh, New York, Miscellaneous Records, Reel 94

Coats	314	Various Colours and Facings
Vests	380	White, made of Trecot (tricot) * (Defined in notes)
Linen Vests	260	
Baize* Vests	3100	
Baize Overalls	174	
Breeches	131	White, made of Moleton (melton)*

Breeches	1172	Drilling and Russia Sheeting*	
Shirts	924		
Shoes	3572		
Hose	10,532	Woolen	
Ditto	1242	Thread	
Hatts and Infantry Caps	4110		
Blankets	532		
Watch Coats	244		
Boots	280		
Mitts	2554		
Socks	2840		
Black Stocks	532		
Shoe Buckles	2582		
Dozens Coat Buttons	1665		
Do.		Vest Do	2364
pairs of Spurs	170		

Yards of Moleton (melton)	9920 for Breeches and Overalls			
Do.	Trecot (tricot)	2451	Do. Vests	
Do.	Blue Cloth	114	Do. Coats	
Do.	White	do	399	Do. Music Coats and Facings to blue cloth
Do.	Buff	103	Do. Facings	
Do.	Serge*	3216	Do. Lining (illegible)	
Do.	Osnaburg*	2230	Do. Pockets, Sleeve Linings (illegible)	
Do.	Ticking*	20,460		for Overalls

Yards of Moleton (melton)	9920 for Breeches and Overalls			
Pieces of Buckram*	74 34			

baize—a course woolen stuff having a long nap
buckram—a kind of course linen or cloth stiffened with cloth or paste
drilling—a course twilled linen or cotton fabric
melton—a stout smooth cloth having the nap cut very close and the face finished without pressing or glossing
Osnaburg—a kind of course linen originally made in Osnabruck
Russia sheeting—a fine bleached linen canvas
serge—a woolen fabric, now a very durable twilled cloth of worsted or with the warp of worsted and the woof of wool, used extensively for clothing
ticking—strong hard linen or cotton material used for making cases for mattresses or pillows
tricot—a woolen fabric, knitted by hand or by machinery in imitation of hand knitting

12. Howard C. Rice, Jr., and Anne S.K. Browne, trans., eds., *The American Campaigns of Rochambeau's Army 1780, 1781, 1782, 1783*, 2 vols. (Jointly published by Princeton University Press and Brown University Press, 1972), "The Journal of Jean Baptiste-Antoine de Verger,"1:166 (hereafter "de Verger Journal"); *Sinews of Independence*, 234–235; General Orders, September 14, 1782, *Washington Writings*, 25:158; General Orders, August 21, 1782, *Washington Writings*, 25:46–48; and Disposition for the Maneuver, September 21, 1782, Washington Papers.

13. To Clothier General John Moylan, October 31, 1782, *Washington Writings*, 25:313; and General Orders, January 8, 1783, *Washington Writings*, 26:23. Fortunately, a new shipment of thread arrived in January at the "Clothiers Store" in Newburgh. Barber Report; and Stewart Report.

14. General Orders, December 6, 1782, *Washington Writings*, 25:402; General Orders, April 14, 1783, *Washington Writings*, 26:315; and General Orders, February 24, 1783, *Washington Writings*, 26:159.

15. General Orders, March 3, 1783, *Washington Writings*, 26:181.

16. To Major Thomas Lansdale, January 25, 1783, *Washington Writings*, 26:67–69. The 3rd Maryland Detachment was attached to the New Jersey Brigade. A detachment was a portion of a regiment; To Major Thomas Lansdale, February 7, 1783, *Washington Writings*, 26:106–107.

17. To Colonel Michael Jackson or Officer Commanding Eighth Massachusetts Regiment, February 7, 1783, *Washington Writings*, 26:105–106; To Lieutenant Colonel Ezra Newhall or Officer Commanding Fifth Massachusetts Regiment, February 8, 1783, *Washington Writings*, 26:108–109; and

Regimental Orders, February 28, 1783, 8th Mass. Orderly Book.

18. Philip Katcher, *Uniforms of the Continental Army* (York, PA, 1981), 101–102. The 1781 specifications below for the Massachusetts Line unform were for officer uniforms. Soldier clothing was of similar design but normally not as finely finished. Though depending on the skill of the regimental tailors, some of them might have also had very well-made garments incorporating the most exquisite details.

> The color of the coats, waistcoat, linings and buttons, to be agreeable to the General Orders of the 2nd of October, 1779. The length of the coat, to the upper part of the knee-pan, and to be cut high in the neck. As 3 is to 5, so is the skirt to the waist of the coat; or divide the whole length of the coat into 8 equal parts, take 5 for the waist and 3 for the skirts. The lappel, at the top of the breast, to be 3 inches wide, and the bottom 2³⁄₁₀ inches; the lapel to be as low as the waist, and its wing to button within an inch of the shoulder seam with a small button on the cape. The epaulette to be worn directly on the top of the shoulder joint on the same button with the wing of the lappel. A round and close cuff, three inches wide, with four close worked buttonholes. The cape to be made with a peak behind, and its width in proportion to the lapels. The pocket flaps to be scollopped, four buttonholes, the two inner close worked, the two outer open worked, and to be seton in a curved line from the bottom of the lapel to the button on the hip. The coat to be cut full behind, with a fold on each back skirt, and two closed worked buttonholes on each. Ten open worked buttonholes on the breast of each lappel, with ten large buttons, at equal distance; four large buttons on each cuff, four on each pocket flap, and four on each fold: Those on the cuffs and pocket flaps to be placed agreeable to the buttonholes; and those on the folds, one on the hip, one at the bottom, and two in the centre, at an equal distance with those on the lapel. The coat is to be flaunt at the bottom with a genteel and military air. Four hooks and eyes at the breast as low as the coat allow to button. The skirt to hook up with a blue heart at each corner, with such devise as the Field Officers of each Regiment shall direct. The bottom's of the coat to be cut square. The waistcoat to be single-breasted, with twelve buttons, and four buttons, which shall appear below the flaps. The breeches are to be made with a half fall; four buttons on each knee. The small buttons on the waistcoat to be the same kind with the large ones on the coat. The number of the Regiment is to be in the centre of the button, with such device as the Field Officers shall direct.... A fashionable military cock'd hat, with a silver button loop and a small button with the number of the Regiment. To wear a black stock when on duty and on Parade.

Brigade Orders, January 3, 1783, 2nd Mass. Orderly Book.

19. To The President of Congress, January 30, 1782, *Washington Writings*, 23:471.

20. Massachusetts Supply Committee to Major General William Heath, December 21, 1781, Washington Papers. Massachusetts officials offered excuses for not depositing the clothing they procured into the Continental Store. They would continue to equivocate despite Congress's affirmation that Continental clothiers would issue all clothing. JCC, February 11, 1782, 22:71; and General Orders, April 10, 1782, *Washington Writings*, 24:106–107.

21. To the President of Congress, April 3, 1780, *Washington Writings*, 18:209; and *Private Yankee Doodle*, 197. In addition to being synonymous with "rag," another meaning of "jag" is "uneven."

22. To Major General William Heath, January 22, 1782, *Washington Writings*, 23:457; and To Comfort Sands, May 4, 1782, *Washington Writings*, 24:222.

23. General Orders, December 15, 1782, *Washington Writings*, 25:432. Washington desired that "commanding officers of the different lines and corps would agree among themselves on such distinctions as may be deemed proper in the fashion of the Lapels, Cuffs, buttons & ca." Brigade Orders, January 26, 1783, 2nd New Hampshire Regiment Orderly Book, New Hampshire Archives, New Hampshire Historical Society, quoted in Marko Zlatich and Bill Younghusband, *General Washington's Army (2) 1779–1783* (London, 1995), 44; and General Orders, February 24, 1783, *Washington Writings*, 26:158.

24. To Otis and Andrews, September 14, 1778, *Washington Writings,* 12:451.

25. Button from the 60th Regiment of Foot, Washington's Headquarters State Historic Site Collection.

26. John R. Elting, ed., "Light Infantry Company, 4th Massachusetts Regiment, Continental Line, 1781–1782," in *Military Uniforms in America the Era of the American Revolution, 1755–1795* (San Rafael, CA, 1974), 82 (hereafter 4th Massachusetts Light Infantry); and Diana Ross McCain, "Private Deborah Sampson of the Continental Army," *Early American Life* 24, no. 2 (April 1993): 16–18, 74–75.

27. To Major General William Heath, February 28, 1782, *Washington Writings*, 24:25–26.

28. *Gilbert Diary*, February 1, 1783; and *NY Packet*, December 26, 1782, and February 27, 1783.

29. To Major General William Heath, February 28, 1782, *Washington Writings*, 24:25–26; and *JCC*, February 28, 1781, 19:206–207.

30. *Gilbert Diary*, December 31, 1782, October 30, 1782. and January 1, 1783; To his Father, January 18, 1783, *Gilbert Letters*, 80; Directions Given Lieutenant Joseph Smith, *Gilbert Letters*, 75; and *Gilbert Diary*, May 9, 1783, May 10, 1783, and January 6, 1783. He "received a pattern for westcoat & breeches, of corduroy," on December 31, 1782. Having had to borrow an overcoat earlier in the year, Gilbert's father sent him cloth for a "loose Coat" that arrived the following day. In January,

Gilbert requested "some white woolen yarn (to mend Stockings with)." Hating to continue bothering his father for trifles, he apologized and would "not have made this application if ... [he] could purchase any in this place." In his instructions, given in mid-December, to Lieutenant Joseph Smith of his regiment, going on furlough to Boston, Gilbert requested that he buy him a silver epaulette and linen for two shirts. In May, Gilbert "bought some Course Linen for pockets." The day before he purchased a pattern for breeches.

31. 6th Massachusetts Regiment button mold, Washington's Headquarters State Historic Site Collection; Deborah A. Sprouse, "Button Manufacturing in the Hudson Highlands," *Military Collector and Historian* 48, no. 1 (Spring 1995): 43–45; *Insignia of Independence*, 225–226 and 232–233; and *American Revolution Buttons*, 120–121.

32. General Orders, May 14, 1782, *Washington Writings*, 24:254.

33. *Gilbert Diary*, January 16, 1783.

34. General Orders, June 18, 1780, *Washington Writings*, 19:21–22; General Orders July 14, 1780, *Washington Writings*, 19:172–173; and Alan H. Archambault and Marko Zlatich, "4th Massachusetts Regiment of the Continental Line, Battalion Companies, 1782–1783" (Plate No. 601), *Military Collector and Historian* 34, no. 1 (Spring 1987) 30 (hereafter 4th Massachusetts Battalion Companies).

35. General Orders, October 1, 1782, *Washington Writings*, 25:224–225.

36. General Orders, May 14, 1782, *Washington Writings*, 24:254; Regimental Orders, December 8, 1782, 2nd Mass. Orderly Book; Regimental Orders, March 17, 1783, 1st NY Orderly Book; Barber Report; 4th Massachusetts Battalion Companies; and *Gilbert Diary*, February 19, 1783.

37. 4th Massachusetts Light Infantry.

38. General Orders, July 19, 1780, *Washington Writings*, 19:210.

39. Regimental Orders January 19, 1783, 1st New York Orderly Book; General Orders, August 12, 1782, *Washington Writings*, 25:9; Regimental Orders February 18, 1783, 1st NY Orderly Book; Regimental Orders February 3, 1783, 2nd Mass. Orderly Book; and Regimental Orders, January 27, 1783, 2nd Mass. Orderly Book. Sometimes Sproat's last name was spelled Sprout. 2nd Massachusetts Regiment women were paid for washing and ironing, as follows:

	Coppers
a ruffled fhirt	4
plain do	3
cloth vest & breeches each	3
cloth overalls	4
linnen do	3

	Coppers
handerkercheif	1
stocks	1
pair of hofe	2
linen vest & breeches each	2

40. General Orders, August 27, 1782, *Washington Writings*, 25:70. The cape of the hunting shirt shed water, and the fringed ends wicked water away from the wearer. Regimental Orders, February 25, 1783, 1st NY Orderly Book.

41. To Clothier General John Moylan, October 31, 1782, *Washington Writings*, 25:313; General Orders, January 10, 1783, *Washington Writings*, 26:30; and Advertisement, February 16, 1783, 1st NY Orderly Book. Assistant Adjutant General Captain John Carlisle from Hazen's Regiment advertised on February 16, 1783, that he "lost last Evening on the road between the Adjutants Generals Quarters and Williams Tavern a light coloured watch Coat with a red Cape."

42. To Clothier General John Moylan, October 31, 1782, *Washington Writings*, 25:313.

43. *Chastellux Travels*, 1:134, 298 notes; and James A. Lewis, *The Final Campaign of the American Revolution Rise and Fall of the Spanish Bahamas* (Columbia, SC, 1991), 11–17 and 33–34. Taking an interminable amount of time to recruit a crew, Gillon eventually sailed to Havana, Cuba, from which he escorted a Spanish flotilla that seized the Bahamas in May 1782. Forced to turn over the *South Carolina* to his second-in-command Captain John Joyner later that year by American officials at the behest of the French minister to America, the Chevalier de la Luzerne, Gillen's vessel was captured off New York in December 1782 by a squadron consisting of two British frigates and a 44-gun ship.

44. To Major General Benjamin Lincoln, December 11, 1780, *Washington Writings*, 20:313; JCC, January 31, 1780, 16:112–113; and To Brigadier General Henry Knox, January 7, 1781, *Washington Writings*, 21:67. In December 1780, Washington vented to General Lincoln that "ten thousand compleat suits ready in France ... [had sat] there because ... [the] public Agents ... [could not] agree whose business it ... [was] to ship them; [a quantity ... [had] also lain in the West Indies for more than Eighteen Months owing probably to some such cause." This flippant attitude was astounding considering that "supplies of clothing, of tents, of arms and warlike stores ... [had] to be principally obtained from foreign nations." But "so often disappointed from that quarter, that prudence dictate[d] the impolicy of placing dependence upon it." Governor Jonathan Trumbull to George Washington, November 21, 1780, Washington Papers; and Clerk to the Navy Board Eastern Department William Story to General George Washington, November 22, 1780, Washington Papers.

45. To the Secretary at War Major General Benjamin Lincoln, February 24, 1783, *Washington Writings*, 26:158; To Clothier General John Moylan, January 12, 1783, *Washington Writings*, 26:32; and General Orders, December 23, 1782, *Washington Writings*, 25:457.

46. Regimental Orders, February 25, 1783, 1st NY Orderly Book. Colonel Van Schaick wanted "to See the Men make more use of their overhalls, to prevent the wearing out of their Breeches." The troops at New Windsor badly needed woolen overalls because "the building of the Hutts has almost entirely destroyed their last Years breeches." To the Secretary at War Major General Benjamin Lincoln, February 24, 1783, *Washington Writings*, 26:157.

47. Regimental Orders, February 17, 1783, 1st NY Orderly Book. In the 18th century, the term "cloth" usually referred to wool, while the term "thread" referred to linen. "de Verger Journal," 1:166. The American light infantry wore "white linen pantaloons tucked into black gaiters reaching to the calf."

48. General Orders, January 22, 1783, *Washington Writings*, 26:61. The general officers and others who deemed it proper went "into Mourning one month ... by wearing a Crape or Weed." Crepe is "a silk fabric, usually black, used for mourning veils, bands, etc.," while a weed is "a mourning band of black crepe or cloth, as worn on a man's hat or coat sleeve." Laurence Urdang, ed., *The Random House College Dictionary*, 1st ed. (New York, 1980), 315, 492.

49. Regimental Orders, 9th June 1782, 8th Mass. Orderly Book; General Orders, August 7, 1782, *Washington Writings*, 24:487; General Orders, September 19, 1782, 25:181–182; General Orders, February 8, 1783, *Washington Writings*, 26:109–110; and General Orders, March 5, 1783, *Washington Writings*, 26:191.

50. "The Inspector General [Major General von Steuben] (or in his absence the inspector of the Northern army [Colonel Walter Stewart]), the Adjutant general [Brigadier General Edward Hand], Brigadier General [Ebenezer] Huntington, Colonel [John] Greaton and Lieutenant Colonel [Francis] Barber or any three of them are appointed a Board, to examine the pretensions of the noncommissioned officers and soldiers who are Candidates for the Badge of Merit." There is no record of this group holding any meetings. Brown and Churchill were selected by Brigadier General John Greaton, Colonel Walter Stewart, Lieutenant Colonel Ebenezer Sproat, Major Nicholas Fish, and Major Lemuel Trescott, who met in the Temple Building, at 10:00 a.m. on April 19, 1783. General Orders, April 17, 1783, *Washington Writings*, 26:329–330. This board was ordered to meet again in the Temple on June 10, 1783, but if it did, no candidates were recommended. General Orders, June 8, 1783, *Washington Writings*, 26:482; General Orders, June 9, 1783, *Washington Writings*, 26:498; and General Orders, August 7, 1782, *Washington Writings*, 24:488.

51. Major Edward C. Boynton, ed., *General Orders of George Washington Issued at Newburgh on the Hudson, 1782–1783* (Harrison, NY, 1973), 109; and Anonymous to Continental Army Officers, March 10, 1783, Washington Papers.

52. Colonel Walter Stewart to Major General Horatio Gates, June 20, 1783, Gates Papers, Reel 13; and To Colonel Matthias Ogden, April 19, 1783, *Washington Writings*, 26:340.

53. Bradford Adams Whittemore, *Memorials of the Massachusetts Society of the Cincinnati* (Boston, 1964), xxiv–xxx (hereafter and *Cincinnati Memorials*).

54. To Colonel Lewis Nicola, May 22, 1782, *Washington Writings*, 24:272–273; and *Heath Memoirs*, 384. Knox was selected secretary pro tempore, and Major General Alexander McDougall was selected as treasurer. To Barbe Marbois, April 4, 1788, *Washington Writings*, 29:457. "For, having by a circular letter to the several State Societies requested that I might not be re-elected President on account of my numerous avocations: the last Genl. Meeting was pleased so far to indulge me, as to make it a condition for inducing my acceptance, that I should be absolutely excused from all trouble and application incident to the office; and the whole business should devolve on the Vice President, viz, General Mifflin." Society of Cincinnati members desperately needed Washington's prestige, protection, and unquestioned right to the leading role, so they were willing to grant him any indulgence to accept. They knew that the inevitable bitter rivalry between potential successors would result in a schism destructive of their fellowship.

55. *Cincinnati Memorials*, xxxiii; "IV. Jefferson's Observations on DéMeunier's Manuscript, 22 June 1786," Founders Online, National Archives, accessed April 11, 2019, https://founders.archives.gov/documents/Jefferson/01-10-02-0001-0005 (Original source: *The Papers of Thomas Jefferson*, Vol. 10, *22 June–31 December 1786*, ed. Julian P. Boyd [Princeton University Press, 1954], 30–61). "They laid them up in their bureaus with the medals of American independence, with those of the trophies they had taken and the battles they had won. But through all the United States no officer is seen to offend the public eye with the display of this badge." Markus Hunemorder, *The Society of the Cincinnati: Conspiracy and Distrust in Early America* (New York, 2006), 134; and *Heath Memoirs*, 382.

56. General Orders, August 2, 1780, *Washington Writings*, 19:304. Shortages of bayonet belts forced Washington in August 1780 to order "that the troops keep their bayonets constantly fix'd except when cleaning as well in camp as on every kind of duty whatever with arms. This is to be considered as a standing order." General Orders, August 16, 1780, *Washington Writings*, 19:386; and General Orders, August 31, 1780, *Washington Writings*, 19:478.

57. *Gilbert Diary*, 36.

58. *Gilbert Letters*, 19; and *NY Packet*, December 12, 1782.

59. General Orders, January 18, 1778, *Washington Writings*, 10:314; and General Orders, August

9, 1782, *Washington Writings*, 24:491–492. "The acting Quartermaster with the army will have a sufficient number of Espontoons made to furnish each platoon officer who has never received one.... The general expects those officers who have once been supplied will keep themselves equipp'd with that useful and ornamental Weapon."

60. Washington's Headquarters State Historic Site Collection.

61. *Private Yankee Doodle*, 63. Joseph Plumb Martin observed that the government "was always careful to supply us with [arms and accoutrements] ... even if ... [it] could not give us anything to eat, drink or wear."

62. Assistant Quartermaster and Storekeeper Christopher Meng to Deputy Quartermaster at Fishkill Mr. John Fisher, May 8, 1782, and Christopher Meng Ledger, October 2, 1781, to October 2, 1782, Massachusetts Historical Society (hereafter Meng Ledger). Archaeologist Jack Mead excavated one hut from the 4th Massachusetts Regiment at New Windsor in which among other artifacts he found French gun parts and musket balls for those firearms. New Windsor Cantonment has in its collection, however, a .72-caliber musket ball for a British musket found by Oscar T. Barck at an unidentified location at the cantonment in 1936. Additionally, a buttplate fragment, two escutcheon plates, and numerous .72-caliber musket balls for the British Brown Bess musket were found on the Town of New Windsor land that encompasses large sections of the Massachusetts Line and the Maryland, New Hampshire, New Jersey, and New York hut sites. New Windsor Cantonment State Historic Site Collection; New Windsor Cantonment State Historic Site Collection NC.1996.11; and Town of New Windsor, New York Collection. A buttplate was a metal covering for the bottom of the stock that protected the wood when the musket was rested on the ground in a vertical position. An escutcheon plate was a decorative piece on British-style muskets set into the wood below the barrel breech to reinforce the thinnest part of the stock. To Brigadier General Alexander McDougall, April 17, 1777, *Washington Writings*, 7:424. "Congress ... resolved that all [arms] belonging to the Public, with their accoutrements, shall be stamped with the words *United States*, and that they shall be seizable wheresoever they are afterwards found."

63. General Orders, February 16, 1783, *Washington Writings*, 26:137; General Orders, August 27, 1782, *Washington Writings*, 25:70; Regimental Orders, April 9, 1783, 2nd Mass. Orderly Book; *Von Steuben Regulations*, 154; and General Orders, July 5, 1777, *Washington Writings*, 8:350.

64. To Major General William Heath, May 8, 1782, *Washington Writings*, 24:233; To Major General Henry Knox, September 9, 1782, *Washington Writings*, 25:140; To the Secretary at War Major General Benjamin Lincoln, November 27, 1782, *Washington Writings*, 25:377; Queries Submitted to the Secretary at War Major General Benjamin Lincoln, February 17, 1783, *Washington Writings*, 26:140 notes (hereafter Secretary at War Queries); Stewart Report; and General Orders, July 11, 1782, *Washington Writings*, 24:424. Washington noted that "many of the locks where the flints are good and well fastened do not give fire and that the fault is in the softness of the Hammers, which must be remided by having them properly hardened." General Orders, June 8, 1782, *Washington Writings*, 24:322. Washington first noticed an issue with the arms during a review in June 1782, observing that "the Locks or flints of the Musketts were in bad order, as many of them missed fire."

65. *Cuthbertson's System*, 93.

66. General Orders, July 11, 1782, *Washington Writings*, 24:424.

67. *Chastellux Travels*, 2:579 notes.

68. *NY Packet*, December 12, 1782. 1st Massachusetts Brigade commander General Paterson lost "an ELEGANT HOLSTER PISTOL; the maker's name (Wilfon) [Wilson] engraved on the lock, and on the barrel, London," somewhere between Peekskill and the large American campground on the Beverly Robinson farm, located in what is now Garrison, New York.

69. General Orders, May 19, 1779, *Washington Writings*, 15:103; Colonel Timothy Pickering Memorandum of matters to be attended to by the gentlemen in my office, November 1782, Pickering Letters, 29; Round Captain William Hawes Inspected Cartridge Box, New Windsor Cantonment Collection, NC.1996.103; and General Orders, July 4, 1782, *Washington Writings*, 24:399.

70. Barber Report; and Secretary at War Queries.

71. *Gilbert Diary*, 46. While on leave in March 1779, Benjamin Gilbert "rid to Town to get some Black Ball Made." Distribution of Clay to the troops of the New Windsor Cantonment, April 8, 1783, Estimates and Returns of Supplies, Funds, and Personnel, Quartermaster General's Department and Commissary General of Military Stores, 1780–1793, National Archives Microfilm Publication M853, Roll 29, Vol. 148, RG 93, National Archives, Washington, DC (hereafter Quartermaster Estimates).

72. General Orders, October 6, 1777, *Washington Writings*, 9:313.

73. Commissary General of Military Stores Samuel Hodgdon to Charles Hall, May 18, 1782, Letters Sent by Samuel Hodgdon, Richard Frothingham, and Benjamin Flower, July 19, 1778—May 24, 1784, in the Records of the War Department, The Adjutant General's Office Revolutionary War Records, National Archives Microfilm Publication M853, Roll 33, RG 93, National Archives, Washington, DC.

74. Instructions to Brigadier General Henry Knox, January 8, 1778, *Washington Writings*, 10:277; and General Orders, March 26, 1778, *Washington Writings*, 11:156.

75. Voucher 816, April 4, 1781, and Voucher 826, April 11, 1781, Letters, Orders For Pay, Accounts, Receipts, and Other Supply Records Concerning

Weapons and Military Stores 1776–1801, in the Records of the War Department, The Adjutant General's Office Revolutionary War Records, National Archives Microfilm Publication M927, Roll 1, RG 93, National Archives, Washington, DC (hereafter and Military Stores Records).

76. Assistant Quartermaster and Storekeeper Christopher Meng to Deputy Quartermaster at Fishkill Mr. John Fisher, May 8, 1782, Meng Ledger. "You will receive nine down knapsacks.... As the cloth is very thin & fleasy it will be necessary for the painter to size them a composition of glue paste &c.to fill it before the paint is put on. Old leather will answer for button Equals to anything."

77. To Colonel Timothy Pickering, January 1, 1781, *Washington Writings*, 21:42; *Von Steuben Regulations*, 118–119; To Colonel Timothy Pickering, January 1, 1781, *Washington Writings*, 21:42; and General Orders, March 4, 1783, *Washington Writings*, 26:189.

78. Commissary General of Military Stores Samuel Hodgdon to the Secretary at War Major General Benjamin Lincoln, July 2, 1782, Quartermaster Estimates, Reel 29, Vol. 148; and To the Secretary at War Major General Benjamin Lincoln, August 2, 1782, *Washington Writings*, 24:454.

79. Secretary at War Queries; To Colonel Timothy Pickering, March 10, 1783, *Washington Writings*, 26:205; Colonel Timothy Pickering to Lieutenant Colonel Jonathan Trumbull, Jr., March 10, 1783, Washington Papers; To the Secretary at War Major General Benjamin Lincoln, March 11, 1783, *Washington Writings*, 26:207; General Orders, March 14, 1783, *Washington Writings*, 26:222; Military Stores Records, Roll 1, Vol. 35; Military Stores Record, Roll 39, Vol. 151; and Military Stores Records, Roll 1, Vol. 35. Finding out in the second week of March that "the Standards are in the Hands of the Q Master at Camp, and have been there for some Time," made Washington demand an explanation from Pickering. The quartermaster general explained that Richard Frothingham, the field commissary of military stores, received them in a box with other articles in camp at the store, one of the rooms in the Temple Building, and distributed everything else "but left the standards." Quite annoyed that a letter from the secretary at war "was the first Notice ... [he] had, of their being near" him, Washington ordered on March 14 that "the regiments which are not furnished with Colours will immediately make application for them." On November 24, 1782, Hodgdon received from John Poole "18 Silk, Division Colours, 18 Setts Silk Tassels for D[itt]o and 10 Setts Standard Mounting." A division is an arbitrary subset of a military formation and in this instance means a regiment. Were there two colors available for each unit, there would be one for each subdivision, the two battalions of a regiment. From this stock a "Standard & Mounting" were delivered to the following regiments in March 1783: the 1st, 3rd, 4th, 5th, 6th, 7th, and 8th Massachusetts; 1st and 2nd New Hampshire; and the 2nd New Jersey, which drew two, the other for its 1st Regiment. Two more were received by the 1st and 3rd Connecticut Regiments stationed at West Point. *Van Cortlandt Memoir*, 1:68. In compliance with the resolution of the officers of the New York Line, 2nd New York Regiment commander Colonel Philip Van Cortlandt traveled to Poughkeepsie in June 1783 and presented "the stand of Colours and Instruments of musick belonging to the Brigade" to Governor George Clinton.

80. Almon W. Lauber, ed., Orderly Books of the Fourth New York Regiment, 1778–1780, the Second New York Regiment, 1780–1783, by Samuel Tallmadge and Others with Diaries of Samuel Tallmadge, 1780–1782, and John Barr, 1779–1782 (Albany, NY, 1932), 633.

Chapter 6

1. General Orders, November 14, 1782, *Washington Writings*, 25:344–345; General Orders, November 27, 1782, *Washington Writings*, 25:375; and Foster Journal, November 28th, 1782, Thanksgiving Day. "This Day I went to Meeting at New Windsor and heard a fine Sirmon Preached by Mr. Evens—the Sarvices of the Day was Cared on With as Great Deasonсy as Ever I saw a thanksgiving—a band Was placed in the front Gallery & ye Singers in ye 2 Side Gallereys—the Assembly was Larg & Graced by his Excelency & Gaurds—the Day Was Clear but very Cold."

2. Foster Journal, November and December 1782.

3. Foster Journal, January 10 and 11, 1783; General Orders, February 12, 1783, *Washington Writings*, 26:128; General Orders, January 8, 1783, *Washington Writings*, 26:23; General Orders, February 11, 1783, *Washington Writings*, 26:120; and General Orders, April 20, 1783, *Washington Writings*, 26:343–344.

4. To Major General Henry Knox, January 15, 1783, *Washington Writings*, 26:38.

5. Foster Journal, January to May 1783; and *Gilbert Diary*, February 7 and 9, 1783.

6. *NY Packet*, July 18, 1782.

7. *Officer Register*, 80; and *Massachusetts Soldiers and Sailors*, 5:513. Sergeant Major Jonathan Farnam of the 2nd Massachusetts Regiment lived in Duxbury, Massachusetts. On the way there he would have passed through Foster's home in Middleborough, Massachusetts. *Massachusetts Soldiers and Sailors*, 3:677; Foster Journal, July 28, 1782, March 2, 1783, January 13, 1783, and October 16, 1782; *Gilbert Diary*, May 17, 1783; and *Massachusetts Soldiers and Sailors*, 11:642. Peter Oliver was a soldier in the Massachusetts Line, but it is not stated in which regiment he served.

8. General Orders, January 3, 1783, *Washington Writings*, 26:5–6; and *NY Packet*, January 9 and January 29, 1783.

9. *Gilbert Diary*, December 17, 1782; and *Heath Memoirs*, 359.

10. General Orders, March 22, 1783, *Washington Writings*, 26:250; General Orders, March 28, 1783, *Washington Writings*, 26:264; and General Orders, April 17, 1783, *Washington Writings*, 26:330.

11. To the President of Congress, February 3, 1781, *Washington Writings*, 21:179–180; General Orders, December 11, 1782, *Washington Writings*, 25:422–423; General Orders, August 4, 1782, *Washington Writings*, 24:463; and To Major General Horatio Gates, February 10, 1783, *Washington Writings*, 26:113–114.

12. To Colonel Matthias Ogden, April 19, 1783, *Washington Writings*, 26:340.

13. To Major General Robert Howe, February 10, 1783, *Washington Writings*, 26:114.

14. To Major Hodijah Baylies, January 8, 1783, *Washington Writings*, 26:21–22.

15. General Orders, December 11, 1782, *Washington Writings*, 25:421–423; and To his Father, December 18, 1782, *Gilbert Letters*, 75.

16. General Orders, December 11, 1782, *Washington Writings*, 25:422–423.

17. *Private Yankee Doodle*, 155.

18. *Gilbert Diary*, March 7, April 8, and April 17, 1783.

19. *Gilbert Diary*, January 8, January 30, March 3, February 27, and June 20, 1783.

20. *Thacher Journal*, 280.

21. General Orders, December 25, 1782, *Washington Writings*, 25:464; and Major General Horatio Gates' Orders, December 26, 1782, Gates Papers, Reel 13.

22. Benson J. Lossing, *Pictorial Field-Book of the Revolution*, 2 vols. (New York, 1855); 1:686 (hereafter *Lossing Fieldbook*); and Colonel Timothy Pickering to Rebecca Pickering, February 6, 1783, quoted in *Pickering Life*, 1:400.

23. Foster Journal, February 3 and 4 and May 11, 1783.

24. David Fordyce, *The Temple of Virtue: A Dream*, 2nd ed. (London, 1775), 52–54 and 58–59. As editor, James Fordyce did add new material and make changes to the original text in both the first and second editions.

25. Foster Journal, January 24, 1783; and Tupper Report.

26. Major General Gates' Orders, January 6, 1783, 1st NY Orderly Book; and Foster Journal, January 12 and 14, 1783.

27. To Lieutenant Colonel David Humphreys, January 16, 1783, Gates Papers, Reel 13; Major Robert Oliver to Major General Horatio Gates, January 16, 1783, Gates Papers, Reel 13; Major General Horatio Gates' Orders, January 26, 1783, Gates Papers, Reel 13; and Regimental Orders, January 23, 1783, 2nd Mass. Orderly Book.

28. Colonel Benjamin Tupper to Major General Horatio Gates, January 31, 1783, Gates Papers, Reel 13; and Major General Horatio Gates' Orders, January 15, 1783, Gates Papers, Reel 13.

29. Colonel Benjamin Tupper to Major General Horatio Gates, January 31, 1783, Gates Papers, Reel 13; Major General Horatio Gates' Orders, February 4, 1783, 2nd Mass. Orderly Book; and Major General Horatio Gates' Orders, February 8, 1783, 2nd Mass. Orderly Book.

30. General Orders, January 29, 1783, *Washington Writings*, 26:75–76; General Orders, February 4, 1783, *Washington Writings*, 26:94; General Orders, *Washington Writings*, February 5, 1783, 26:102; Foster Journal, February 6, 1783; *Gilbert Diary*, February 6, 1783; To Elizabeth Gates, February 6, 1783, Gates Papers, Reel 13; and *NY Packet*, February 13, 1783.

31. To Colonel Michael Jackson or Officer Commanding Eighth Massachusetts Regiment, February 7, 1783, *Washington Writings*, 26:105–106; and To Lieutenant Colonel Ezra Newhall or Officer Commanding Fifth Massachusetts Regiment, *Washington Writings*, 26:108–109.

32. Colonel Timothy Pickering to Rebecca Pickering, February 6, 1783, quoted in *Pickering Life*, 1:400. The war made him appreciate his wife.

33. General Orders, March 6, 1783, *Washington Writings*, 26:196; To Abel Belknap Esqr., March 8, 1783, Pickering Letters, Reel 27, Vol. 86; and General Orders, March 31, 1783, *Washington Writings*, 26:278.

34. *Heath Memoirs*, 358; and *Lossing Fieldbook*, 685–686. In his early 90s, Burnet was the last-surviving Continental Army officer and an original member of the Society of Cincinnati.

35. Stephen A. Dafoe, MasonicDictionary.com; and H.A. Kingsbury, "The Symbolism of Numbers," in Stephan A. Dafoe, MasonicDictionary.com.

36. Benjamin Blayney, ed., *The Holy Bible Containing the Old and New Testaments: Translated Out of the Original Tongues; and with the Former Translations Diligently Compared and Revised, by His Majesty's Special Command* (Oxford, 1769), 1 Kings 6:2. A short cubit is 17.5 inches long, and a cubit is 20.4 inches long. Solomon used 1,244 inches long (102 feet), 405 inches wide (34 feet), and 612 inches high (51 feet). Foster Journal, March 3, 1783.

37. Rev. A. Elwood Corning, *Address of Rev. A. Elwood President of the National Temple Hill Association Delivered at the Forty-Third Congress, Daughters of the American Revolution, Washington, D.C., April 16, 1934*, Printed in the Congressional Record of May 24, 1934 (U.S. Government Printing Office, 1934); and New Windsor Cantonment State Historic Site Collection.

38. J.O. Dykman, "The Historic Temple at New Windsor, 1783, a Picture Made at That Time and Never before Published," *Magazine of American History* 24 (October 1890), 283–286.

39. I. Finch, *From Travels in the United States of America and Canada, containing some account of the Scientific Institutions and a few Notices of the Geology and Mineralogy of those Countries* (London, 1833), 47 (hereafter *Finch Travels*).

40. *Lossing Fieldbook*, 1:686.

41. *Newburgh News*, June 7, 1960; Ernest A. Rodman, "Digging for History in the Newburgh Area of Temple Hill," Prepared for the Association

of Town Historians Meeting, University of the State of New York, February 4 and 5, 1963, 9–21, New Windsor Cantonment State Historic Site Collection (hereafter "Digging for History").

42. *Gilbert Diary*, March 6, 1783.

43. "Digging for History," 9–21; and "Temple Hill Vicinity," 24.

44. Building Auction; Deputy Quartermaster General Peter Anspach to Colonel Timothy Pickering, July 23, 1783, Miscellaneous Records, Reel 83; and Major General Horatio Gates to General George Washington, December 31, 1782, Washington Papers.

45. *Finch Travels*, 47; and Foster Journal, March 3, 1783.

46. *Heath Memoirs*, 358; Foster Journal, April 6, 1783; General Orders, February 15, 1783, *Washington Writings*, 26:135; New York Brigade Orders, February 22, 1783, 1st NY Orderly Book; *Gilbert Diary*, February 23, 1783; and Foster Journal, May 25, 1783.

47. Foster Journal, April 19, 1783; and Lieutenant Colonel David Cobb to Colonel Timothy Pickering, November 9, 1825, quoted in *Pickering Life*, 1:431.

48. Major General Horatio Gates' Orders, February 4, 1783, 2nd Mass. Orderly Book; and Regimental Orders, February 28, 1783, 1st NY Orderly Book.

49. To Major General Nathanael Greene, September 23, 1782, *Washington Writings*, 25:194; Foster Journal, August 18, 1782; and To the Secretary at War Major General Benjamin Lincoln, September 24, 1782, *Washington Writings*, 25:201.

50. General Orders, February 26, 1783, *Washington Writings*, 26:168; General Orders, February 26, 1783, *Washington Writings*, 26:168–169; General Orders, February 27, 1783, *Washington Writings*, 26:171; and General Orders, March 18, 1783, *Washington Writings*, 26:235.

Chapter 7

1. To the Secretary at War Major General Benjamin Lincoln, May 15, 1782, *Washington Writings*, 24:255–256; To Colonel Timothy Pickering, May 15, 1782, *Washington Writings*, 24:257–258; Secretary at War Major General Benjamin Lincoln to General George Washington, May 21, 1782, Washington Papers; Colonel Timothy Pickering to General George Washington, May 29, 1782, Washington Papers; and Conference at Hartford, September 22, 1780, *Washington Writings*, 20:78.

2. General Orders, November 8, 1782, *Washington Writings*, 25:325; To Colonel Timothy Pickering, December 25, 1782, *Washington Writings*, 25:465–466; and Colonel Timothy Pickering to General George Washington, November 12, 1782, Washington Papers.

3. *NY Packet*, December 12, 1782.

4. General Orders, March 27, 1783, *Washington Writings*, 26:261; and General Orders, May 19, 1783, *Washington Writings*, 26:445.

5. Chief Justice of the New York Supreme Court Richard Morris to Ulster County, New York, Sheriff, October 26, 1782, Warrant, Washington Papers; Colonel Timothy Pickering to Rebecca Pickering, January 19, 1783, quoted in *Pickering Life*, 1:431; Colonel Timothy Pickering to Commissary General of Military Stores Samuel Hodgdon, January 21, 1783, quoted in *Pickering Life*, 1:398; and Colonel Timothy Pickering to Rebecca Pickering, April 2, 1783, quoted in *Pickering Life*, 1:398.

6. To John Parke Custis, February 28, 1781, *Washington Writings*, 21:320; To Lieutenant Colonel John Laurens, January 15, 1781, *Washington Writings*, 21:105–110; To his brother-in-law Joseph Dane, December 17, 1782, *Gilbert Letters*, 73; To Captain Jonathan Stone, March 1, 1783, *Gilbert Letters*, 86; Circular to the Governors of the States, May 16, 1782, in E. James Ferguson, John Catanzariti, et al. eds., *The Papers of Robert Morris, 1781–1784*, 9 vols. (Pittsburgh, PA, 1973–1999), 5:190–192 (hereafter *Morris Papers*).

7. To Major General John Armstrong, January 10, 1783, *Washington Writings*, 26:26–27.

8. To Major Benjamin Tallmadge, October 21, 1780, *Washington Writings*, 20:224; *Chastellux Travels*, 1:333 notes; Commissary General of Military Stores Samuel Hodgdon to Colonel Timothy Pickering, December 23, 1782; and Colonel Timothy Pickering to Commissary General of Military Stores Samuel Hodgdon, December 24, 1782, quoted in *Pickering Life*, 1:387–388.

9. *Chastellux Travels*, 1:333 notes; *Chastellux Travels*, 2:572 notes; and To John Sullivan, February 4, 1781, *Washington Writings*, 21:183. The former major general retired in 1779.

10. *Thacher Journal*, 31.

11. E. James Ferguson, *The Power of the Purse: A History of American Public Finance, 1776–1790* (Chapel Hill, NC, 1961), 46–69. Ferguson ably describes Congress's plan to make paper currency a viable circulating medium and the forces that interfered with that effort. *Chastellux Travels*, 1:333 notes. George Grieve commented that "its extraordinary depreciation, and total disappearance without producing any great shock or convulsion ... will certainly form an epocha in the general history of finances ... [and] balanced, by alternate profit and loss among all classes of citizens, that on casting up the account, some very unfortunate cases excepted, it seems to have operated only as a general tax on the public."

12. *Chastellux Travels*, 1:300 notes.

13. James Madison to Benjamin Harrison, January 7, 1783, *Congress Delegates Letters*, 19:558.

14. Congressional Resolution, August 14, 1782, *Washington Writings*, 25:3; Edward C. Skeen, *John C. Armstrong, Jr., 1758–1843* (Syracuse, NY, 1981); and Clayton C. Hall et al., eds., *Muster Rolls of Maryland Troops in the American Revolution (1775–1783)* (Baltimore, Maryland, 1972 [reprint of 1900 edition]), 5, 155, 363, 379, 478, 479, and 521.

15. Major General Horatio Gates to Colonel Timothy Pickering, December 22, 1782, Gates

Papers, Reel 13; Major General Horatio Gates to Colonel Timothy Pickering, December 27, 1782, Gates Papers, Reel 13; *NY Packet*, December 12, 1782; and Major John Armstrong to Colonel Timothy Pickering, January 20, 1783, Gates Papers, Reel 13. Joseph King* and a Mr. Evans issued corn, buckwheat, rye, and hay to Gates and his staff in February and March 1783. Major General Gates' + [military] family forage February and March 1783, Gates Papers, Reel 13; Account of Planks and Boards, November 23, 1782, Washington's Headquarters State Historic Site Collection; and Deputy Quartermaster General Peter Anspach to Major Christopher Richmond, December 15, 1782, Gates Papers, Reel 13. *Probably the former artillery artificer officer.

16. Major General Horatio Gates' Orders, December 29, 1782, Jersey Brigade Orderly Book; To Lieutenant Colonel David Humphreys, January 9, 1783, Gates Papers, Reel 13; and Lieutenant Colonel David Humphreys to Major General Horatio Gates, January 9, 1783, Gates Papers, Reel 13.

17. To General Washington, December 31, 1782, Gates Papers, Reel 13; and General Orders, December 22, 1782, *Washington Writings*, 25:456.

18. To Elizabeth Gates, January 26 and January 17, 1783, Gates Papers, Reel 13.

19. General Orders, February 6, 1782, *Washington Writings*, 26:102–103; and General Orders, February 18, 1783, *Washington Writings*, 26:141–143.

20. At meetings in the Horton House on nearby Murderer's (Moodna) Creek in New Windsor, a group of officers, led by Major General Henry Knox, drafted the army's memorial to Congress. Quoted in Thomas Egleston, *The Life of John Paterson, Major-General in the Revolutionary Army* (New York, 1898), 280–281 (hereafter *Paterson Life*).

21. Major John Armstrong to Major General Horatio Gates, May 9, 1783, Gates Papers; Major General Alexander McDougall to Congressional Committee, January 13, 1783, quoted in "Notes on Debates, January 13, 1783," in William T. Hutchinson and M.E. Rachal, eds., *Papers of James Madison*, 14 vols. (Chicago, 1969), 6:32 (hereafter *Madison Papers*).

22. To Pennsylvania Congressman Richard Peters, February 20, 1783, Gates Papers, Reel 13; *Morris Papers*, 7:345, 400; Superintendent of Finance Robert Morris to His Excellency The President of Congress, Gates Papers, 7:368; Gouverneur Morris to John Jay, January 1, 1783, quoted in *Paterson Life*, 282–283; and To Alexander Hamilton, April 22, 1783, *Washington Writings*, 26:351–352.

23. To Joseph Jones, December 14, 1782, *Washington Writings*, 25:430–431. While the military suffered with wages that was months in arrears, civilian government officials were always paid promptly, so "it would not be more difficult to still the raging Billows in a tempestuous Gale, than to convince the Officers of this Army of the justice or policy of paying men in Civil Offices full wages, when they cannot obtain a Sixtieth part of their dues." To James McHenry, October 17, 1782, *Washington Writings*, 25:269–270.

24. To Alexander Hamilton, March 4, 1783, *Washington Writings*, 26:185–188.

To you who have seen the danger, to which the Army has been exposed, to a political dissolution for want of subsistence ... that it would at this day be productive of Civil commotions and end in blood. Unhappy situation this! God forbid we should be involved in it.

The predicament in which I stand as Citizen and Soldier, is as critical and delicate as can well be conceived. It has been the Subject of many contemplative hours. The sufferings of a complaining Army on one hand, and the inability of Congress and the tardiness of the States on the other, are the forebodings of evil, and may be productive of events which are more to be deprecated than prevented; but I am not without hope, if there is such disposition shewn as prudence and policy will dictate, to do justice, that your apprehensions, in case of Peace, are greater than there is cause for. In this however I may be mistaken, if those ideas, which you have been informed are propogated in the Army should be extensive; the source of which may be easily traced as the old leven, [Gates] *it is said*, for I have no proof of it, is again, beginning to work, under a mask of the most perfect dissimulation, and apparent cordiality.

David Head, *A Crisis of Peace: George Washington, the Newburgh Conspiracy, and the Fate of the American Revolution* (New York, 2019), 182; Thomas Fleming, *The Perils of Peace: America's Struggle for Survival after Yorktown* (New York, 2007), 266; William M. Fowler, Jr., *American Crisis: George Washington and the Dangerous Two Years after Yorktown, 1781–1783* (New York, 2011), 180; Dave Richards, *Swords in Their Hands: George Washington and the Newburgh Conspiracy* (Candler, NC, 2013), 193; and Alexander Hamilton to General Washington, April 8, 1783, Founders Online, National Archives, https://founders.archives.gov/documents/Hamilton/01-03-02-0204 (Original source: *The Papers of Alexander Hamilton*, Vol. 3, *1782–1786*, ed. Harold C. Syrett [New York: Columbia University Press, 1962], 317–321, hereafter *Hamilton Papers*).

25. *JCC*, October 21, 1780, 18:958–959.

26. Quoted in Edward C. Skeen, "The Newburgh Conspiracy Reconsidered with a Rebuttal by Richard H. Kohn," *William and Mary Quarterly*, 3rd Ser., vol. 31, no. 2 (April, 1974): 275–276; *Officer Register*, 307, 400, and 227; To Elizabeth Gates, February 11, 1783, Gates Papers, Reel 13; *Officer Register*, 311; Sons of the American Revolution Society, *An Account of the Action at Tarrytown on July Fifteenth, 1781, and of Its Commemoration by the Sons of the American Revolution of Tarrytown on July Fifteenth, 1899* (New York, 1899); Captain George Hurlbut to General George Washington, March 26, 1783, Washington Papers; To Captain

George Hurlbut, March 27, 1783, *Washington Writings*, 26:262–263; To Rear Admiral Robert Digby, April 11, 1783, *Washington Writings*, 312; and Major Christopher Richmond to Major General Horatio Gates, May 29, 1783, Gates Papers, Reel 13. Hurlbut stayed at the Ellison house because it was the closest one to his attending physicians from the nearby Continental Army hospital. Declining quickly and knowing that he was not up to an overland journey, he petitioned the commander in chief on March 26, 1783, to arrange a ship to take him home. Obtaining the assent of British officials in New York City for this vessel to pass through their lines, Washington sent Captain William Colfax, the commander of his guard, to escort the young cavalry officer to New London, Connecticut. Surrounded by family and friends, George Hurlbut died three weeks later.

27. Quoted in George Bancroft, *History of the Formation of the Constitution of the United States of America*, 2 vols. (New York, 1882), 1:318, hereafter *Constitution History*. This document is not included in the New-York Historical Society microfilm edition of the Horatio Gates Papers. Superintendent of Finance Robert Morris to the Governors of the States, January 3, 1782, in Francis Wharton, ed., *The Revolutionary Diplomatic Correspondence of the United States*, 6 vols. (Washington, DC, 1889), 5:85.

28. Quoted in *Morris Papers*, 7:468. An officer in the Pennsylvania Line, Stewart had also been an aide to Gates. Stewart left his recently betrothed, Deborah McClenachan, the daughter of a wealthy Philadelphia merchant, to join the forces under General Anthony Wayne in early 1781. Stewart led his men at Green Springs, Virginia, and finally at the Battle of Yorktown. *Private Yankee Doodle*, 187. He was considered the handsomest man in the Continental Army and one of its most eligible bachelors, and the rest of the city's belles lost the fight for his affection. Joseph Plumb Martin recorded that "this Colonel Stewart was an excellent officer, much beloved and respected by the troops of the line he belonged to. He possessed great personal beauty; the Philadelphia ladies styled him the *Irish Beauty*." George Washington Park Custis, *Recollections and Private Memoirs of the Life and Character of Washington by His Adopted Son, George Washington Parke Custis, with a Memoir of the Author, by His Daughters; And Ilustrative and Explanatory Notes by Benson J. Lossing* (New York, 1860), 360n. "Colonel Walter Stewart was of Irish descent, had a fair and florid complexion, vivacious, intelligent and well educated, and, it was said, was the handsomest man in the American army." General Orders, February 11, 1782, *Washington Writings*, 23:495. Recognizing the talents of this officer, Washington recommended Stewart for the position of inspector of the northern department, a deputy of inspector general Major General Friedrich von Steuben. Subsequent events made the commander in chief rue his offer. After performing his duties throughout the campaign season of 1782, Stewart went back to Philadelphia to recover from a prolonged ailment. Taking a long time to finally arrive in the Highlands to resume his position, he was more interested in politics than troop returns, drill, and equipment deficiencies.

29. Quoted in *Morris Papers*, 7:332; To Governor George Clinton, February 17, 1783, *Washington Writings*, 26:138–139; To Brigadier General Edward Hand, February 14, 1783, *Washington Writings*, 26:133; General Orders, February 14, 1783, *Washington Writings*, 26:132; To his Father, March 6, 1783, *Gilbert Letters*, 83; General Orders, March 2, 1783, *Washington Writings*, 26:177; To his Father, March 6, 1783, *Gilbert Letters*, 83; and *Private Yankee Doodle*, 222–223. Furthermore, like everyone else, he received Morris Notes for three months' pay redeemable in six months when furloughed in June. After his discharge, Martin eventually received an interest-bearing certificate of indebtedness from the "Commissioner for settling the accounts of the Army," John Pierce, the former paymaster, for his remaining arrearages and $80 gratuity promised to all enlisted men who served until the end of the war. General Orders, July 8, 1783, *Washington Writings*, 27:53–54; *Morris Papers*, 7:334; and *Gilbert Diary*, April 9, 1783.

30. To his Father, March 6, 1783, *Gilbert Letters*, 83; To Captain Nathan Goodale, January 31, 1783, *Gilbert Letters*, 82; To Captain Jonathan Stone, March 1, 1783, *Gilbert Letters*, 86; and *Morris Papers*, 7:327, 335.

31. To the Superintendent of Finance Robert Morris, March 12, 1783, *Washington Writings*, 26:213; Superintendent of Finance Robert Morris to General Washington, March 25, 1783, Washington Papers; To the Superintendent of Finance Robert Morris, April 9, 1783, *Washington Writings*, 26:309.

32. General George Washington to Brigadier General Thomas Conway, November 9, 1777, Washington Papers; and General George Washington to Major General Horatio Gates, January 4, 1778, Washington Papers.

33. Anonymous to Continental Army Officers, March 10, 1783, Washington Papers.

34. To the Secretary at War Major General Benjamin Lincoln, October 2, 1782, *Washington Writings*, 25:228. Presciently, Washington had warned Secretary at War Lincoln the previous October that "the patience and long sufferance of this Army are almost exhausted, and that there never was a so great a spirit of Discontent as at this instant: While in the field, I think it may be kept from breaking out into Acts of Outrage, but when we retire into Winter Quarters (unless the Storm is previously dissipated) I cannot be at ease, respecting the consequences. It is high time for a Peace." To Joseph Jones, March 12, 1783, *Washington Writings*, 26:213–216; and General Orders, March 11, 1783, *Washington Writings*, 26:208–209. Disconcerted that his officers were adding to the unrest, Washington countered the first letter by expressing his

"disapprobation of such disorderly proceedings" and directed that they meet instead on March 15 to hear the report of the committee of the army to Congress to "rescue the foot, that stood wavering on the precipice of despair, from taking those steps which would have lead to the abyss of misery while the passions were inflamed, and the mind tremblingly alive with the recollection of past sufferings, and their present feelings. I did this upon the principle that it is easier to divert from a wrong to a right path, than it is to recall the hasty and fatal steps which have already been taken." He then directed the officers to deliberate on the report and "devise what further measures ought to be adopted as most rational and best calculated to attain the just and important object in view. The senior officer in Rank present will be pleased to preside and report the result of the Deliberations to the Commander in Chief." Lieutenant Colonel Benjamin Walker to Major General Friedrich von Steuben, March 13, 1783, von Steuben Papers, Reel 6; and Anonymous to Continental Army Officers, March 12, 1783, Washington Papers.

35. To Joseph Jones, March 12, 1783, *Washington Writings*, 26:213–216; To Alexander Hamilton, March 12, 1783, *Washington Writings*, 26:216–218; Alexander Hamilton to General George Washington, March 17, 1783, *Hamilton Papers*, 3:290–293.

36. *Van Cortlandt Memoir*, 1:68.

37. To Alexander Hamilton, March 4, 1783, *Washington Writings*, 26:185–188; and To Joseph Jones, March 12, 1783, *Washington Writings*, 26:214. "It also appears, that upon the arrival of a certain Gentleman from Phila. [Colonel Walter Stewart] in Camp, whose name, I do not, at present, incline to mention such sentiments as these were immediately and industriously circulated." Colonel Walter Stewart to General George Washington, February 18, 1783, Washington Papers. Stewart was also delayed by his attempt to stay an officer in line, entitling him to command troops. Deprived of his regiment by the reorganization of the army that took effect on January 1, 1783, he wrote to Washington that he "endeavored a compromise, with Colonel [Richard] Humpton [but he] was unfortunate enough to fail." In the new arrangement, Humpton, senior in grade, replaced Stewart as commander of the 2nd Pennsylvania Regiment when his own 6th Regiment was disbanded.

38. General Orders, March 13, 1783, *Washington Writings*, 26:221–222. Robert Morris was directed to liquidate the accounts "as soon as the state of the public finances will permit." Congress pledged to use every means within "their power to obtain from the respective states substantial funds, adequate to the object of funding the whole debt of the United States."

39. Lieutenant Colonel Benjamin Walker to Lieutenant Colonel William Stephens Smith, March 16, 1783, New Windsor Cantonment State Historic Site Collection; and To the Officers of the Army, March 15, 1783, *Washington Writings*, 26:222–227. The original copy of the speech is in the collection of the Massachusetts Historical Society.

40. Josiah Quincy, *The Journals of Major Samuel Shaw, the First American Consul at Canton* (Boston, 1847), 104 (hereafter *Shaw Journal*); and To David Rittenhouse, February 16, 1783, *Washington Writings*, 26:136–137. Washington's spectacles were made by eminent Philadelphia precision instrument maker David Rittenhouse, who also made clocks, astronomical models, and surveying equipment. Lieutenant Colonel David Cobb to Colonel Timothy Pickering, November 9, 1825, quoted in *Pickering Life*, 1:431.

41. *Shaw Journal*, 104.

42. Colonel Timothy Pickering to Commissary General of Military Stores Samuel Hodgdon, March 16, 1783, quoted in *Pickering Life*, 1:438; Joseph Jones to General George Washington, February 27, 1783, Washington Papers; and Timothy Pickering to Dudley A. Tyng, August 2, 1819, in a bound volume titled *George Washington—Address to the Officers of the American Army, March 15, 1783*, Massachusetts Historical Society.

> After this the General [Washington] read a private letter of the 27th of February (I imagine from Mr. Jones, of Virginia) from a member of Congress, written without the most distant expectation of its being used on such an occasion, he thought himself justified in the communication of it. This letter was written with calmness and great good sense; mentioning the measures Congress were pursuing to obtain permanent revenues, and his hopes of their succeeding, the reasons which prevented prompt decisions, and his wishes that the army might a little longer persevere in that line of patient endurance which had hitherto done them so much honor.

43. *JCC*, April 29, 1783, 24:310–311..

44. *JCC*, January 25, 1783, 24:93; *Officer Register*, 288; and [Brigadier General Rufus Putnam] To the Officers of the Army, March 13 or 14, 1783, GLC02437.10105, Gilder Lehrman Institute of American History, New York. The Captain John Lillie copy is in the Henry Knox Papers.

45. Don R. Gerlach, *Proud Patriot Philip Schuyler and the War for Independence, 1775–1783* (Syracuse, NY, 1987), 494n16 and 496n23; and Philip Schuyler to Stephen Van Rensselaer, March 17, 1783, quoted in Benson J. Lossing, *The Life and Times of Philip Schuyler*, 2 vols. (New York, 1872–73 [Di Capo Press edition, New York, 1973]) 2:427.

46. Colonel Timothy Pickering to Rebecca Pickering, March 16, 1783, quoted in *Pickering Life*, 1:442; and Colonel Timothy Pickering to Commissary General of Military Stores Samuel Hodgdon, March 16, 1783, quoted in, *Pickering Life*, 1:439–441.

47. *JCC*, March 22, 1783, 24:207–210; *Morris Papers*, 7:399; and *JCC*, October 16, 1782, 22:659. "That the estimate for the service of the year 1783, be as follows:

• For the pay of the army, ... $2,609,320" *JCC*, September 17, 1783, 25:577–579.

48. To the President of Congress, March 30, 1783, *Washington Writings*, 26:273; General Orders, April 16, 1783, *Washington Writings*, 26:328; Officers of Massachusetts Line acceptance of commutation, April 18, 1783, Heath Papers, Reel 26; and To the Secretary at War Major General Benjamin Lincoln, April 30, 1783, *Washington Writings*, 26:368.

49. To Joseph Jones, March 18, 1783, *Washington Writings*, 26:232–233. Washington warned Jones that "the storm which seemed to be gathering with unfavorable prognostics, when I wrote you last, is dispersed: and we are again in a state of tranquility. But do not, My dear Sir, suffer this appearance of tranquility to relax your endeavors to bring the requests of the Army to an issue."

50. To Alexander Hamilton, April 4, 1783, *Washington Writings*, 26:292–293; and To Alexander Hamilton, April 16, 1783, *Washington Writings*, 26:324. As Washington observed,

> For these reasons I said, or meant to say, the Army was a dangerous Engine to Work with, as it might be made to cut both ways; and, considering the Sufferings of it, would, more than probably, throw its weight into that Scale which seemed most likely to preponderate towards its immediate relief, without looking forward (under the pressure of present want) to future consequences with the eyes of Politicians. In this light also I meant to apply my observation to Mr. [Robert] Morris, to whom, or rather to Mr. G-[ouverneur] M-[orris] is ascribed, in a great degree, the ground work of the superstructure which was intended to be raised in the Army by the Anonymous Addresser.

Morris Papers, 7:470; and Superintendent of Finance Robert Morris to General George Washington, May 29, 1783, Washington Papers.

51. Major General Horatio Gates to Major John Armstrong, June 22, 1783, quoted in *Constitution History*, 1:318.

> That Stewart was a kind of agent from our friends in congress and in the administration, with no object, however, beyond that of getting the army to co-operate with the civil creditors, as the way most likely for both to obtain justice; and that the letters were written in my quarters by you, copied by [Christopher] Richmond and circulated by [William] Barber, and were intended to produce a strong remonstrance to congress in favor of the object prayed for in a former one; and that the conjecture that it was meant to offer the crown to Caesar, was without any foundation; referring him to his townsman or neighbor, Dr. Eustis, for further information, as well as for the correctness of this.

To Colonel Timothy Pickering, May 19, 1783, Gates Papers, Reel 13.

52. Major John Armstrong to Major General Horatio Gates, May 31, 1783, Gates Papers, Reel 13; To Brigadier General Elias Dayton, March 31, 1783, *Washington Writings*, 26:274; To Colonel Matthias Ogden, April 7, 1783, *Washington Writings*, 26:305; To Colonel Matthias Ogden, April 19, *Washington Writings*, 26:340; Report of the Committee to Congress (Major General Alexander McDougall and Colonel Matthias Ogden) to Major General Henry Knox, February 8, 1783, quoted in *Clinton Papers*, 8:115–118; and *Madison Papers*, Notes on Debates, January 13, 1783, 6:32.

53. Major John Armstrong to Major General Horatio Gates, April 29, 1783, Gates Papers, Reel 13; New Jersey Brigade officers to the New Jersey Assembly, April 17, 1779, Letters from Gen. George Washington, Commander in Chief of the Army, 1775–84, Vol. 7: Dec 16, 1778–September 12, 1779, Continental Congress Papers, 325–327, M247, Roll 169, RG 360, www.fold3.com/images/344395-344397 ; General William Maxwell to General Washington, May 6, 1779, Continental Congress Papers, 315–316, M247, Roll 169 RG 360; 1st New Jersey Regiment officers to General Washington, May 8, 1779, Continental Congress Papers, 323–324A, M247, Roll 169, RG 360; and To the President of Congress, May 11, 1779, *Washington Writings*, 15:42–44.

54. Report of the Committee to Congress to Major General Henry Knox, February 8, 1783, quoted in *Clinton Papers*, 8:115–118; Gouverneur Morris to Major General Henry Knox, February 7, 1783, quoted in *Morris Papers*, 7:417–418; and Gouverneur Morris to Major General Nathanael Greene, February 11, 1783, *Greene Papers*, 12:432–434.

55. Report of the Committee of Congress to Major General Henry Knox, February 8, 1783, quoted in *Clinton Papers*, 8:115–118; Brutus (Major General Alexander McDougall) to Major General Henry Knox, February 12, 1783, Knox Papers, Reel 11; Brutus (Major General Alexander McDougall) to Major General Henry Knox February 27, 1783, Knox Papers, Reel 11; Major General Henry Knox to Major General Alexander McDougall, February 21, 1783, Alexander McDougall Papers, New-York Historical Society, Reel 4; Alexander Hamilton to General George Washington, February 13, 1783, Washington Papers; and Major John Armstrong to Major General Horatio Gates, May 31, 1783, Gates Papers, Reel 13..

Chapter 8

1. General Orders, February 5, 1781, *Washington Writings*, 21:186; Circular to the States, December 19, 1781, *Washington Writings*, 23:399; and JCC, October 3, 1780, 18:895.

2. Alice F. Jackson and Bettina Jackson, *Three Hundred Years American: The Epic of a Family from Seventeenth-Century New England to Twentieth-Century Midwest* (The State Historical Society of Wisconsin, 1951), 115–116 and 121; *Massachusetts Soldiers and Sailors*, 8:658–659, 661, 663, 681, and 688; and *Officer Register*, 315 and 316.

3. General Orders, August 1, 1782, *Washington Writings*, 24:452; To Lieutenant Colonel John Popkin, September 16, 1782, *Washington Writings*, 25:165; and To Marquis de Vaudreuil, *Washington Writings*, 25:166–167.

4. To Brigadier General Moses Hazen, December 25, 1782, *Washington Writings*, 25:467.

5. To Jonathan Hobby, February 7, 1783, *Washington Writings*, 26:107–108.

6. *Sinews of Independence*, 156–186.

7. *Thacher Journal*, 254–255; Commonwealth of Massachusetts, In the House of representatives, December 2, 1780, Whereas the Congress of the United States have required of this Commonwealth to supply the deficiency of our proportion of the Continental army ... (Boston: Printed by Benjamin Edes and son, 1780); and To Major General Horatio Gates, October 8, 1780, *Washington Writings*, 20:137–138.

8. To his Father and Stepmother, October 15, 1780, *Gilbert Letters*, 25–26; To John Mathews, October 4, 1780, *Washington Writings*, 20:114–111; and *JCC*, October 3, 1780, 18:895.

9. To the Secretary at War Major General Benjamin Lincoln, April 25, 1782, *Washington Writings*, 24:166–167.

10. To Lieutenant Colonel Frederick Weissenfels, May 20, 1782, *Washington Writings*, 24:267.

11. General Orders, August 10, 1782, *Washington Writings*, 24:494.

12. *Massachusetts Soldiers and Sailors*, 11:838; and To Major General Benjamin Lincoln, February 27, 1781, *Washington Writings*, 21:308.

13. General Orders, January 19, 1782, *Washington Writings*, 23:450–452; and General Orders, November 23, 1782, *Washington Writings*, 25:369.

14. *Von Steuben Regulations*, 6–7; General Orders, September 13, 1782, *Washington Writings*, 25:157; and *Von Steuben Regulations*, 8.

15. General Orders, February 1, 1781, *Washington Writings*, 21:169–170. Washington preferred "well made men from five feet six to five feet ten inches stature." The assistant inspector general was ordered "to review each company and reject every man" who did not have the requisite appearance and discipline. General Orders, March 23, 1783, *Washington Writings*, 26:250; and General Orders, June 8, 1782, *Washington Writings*, 24:322. The light infantrymen were reminded of the "necessity of taking deliberate aim," because it is "the effect of the shot not the report of the Gun that can discomfort the Enemy and if a bad habit is acquired at exercise it will prevail in real Action and so vice versa."

16. General Orders, August 25, 1780, *Washington Writings*, 19:438–439. Washington advised his officers to watch their soldiers so they did not expend their ammunition "at too great a distance" and then plead "the want of it" to leave the field. In the event they ran out, they were to "depend upon their Bayonets 'till the Conflict" was decided.

17. *Von Steuben Regulations*, 49.

18. Major General Nathanael Greene to General George Washington, May 1, 1781, Washington Papers.

19. General Orders, *Washington Writings*, 25:179.

20. To the President of Congress, November 28, 1780, *Washington Writings*, 20:419; and *Von Steuben Regulations*, 88.

21. General Orders, March 20, 1783, *Washington Writings*, 26:248.

22. To Major General William Heath, February 5, 1783, *Washington Writings*, 26:97; and General Orders, February 5, 1783, *Washington Writings*, 26:101–102.

Chapter 9

1. General Orders, March 9, 1783, *Washington Writings*, 26:202; and General Orders, March 28, 1783, *Washington Writings*, 26:264.

2. General Orders, February 10, 1783, *Washington Writings*, 26:111–112; General Orders, February 18, 1783, *Washington Writings*, 26:142–143; and General Orders, March 12, 1783, *Washington Writings*, 26:209–210.

3. General Orders, February 10, 1783, *Washington Writings*, 26:111–112; Regimental Orders, April 22, 1783 and March 25, 1783, 2nd Mass. Orderly Book; General Orders, March 19, 1783, *Washington Writings*, 26:247; and Regimental Orders, February 17, 1783, 1st NY Orderly Book.

4. General Orders, March 18, 1783, *Washington Writings*, 26:235; and "Soil Investigations," 24.

5. General Orders, March 12, 1783, *Washington Writings*, 26:209–210; and General Orders, November 22, 1782, *Washington Writings*, 25:367.

6. General Orders, March 28, 1783, *Washington Writings*, 26:264.

7. *JCC*, June 30, 1775, 112–123.

8. General Orders, July 5, 1781, *Washington Writings*, 22:329; General Orders, April 14, 1783, *Washington Writings*, 26:314–315; General Orders, May 7, 1783, *Washington Writings*, 26:410; and General Orders, June 11, 1783, *Washington Writings*, 27:7.

9. Regimental Orders, December 2, 1782, 8th Mass. Orderly Book; *Gilbert Diary*, December 28, 1782; and *Massachusetts Soldiers and Sailors*, 8:429.

10. Regimental Orders, December 8, 1782, 8th Mass. Orderly Book.

11. General Instructions for the Colonels and Commanding Officers of Regiments in the Continental Service, 1777, *Washington Writings*, 10:242; Regimental Orders, March 6 and 8, 1783, 8th Mass. Orderly Book; and Regimental Orders, March 6 and 19, 1783, 2nd Mass. Orderly Book.

12. Foster Journal, January 12, 1783. Foster believed that "our Marshal Laws are Very Good but to See how Parshally they are Put into Execution." Though a violation of military law, he was very concerned that "profain swaring and Blasspheaming the Almighty which is frequently & not

ye Lest Notice taken of it" would bring the wrath of God down on the American people. Foster Journal, February 16, 1783. On February 16, there was no labor that made it "appeair Like Saboth Day although Meny Notorious Profanations are planly to be Observed in Many hear in the Armey."

13. To Major General Horatio Gates, February 16, 1783, *Washington Writings*, 26:137.

14. General Orders, December 9, 1782, *Washington Writings*, 25:410; and General Orders, December 19, 1782, *Washington Writings*, 25:452.

15. To Colonel Joseph Vose, January 21, 1783, *Washington Writings*, 26:55; To Joseph Chandler, January 21, 1783, *Washington Writings*, 26:56–57; and General Orders, April 6, 1778, *Washington Writings*, 11:224.

16. General Orders, March 1, 1783, *Washington Writings*, 26:174–175; and General Orders, March 7, 1783, *Washington Writings*, 26:197.

17. General Orders, January 19, 1783, *Washington Writings*, 26:49; To Captain Nathan Goodale, January 31, 1783, *Gilbert Letters*, 82; *Massachusetts Soldiers and Sailors*, 11:367; and *Gilbert Diary*, February 12 and 13, 1783.

18. General Orders, April 23, 1783, *Washington Writings*, 26:356.

19. General Orders, October 30, 1782, *Washington Writings*, 25:309; General Orders, November 14, 1782, *Washington Writings*, 25:343–344; *Gilbert Diary*, January 23, 1783; and *Officer Register*, 159. Captain Peter Clayes was in the 6th Massachusetts Regiment.

20. General Orders, November 19, 1782, *Washington Writings*, 25:354–355; General Orders, December 2, 1782, *Washington Writings*, 25:386; General Orders, December 25, 1782, *Washington Writings*, 25:464; and General Orders, February 12, 1783, *Washington Writings*, 26:129.

21. General Orders, April 16, 1783, *Washington Writings*, 26:327.

22. General Orders, April 22, 1783, *Washington Writings*, 26:354.

23. *Sinews of Independence*, 238–253.

24. *Greenman Journal*, 172.

25. General Orders, October 4, 1781, *Washington Writings*, 23:171; Frederick Mackenzie, *Diary of Frederick Mackenzie: Giving a Daily Narrative of His Military Service as an Officer of the Regiment of Royal Welch Fusiliers during the Years 1775–1781 in Massachusetts, Rhode Island, New York*, 2 vols. (New York Times/Arno Press, 1968 [1930]), 2:685; General Orders, October 28, 1781, *Washington Writings*, 23:283–284; General Orders, November 3, 1781, *Washington Writings*, 23:320–323; and To Major General William Heath, January 29, 1782, *Washington Writings*, 23:469.

26. General Orders, December 12, 1782, *Washington Writings*, 25:424..

27. General Orders, March 5, 1783, *Washington Writings*, 26:191–192; and General Orders, February 6, 1783, *Washington Writings*, 26:103.

28. General Orders, February 24, 1780, *Washington Writings*, 18:48; General Orders, February 6, 1783, *Washington Writings*, 26:103; and General Orders, June 2, 1783, *Washington Writings*, 26:465.

29. Rhode Island Delegates to Governor William Greene, March 12, 1783, *Congress Delegates Letters*, 20:21; To the General Officers of the Army, April 17, 1783, *Washington Writings*, 26:328–329; and Foster Journal, April 9, 1783.

30. *Gilbert Diary*, March 26–28, 1783; Lieutenant Colonel Hugh Maxwell to his wife Bridget, March 27, 1783, in Priscilla Maxwell, *The Christian Patriot, Some Recollections of the Late Col. Hugh Maxwell, of Massachusetts. Collected and Preserved by a Daughter* (New York, 1833), 110–111 (hereafter *Maxwell Recollections*); General Orders, March 28, 1783, *Washington Writings*, 26:263; *Gilbert Diary*, March 29, 1783; Foster Journal, March 29, 1783; General Orders, April 4, 1783, *Washington Writings*, 26:296; Foster Journal, April 5, 1783; Foster Journal, April 8 and 16, 1783; To Captain John Pray, March 30, 1783, *Washington Writings*, 26:272; To Major General Henry Knox, April 21, 1783, *Washington Writings*, 26:344–345; and *Heath Memoirs*, 371.

31. To Ralph Izard, June 14, 1783, *Washington Writings*, 27:10.

32. Foster Journal, April 17, 1783.

33. General Orders, April 18, 1783, *Washington Writings*, 26:337.

34. General Orders, April 2, 1783, *Washington Writings*, 26:281–282; General Orders, March 29, 1783, *Washington Writings*, 26:269; and General Orders, April 13, 1783, *Washington Writings*, 26:314.

35. *Heath Memoirs*, 371; *Gilbert Diary*, April 19, 1783; Foster Journal, April 19, 1783; and William Heath Diaries, April 19, 1783, Massachusetts Historical Society, Reel 30.

36. Rev. E.B. Hillard, *The Last Men of the American Revolution: A Photograph of Each from Life Together with Views of Their Homes Printed in Colors. Accompanied by Brief Biographical Sketches of the Men* (Hartford, CT, 1864), in Don N. Hagist, *The Revolution's Last Men: The Soldiers behind the Photographs* (Yardley, PA, 2015), 25 (hereafter *Revolution's Last Men*).

37. Tarbell Drawing ; and Foster Journal, April 19, 1783.

38. Order of Exhibition of the FIRE-WORKS, on Monday Evening the first of December 1783, Knox Papers, Reel 16. The first is crossed out, and "2d." is written above it.

39. General Orders, April 18, 1783, *Washington Writings*, 26:335–336. Every man received "an extra ration of liquor ... to drink Perpetual Peace, Independence and Happiness to the United States of America." Foster Journal, April 19, 1783. This additional issue of alcohol was fortuitous because it was a very cold day, and with the previous day being so hot, the drastic change could have been "very hartful to the hilth of Many in the Armey if Not fatal." Not placated by this contrived celebration, Foster felt "the formal aclemations of Joy Maks Such a Confussion that I am Almost tired

Out; and it Mak Me Wish that fuads of Joy Ware Ended So that My Wished for Discharg Might Come Which would afford me More Joy than to Continue hear in Such a Confution."

40. General Orders, April 19, 1783, *Washington Writings*, 26:338; General Orders, April 21, 1783, *Washington Writings*, 26:344; General Orders, April 25, 1783, *Washington Writings*, 26:361; General Orders, May 16, 1783, *Washington Writings*, 438; and To Daniel Parker Esq., April 28, 1783, Pickering Letters, Reel 27, Vol. 86.

41. To his Father, May 5, 1783, *Gilbert Letters*, 104; Major Leonard Bleecker to Peter Elmendorph, May 1, 1783, General Peter Gansevoort Military Papers, Gansevoort-Lansing Collection, New York Public Library; Karie Diethorn, "Charles Willson Peale's Philadelphia Museum Portraits, 1782 to 1827," *Bulletin du Centre de recherche du château de Versailles* [Online], 2017; To the Chevalier de La Luzerne, May 13, 1783, *Washington Writings*, 26:428; and Major General Friedrich von Steuben to [Lieutenant Colonel William North?] 1783, quoted in *Revolutionary People*, 352.

42. Major John Armstrong to Major General Horatio Gates, May 9, 1783, Gates Papers; and To Major General Henry Knox, May 14, 1783, *Washington Writings*, 26:430."

43. To Brigadier General Jedidiah Huntington, May 14, 1783, *Washington Writings*, 26:429; To Alexander Hamilton, April 22, 1783, *Washington Writings*, 26:351; and To the President of Congress, April 18, 1783, *Washington Writings*, 26:332.

44. Brigadier General Jedidiah Huntington to General George Washington, May 16, 1783, Washington Papers; General Orders, May 11, 1783, *Washington Writings*, 26:424; and General Orders, May 17, 1783, *Washington Writings*, 26:439–440. Corporals, Robert (?) Kelly and Cornelius Amberman, from the 2nd New York Regiment, were both convicted of the "willfull disobedience of orders."

45. Sewall Journal, April 29, May 19, May 22, June 14, and June 19, 1783.

46. To the Superintendent of Finance Robert Morris, February 25, 1783, *Washington Writings*, 26:161–162; To William Duer and Daniel Parker, May 29, 1783, *Washington Writings*, 26:459–460; Brigadier General Elias Dayton to Major General William Heath, May 28, 1783, Washington Papers; Brigadier General John Paterson to Major General William Heath, May 28, 1783, Washington Papers; Brigadier General John Stark to Major General William Heath, May 28, 1783, Washington Papers; To William Duer and Daniel Parker, May 29, 1783, *Washington Writings*, 26:459–460; To William Duer and Daniel Parker, June 3, 1783, *Washington Writings*, 26:466; and General Orders, June 4, 1783, *Washington Writings*, 26:468.

47. Foster Journal, May 8, 1783. "There is a Very Great Uneslyness in the Armey Arising from the Not Discharging the During Wars Men & I fear the Consiquenc of the Same." Foster Journal, May 14 and May 18, 1783. "Do Many of [us] Wonder We Should be Detained hear & Dayly to Increas the Publick Debt When the Cuntery are Growning under the Burden already Which is heavey."

48. To Major General Henry Knox, May 14, 1783, *Washington Writings*, 26:430; Foster Journal, May 29, 1783; and *Massachusetts Soldiers and Sailors*, 7:634.

49. Foster Journal, June 2, 1783 and May 12, 1783. Trescott led the raid against Fort Slongo on Long Island in early October 1781, one of the actions for which Sergeant Elijah Churchill was awarded the Badge of Military Merit.

50. Foster Journal, May 31, 1783.

Chapter 10

1. To Major General Marquis de Lafayette, June 15, 1783, *Washington Writings*, 27:14.

2. Major General William Heath to General George Washington, June 5, 1783, Washington Papers; To Major General William Heath, June 6, 1783, *Washington Writings*, 26:472–475; General Orders, June 6, 1783, *Washington Writings*, 26:471; and To Colonel Timothy Pickering, September 3, 1783, *Washington Writings*, 27:129.

3. JCC, July 26, 1783, 24:447–451; Superintendent of Finance Robert Morris to General George Washington, May 29, 1783, Washington Papers; and Superintendent of Finance Robert Morris to a Committee of Congress, April 14, 1783, *Morris Papers*, 7:701–702.

4. To the Superintendent of Finance Robert Morris, April 9, 1783, *Washington Writings*, 26:309; To the Superintendent of Finance Robert Morris, June 3, 1783, *Washington Writings*, 26:467; and *Gilbert Diary*, June 14, 1783.

5. JCC, July 26, 1783, 24:447–451; and George Fisher to Governor George Clinton, July 1783, *Clinton Papers*, 8:217–219.

6. General Orders, May 21, 1783, *Washington Writings*, 26:446–447. "The General thinks it necessary to caution the soldiers against the foolish practice, which he is informed has prevailed in some instances, of disposing of their Notes and securities of pay, at a very great discount, when it is evident the Speculators on those securities must hereafter obtain the full payment of their nominal value."

7. Major John Graham to Major General William Heath, May 22, 1783, Heath Papers, Reel 26; and General Orders, July 8, 1783, *Washington Writings*, 27:53–54.

8. To the President of Congress, April 18, 1783, *Washington Writings*, 26:333; and Colonel John Lamb to Governor George Clinton, May 2, 1783, *Clinton Papers*, 8:163.

9. To Colonel Henry Jackson, June 8, 1783, *Washington Writings*, 26:483.

10. General Orders, June 5, 1783, *Washington Writings*, 26:469.

11. To William Duer and Daniel Parker, June 3, 1783, *Washington Writings*, 26:466; and Major Christopher Richmond to Major General Horatio Gates, June 15, 1783, Gates Papers, Reel 13.

12. General Orders, June 6, 1783, *Washington Writings*, 26:471-472.
13. To his Father, c. June 6, 1783, *Gilbert Letters*, 106; *Gilbert Diary*, June 12, 1783; To his Father, January 18, 1783, *Gilbert Letters*, 79; and To his Father, March 26, 1783, *Gilbert Letters*, 103. Gilbert spent the entire winter writing to his father about how to dispose of his securities and borrow money, giving his desired discount rate and the lowest that he would accept.
14. To his Father, c. June 6, 1783, *Gilbert Letters*, 106-107; and To his Brother-in-Law Charles Bruce, June 10, 1783, *Gilbert Letters*, 107. "If this Continent and its inhabitants were worth fighting for, one could not be so ungenerous as to suppose it would not reward its protectors. I am at some times almost tempted to wish I had not lived to see the day when those brave heroes the deliverers of my Country should be drove from the field of Glory without one farthing of reward for their services. Where is the Justice, where is the propriety of the Army's bearing the whole burthen of the war.".
15. Colonel Timothy Pickering to Commissary General of Military Stores Samuel Hodgdon, June 12, 1783, quoted in *Pickering Life*, 1:473.
16. General Orders, June 3, 1783, *Washington Writings*, 26:468; To Major Thomas Lansdale, June 5, 1783, *Washington Writings*, 26:470; *Heath Memoirs*, 374 and 382-383; and *Gilbert Diary*, June 4-10, 1783.
17. General Orders, June 10, 1783, *Washington Writings*, 26:501.
18. *Heath Memoirs*, 351; *Van Cortlandt Memoir*, 1:68; and Colonel David Humphreys to Colonel Timothy Pickering, June 8, 1783, Miscellaneous Records, Reel 83. Upon reaching their destination, the soldiers returned it to Pickering's agent in that city.
19. General Orders, June 8, 1783, *Washington Writings*, 26:482.
20. Brigadier General Moses Hazen to General George Washington, June 7, 1783, Washington Papers; General Orders, February 21, 1783, *Washington Writings*, 26:149-152; To Brigadier General Moses Hazen, June 9, 1783, *Washington Writings*, 26:498; Brigadier General Moses Hazen to General George Washington, June 12, 1783, Washington Papers; To Brigadier General Moses Hazen, June 12, 1783, Pickering Letters, Reel 27, Vol. 86; To Brigadier General Moses Hazen, June 30, 1783, *Washington Writings*, 27:38-39; and To Brigadier General Moses Hazen, June 24, 1783, *Washington Writings*, 27:31.
21. To Lieutenant Colonel Jeremiah Olney, June 4, 1783, *Washington Writings*, 26:468-469.
22. Circular to the States, June 8, 1783, *Washington Writings*, 26:483-496; and David Howell to Thomas G. Hazard, August 26, 1783, *Congress Delegates Letters*, 20:595.
23. To Alexander Hamilton, April 22, 1783, *Washington Writings*, 26:350-351. A few days after the formal announcement of peace in mid-April, he desired "most fervently that all the Troops ... not retained for a Peace Establishment were ... discharged immediately." He believed it "was not in the power of Congress or their Officers, to hold them much, if any longer; for we are obliged at this moment to increase our Guards to prevt. Rioting, and the Insults which the Officers meet with in attempting to hold them to their duty." To the President of Congress, June 18, 1783, *Washington Writings*, 27:20. That the army was disbanded without major incident "and the business got more happily over than could be expected."
24. To the President of Congress, June 24, 1783, *Washington Writings*, 27:34; and *Sinews of Independence*, 255; *Gilbert Diary*, June 11, 1783; and *Heath Memoirs*, 384.
25. General Orders, January 18, 1783, *Washington Writings*, 26:48; To Quartermaster Lieutenant Ebenezer Brown, 1st Massachusetts Brigade, June 21, 1783, Pickering Letters, Reel 27, Vol. 8; To Brigadier General John Paterson, June 20, 1783, Pickering Letters, Reel 27, Vol. 86; and To Brigadier General John Paterson, June 21, 1783, Pickering Letters, Reel 27, Vol. 86.
26. General Orders, June 10, 1783, *Washington Writings*, 26:501; and General Orders, June 7, 1783, *Washington Writings*, 26:477..
27. Sewall Journal, June 22, 1783; General Orders, June 20, 1783, *Washington Writings*, 27:25; General Orders, June 21, 1783, *Washington Writings*, 27:26-27; and *Heath Memoirs*, 385-386.
28. To his Father, late June 1783, *Gilbert Letters*, 108.
29. Lieutenant Colonel Benjamin Walker to Colonel Timothy Pickering, June 19, 1783, Miscellaneous Records, Reel 83.

Chapter 11

1. Instructions to Major General Robert Howe, June 25, 1783, *Washington Writings*, 27:35-36; and Lieutenant Colonel Jonathan Trumbull, Jr., to Lieutenant Thomas Edwards, July 7, 1783, Washington Papers.
2. General Orders, June 20, 1783, *Washington Writings*, 27:26.
3. Elizabeth Cometti, trans., ed., *Seeing America and Its Great Men: The Journal and Letters of Count Francesco dal Verme* (Charlottesville, VA, 1969), 11-19 (hereafter *Dal Verme Journal*); and Major General Henry Knox to Paymaster John Pierce, July 19, 1783, West Point, Knox Papers, Reel 13. Washington left the day before and returned on August 5, 1783. To Daniel Parker, July 26, 1783, *Washington Writings*, 27:72; and To the Continental Congress, August 6, 1783, *Washington Writings*, 27:83.
4. Colonel Timothy Pickering to Rebecca Pickering, September 8, 1783, quoted in *Pickering Life*, 1:478.
5. *Dal Verme Journal*, 14; and Colonel Timothy Pickering to Commissary General of Military Stores Samuel Hodgdon, August 27, 1783, *Pickering Life*, 1:476.

6. Colonel Timothy Pickering to Major General Horatio Gates, June 17, 1783, Gates Papers, Reel 13.

7. To the Superintendent of Finance Robert Morris, March 13, 1783, Pickering Letters, Reel 27, Vol. 86; Joseph Davis and Joshua Sears Statement to Colonel Timothy Pickering, March 18, 1783, Quartermaster Estimates, Reel 29, Vol. 103; and William Dennings, John Robinson and Daniel Niven to Colonel Timothy Pickering, May 21, 1783, Quartermaster Estimates, Reel 29, Vol. 103; and To Commissary General of Military Stores Samuel Hodgdon, October 9, 1783, Pickering Letters, Reel 28, Vol. 87.

8. Colonel Timothy Pickering Estimate of Monies Wanted for the Quartermaster Department to Superintendent of Finance Robert Morris, August 15, 1783, Pickering Letters, Reel 28, Vol. 87.

9. Colonel Michael Jackson to Colonel Timothy Pickering, June 30, 1783, Miscellaneous Records, Reel 83; Major Job Sumner to Colonel Timothy Pickering, June 22, 1783, Miscellaneous Records, Reel 83; and Lieutenant Colonel Hugh Maxwell to Colonel Timothy Pickering, August 26, 1783, Miscellaneous Records, Reel 83.

10. *NY Packet*, August 26, 1783; Building Auction; Deputy Quartermaster General Peter Anspach to Colonel Timothy Pickering, July 23, 1783, Miscellaneous Records, Reel 83; and Foster Journal, May 11, 1783. "[O]ur famous Tempel of Vertue & Libberty was yesterday almost Washed Down With a Sevear Storm of Wind & Rain," *Heath Memoirs*, 383; and Building Auction.

11. Washington's Headquarters State Historic Site Collection.

12. Colonel Timothy Pickering to General George Washington, August 28, 1783, Washington Papers; To Joseph Davis, October 27, 1783, Pickering Letters, Reel 28, Vol. 87; and Estimate of damages done by the army to the following Farms.viz., October or November 1783, Quartermaster Estimates, Reel 29, Vol. 103.

13. Colonel Timothy Pickering to General George Washington, August 28, 1783, Washington Papers; Hospital Surgeon William Eustis to Colonel Timothy Pickering, September 2, 1783, Pickering Letters, Reel 28, Vol. 87; To Assistant Commissary of Forage Joseph King, September 5, 1783, Pickering Letters, Reel 28, Vol. 87; and To The Contractors for New Jersey & New York, October 12, 1783, Pickering Letters, Reel 28, Vol. 87.

14. To Mr. Horr, October 28, 1783, Pickering Letters, Reel 28, Vol. 87; and To Governor George Clinton, February 17, 1783, *Washington Writings*, 26:138–139.

15. To Major General Henry Knox, November 1, 1783, Pickering Letters, Reel 28, Vol. 87; and To Captain Elnathon Haskins, November 1, 1783, Pickering Letters, Reel 28, Vol. 87.

16. *JCC*, August 26, 1783, 24:521–522.

17. *JCC*, October 18, 1783, 25:703; To Lieutenant General Comte de Rochambeau, November 1, 1783, *Washington Writings*, 27:218–219; Farewell Orders to the Armies of the United States, November 2, 1783, *Washington Writings*, 27:222–227; and Peter Adams Pension File, Revolutionary War Pension and Bounty-Land Warrant Application Files, National Archives Microfilm Publication M804, Roll 14, Massachusetts, Records of the Veterans Administration RG15, National Archives, Washington, DC. In 1778, Private Adams served nine months in Captain James Cooper's Company of Colonel Gamaliel Bradford's 14th Massachusetts Regiment. In May 1781, Adams enlisted for three years and was assigned to Captain Jeremiah Miller's Company in Colonel Joseph Vose's 1st Massachusetts Regiment. *Officer Register*, 259.

18. Address to Congress on Resigning His Commission, December 23, 1783, *Washington Writings*, 27:284–286; *JCC*, December 23, 1783, 25:838–839.

19. *Washington Writings*, June 2 and 3, 1784, 27:524 and 538–540.

20. James L. Mooney, *Dictionary of American Naval Fighting Ships*, 8 vols. (Washington, DC, 1959–1981), 1:149; and General Orders, March 9, 1783, *Washington Writings*, 26:202.

21. Brigadier General Rufus Putnam to General George Washington, June 16, 1783, Washington Papers; Archer Butler Hulbert, ed., *Ohio Company Series: The Records of the Original Proceedings of the Ohio-Company*, 2 vols. (Marietta, OH, 1917), 1:xxvi–xxviii, 50–51, 26, 61, 65, 76, and 117.

22. *Officer Register*, 189; *Massachusetts Soldiers and Sailors*, 13:826; Leonard L. Richards, *Shays's Rebellion: The American Revolution's Final Battle* (University of Pennsylvania Press, Philadelphia, 2002); and David P. Szatmary, *Shays' Rebellion: The Making of an Agrarian Insurrection* (University of Massachusetts Press, Amherst, 1980).

23. *Maxwell Recollections*, 122–139.

24. Glenn A. Knoblock, *"Strong and Brave Fellows": New Hampshire's Black Soldiers and Sailors of the American Revolution, 1775–1784* (Jefferson, NC, 2003), 119–122, 109–110, and 102–103.

25. "Indian Patriots."

26. Quoted in William H. Guthman, *March to Massacre: A History of the First Seven Years of the United States Army, 1784–1791* (New York, 1970), 24. Some Indians did, however, fight in the volunteer regiments during the Civil War, and Seneca sachem Colonel Ely S. Parker was on General Ulysses S. Grant's staff. Others joined volunteer units during the Spanish-American War.

27. *Revolution's Last Men*, 1–29 and 89–114; Ken Raymond, *Eleazer Blake*, rindgehistoricalsociety.org, 2018; and *Massachusetts Soldiers and Sailors*, 2:127.

28. *Massachusetts Soldiers and Sailors*, 9:339; General Orders, October 20, 1781, *Washington Writings*, 23:247; *Massachusetts Soldiers and Sailors*, 9:339; Kneeland Pension Files; Town of Bedford, Massachusetts, Tax Rolls for 1785 and 1786; W.T.R. Saffel, comp., *Records of the Revolutionary War Containing the Military and Financial Correspondence of Distinguished Officers, etc.* (New York, 1858), 511–514 (hereafter *Revolutionary*

Records); and Kneeland Pension Files. His death notice in Pomroy Jones, *Annals and Recollections of Oneida County* (Oneida County, NY, 1851), 777, gives his age as 100:

> Died.—At Westmoreland, on the 17th of October 1846, Henry Francis Aaron Keckland, aged 100 years and 5 months. Mr. Keckland was a native of Germany, came to this country as a soldier in the army of Gen. Burgoyne, was made prisoner at Saratoga, afterwards enlisted into the American service, continued a faithful soldier during the war, and, as he was proud to say, marched into New York with Gen. Washington, when the city was evacuated by the British, and was honorably discharged.

Revolutionary Records, 524; and Kneeland Pension Files.

29. *Revolution Remembered*, 240–250; *NY in Revolution*, 1:157; and Richard Eldred, "The Heroine of Yorktown," *Daughters of the American Revolution Magazine* 118 (November 1984), 634, 635, and 698.

30. *Gilbert Letters*, 13–14 and 100–101.

31. *New Windsor Centennial*.

32. Orange County, New York Clerk, Deed August 15, 1891, Book 385 of Deeds, p. 337, Orange County Clerk Office, Mary E. Smith Deed November 13, 1916, conveying property to The Historical Society of Newburgh Bay and the Highlands, Book 569 of Deeds, p. 531, Orange County Clerk Office, Assignment of Lease Joseph M. Dickey and Others to The Historical Society of Newburgh Bay and the Highlands, December 13, 1916, Liber 570 of Deeds, p. 1 and The Historical Society of Newburgh Bay and the Highlands convey to the State of New York January 31, 1918, Recorded June 19, 1918, Book 581 of Deeds, p. 208, Office, New Windsor Cantonment Collection.

33. *Newburgh News*, May 31, 1932.

34. New Windsor Cantonment State Historic Site Collection.

Appendix 2

1. General Orders, June 7, 1778. John C. Fitzpatrick, ed., *The Writings of George Washington from the Original Manuscript Sources, 1745–1799*, 39 vols. (Washington, DC, 1931–1944) 12:30, (hereafter *Washington Writings*).

2. General Orders, June 7, 1778, *Washington Writings*, 12:32.

3. General Orders, April 7, 1782, *Washington Writings*, 23:101.

4. General Orders, April 30, 1782, *Washington Writings*, 24:189.

Appendix 6

1. *Newburgh News*, November 8, 1934; Rev. A. Elwood Corning, Summary of Documentation on Mountainville Hut, undated, probably mid-1930s, New Windsor Cantonment State Historic Site Collection (hereafter Hut Documentation); and Donald Fangboner, Mr. John T. Hand November 5, 1974, Interview Concerning Officers' Hut Donated by Mr. John T. Hand to National Temple Hill Association, New Windsor Cantonment State Historic Site Collection (hereafter Hand Hut Interview).

2. Susan E. Smith, *The Mountainville Hut Structure Report* (Peebles Island, NY, 1981), Appendix B, 3 and 4 (hereafter *Hut Structure Report)*; and *Newburgh News*, November 28, 1934.

3. Hut Documentation; *NY in Revolution*, 1:253; Program: Ceremonies Dedicating Revolutionary Hut at Temple Hill in the Town of New Windsor, October 7, 1934, Under the Auspices of National Temple Hill Association, Inc., Newburgh, N.Y. (Newburgh, 1934), New Windsor Cantonment State Historic Site Collection; *Newburgh News*, November 28, 1934; Baptismal Certificate of Mary Patricia Hunt, August 28, 1928, Baptism performed by Minister A. Elwood Corning, Possession of Patricia Hunt Perry, Newburgh New York, Copy of certificate in New Windsor Cantonment State Historic Site Collection; *Newburgh News*, April 17, 1941; and Mildred Parker Sees, *Old Orange Houses*, 2 vols. (Middletown, NY, 1941–1943) 2:73.

4. *Hut Structure Report*, Appendix B, 6.

5. General Orders, May 13, 1782, *Washington Writings*, 24:250.

6. *Newburgh News*, November 28, 1934; and Hand Hut Interview.

Bibliography

Manuscript Orderly Books

8th Massachusetts Regiment Orderly Book, The Huntington Library, San Marino, CA.
Jersey Brigade Orderly Book, Regimental Orders for the Jersey Brigade, November 9–December 31, 1782, The Huntington Library, San Marino, CA.
Orderly Book of Sergeant Peter Gaspar, Captain John C. Ten Broeck's Company, First New York Regiment, January 1, 1783 to April 19, 1783. United States Military Academy Library Special Collections Division, West Point, New York.
The Papers of William Torrey (Adjutant 2nd Massachusetts), 2nd Massachusetts Regiment Orderly Book, September 6, 1777–May 31, 1783, 24 vols., microfilm edition, 1976, Library of Congress.
Return of the 5th Massachusetts Regiment of Foot Commanded by D. Cobb Esqr., 14th Feb 1783. Rufus Putnam, Weekly Returns, 5th Massachusetts Regiment, January 1781–April 1783. United States Military Academy Library Special Collections Division, West Point, New York, Microfilm Archives.
2nd New Hampshire Regiment Orderly Book, New Hampshire Archives, New Hampshire Historical Society.

Manuscript Collections

Adams, Peter, Pension File, Revolutionary War Pension and Bounty-Land Warrant Application Files, Microfilm Publication M804, Roll 14, Massachusetts, Records of the Veterans Administration RG 15, National Archives, Washington, DC.
Adams, Samuel, Samuel Adams's Private Miscellaneous Diary Kept Ann. Dom. 1781 When he was Surgeon to the Massachusetts Regt. Of Artillery Which did duty at the several places of New Windsor, Philipsburgh West-Point . . . , February 1, 1781. Samuel Adams Papers, Manuscripts and Archives Division, New York Public Library.
Bedford, Massachusetts, Tax Rolls for 1785 and 1786.
Estimates and Returns of Supplies, Funds, and Personnel, Quartermaster General's Department and Commissary General of Military Stores, 1780–1793, Microfilm Publication M853, Roll 29, Vol. 148, RG 93, National Archives, Washington, DC.
Fogg, J.H.S., Autograph Collection, Maine Historical Society.
Force, Peter, Collection, Transcripts, 1520s–1880s, Series 7D, Library of Congress.
Gansevoort, Peter, Military Papers, Gansevoort-Lansing Collection, New York Public Library.
Gates, Horatio, Papers, New-York Historical Society.
Gilbert, Benjamin, Diary, 1782–1786, Diaries G372, Manuscript Collection, New York State Historical Association Research Library, Cooperstown, New York.
Heath, William, Papers, Massachusetts Historical Society.
Letters Sent by Samuel Hodgdon, Richard Frothingham, and Benjamin Flower, July 19, 1778–May 24, 1784, in the Records of the War Department, Adjutant General's Office, Revolutionary War Records, Microfilm Publication M853, Roll 33, RG 93, National Archives, Washington, DC.
Kneeland, Henry, Pension File, Revolutionary War Pension and Bounty-Land Warrant Application Files, Microfilm Publication M804, Roll 1501, Massachusetts, Records of the Veterans Administration, RG 15, National Archives, Washington, DC.
Knox, Henry, Papers, Massachusetts Historical Society.
Lehrman, Gilder, Institute of American History.
Letters, Orders for Pay, Accounts, Receipts, and Other Supply Records Concerning Weapons and Military Stores, 1776–1801, in the Records of the War Department, Adjutant General's Office Revolutionary War Records, Microfilm Publication M927, Roll 1, RG 93, National Archives, Washington, DC.

Letters, Orders for Pay, Accounts, Receipts, and Other Supply Records Concerning Weapons and Military Stores, 1776–1801, in the Records of the War Department, Adjutant General's Office Revolutionary War Records, Microfilm Publication M927, Roll 1, RG 93, National Archives, Washington, DC.

Letters and Reports from Maj. Gen. Benjamin Lincoln, Secretary at War, 1781–83, Papers of the Continental Congress, compiled 1774–1789, p. 693–694, M247, Roll 162, RG 360, https://www.fold3.com/images/424632 and & 424635.

Letters from Gen. George Washington, Commander in Chief of the Army, 1775–84, Vol. 7, December 16, 1778–September 12, 1779, Continental Congress Papers, pp. 325–327, M247, Roll 169, RG 360.

McDonald, Robert, trans. The Revolutionary War Journal of Private Thomas Foster 7th Massachusetts Regiment at West Point, Verplanck's Point and Cantonment New Windsor May 1782–June 1783, The Huntington Library, San Marino, CA.

McDougall, Alexander, Papers, New-York Historical Society.

Memorandum of Officers Quarters in the Neighbourhood of New Windsor & Newburgh during the Winter of 1780_81_&83. Photostat of an original memorandum in the research collection at the New Windsor Cantonment State Historic Site. Originally in the Adjutant General's Office in the War Department, this record was subsequently transferred to the National Archives.

Meng, Christopher, Ledger, October 2, 1781, to October 2, 1782, Massachusetts Historical Society.

Miscellaneous Number Records (The Manuscript File) in the War Department Collection of Revolutionary War Records, 1775–1790s, Microfilm Publication, M859, Roll 80, RG 93, National Archives, Washington, DC.

Muster of 1st and 2nd Regiments, New Jersey Continental Line, from January 1782 to April 1783. Photostat of an original form in the research collection at the New Windsor Cantonment State Historic Site. Originally in the Adjutant General's Office in the War Department, this record was subsequently transferred to the National Archives.

New Windsor Cantonment State Historic Site Collection.

New Windsor, New York, Collection.

Orange County, New York Clerk, Deed, August 15, 1891, Book 385 of Deeds, p. 337, Orange County Clerk Office, Mary E. Smith Deed, November 13, 1916, conveying property to the Historical Society of Newburgh Bay and the Highlands, Book 569 of Deeds, p. 531, Orange County Clerk Office, Assignment of Lease Joseph M. Dickey and Others to the Historical Society of Newburgh Bay and the Highlands, December 13, 1916, Liber 570 of Deeds, p. 1, and the Historical Society of Newburgh Bay and the Highlands convey to the State of New York, January 31, 1918, Recorded June 19, 1918, Book 581 of Deeds, p. 208, New Windsor Cantonment Collection.

Pickering, Timothy, Letters of Col. Pickering in the Records of the War Department, Adjutant General's Office Revolutionary War Records, Microfilm Publication M853, Roll 28, Vol. 87, RG 93, National Archives, Washington, DC.

Pickering, Timothy, Papers, Huntington Historical Society, Huntingdon, Long Island, New York.

Pickering, Timothy, Papers, Reel 56, Military Papers, 1767–1792, Massachusetts Historical Society.

Pickering, Timothy, to Dudley A. Tyng, August 2, 1819, in a bound volume titled *George Washington—Address to the Officers of the American Army, March 15, 1783*. Massachusetts Historical Society.

Revere, Paul, to his congressman Representative William Eustis, February 20, 1804, Miscellaneous Bound Manuscripts, Massachusetts Historical Society.

Sewall, Henry, Journal, Maine State Library, Miscellaneous Manuscripts Collection.

Washington, George, Papers at the Library of Congress, 1741–1799, Series 2, Letterbooks.

Washington, George, The George Washington Papers at the Library of Congress, 1741–1799, Series 4, General Correspondence, 1697–1799.

Washington's Headquarters, State Historic Site Collection.

Wolfe, Michael, ed. A Memoir of the Revolutionary War (Sergeant James Selkirk, 1756–1820). Draft, New York State Library, 1993.

Zemensky, Edith von, ed. The Papers of General Friedrich Wilhelm von Steuben, 1777–1794, 7 reels with printed guide (Millwood, New York, 1983).

Memoirs, Published Papers, and Related Items

"An Act for the Relief of the Heirs of Deborah Gannett, a Soldier of the Revolution, Deceased." House Resolution 184, June 18, 1838. *Bills and Resolutions, House of Representatives*, 25th Congress, 2nd Session, House Resolution 184.

"A Bill for the Relief of Benjamin Gannett, Widower of Deborah Gannett, a Soldier of the Revolution." House Resolution 890, January 31, 1837. *Bills and Resolutions, House of Representatives*, 24th Congress, 2nd Session.

Blayney, Benjamin, ed. *The Holy Bible Containing the Old and New Testaments: Translated Out of the Original Tongues; and with the Former Translations Diligently Compared and Revised, by His Majesty's Special Command*. Oxford, 1769.

Boyd, Julian P., et al., ed. *The Papers of Thomas Jefferson*, 60 vols. Princeton University Press, 1950-2009.
Boynton, Edward C., ed. *General Orders of George Washington Issued at Newburgh on the Hudson 1782-1783*. Harrison, NY: Harbor Hill Books, 1973.
Bray, Robert C., and Paul E. Bushnell, eds. *Diary of a Common Soldier in the American Revolution, 1775-1783: An Annotated Edition of the Military Journal of Jeremiah Greenman*. DeKalb: Northern Illinois University Press, 1978.
Cometti, Elizabeth, ed. *Seeing America and Its Great Men: The Journal and Letters of Count Francesco dal Verme*. Charlottesville: University Press of Virginia, 1969.
Commonwealth of Massachusetts. "In the House of Representatives, December 2, 1780. Whereas the Congress of the United States Have Required of This Commonwealth to Supply the Deficiency of Our Proportion of the Continental Army...." Boston: Printed by Benjamin Edes and Son, 1780.
Conrad, Dennis M., ed. *The Papers of Nathanael Greene*. 13 vols. Chapel Hill: University of North Carolina Press, 1976-2005.
Cuthbertson, Bennett. *Cuthbertson's System for the Complete Interior Management and Oeconomy of a Battalion of Infantry*. Bristol, UK, 1776.
Dann, John C., ed. *The Revolution Remembered: Eyewitness Accounts of the War for Independence*. Chicago: University of Chicago Press, 1980.
Diderot, Denis, and Jean D'Alembert. *Le Encyclopedie, Fabrication Des Canons*. Reprint ed. Inter-Livres, 2002 (1762-1772).
Ellis, William A., ed. "The Diary of William S. Pennington" (Part 2 of 2). In *The Proceedings of the New Jersey Historical Society* 64, no. 1 (January 1946). Newark, NJ, 1946.
Elmer, Ebenezer. "Journal of Lieutenant Ebenezer Elmer, 2nd New Jersey Regt." In *Proceedings of the New Jersey Historical Society*, Vol. 3, 1848-1849.
Ferguson, E. James, et al., eds. *The Papers of Robert Morris, 1781-1784*. 9 vols. Pittsburgh: University of Pittsburgh Press, 1973-1999.
Fitzpatrick, John C., ed. *The Writings of George Washington from the Original Manuscript Sources, 1745-1799*. 39 vols. U.S. Government Printing Office, 1931-1944.
Ford, Worthington C., ed. *Journals of the Continental Congress, 1774-1789*. 34 vols. Washington, DC, 1904-1937.
Fowler, David J. *Guide to the Sol Feinstone Collection of the David Library of the American Revolution*. Washington Crossing, PA, 1994.
Gannett, Deborah Sampson. *An Address, Delivered with Applause, at the Federal Street Theatre, Boston, Four Successive Nights of the Different Plays, Beginning March 2, 1802; and After, at Other Principal Towns, a Number of Nights Successively at Each Place; By Mrs. Deborah Gannett, the American Heroine, Who Served Three Years with Reputation (Undiscovered as a Female) in the Late American Army*. Dedham, Massachusetts, 1802.
Hall, Clayton C., et al., eds. *Muster Rolls of Maryland Troops in the American Revolution (1775-1783)*. Reprint ed. Baltimore, d, 1972 (1900).
Hastings, Hugh, comp. *Public Papers of George Clinton First Governor of New York War of the Revolution Series*. 8 vols. Albany, NY: W.H. Crawford, 1899-1904.
Heath, William. *Memoirs of Major-General Heath Containing Anecdotes, Details of Skirmishes, Battles, and Other Military Events, during the American War* (Boston, 1798).
Heitman, Francis B., ed. *Historical Register of Officers of the Continental Army during the War of the Revolution April 1775, to December 1783 with Addenda by Robert Kirby, 1932*. Reprint ed. Baltimore: Genealogical Publ. Co., 1967 (1914).
Hervey, James. *Theron and Aspasio: or, a Series of Dialogues and Letters, upon the Most Important and Interesting Subjects*. London, 1755.
Hulbert, Archer Butler, ed. *Ohio Company Series: The Records of the Original Proceedings of the Ohio-Company*. 2 vols. Marietta, OH: Marietta Historical Commission, 1917.
Hutchinson, William T., and M.E. Rachal, eds. *Papers of James Madison*. 14 vols. Chicago: University of Chicago Press, 1969.
Jones, John, M.D. *Plain Concise Practical Remarks, on the Treatment of Wounds and Fractures; To which Is Added, an Appendix, on Camp and Military Hospitals; Principally Designed for the Use of Young Military and Naval Surgeons, in North-America*. Philadelphia, 1776.
Jordan, John W., comp. "Continental Hospital Returns 1777-1780." *Pennsylvania Magazine of History and Biography*, April 1899.
Journal of the House of Representatives of the United of States, Being the First Session of the Fifth Congress: Begun and Held at the City of Philadelphia, May 15, 1797, and in the Twenty-First Year of the Independence of the Said States. Washington, DC, 1826.
Judd, Jacob, ed. *The Revolutionary War Memoir and Selected Correspondence of Philip Van Cortlandt*. 2 vols. Tarrytown, NY: Sleepy Hollow Restorations, 1976.
Lauber, Almon W., ed. *Orderly Books of the Fourth New York Regiment, 1778-1780, the Second New York Regiment, 1780-1783, by Samuel Tallmadge and Others with Diaries of Samuel Tallmadge, 1780-1782 and John Barr, 1779-1782*. Albany, NY: University of the State of New York, 1932.

Lesser, Charles H., ed. *The Sinews of Independence: Monthly Strength Reports of the Continental Army*. Chicago: University of Chicago Press, 1976.

Mackenzie, Frederick. *Diary of Frederick Mackenzie: Giving a Daily Narrative of His Military Service as an Officer of the Regiment of Royal Welch Fusiliers during the Years 1775–1781 in Massachusetts, Rhode Island, New York*. 2 vols. Reprint ed. New York Times/Arno Press, 1968 (1930).

Massachusetts Office of the Secretary of State, Secretary of the Commonwealth. *Massachusetts Soldiers and Sailors of the Revolutionary War: A Compilation from the Archives*. 17 vols. Boston, 1896–1908.

Mead, John H. "Summary of Archaeological Surveys, Excavations, Etc. at the New Windsor Cantonment; Prepared by John H. Mead, November 24, 1980." New Windsor Cantonment State Historic Site Collection.

Pickering, Octavius, and Charles Wentworth Upham. *The Life of Timothy Pickering*. 4 vols. Boston, 1867–1873.

Quincy, Josiah. *The Journals of Major Samuel Shaw: The First American Consul at Canton*. Boston, 1847.

Rice, Howard C., Jr., ed. *Travels in North America in the Years 1780, 1781 and 1782 by the Marquis de Chastellux*. 2 vols. Chapel Hill: University of North Carolina Press, 1963.

Rice, Howard C., Jr., and Anne S.K. Browne, trans. and eds. *The American Campaigns of Rochambeau's Army 1780, 1781, 1782, 1783*. 2 vols. (Princeton University Press and Brown University Press, 1972.)

Riling, Joseph B. *Baron von Steuben and His Regulations Including a Complete Facsimile of the Original Regulations for the Order and Discipline of the Troops of the United States*. Philadelphia: Ray Riling Arms Books Co., 1966.

Roberts, James A., comp. *New York in the Revolution as Colony and State*. 2 vols. Albany, NY: J.B. Lyon Co., 1904.

Rush, Benjamin. "The Results of Observations Made upon the Diseases Which Occurred in the Military Hospitals of the United States, during the Late War." In *Medical Inquiries and Observations*. 2nd ed., 4 vols. Philadelphia, 1805.

Saffel, W.T.R., comp. *Records of the Revolutionary War Containing the Military and Financial Correspondence of Distinguished Officers, Etc*. New York, 1858.

Scheer, George F., ed. *Private Yankee Doodle Being a Narrative of Some of the Adventures, Dangers and Sufferings of a Revolutionary Soldier by Joseph Plumb Martin*. Reprint ed. New York: Eastern Acorn Press, 1988 (1962).

Shy, John, ed. *Winding Down: The Revolutionary War Letters of Lieutenant Benjamin Gilbert of Massachusetts, 1780–1783*. Ann Arbor: University of Michigan Press, 1989.

Simms, Jeptha R. *Trappers of New York: or, a Biography of Nicholas Stoner and Nathaniel Foster; Together with Anecdotes of Other Celebrated Hunters, and Some Account of Sir William Johnson, and His Style of Living*. Reprint ed. Harrison, NY: Harbor Hill Books, 1980 (1871).

Smith, George. *An Universal Military Dictionary, a Copious Explanation of the Technical Terms & c. Used in the Equipment, Machinery, Movements, and Military Operations of an Army*. Reprint ed. Museum Restoration Service, Ottawa, Ontario, 1969 (1779).

Smith, Paul H., et al., eds. *Letters of Delegates to Congress, 1774–1789*. 25 vols. US Government Printing Office, 1976–2000.

Symmes, Rebecca D., ed. *A Citizen-Soldier in the American Revolution: The Diary of Benjamin Gilbert in Massachusetts and New York*. Cooperstown, NY: New York State Historical Association, 1980.

Syrett, Harold C., ed. *Papers of Alexander Hamilton*. 26 vols. New York: Columbia University Press, 1962.

Thacher, James. *Eyewitness to the American Revolution: The Battles and Generals as Seen by an Army Surgeon*. Reprint ed. Stamford, CT: Longmeadow Press, 1994 (1862).

Wharton, Francis, ed. *The Revolutionary Diplomatic Correspondence of the United States*. 6 vols. Washington, DC, 1889.

Willett, William M. *A Narrative of the Military Actions of Colonel Marinus Willet, Taken Chiefly from His Own Manuscript*. Reprint ed. New York Times, 1969 (1831).

Wolf, Simon, and Louis Edward Levy, eds. *The American Jew as Patriot, Soldier and Citizen*. Philadelphia, 1895.

Secondary Sources

Archambault, Alan H., and Marko Zlatich. "4th Massachusetts Regiment of the Continental Line, Battalion Companies, 1782–1783." *Military Collector and Historian* 39, no. 1 (Spring 1987): Plate no. 601.

Bancroft, George. *History of the Formation of the Constitution of the United States of America*. 2 vols. New York, 1882.

Beach, Lewis. *Cornwall*. Newburgh, NY, 1873.

Billias, George A. *General John Glover and His Marblehead Mariners*. New York: Holt, 1960.

Brown, Abraham English. *History of the Town of Bedford, Middlesex County, Massachusetts, from Its Earliest Settlement to the Year of Our Lord 1891*. Bedford, MA, 1891.

Brown, Louise K. *A Revolutionary Town*. Canaan, NH: Phoenix Pub., 1975.

Bibliography

Burnet, Joseph B., et al. *New Windsor Centennial Temple Hill, June 22, 1883.* Newburgh, NY, 1883.
Corning, A. Elwood. *Address of Rev. A. Elwood President of the National Temple Hill Association Delivered at the Forty-Third Congress, Daughters of the American Revolution, Washington, D.C., April 16, 1934.* Printed in the Congressional Record of May 24, 1934. U.S. Government Printing Office, 1934.
Custis, George Washington Park. *Recollections and Private Memoirs of the Life and Character of Washington by His Adopted Son, George Washington Parke Custis, with A Memoir of the Author, by His Daughters; And Ilustrative and Explanatory Notes by Benson J. Lossing.* New York, 1860.
Dykman, J.O. "The Historic Temple at New Windsor, 1783, a Picture Made at That Time and Never Before Published." *Magazine of American History* 24 (October 1890), 283–286.
Egleston, Thomas. *The Life of John Paterson, Major-General in the Revolutionary Army.* New York, 1898.
Egly, T.W., Jr. *Goose Van Schaick of Albany, 1736–1789: The Continental Army's Senior Colonel*, Privately Printed, 1992.
Eldred, Richard. "The Heroine of Yorktown." *Daughters of the American Revolution Magazine* 118 (November 1984), 634–635, 698.
Elting, John R., ed. *Military Uniforms in America: The Era of the American Revolution, 1755-1795.* San Rafael, CA: Presidio Press, 1974.
Ferguson, E. James. *The Power of the Purse: A History of American Public Finance, 1776–1790.* Chapel Hill: University of North Carolina Press, 1961.
Finch, I. *Travels in the United States of America and Canada, Containing Some Account of the Scientific Institutions and a Few Notices of the Geology and Mineralogy of Those Countries.* London, 1833.
Fleming, Thomas. *The Perils of Peace: America's Struggle for Survival after Yorktown.* New York: Smithsonian Books/Collins, 2007.
Fordyce, David. *The Temple of Virtue: A Dream.* 2nd ed. Published by James Fordyce, DD, London, 1775.
Fowler, William M., Jr. *American Crisis: George Washington and the Dangerous Two Years after Yorktown, 1781–1783.* New York: Walker, 2011.
Gordon, Donald C. *The New Windsor Cantonment National Temple Hill Association, Inc., Annual Report 1963.* New Windsor Cantonment State Historic Site Collection.
Guthman, William H. *March to Massacre: A History of the First Seven Years of the United States Army, 1784–1791.* New York: McGraw-Hill, 1970.
Hagist, Don N. *The Revolution's Last Men: The Soldiers behind the Photographs.* Yardley, PA: Westholme, 2015.
Head, David. *A Crisis of Peace: George Washington, the Newburgh Conspiracy, and the Fate of the American Revolution.* New York: Pegasus Books, 2019.
Hillard, E.B. *The Last Men of the American Revolution: A Photograph of Each from Life Together with Views of Their Homes Printed in Colors, Accompanied by Brief Biographical Sketches of the Men.* Hartford, CT, 1864.
Historical Society of Newburgh Bay and the Highlands. "Temple Hill and Its Vicinity," XIX, 1924.
Hunemorder, Markus. *The Society of the Cincinnati: Conspiracy and Distrust in Early America.* New York: Berghahn Books, 2006.
Jackson, Alice F., and Bettina Jackson. *Three Hundred Years American: The Epic of a Family from Seventeenth-Century New England to Twentieth-Century Midwest.* State Historical Society of Wisconsin, 1951.
Jones, Pomroy. *Annals and Recollections of Oneida County.* Oneida County, NY, 1851.
Katcher, Philip. *Encyclopedia of British, Provincial, and German Army Units, 1775–1783.* Harrisburg, PA: Stackpole Books, 1973.
Katcher, Philip. *Uniforms of the Continental Army.* York, PA: G. Shumway, 1981.
Knoblock, Glenn A. *"Strong and Brave Fellows": New Hampshire's Black Soldiers and Sailors of the American Revolution, 1775–1784.* Jefferson, NC: McFarland, 2003.
Lewis, James A. *The Final Campaign of the American Revolution Rise and Fall of the Spanish Bahamas.* Columbia: University of South Carolina Press, 1991.
Lossing, Benson J., ed. "The American Historical Record and Repertory of Notes and Queries, Concerning the History and Antiquities of America and Biography of Americans." *Potter's American Monthly: An Illustrated Magazine of History, Literature, Science and Art* 3, no. 29 (May 1874), 299. J.E. Potter and Company, Philadelphia, 1874.
Lossing, Benson J. *The Life and Times of Philip Schuyler.* 2 vols. New York, 1872–1873 (Da Capo Press ed., New York, 1973).
Lossing, Benson J. *Pictorial Field-Book of the Revolution.* 2 vols. New York, 1855.
Mailler, Marion M., and Janet Dempsey. *18th Century Homes in New Windsor and Its Vicinity as Depicted by Simeon De Witt, Geographer to the Army, on His Map of the Cantonment 1783.* Vails Gate, NY: National Temple Hill Association, 1968.
Maxwell, Priscilla. *The Christian Patriot: Some Recollections of the Late Col. Hugh Maxwell, of Massachusetts; Collected and Preserved by a Daughter.* New York, 1833.
McCain, Diana Ross. "Private Deborah Sampson of the Continental Army." *Early American Life*, 24, no. 2, April 1993, 16–18 and 74–75.

McGurty, Michael S. "'A tolerably decent appearance': The Clothing of the Continental Army at the New Windsor Cantonment, 1782–83." *Military Collector & Historian* 63, no. 2 (Summer 2011): 89–100.
McGurty, Michael S. "Henry Kneeland one of Bergoines troops & defected from Winterhill." *Hudson River Valley Review* 30, no. 1 (Autumn 2013): 47–60.
Mooney, James L. *Dictionary of American Naval Fighting Ships*. 8 vols. U.S. Government Printing Office, 1959–1981.
Nell, William C. *Colored Patriots of the American Revolution*. Boston, 1855.
Nutt, John J. *Newburgh: Her Institutions, Industries and Leading Citizens*. Newburgh, NY, 1891.
Purvis, Thomas L. *Colonial America to 1763*. New York: Facts on File, 1999.
Richards, Dave. *Swords in Their Hands: George Washington and the Newburgh Conspiracy*. Candler, NC: Pisgah Press, 2013.
Richards, Leonard L. *Shays's Rebellion: The American Revolution's Final Battle*. Philadelphia: University of Pennsylvania Press, 2002.
Rodman, Ernest A. "Digging for History in the Newburgh Area of Temple Hill." Prepared for the Association of Town Historians Meeting, University of the State of New York, February 4–5, 1963, 9–21.
Royster, Charles. *A Revolutionary People at War: The Continental Army and American Character, 1775–1783*. New York: Norton, 1979.
Ruttenber, Edward M. *History of the Town of New Windsor, Orange County, N.Y.* Newburgh, NY: Historical Soc. of Newburgh Bay and the Highlands, 1912.
Ruttenber, Edward M., and Lewis H. Clark, comps. *History of Orange County, New York with Illustrations and Biographical Sketches of Many of the Pioneers and Prominent Men*. Philadelphia, 1881.
Saffron, Morris H. *Surgeon to Washington: Dr. John Cochran, (1730–1807)*. New York: Columbia University Press, 1977.
Skeen, Edward C. *John C. Armstrong, Jr., 1758–1843*. Syracuse: Syracuse University Press, 1981.
Skeen, Edward C. "The Newburgh Conspiracy Reconsidered with a Rebuttal by Richard H. Kohn." *William and Mary Quarterly*, 3rd ser., vol. 31, no. 2 (April, 1974): 273–298.
Simpson, J.A., and E.S.C. Weiner, eds. *The Compact Oxford English Dictionary*. 2nd ed. New York, 2000.
Sons of the American Revolution Society. *An Account of the Action at Tarrytown on July Fifteenth, 1781, and of Its Commemoration by the Sons of the American Revolution of Tarrytown on July Fifteenth, 1899*. New York, 1899.
Sopko, Joseph. "Geophysical and Soil Chemical Investigations at New Windsor Cantonment." 1983 Symposium on Archaeology of the Revolutionary War Period Held at the New Windsor Cantonment State Historic Site, New Windsor, New York, Charles L. Fisher, ed. *Northeast Historical Archaeology* 12 (1983): art. 6.
Sprouse, Deborah A. "Button Manufacturing in the Hudson Highlands." *Military Collector and Historian* 47, no. 1 (Spring 1995): 43–45.
Strachan, Hew. *British Military Uniforms 1768–96: The Dress of the British Army from Official Sources*. London: Arms and Armour Press, 1975.
Szatmary, David P. *Shays' Rebellion: The Making of an Agrarian Insurrection*. Amherst: University of Massachusetts Press, 1980.
Troiani, Don. *Military Buttons of the American Revolution*. Gettysburg, PA: Thomas Publications, 2001.
Troiani, Don, and James L. Kochan. *Don Troiani's Soldiers of the American Revolution*. Mechanicsburg, PA: Stackpole Books, 2007.
Troiani, Don, and James L. Kochan. *Insignia of Independence: Military Buttons, Accoutrement Plates, & Gorgets of the American Revolution*. Gettysburg, PA: Thomas Publications, 2012.
Trussell, John B.B., Jr. *Birthplace of an Army: A Study of the Valley Forge Encampment*. Harrisburg, PA: Pennsylvania Historical and Museum Commission, 1976.
Urdang, Laurence, ed. *The Random House College Dictionary*. New York, 1980.
Warner, John. *Historical Collections Being a General Collection of Interesting Facts, Traditions, Biographical Sketches, Anecdotes &c., Relating to the History and Antiquities of Every Town in Massachusetts, with Geographical Descriptions*. Worcester, MA, 1841.
Weigley, Russell F. "A War of Posts: The Morristown Encampment and the American Revolution." *Morristown: A History and Guide*. Washington, DC: National Park Service, 1983. 14–83.
Whittemore, Bradford Adams. *Memorials of the Massachusetts Society of the Cincinnati*. Boston, 1964.
Young, Alfred F. *Masquerade: The Life and Times of Deborah Sampson, Continental Soldier*. New York: Knopf, 2004.
Zlatich, Marko. *New England Soldiers of the American Revolution*. Santa Barbara: Bellerophon, 1981.
Zlatich, Marko, and Bill Younghusband. *General Washington's Army (2), 1779–1783*. London: Osprey, 1995.

Newspapers

The Independent Gazette, or, The New York Journal Revived (New York, Dec. 13, 1783—March 11, 1784), J. Holt, publisher, New York Public Library

Newburgh Daily Journal
Newburgh Gazette
Newburgh News
The New York Packet and The American Advertiser, 1776–1783, December 12, 1782, Edited by Samuel Loudon, New-York Historical Society, University Microfilm
The Pennsylvania Packet or the General Advertiser, Philadelphia, Pennsylvania, February 27, 1783, America's Historical Newspapers

Unpublished Source

Manager of New Windsor Cantonment Jane Townsend to Regional Historic Preservation Supervisor Wallace Workmaster, January 25, 1987, Memorandum: The Soldiers' Graves at NWC. New Windsor Cantonment State Historic Site Collection.

Internet Sources

Diethorn, Karie. "Charles Willson Peale's Philadelphia Museum Portraits, 1782 to 1827." *Bulletin du Centre de recherche du château de Versailles* (2017), https://doi.org/10.4000/crcv.14059.
Kingsbury, H.A. "The Symbolism of Numbers." Masonic World (www.masonicworld.com).
Masonic Dictionary, 2005–2007, https://www.masonicworld.com/education/files/masonicdictionary.htm.
Tortora, Daniel J. "Indian Patriots from Eastern Massachusetts: Six Perspectives," *Journal of the American Revolution*, February 4, 2015, https://allthingsliberty.com/2015/02/indian-patriots-from-eastern-massachusetts-six-perspectives/.

Index

Abel, John (private) 28
absences, unauthorized 28, 35, 36, 79, 80, 129–131; *see* cashiering; desertion
accoutrements: prevention of trading away 46; stoppages of pay for abused or missing 19, 75
acquittals 28, 93, 130
Adams, John 71
Adams, Margaret (Peggy; née Harden; wife of Peter Adams) 151
Adams, Peter (private) 151
Adams, Samuel (surgeon) 49, 53, 71
African Americans 9, 37, 40, 43, 54, 78, 119, 128, 151, 153, 157, 158
Albany, New York 9, 10, 22, 30, 36, 41, 45, 50, 59, 60, 67, 106, 115, 144, 148
Albany Post Road 10, 73
alcohol abuse 47, 80, 83
Allen, Ethan 155
Allen, Jeremiah (drum major; private) 128
Allen, Noah (private) 132
Alvey, John D. (deputy postmaster) 79
ammunition 73–75, 83, 123, 133, 144
amputation 53, 54, 148, 152
Amsterdam, Dutch Republic 66
André, John (major) 27
Annapolis, Maryland 151
anonymous letters *see* Newburgh Conspiracy
Anspach, Peter (deputy quartermaster) 148
Apothecary's Store, New Windsor, New York 142
archways 27
Ark 88
Armand, Charles (colonel) 91
Armand's Legion 91
armorers 72

Armstrong, John (major) 97, 101, 102, 108, 109, 110, 111, 114, 115, 116, 117
Armstrong, John, Sr. (major general) 29, 97
army organization 22, 23, 121, 122, 145
Arnold, Benedict (major general) 41
Articles of War 127, 128
artificers 27, 31, 33, 55, 77
artillery 8, 11, 15, 27, 29, 42, 75, 84, 85, 121, 123, 142, 147, 151, 155; New Windsor 1780–81 huts 10, 27, 49, 50, 150; 2nd Regiment of Artillery 31, 42; 3rd Regiment 19, 80
Artillery Artificer Regiment 27
artillery encampment of 1780–81 10, 27, 53
assaults 28, 35, 130, 137
auction of structures 31, 90, 150, 151
Azores islands 58

Badge of Military Merit 68, 69, 162
Badlam, Ezra (lieutenant colonel) 119
Bagnell, Richard (lieutenant) 78
Bailey, Ephrain (private) 36
Baker, Beney (private) 36
Ballard, Jeremiah (captain) 43
Baltimore, Maryland 143
Bancroft, George (author): *History of the Formation of the Constitution of the United States of America* 102
Bank of North America 94, 96
Barber, Francis (lieutenant colonel; colonel) 14, 30, 55, 56
Barber, Mary (Ogden) 56
Barber, William (major; assistant inspector for the northern army) 60, 74, 101, 102

Barlow, Joel (chaplain) 37, 157
Barnett, John (chaplain) 37
Barns, Samuel (?) (corporal; private) 137
Baylies, Hodijah (major) 80
bayonets 23, 24, 54, 63, 71–73, 122, 123
beacons 17
Beaks, John 75
Beals, Elijah (private) 56
Beaver Dam (Silver) Stream 10, 11, 15, 19, 26, 51, 91, 124
Bedford, Massachusetts 34, 159
Bedford, New York 16
Bedlow, William 133
Belknap, Squire Abel 83
Belknap house 13, 46
Bell, William 11
belts 71, 72, 74
Benjamin, John 160
Benjamin, Samuel (lieutenant) 37
Bennington, Vermont 148
Bennington, battle of 133
Benson, Egbert (attorney general of New York) 149
Benton, Selah (captain; superintendent of New Windsor hospital) 49
Berkshire County, Massachusetts 154
Bethlehem Meeting House 37
Bible 36–38, 87, 88, 99
Billings, William (composer: "Independence") 134
Birch, Warren (corporal) 137
Birdsall, Daniel 79
Bissell, Daniel (sergeant) 69
Black Horse (Columbus), New Jersey 40
Black Prince (ship) 150
blacksmith shops 32, 150
Blaisdell, John (sergeant; private) 28
Blake, Eleazer (sergeant) 159
blankets 28, 75, 126
blaspheming *see* profanity
bleeding 51, 54; internal 54

221

Index

blistering 51
Blooming Grove, New York 40, 160
Board of War 74, 99, 107
boats 9, 16, 33, 64, 79, 144, 148; ice 16
Bonetta (ship) 132
boots *see* shoes
Bordone, Count Francesco dal Verme (translator and servant) 148
Boston, Massachusetts 8, 24, 35, 58, 66, 90, 146, 151, 154
Boston Gazette (Benjamin Edes, publisher) 59
Boudinot, Elias (president of Congress) 115, 133
Bowman, Phineas (captain) 130
Boyd, Robert, Jr. 150
Boynton, Edward C. (major; West Point historian) 89
Bradford (DD-545; destroyer) 152
Bradford, Gamaliel (lieutenant) 126, 152
Brandywine, Pennsylvania, battle of 97, 159
breeches 58, 59, 62, 67
Brewster, Deacon Samuel 150; house 12, 45, 150
Brewster, Samuel, Jr. 150; house 15
Bronx, New York 156
Brookfield, Massachusetts 38, 39, 161
Brooks, David (assistant clothier general) 133
Brooks, John (lieutenant colonel) 99, 98, 104, 113, 116, 117, 157
Brown, John (steward) 49
Brown, William (sergeant) 68
Brutus *see* McDougall, Alexander (major general)
Bunker Hill, Charlestown, Massachusetts, battle of 39, 156, 159
Burlington Gazette, New Jersey 40
Burnet, Robert (lieutenant) 84, 85, 89
Burr, Aaron 116, 156
Butter Hill (Storm King Mountain) 9, 17, 146
buttons 59, 63, 64, 129
Byard house (Brig. Gen. Edward Hand headquarters) 13

Cadiz, Spain 58
Caesar, Julius (dictator) 110
Caffieri, Jean-Jacques (Brig. Gen. Richard Montgomery monument sculptor) 157

Caldwell & Garrison (engineers) 89
Camden, South Carolina, battle of 96, 97 108
Canada 8, 107, 148
Canadian Regiment (Hazen's) 9, 15, 17, 60, 104, 131, 144
cancer 54
canteens 71, 75
caps 65, 66
Caribbean 7, 8, 97
Carleton, Guy (general; governor) 16, 148, 155
Carlton, Moses (lieutenant) 78
Carter, John (Church) 44
cartridge boxes 24, 71, 74, 75, 122
cashiering 129
catchrolls 19, 130, 131
causeway 20, 89, 91
Centennial New Windsor encampment celebration 161, 162
chaplains 37, 38, 77, 90, 157; *see also* Evans, Israel; Gano, John
Charles III (king of Spain) 7
Charleston, South Carolina 6, 8, 108, 124
Chastellux, chevalier Francois-Jean de (major general) 29, 32 49
Chester, New York 9
children 31, 41, 42, 53, 151, 160
Churchill, Elijah (sergeant) 68
circular letter 144, 145
Civil War, American 159, 161, 162
Clausewitz, Carl von (major general) 20
Clinton, George (brigadier general and New York governor) 17, 33, 104, 142–144, 148, 150
Clinton, James (brigadier general) 52, 148
Close, John (the reverend, Presbyterian church of New Windsor; Presbyterian church of Newburgh; Bethlehem Meeting House) 37, 150
clothier's store, Newburgh, New York 28
clothing 46, 58, 60, 67, 75
coats 57, 59–63, 66
Clove blockhouse 9, 15
Clove Road 11, 12, 26, 49
coats 57–63, 66
Cobb, David (lieutenant colonel) 10, 80, 91, 111
Cobb, Melatiah (sergeant) 78
Coburn, Asa (captain) 153
Cochran, John (director general

of the hospital of the United States) 31, 51, 55, 79
Cochran, Robert (lieutenant colonel) 51, 54
cockade for hats and caps 65, 66
Cogdon, John (private) 28
Cogswell, Thomas (wagonmaster general) 148
Cogswell, William (surgeon's mate) 49, 150
coins 44, 94, 95, 104, 128, 129, 141
collation 83
Comfort Sands & Company (contractor) 43, 44, 63
Commander-in Chief's Guard 51, 77, 146, 159
Commissary Bell's *see* Bell, William
commission, officer 38, 39, 151
Congress: pensions 40, 156, 159–161
Connecticut 22
Connecticut 5th Regiment 49, 68
Connecticut Line 8, 9, 15, 19, 20, 23, 58, 60, 120, 137, 145
Constitutional Convention 26, 155
Continental Congress 19, 33, 35, 55, 57, 62, 64, 70, 93–95, 116, 128; Annapolis, Maryland relocation 151; army committee 98, 99, 109, 116, 117; army northern command dispute 106, 107; army structure 23, 34, 48, 151, 152; army women and children 31, 41, 42; *Articles of War* 127, 128; blame for doing little for army 143; Board of War 74, 107; Canadian Regiment 144; circular letter 144, 145; commissions 38, 39, 151; dal Verme introduction letter 148; enemy communication 16; frontier posts 148, 149; furloughs/discharges 79, 140; Gates defeat inquiry repeal 96, 108; hospital department 48; invalids 51; mail 79; monument for Brigadier General Richard Montgomery 157; musket and musical instrument gratuity 142; officer pension 69, 98, 103, 115; Ohio land grand petition 152; peace announcement 132, 133; powers 93, 94; Princeton, New Jersey, withdrawal

to 183; Robert Morris resignation threat 99, 141; settlement of army accounts 110, 115, 141; Shay's Rebellion 154; taxation 8, 45, 93, 94, 96, 113; thanksgiving 77; Washington commission return 151; Washington refusal to pressure 108, 110, 143; Washington visit 151
Converse, James (colonel; father of Patience) 39
Converse, Patience 39
Conway, Thomas (brigadier general) 107, 154, 156, 157
Conway Cabal 107, 110, 156, 157
Corning, Elwood A. 88
corruption 94, 142
Cortlandt, Philip Van (colonel) 57, 143, 144
counterfeiting 94, 95, 141
courts-martial hut 27
Crompond, New York 8
Cromwell, Oliver (private) 40
Crook, Joseph (lieutenant; superintendent of New Windsor hospital) 49
crosses of St. Louis 71
Croton River 15, 16
Crown Point, New York 148
Crystal Palace Exhibition, London, England 161
cupping 51
currency (bills of credit) 95, 96, 141, 153
Currie, John (merchant) 63, 64, 79
Cushing, Nathaniel (captain) 153
Cuthbertson, Bennett (captain): *Cuthbertson's System for the Complete Interior Management and Oeconomy of a Battalion of Infantry* 73
Cutler, Rufus (son of Tobias) 158
Cutler, Tobias (private) 158

Daily, London (private) 158
Danbury, Connecticut 9, 39, 161
dancing 37, 80, 81, 132
Dartmouth, Massachusetts 35
Davis, Joseph 150
Davis, William 75
Day, Luke (captain) 153, 155
Dayton, Elias (colonel and brigadier general) 138
Dayton, fort 148
Dean, Thomas (chairman for Class III of the Town of Bedford, Massachusetts) 34
Dearborn, Henry (lieutenant colonel; major general) 157

deaths 56, 151
Denniston, John 14, 56
De Peyster, Abraham (director general of the Hospital of the United States John Cochran headquarters) 55
depreciation certificates 94, 154, 156
desertion 18, 23, 31, 42, 48, 80, 119, 127, 131, 132, 138; encouragement in German auxiliaries and royalists 35, 132, 146; pardon 132; prohibition enlisting French and enemy deserters 35, 119, 160; recovery 59, 120
Detroit, fort 149
De Witt, Simeon (geographer of the United States) 11–15
disability benefits 40, 51, 156
disbandment of army 136, 140–147, 151, 152
discharges 137, 140
dismissal 119
disputes 130, 138
disrespect to superior 35, 130, 137
Dobbs Ferry, New York, blockhouse 15, 17
docks 20, 64, 79
Dodge, Samuel (ensign) 137
Downing, Samuel (private) 134, 159
duels 55, 116, 129, 156
Duer, William 45
Duer & Parker contractor 104, 138, 142
Duerzen, Abraham Van (tavern keeper) 78
Duportail, Louis le Bègue de Presle (major general) 14
Dusenberry (widow) 150
Dutch Republic 7, 10, 64, 66 151

Eastchester, New York 35
Edes, Benjamin (publisher, *Boston Gazette*) 59
Edinburgh, Scotland 74
Edmonston, James 12, 15, 55
Edmonston, William 12, 15, 55, 97, 98
Edwards, John (private) 132
Edwards, Thomas (lieutenant; judge advocate general) 27, 144
effigy 138
Ellison family 52
Ellison, John 36, 97, 149, 150; house (headquarters for generals Nathanael Greene, Henry Knox and Horatio Gates) 11, 27, 55, 97, 101, 102, 108

Ellison, Thomas, house (Washington's headquarters mid-1779 and winter 1780–81) 100
Ellison, William 20, 64, 79, 149
Elmer, Daniel 79
embargoes 95, 96
Emerson, Ralph Waldo 76
encampment 8, 10, 11, 15, 18, 20, 25–32, 61, 81, 89, 126, 127, 129–131, 144, 149, 150, 160
engrossers 95
epaulettes 65, 70
entertainment 77–81; *see* games; health; music; religious services; Wyoma
Eustis, William (surgeon) 49, 101, 148
Eutaw Springs, South Carlina, battle of 124
evacuation of British 146, 148
Evans, Israel (chaplain) 37, 77, 83, 88, 146
Evans, Samuel (forage master) 93
Everett, Pelathiah (lieutenant) 78
Eysandeau, William (lieutenant) 80

Fairlie, James (captain; Maj. Gen. Friedrich von Steuben aide) 148
farms 10, 33, 74
Farnam, Jonathan (sergeant major) 78
fatigues 19, 20, 27, 35, 50, 66, 78, 81, 91, 131, 134, 136
feathers for hats and caps 64–66
Federalist Party 156
fence rails 77, 123, 150
feu de joie 83, 136
Finch 89, 90
fines 55, 93
Finley, James Burr (surgeon) 40
firewood 8, 10, 18, 49, 50, 66, 77, 98, 149–151
fireworks 20, 26, 27, 134–136
1st American Regiment 151, 152, 154, 159
Fish, Hamilton (former New York governor) 161
Fish, Nicholas (major) 102
fish spear 46
Fisher, Bartholomew (forage master) 93
fishing 46
Fishkill, New York 10, 15, 46, 72, 138; depot 20
Fishkill Landing (Beacon) New York 17, 20, 72

Index

Fisk, Cato (fifer) 158
flags 16, 23, 24, 84, 86, 150; regimental 26, 75, 76, 143, 144
flints 72, 73
flogging *see* lashing
Florida 7
forage 97, 98; allowance 92, 93, 97, 98, 142, 150; shortage 92, 93, 97, 98
Fordham University, Bronx, New York 156
Fordyce, the Rev. David (author: *The Temple of Virtue: A Dream*) 81, 82
Fordyce, James (publisher: *The Temple of Virtue: A Dream*) 81
forgiveness solicitation in front of unit 130
Foster, Thomas (private) 34, 77, 78; belief of fairness of military regulations, but not enforcement 129; blacksmithing nails 32; chaplains and sermons commentary 37, 38, 90; desire to leave service and 132; furlough overstay and reduction in rank 35, 36, 129; increasing conflicts between officers and soldiers 138; Irish contempt for 47; Middleborough, Massachusetts, home 35, 161; Middlebury, Vermont, move 161; peace announcement 132, 134–136, religiosity 36, 37; shooting by camp guards 53, Temple of Virtue 36, 81, 82, 88, 90, 150; Thanksgiving service at Presbyterian Church in New Windsor 77; unrest over delay in discharging army 138
fox hunt 93, 97
fractures 53
France 5–8, 57, 58, 62, 64, 66, 67, 70, 72, 83, 94, 97, 101, 133, 136, 148, 151, 153, 157; expeditionary force 6, 8, 11, 39, 44, 58, 67, 109, 119, 124
Franklin, Benjamin 26, 27, 157
fraud 93–95
Fraunces, Samuel, tavern, New York City, New York 151
Frederick the Great, king of Prussia 121
Freeman, Thomas D. (lieutenant) 130, 138
French alliance anniversary celebration 82, 83, 98, 100, 132

French and Indian War 6, 55, 97
French Revolution 7, 71
frontier posts 148, 149
Frothingham, Richard (field commissary of military stores) 14, 76
Frye, Ebenezer (captain) 129
furloughs 35, 36, 79, 80, 129, 138; end of war 137, 140, 141, 143, 144, 146
Furman, John (lieutenant) 150

gaiters 67
Gamboll, George (private) 137
games 78, 128, 129
gangrene 53
Gannett, Benjamin 40
Gano, John (chaplain) 37, 38, 134
gardens 25, 46
Gates, Elizabeth (Betsy) 31, 80, 98, 116, 156
Gates, Horatio (major general) 12, 13, 20, 33, 34, 69, 70, 84, 97, 107, 156; artificer made bed 31, 55; Camden, South Carolina, defeat, dismissal and reinstatement 96, 98, 108; declining health and death of wife 116, 156; effort to replace General Schuyler as commander of northern army 106, 107; forage shortage 97, 98; General Chastellux visit headquarters 29; headquarters guard 98; John Ellison house headquarters 11, 12, 15, 55, 64, 97, 101; loss of horses due to forage shortage 92; Newburgh Conspiracy 97, 99, 100, 102, 105, 108, 110, 114, 116, 117; officer furlough authorization 80; perilous financial condition 116; plea for wife to join him in camp 31, 98; possible feigned sickness on anniversary of French alliance 100; remarriage 156; sale of wagon and team 149; sickness during anniversary of French alliance celebration 83, 100; stable for headquarters 98; Surgeon General Cochran occupation of desired headquarters 55; Temple of Virtue 81–83; Trinity Churchyard Cemetery unmarked grave, New York City 156, 157; Washington relationship deterioration 99, 100, 105–108

George, fort, Lake George 148
German auxiliaries 72, 146; *see also* Kneeland, Henry (private)
Germantown, Pennsylvania, battle of 97
Gerould, Jerusha 159
Gibbs, Caleb (captain) 51
Gibraltar 152; siege of 7, 79
Gilbert, Benjamin (lieutenant) 24, 27, 34, 38–40, 46, 47, 56, 63, 64, 65, 71, 72, 78, 80, 81, 90, 104, 119–120, 131, 132, 142–143, 152, 153, 161; alcohol abuse 47, 83; courtmartial of commander Lieutenant Colonel Newhall 130; deterioration of physical condition by war 143; failure to purchase sequestered royalist estate 143; illness Danbury, Connecticut 39; marriage to Mary Cornwall 161; pay 45, 46, 104, 105, 141; promiscuity 38, 39; surveying 152, 161; Wyoma, brothel 39, 40, 81, 142
Gilbert, Daniel 39
Gilbert, Mary (Cornwall) (wife of Lieutenant Benjamin Gilbert) 161
Giles, Samuel (private) 137
Gillon, Alexander (commodore) 66
glasshouse 29
Goodale, Nathan (captain) 80, 130, 143, 153
Goodwill Church Cemetery, Montgomery, New York 56
Gorham (New York) Purchase *see* Maxwell, Hugh (lieutenant colonel)
Goshen, New York 79
Goshen Road 11, 12, 14, 124
Gouvion, Jean Baptiste (colonel) 13, 14, 136
Grand Armee 157
Grand Parade 90, 131, 134, 146
gratuity 119
Great Britain 5–8, 36, 58, 79, 88, 102, 143, 148, 151
Great Lakes 5, 148
Greaton, John (brigadier general) 61, 145, 151
Greene, Christopher (colonel) 16
Greene, Nathanael (major general) 9, 11, 21, 45, 117, 124
Greenman, Jeremiah (ensign) 24
Gregg, James (captain) 41, 54
Grieve, George (translator, *Chastellux's Travels*) 96

Index

gristmills 10
guards 19, 26, 28, 46, 49, 53, 66, 78, 98, 120, 121, 130, 131, 145, 146, 150, 151; irregular march 126, 152

Haldimand, Frederick (general and governor of Canada) 148
Hall, Jude (private) 158
Hamilton, Alexander 99–102, 108, 110, 115, 116, 117, 156, 157
Hand, Edward (brigadier general; adjutant general) 13, 20, 31, 48, 70, 83, 113, 148
Hand, Katherine 13, 31, 83
Harrison, Richard (Continental agent) 58
Hartford, Connecticut 144, 156
Hasbrouck, Tryntje 11, 13, 79, 109, 148, 149, 163
Haskell, Elnathon (captain; aide to Maj. Gen. Robert Howe) 150–151
hats 65
haversacks 71, 75
Hawes, William (captain) 74
Haws, Pelatiah (justice of peace Westchester County) 17
Hayward, William (sergeant) 138
Hazen, Moses (brevet brigadier general) 15, 144
Heath, William (major general) 9, 43, 58, 137, 138, 146; peace proclamation 134; Society of Cincinnati opposition and withdrawal 71; Squire Abel Belknap house headquarters 12, 13, 46; Temple description 84, 90
Heer, Bartholomew von (captain) 9
helions 39
Hendry, Daniel (ward master) 49
Henry V 129
Henry, Patrick (governor) 52
Herkimer, George 148
Herkimer, Nicholas 148
Herkimer, fort 148
Hervey, the Rev. James (author: *Theron and Aspasio or, a Series of Dialogues and Letters*) 36
hewing 32, 82
Heyward, Benjamin (captain) 113
Higby, Moses (doctor) 52
Hillegas, Michael (United States treasurer) 46
Hillegas Notes 46
Hillsborough, North Carolina 108

Hiram Abif 88
Hiram of Tyre 88
Historical Society of Newburgh Bay and the Highlands 162
Hitchcock, Luke (captain) 129
Hiwell, John (music inspector and superintendent; 3rd Artillery Regiment Lieutenant) 19, 80
Hobby, Jonathan (captain) 119
Hodgdon, Samuel (commissary general of military stores) 76, 94, 95, 113, 114, 143, 149
Holland, Park (lieutenant) 39, 80
Holt, John (publisher, *Independent Gazette or, The New York Journal Revived*, New York City, New York) 40
Holy Royal Arch 86
homosexuality 38
Honorary Badge of Distinction 67–69, 80, 158; public removal punishment 67, 68, 128, 132, 137
Hooker, Zibeon (lieutenant) 46
Horr, Mr. (blacksmith) 150
Horr's Blacksmith Shop, Nine Partners, New York 150
horses 25, 31, 41, 71, 92, 97, 98, 125, 134–135, 149, 150, 155, 156, 160; death of Colonel Barber's 56; forage shortage 91–93, 97, 98
Hosmer, Joseph (superior for Middlesex County, Massachusetts) 34
hospital in New Windsor 10, 37, 41, 46, 48–51, 53, 55, 56, 77, 90, 121, 150
Howe, Robert (major general) 12, 45, 79, 80, 150, 151
Hubbard, Humphrey (private) 128
Hudson Highlands 5, 6, 27, 35, 39, 55, 58, 62, 64, 79, 108, 148, 159
Hudson River 5, 6, 8, 9–11, 15–17, 39, 45, 46, 64, 78, 79; chain at West Point, 5, 133
Hudson Valley 8, 41, 45, 55, 97, 117, 119
Hughes, James Miller (lieutenant colonel) 101
Hull, William (lieutenant colonel) 148, 157
humiliation *see* shaming
Humphreys, David (lieutenant colonel) 98, 144
Hunter, Andrew (chaplain) 37
hunting: prohibition 46

Huntington, Jedediah (brigadier general) 70, 137
Hurlbut, George (captain) 102
hygiene 19, 79, 126

Ides of March, March 15, 1783 110
illumination frame 20, 136
impetigo 19, 52, 80
Impost 96, 104
Impressment 9, 95
"Independence" (song) 134
Independent Gazette or, The New York Journal Revised 40
India 7
inflation 72, 95, 116, 154
inoculation 52, 53
inspections 59, 60, 61, 65–67, 74, 83, 124
insubordination 137
Invalid Corps 8, 15, 17, 27, 51, 70
invalid inspection 50, 51
invigoration 52
Irish 47

Jackson, Henry (colonel) 10, 146, 151, 154, 159
Jackson, Michael (colonel) 45, 61, 118, 128, 145, 149
Jacobin 71
Jay, John 58, 71, 99
Jefferson, Thomas 71, 156, 157
Job (Biblical prophet) 86
Joel, Richard (private) 132
Jones, John (brother) 149
Jones, John (doctor; professor of surgery, King's College, New York City) 49, 54
Jones, John Paul (captain) 67
Jones, Joseph (congressman) 111, 113, 115
Jones, Thomas 149
Journals of the Continental Congress 33

Keith, James (major) 65
Kempenfelt, Richard (admiral) 79
King, Joseph 27
King, Philip (private) 28
Kingston, New York 114
kitchens 25, 126; for officers 25, 31, 43
knapsacks 24, 71, 75, 151
Kneeland (Kickeland), Henry (private) 34, 35, 159, 160
Knox, Henry (major general) 8, 11, 17, 20, 45, 70, 75, 79, 83, 113, 114, 117, 133, 148, 150–152, 154, 156, 158, 160
Knox, Lucy 83
Knox's Headquarters State Historic Site 88, 163

Index

Lafayette, fort 16, 20; *see also* Verplanck's Point, New York
Lafayette, Marquis de (major general) 39, 20, 21, 71, 105, 107, 140, 153
Lake, Mary (matron) 49
Lake Champlain 5, 6, 106
Lake George 5, 148
La Luzerne, chevalier Antoine de (French minister to United States) 133, 136
Lamb, John (colonel) 142
Lancaster, Pennsylvania 9, 55, 60
land bounty 35, 152
Lansdale, Thomas (major) 61
Lashing 28, 128, 129, 131, 132, 137, 138
Latta, James (geographer of the United States) 14
Latta, James (merchant and highway master for the New Windsor district) 90, 149
laundry 42, 66
Laurens, John (lieutenant colonel) 66, 72, 94
Lawton, William (surgeon's mate) 80
laudable pus 53
laxatives 52
leave 120; *see also* furlough
levee meetings 80, 84, 89, 90, 127
Lexington Green, Massachusetts, battle of 133
Light Dragoons, British 17th 133
Light Dragoons, 2nd Regiment *see* 2nd Light Dragoons
lightning strike of Temple 150
Lillie, John (captain) 114
Lincoln, Benjamin (major general and Secretary at War) 9, 57, 58, 61, 67, 72, 74, 76, 92, 98, 109, 115, 126, 135, 154, 155
the lines (outposts) 14–17, 20, 24, 35, 130, 133
Litchfield, Connecticut 144
Litchfield, New York 160
Little Britain, New York 79, 84
Lockwood, William (chaplain) 37
London, England 48, 161
Long Island, New York, battle of 33, 39, 97
Long Island Sound 9
Lossing, Benson (author, *Pictorial Fieldbook of the American Revolution*) 81, 84, 85, 89, 114
Loudon, Samuel (publisher,

The New York Packet and the American Advertiser) 46, 137, 138
Loudon, William (drum major) 19
Louis XVI (king of France) 7, 66
Lovekins, Joseph (private) 56
Lunt, Daniel (captain) 153
Lunt, Ezra (Massachusetts state clothier) 62

Mackinac, fort 149
Madeira islands 58
Madrid, Spain 58
magazines 33, 43, 63, 77, 133, 144
mail 78, 79
Maine 7, 21, 97
Malaria 50, 52
Mamaroneck, New York 35
Mandeville house 14
Manhattan, New York 17, 151
map 11–15
marauding 28, 130, 131
Marechaussee Corps (provost) 9, 129
Marie Antoinette (queen of France) 153
Marietta, Ohio 153
markets 46
Marquis de Lafayette (ship) 58, 63
Martin, Joseph Plumb (sergeant; author: *Private Yankee Doodle*) 34, 39, 62, 72, 80, 104
Maryland 3rd detachment 6, 9, 15, 16, 28–31, 58–61, 63, 64, 91, 98, 124, 143, 150; attachment to New Jersey Brigade 9; Clove blockhouse 9; French alliance anniversary review 83
Mashpee, Cape Cod, Massachusetts 37, 158
Masonic Order 26, 85–89, 161
Massachusetts 8th Regiment 27, 37, 45, 61, 83, 118, 119, 126, 128, 129, 137, 149, 156
Massachusetts 5th Regiment 27, 39, 46, 56, 61, 83, 90, 120, 126, 128, 130, 152, 153; *see also* Gilbert, Benjamin (lieutenant)
Massachusetts 1st Brigade 26, 31, 34, 73, 83, 91, 124, 150, 153
Massachusetts 1st Regiment 28, 129, 151, 153
Massachusetts 4th Regiment 20, 40, 45, 46, 63, 65, 66, 126, 153–155, 159; *see also* Sampson, Deborah (private)

Massachusetts Line 5, 8, 15, 19, 22, 26–31, 58–65, 98, 120, 143, 147, 148, 152, 153; attrition 119; chaplains 37, 157; consolidation 19, 23; officer pension commutation acceptance 115; reorganization after furlough 145
Massachusetts 9th Regiment 20, 41, 53; pending disbandment 20
Massachusetts 2nd Brigade 15, 31, 59, 61, 82, 130, 150, 151
Massachusetts 2nd Regiment 65, 66, 82, 126, 128, 129, 132, 150, 153
Massachusetts 7th Regiment 56, 126, 129, 130, 137, 138, 152, 153, 155; *see also* Foster, Thomas (private)
Massachusetts 6th Regiment 137, 150, 153
Massachusetts Soldiers and Sailors of the Revolutionary War 130
Massachusetts 10th Regiment 9, 20, 37, 49, 58, 59, 61, 63, 153, 158
Massachusetts 3rd Brigade 26, 31, 34, 91, 124, 131, 149, 150, 153
Massachusetts 3rd Regiment 18, 119, 129, 149
Maxwell, Hugh (lieutenant colonel) 149, 156
McCay, Daniel (ensign) 46
McClenachan, Blair (merchant) 104
McCoy, Mr. 149
McDougall, Alexander (major general) 98, 116, 117
McFingal (John Trumbull, author) 138
McGill, William 89, 162
McKenzie, Henry (author, *Julia de Roubigne*; *Man of Feeling*) 137
McLean, John (corporal; private) 46
Meacham, John (lieutenant) 129
Meadows, ? (corporal; private) 137
measles 47, 50, 138
medical theory 51
Mediterranean Sea 7
Melmoth, Courtney (author: *Emma Corbett*) 137; *see also* Pratt, Samuel Jackson
mental illness 41, 54
Mercer, Hugh (brigadier general) 48, 97

Index

merchant shops *see* store (merchant)
Middleborough, Massachusetts 35, 161
Middlebury, Vermont 161
Middlefield, New York 161
Mifflin, Thomas (president of Congress) 129, 152
militia 9, 21, 22, 27, 39, 47, 108, 124, 135, 148, 153, 154, 155, 161; exemption from service 22; levies 9, 21, 22, 120; New York levies 9, 21, 27, 101, 120
Miller, Henry (corporal) 150
Milliner, Alexander (drummer) 159
Minorca 7
Mitchell, Uriah (captain; deputy quartermaster) 13
Mohawk River 5, 41
Mohawk Valley, New York 148, 159, 160
money *see* coins; currency
Monmouth, New Jersey, battle of 35, 40, 97, 120, 159
Montgomery, Janet (Livingston) 157
Montgomery, Richard (brigadier general) 157
Monticello, Virginia 71
Morris, Gouverneur (assistant to Superintendent of Finance Robert Morris) 99, 102, 115, 117
Morris, Lewis (congressional emissary) 16
Morris, Robert (Superintendent of Finance) 31, 41, 42, 44, 45, 63, 92–94, 96, 99, 102, 104, 105, 110, 115, 116, 141, 144
Morris Notes 63, 96, 104, 105, 141, 142
Morristown, New Jersey 11, 32, 48, 52, 55, 78
Moscow, Russia 157
Moses 88
Mount Ararat 88
Mount Pleasant, Pennsylvania 161
Mount Sinai 88
Mount Vernon, Virginia 12, 79, 99, 151
Mountainville hut 162
Munnel, James 28
murder attempt 28
Murderer's (Moodna) Creek 9, 11, 15, 16, 20, 22, 149
murders 79
music 19, 23, 26, 56, 63, 65, 77, 118, 121, 122, 128, 132, 137, 142–144, 158, 159; drum calls 18, 19, 28, 121; drum shortage 19; instruction 18,
19; orchestra in Temple 84, 90; performances in Temple 80, 90, 134
muskets 24, 25, 29, 46, 66, 71–73, 75, 122, 123, 131, 142, 151, 155
mutiny 39, 127, 137, 147, 148

Napoleon 20, 157
Narragansett Bay, Rhode Island 6
National Park Service 88, 162
National Temple Hill Association 84, 88–90, 162, 163
Native Americans 8, 9, 37, 54, 152, 157, 158
neck stock 67
Nelson, Henry (lieutenant) 82, 83
Nesbitt, Robert 153
New Bedford, Massachusetts 35
New Bridge crossing of Croton River 16
New England 5, 37, 48, 58, 97, 152, 158
New Hampshire Battalion 146, 148
New Hampshire Brigade 5, 9, 12, 22, 28, 30, 31, 58–60, 62–64, 72, 91, 120, 124, 133, 143, 145, 150, 157; acceptance of officer pension commutation 115; chaplain *see* Evans, Israel; desertions 138; French alliance anniversary review 83
New Hampshire 1st Regiment/ New Hampshire Regiment 98, 129
New Hampshire 2nd Regiment/ New Hampshire Battalion 62, 63, 98, 132, 134, 158, 159

New Jersey Brigade 5, 8, 9, 12, 22, 28–31, 37, 46, 47, 60, 61, 64, 72, 83, 91, 115, 137, 143, 150; *see also* Maryland 3rd detachment
New Jersey 1st Regiment 16, 20, 56, 60, 61, 70, 79, 98, 116, 117
New Jersey Line 39, 147
New Jersey 2nd Regiment 43, 98; death of Colonel Francis Barber 14, 55, 56; Private Oliver Cromwell African American soldier 40
New Windsor, New York 5, 9, 10–15, 24
New Windsor Cantonment State Historic Site 163
New York Brigade 5, 8, 9, 12, 22, 28, 29, 31, 41, 42, 46, 51,
60, 61, 63, 72, 83, 90, 91, 124, 143, 144, 150; acceptance of officer pension commutation 115; chaplain *see* Gano, John; presentation of flags and instruments to Governor Clinton 143, 144; uniform 58–61, 63, 64
New York City 5, 6, 8–10, 16, 39, 55, 58, 94, 97, 121, 133, 135, 136, 146, 151, 156, 157, 161; delay in British evacuation 146, 148; illegal trade with 15, 16, 95
New York 1st Regiment 19, 28, 29, 32, 46, 54, 60, 65–67, 98, 141, 144, 150, 159
New York levies 9, 21, 27, 101, 120
New York 140th Volunteer Infantry 159
New York 124th Volunteer Infantry "Orange Blossoms" 161, 162
The New York Packet and the American Advertiser (Samuel Loudon, publisher) 46, 64, 79, 149
New York 2nd Regiment 9, 28, 60, 61, 98, 112, 137
New York State Office of Parks, Recreation and Historic Preservation 163
Newburgh, New York 11, 13, 15, 20, 28, 37, 78–81, 89, 101, 109, 127, 133, 148, 150, 151, 162
Newburgh Conspiracy 99, 100, 102–105, 107, 108, 110, 113–117, 156; anonymous letters 69, 97, 101, 102, 108–110, 114, 115; army committee to Congress 98, 109, 116, 117; Colonel Walter Stewart initiation of crisis 101, 103–105, 110, 117; Philadelphia origins 99, 110, 115; Temple meeting 110–113; Washington response 109–113
Newhall, Ezra (lieutenant colonel) 130
Newport, Rhode Island, battle of 7, 120, 159
Niagara, fort 149
Nicola, Lewis (colonel) 51, 70
Nine Partners Patent, Dutchess County, New York 150
Noah 88
North, Lord (prime minister) 6
North Carolina, regulators 154
North Castle, New York 35
northern lights 133
Northwest Territory 157
nostalgia 49, 50

Index

Oakley, John (sergeant) 137
Ogden, Aaron (captain) 16, 56
Ogden, Matthias (colonel) 16, 70, 79, 98, 99, 116, 117
Ohio Company of Associates 152, 153
Ohio military land grants petition 152
Oliver, Peter (private) 78
Oliver, Robert (major) 82; Ohio Company of Associates 153
Ontario, Lake 9
orchards 10
Oriskany, battle of 148
Osborn, Aaron (sergeant) 41, 146, 160
Osborn, Aaron, Jr. 146, 160
Osborn, Phebe 41, 146
Osborn, Sarah 34, 40, 41, 146, 160, 161
Oswald, Eleazer (publisher, *Independent Gazetteer*, Philadelphia, Pennsylvania) 115
Oswegatchie, fort 149
Oswego, fort 149
Oswego, New York attack 9, 10, 21, 54
Oswego River 9
Otsego, Lake 148, 161
overalls 58, 67

paintings for peace treaty celebration 136
Paoli, Pennsylvania, battle of 73
parade grounds 26, 83, 90, 124, 126, 131, 134, 138, 146
pardons 132, 137
Paris, France 71, 99, 133, 136
Parker, Benjamin (private) 120
Parker, Daniel 45, 104, 105, 136, 138
Parliament 55, 76
Parsons, Eli 155
passes 19; *see also* furloughs
pastures 149
Paterson, John (brigadier general) 40, 61, 67, 73, 138, 145, 150, 154
Paulding, John 27
pay for army 23, 40, 42, 46, 64, 66, 99, 101, 113, 118, 119, 129, 133, 141, 142, 156: advances proposal 105; arrears 8, 57, 79, 94, 99, 103, 116; danger of failure to 98, 115; disability 40, 51, 156; forage allowance 92, 93, 97, 98, 142, 150; gratuity 140, 142; month pay 104, 105; musicians extra 19, 142; pay and depreciation certificates discount 94; sale to 141, 153–156; settlement of accounts 115, 133, 140, 142, 143; Society of Cincinnati relief fund subscription 70; stoppages 19, 28, 31, 55, 75, 93; subsistence allowance 23, 46, 64, 101, 110, 116, 133, 142; three month pay certificates 141; wood cutting for hospital allowance 49, 77
paymaster accounts 46, 133
peace announcement 7, 132, 134, 135
peace celebration April 19, 1783 20, 26, 27, 134, 135
peace treaty celebration preparations 20, 136; cancellation 136
Peale, Charles Willson 136
Peekskill, New York 17, 73, 79
Pembroke, Massachusetts 37
Pennsylvania 22
Penobscot, Maine 8
pensions 34, 137: commutation 113, 115, 142, 156; heirs 40; invalid 40, 51, 156; officer 80, 98, 101, 103, 110; soldier 151, 158–160; widow 40, 161
Peruvian/Jesuit's bark 52
Peters, Richard (congressman) 99
Petersham, Massachusetts 155
Phelps (New York) Purchase *see* Maxwell, Hugh (lieutenant colonel)
Philadelphia, Pennsylvania 12, 20, 40, 48, 54, 56, 57, 64, 67, 73, 75, 77, 90, 92, 94, 97, 99, 104, 105, 110, 115, 132, 136, 141, 143, 147, 149, 150, 155, 156, 159
physicians and surgeons distinction 49
Pickering, Timothy (colonel; quartermaster general) 10, 11, 24, 33, 75, 81, 83, 92–95, 116, 126, 136, 141, 144–146, 148–150, 157: altercation with Heath 12, 13; bed for Gates 31, 55; contempt for Washington and Congress 143; encampment selection 10, 11; flags 76; forage shortage 92, 93, 97, 98; Gates headquarters at John Ellison house 12, 55; Gates sale of public wagon and team 149; headquarters 17; hospital buildings movement to West Point 150; hut specifications 28–32; lawsuit and arrest warrant 46; Newburgh Conspiracy 113–115; wood/fence rails 77, 149–151
pickets 130
Pictorial Fieldbook of the American Revolution (Lossing, Benson, author) 81
Pierce, John (paymaster general and commissioner for settling accounts of the army) 133, 141, 142
Pierce Certificates 141, 142
Pines Bridge crossing of Croton River attack 16
pistols 73, 74, 129
pitching coppers, buttons or dollars 128, 129
Plain, fort *see* Rensselaer, fort
Plum Point, New Windsor, New York 11
Pompton, New Jersey 39, 104, 143, 144
Porta Capena, Rome, Italy 82
post office, army 79
Pratt, Samuel Jackson (author; Courtney Melmoth pen name) 137
Pray, John (captain) 133
prejudice 9, 40, 157–159
Presbyterian Church (First) of Newburgh, First 37
Presbyterian church of New Windsor 37, 77
Prescott, Joseph (surgeon's mate; hospital, New Windsor) 49, 150
price fixing 95
Prince of Luxembourg 66
Princeton, New Jersey 143, 147, 148, 151, 152; battle of 40, 48, 97
prisoners of war 9, 20, 27, 35, 60, 72, 119, 133, 135; Continental army 27, 28, 132
Private Yankee Doodle (Joseph Plumb Martin, author) 34
privateers 58, 96, 152
profanity 37
punishment 128, 132, 137; *see also* desertion
purgatives 52
Purple Heart Medal 68
Putnam, Rufus (colonel and brigadier general) 47, 65, 79, 150, 152, 161; Newburgh Conspiracy 113, 114; Ohio Company of Associates cofounder 152; petition of Ohio for military land grants 152

Quasi-War with France, 1798–1800 101, 152

rank: promotion 38, 39, 46, 47, 79; reduction 36, 129, 137
rations 43, 49, 77, 127: alcohol,

rum or whiskey 20, 47, 77, 82, 83, 135, 136; contractors 22, 43–45; extra allowance for celebrations 77, 83, 135, 136; extra allowance for fatigue 20, 82, 49, 77; haversack 75; issue 31, 41, 42, 44, 62, 143, magazines 43, 45, 143; officer 45, 113, 141, 142; poor quality 138; preparation 19, 44, 45, 79, 126 sick 39, 44, 138, 150
Read, John 41
Reading, Connecticut 9
recruiting 8, 18, 23, 30, 34, 52, 94, 118–120, 158; accounts 133; African-American enlistment 9, 118, 119; bounty 21, 34, 118, 119, 120; British prisoners of war 119; Congress refusal to draft 120; desertion 34, 35; enlistment terms 47, 48, 98, 143; gratuity to soldiers enlisted 140, 142; guidelines/screening 35, 118, 119; musician enlistment bar 19; Native American enlistment 9; recovery of deserters 120; short term enlistments 22, 119, 120; state failure to fund deficiency 120
Regulations for the Order and Discipline of the Troops of the United States (Friedrich von Steuben; major general; author) 24, 61, 75, 121, 123
Reid, James (major) 144
Reign of Terror 71
religious denominations 36, 37
religious services 37, 38–40, 77, 90, 146; capacity 90, 91; music 77, 90; peace announcement celebration 134; Private Thomas Foster summary 37, 38 90; Temple final 146; Temple inaugural 83; Thanksgiving, November 28, 1782 77
Rensselaer, Stephen Van 114
Rensselaer, fort 148
Revere, Paul 40
reviews *see* inspections
Rhode Island 96, 145
Rhode Island Regiment 9, 10, 60, 115, 120, 131, 133, 144, 145
Richmond, Christopher (major) 97, 101, 102
rifle 66, 73, 122
Rindge, New Hampshire 159
Ringwood, New Jersey 104, 135
Roberts, Gilbert 79
Robertson, James (lieutenant general and governor of New York City) 94

Robinson, Beverly 74
Rochambeau, comte Jean de (lieutenant general) 6, 8, 11, 58, 66, 67, 94
Rochefontaine, Etienne de (major) 20, 82
Rockingham Estate, Rocky Hill, New Jersey 151
Rocky Hill Meeting House, Amesbury, Massachusetts 86, 87
"The Rogue's March" 128, 137
roll calls 18, 19, 128
Rome, Italy 82
Rose Hill Farm, Bronx, New York 156
Roxbury, Massachusetts 151
Royal George, HMS 79
Royal Navy (British) 6, 58
royalists 6, 8, 27, 108, 132, 148
Ruddock, John (deputy commissary of military stores) 20
Rush, Benjamin (doctor) 50

St. Clair, Arthur (major general) 9, 12, 27, 80, 157
St. Lawrence, George (corporal; private) 137
St. Patrick's Day 47
St. Paul's Chapel, New York City 157
Sampson, Crocker (lieutenant) 129, 130
Sampson, Deborah (private) 40, 63, 65, 66
Sands, Comfort 43, 44, 62, 63
sanitation 61, 66, 126, 127
Saratoga, New York, battle of 35, 39, 71, 97, 107, 108, 120, 148, 157, 159
Sash, Moses (private) 153
Savannah, Georgia 8; siege of 7
sawmills 10
Sawyer, James (ensign) 129, 130
scabies 52
Schenectady, New York 148
Schuyler, Philip (major general; congressman) 106, 107, 114, 148
Schuyler, fort 41, 106, 148, 159
Scott, William (major) 51, 59, 60
2nd Continental Light Dragoons 9, 68
Sedam, Ricker (ensign) 16
sermons 37, 38, 90, 91
sequestered estate 143
servants 24, 43, 45, 120, 121, 148, 150, 151
Sewall, Henry (major) 137, 138
shaming 28, 122, 124, 126, 128, 130, 152

Sharkey, Joseph (private) 128
Sharon, Massachusetts 40
Shaw, Samuel (major) 70
Shays, Daniel (captain) 152, 155
Shays' Rebellion 142, 153–156
Shepherd, William (colonel) 153, 155
shirts 39, 55, 57, 58, 66, 67; hunting 10, 66
shoes 28, 58, 67, 74, 98
shooting by camp guards 53
Short Hills, New Jersey, battle of 27
Shurtliff, Robert *see* Sampson, Deborah (private)
skull trauma 54
slaughterhouse and pen in Newburgh, New York 44
sleds 77
sleighs 77, 78
Sloat, Polly 160
smallpox 47, 49, 52, 53
Smith, Joseph (lieutenant) 80, 143
Smith, Josiah (lieutenant) 137
Smith, Mary (daughter of William McGill) 162
Smith, Melancton 142
Smith, Nathan 150
Smith, William 149
Snake Hill, New Windsor, New York 10
Society of Cincinnati 57, 70–72
Solomon 88
South Carolina (ship) 66
Spain 6, 7, 58, 95, 151
Sparks, Nicholas 102
speculators 141, 153–156
Spithead, Portsmouth Harbor, England 79
spontoons 72
Springfield, Massachusetts 154
Springfield (Massachusetts) Arsenal 153, 155
Springfield (Massachusetts) Depot 67, 74
Sproat, Ebenezer (lieutenant colonel) 26, 66, 126, 129, 145; Ohio Company of Associates 153
stables 25, 31, 149, 155; Gates' headquarters 98
Stanwix, fort *see* Schuyler, fort
Stapleton, John (captain; deputy adjutant general British army) 133
Stark, John (brigadier general) 133, 138
Starkeans Hall, Masonic Lodge at West Point 89
Steuben, Friedrich von (major general, inspector general) 13, 24, 75, 121; army

disbandment ceremony 136; frontier posts return 148; homosexuality 38; inspection of army 59, 60, 61, 65–67, 74, 83, 124; manual 24, 26, 75, 121, 123, 124; New York Brigade address 143; Samuel Verplanck house headquarters 15, 70; Society of Cincinnati formation 70
Stevens, Ebenezer (lieutenant colonel) 27
Stevens, Thomas (private) 137
Stewart, Walter (colonel; inspector for the northern army) 61, 64, 70, 144; Newburgh Conspiracy 101, 103–105, 110, 117
stimulants 52
Stirling, Lord William Alexander (major general) 67, 107, 156, 157
stockings 58, 67
Stone, Nathaniel (lieutenant) 129
Stoner, Nicholas (fifer) 54
Stony Point, New York 8, 15, 16; battle of 63, 123
store (merchant) 63, 64, 79
subsistence allowance 23, 46, 64, 101, 110, 116, 133, 142
Suffern, New York 9, 15
Sumner, Job (major) 149
surveying of camp 20
suspension of officers 129
Susquehanna River 5, 148
Sutlers 25, 46, 63, 64, 104, 105, 142, 144
sutures 53, 54
Swift, Heman (colonel) 10
swords 56, 72, 107, 108, 111, 134, 135, 153

tailors 33, 60, 62
Tarbell, Luther 89
Tarrytown, New York 102
taxes 34, 45, 63, 93–96, 102, 137, 141, 154, 155
tea 80
Teagues 47
Temple Hill 89, 161
Temple Hill Creamery 161
Temple Hill Day 162
Temple Hill Monument 89, 162, 163
Temple of Honor and Virtue, Rome, Italy 82
Temple of Virtue 20, 46, 51, 88, 127, 131–133: auction sale 149, 150; benches 91, 150; capacity 89, 90; commissary store 84, 89, 90; discovery of site 83, 89; French alliance anniversary and inaugural celebration 83; Gates oversight 81, 82; Heath description 84; levee meetings 80, 84, 89, 90, 127; Lossing depiction 84, 85, 89; Masonic influence and imagery 86–88; Massachusetts Line reorganization meeting 145; materials 32, 82, 83, 85, 90; music performances 80, 134; names for 81; officer meeting and Washington speech 100, 110–115; Ohio land grant petition meeting 152; orchestra/gallery 84, 90; peace announcement and celebration 132–135; peace treaty celebration preparations 136; portico 84–87, 90; proposal for 81; quartermaster store room 84, 89, 90; reconstruction 88–90, 163; rooms 84, 89, 90; sermons 37, 38, 90, 91; Society of Cincinnati meetings 70; Tarbell depiction 26, 85–89; weather damage 36, 150; windows 83, 85–88, 90
Temple of Virtue: A Dream (David Fordyce, author) 81
Ten Broeck, Abraham (brigadier general; Albany, New York mayor) 148
tents 9, 10, 20, 23, 24, 25, 31, 146; for arms 25; bunks 24; chimneys 20, 24
terms of service 47, 48
Thacher, James (surgeon) 41, 53
Thanksgiving, November 28 77
theft 27, 28, 127, 128, 130, 131, 150
39, "40 save one" 128
Thorp, Eliphalet (captain) 35
Ticonderoga, fort 54, 106, 148
Tiebout, Henry (captain) 141
Tilghman, Tench (lieutenant colonel) 80
Tioga, Pennsylvania 148
toothache 54, 55
tour of northern and central New York 148
Townsend, David (surgeon) 79
trade with enemy 15, 16, 65, 95
Trenton, New Jersey, battle of 33, 40, 48
Trescott, Lemuel (major) 138
Trinity Churchyard Cemetery, New York 157
Trumbull, John (*McFingal*, author) 138
Trumbull, Jonathan (lieutenant colonel) 80, 91, 111

Tupper, Anselm (captain) 153
Tupper, Benjamin (colonel) 20, 31, 82, 83, 153
typhoid 47, 50
typhus 50

United Provinces of the Netherlands *see* Dutch Republic

Valley Forge, Pennsylvania 32, 35, 48, 75, 78, 120, 121, 159
Van Schaick, Goose (colonel) 54, 67
Vaudreuil, Louis Marquis de (admiral) 119
venereal disease 55
Verger, Jean-Baptiste Antoine de (lieutenant) 59, 60
Verme, Francesco 148
Vermont 133, 148, 155
Verplanck, Samuel (major general) 15, 70
Verplanck's Point (New York encampment) 8, 16, 20, 58, 60, 109, 124
Versailles, France 151
Villefranche, Chevalier Jean de (major) 148
Virginia 96
Vose, Joseph (colonel) 145

Wadsworth, Jeremiah 44
Wadsworth and Carter (contractor) 44
wagons 11, 24, 25, 33, 41, 56, 67, 74, 149
Walker, Benjamin (lieutenant colonel) 38, 109, 146
walkways 27, 86
Wampanoag Tribe 37, 158
warehouse 64
Warren, John (lieutenant) 39, 80
Warren, Joseph (major general) 48
Washington, George (general) 7, 11, 13, 16, 17, 21, 33, 41, 45, 50, 52, 53, 56, 70, 77, 79, 81, 109, 115, 116, 146, 148, 150, 159, 163; Alexander Hamilton relationship 99–101, 108, 115, 117; arms and accoutrements 71, 72, 74, 75, 122, 123, 142; Badge of Military Merit and Honorary Badge of Distinction 67–69, 80; Christmas Eve 1783 return to Mount Vernon 151; circular letter, 144, 145; clothing 57–67, 70, 76; Colonel Nicola letter 70; confidence in General Knox 110, 113, 117;

Congress 151, 152; Conway Cabal 107, 110, 156, 157; farewell address to army 151; disbandment of army 142, 145, 146; discipline 27, 28, 35, 47, 61, 122, 123, 124, 126, 128–132, 138, 144, 152; final meeting with officers 151; flags 75, 76; forage shortage 92, 93, 97, 98; French alliance anniversary celebration 61, 83; French expeditionary force 8; French Minister La Luzerne invitation to peace treaty celebration 136; furlough of army 137, 138, 140–144, 146, 151; General Gates relationship 12, 99, 100, 108, 108, 156; Great Britain 8, 27, 45, 148, 149; implementation of January 1, 1783 army reorganization 23; leave absences 12, 61, 79–80, 138; the lines 14–17, 20, 24, 130, 133; New Jersey Line request for exemption from taxation 137; New Windsor encampment 10, 11, 27- 29, 61, 124, 126, 127, 144; Newburgh Conspiracy 91, 100, 105, 109–117;Oswego, New York, attack 9, 10; pay for army 75, 104, 105, 133, 141, 142; peace announcement and celebration 132–136; pension request for non-commissioned officers 137; petition for Ohio as location for military land grants 152; Pickering absence and failure to report army logistical status 92, 93; rations 31, 41–47, 138, recall of brigade chaplains 37; recruiting 48, 94, 119, 120; refusal to pressure Congress on army's behalf 108, 143; sanitation 61, 126, 127; servants 43, 121; settling of officer disputes 129; snub by disbanding army 143; Society of Cincinnati presidency 70; Temple of Virtue 81, 91; Thanksgiving, November 28, 1782 77; tour of central and northern New York 144; trade with enemy 15, 16, 95; unrest in army 94, 99, 109, 137; use of proxies to attack enemies 108; Verplanck's Point, New York, encampment 8, 58, 60, 67, 124; West Point 5; women allowed to travel with army 31, 41, 42; Wyoming Valley of Pennsylvania 22

Washington's Headquarters State Historic Site 56, 89, 163
watch coats 66, 98, 131
weight of largest officers 45
Weissenfels, Frederick (lieutenant colonel) 120
West Indies 7, 8, 59, 67, 156
West Point, New York 5, 6, 8, 9, 10, 15, 17, 18, 20, 21, 24, 27, 30, 35, 41, 42, 45, 51, 53, 60, 64, 65, 77, 79, 89, 104, 113, 114, 121, 129, 133, 137, 138, 144, 146–150, 152
Westchester County, New York 17, 35, 40, 133, 148
Westlake, Benjamin 150
Westlake, Samuel 150
Wetmore, Hezekiah (deputy paymaster) 15, 104
Weyman, Abel (captain) 22
Wharves *see* docks

Whig 95, 109
Whig Party 76
Whiskey Rebellion 1794 100, 101
White Plains, New York 35; battle of 159
Whitestown, New York 160
Wickhams, Isaac (private) 37, 158
Wilkins (soldier) 150
Wilkinson, James (lieutenant colonel) 107
Willett, Marinus (colonel) 9, 10, 148
Williams, Jonas 28, 150
Williamsburg, Virginia 8
Wilmington, Delaware 143
windows 29, 83, 85–88, 90
Wing, Jonathan (ensign) 39
women 31, 36, 38–42, 53, 66, 78–83, 137, 142, 149, 150, 151, 153, 156, 157, 159–162
woodlots 10
Wood, Samuel 149
Wood, Samuel, tavern 13, 14, 93, 97
Woolsey, Melancthon L. 93
World's Fair in New York City 161
Worthy, Benjamin (private) 150
Wrights' Mills, New York 35
Wykoff, Henry (major) 138
Wyoma: brothel 39, 81, 142
Wyoming Valley, Pennsylvania 22

yellow fever 50
Yorktown, Virginia 8; siege of 6, 18, 35, 39, 40, 41, 52, 53, 58, 63, 72, 81, 98, 99, 102, 104, 105, 123, 132, 158, 159

www.ingramcontent.com/pod-product-compliance
Lightning Source LLC
Chambersburg PA
CBHW060341010526
44117CB00017B/2921